War on the Ballot

WAR ON THE BALLOT

How the Election Cycle Shapes
Presidential Decision-Making in War

ANDREW PAYNE

COLUMBIA UNIVERSITY PRESS *NEW YORK*

Columbia University Press
Publishers Since 1893
New York   Chichester, West Sussex
cup.columbia.edu
Copyright © 2023 Columbia University Press

Library of Congress Cataloging-in-Publication Data
Names: Payne, Andrew, 1991– author.
Title: War on the ballot : how the election cycle shapes presidential
decision-making in war / Andrew Payne.
Description: New York : Columbia University Press, 2023. |
Includes bibliographical references and index.
Identifiers: LCCN 2022050825 (print) | LCCN 2022050826 (ebook) | ISBN 9780231209649
(hardback) | ISBN 9780231209656 (trade paperback) | ISBN 9780231558044 (ebook)
Subjects: LCSH: Presidents—United States—Election—History—20th century. |
Presidents—United States—Election—History—21st century. | Presidents—
United States—Decision making. | Politics and war—United States. | United States—
History, Military—20th century. | United States—History, Military—21st century.
Classification: LCC JK524 .P39 2023 (print) | LCC JK524 (ebook) |
DDC 324.973—dc23/eng/20230103
LC record available at https://lccn.loc.gov/2022050825
LC ebook record available at https://lccn.loc.gov/2022050826

Cover design: Elliott S. Cairns
Cover image: Everett Collection Inc / Alamy Stock Photo

Contents

[v]

Acknowledgments

This book was researched, written, and completed while I was associated with the University of Oxford, first as a graduate student and then as the Hedley Bull Research Fellow in International Relations. Accordingly, it is to the students, staff, and faculty of that institution that I owe principal thanks for creating the environment in which I could develop the ideas underpinning this book. Above all, I would like to express my deepest gratitude to Louise Fawcett, whose endless support, warm encouragement, and wise counsel have been instrumental in the development both of this book and of my own career. I could not have wished for a more helpful, patient, and reassuring mentor, and I consider myself incredibly lucky to be able to count myself among the many students and scholars whose paths have been shaped by her guidance and example. Special thanks are also due to Janina Dill, William James, Dominic Johnson, and Duncan Snidal, each of whom read significant portions of earlier draft material that made its way into the book. Beyond this, I have benefited immensely from discussions with innumerable friends and colleagues at the Department of Politics and International Relations, including Richard Caplan, Rosemary Foot, Todd Hall, Eddie Keene, Neil MacFarlane, and Andrea Ruggeri.

Merton College generously provided me with several research grants and scholarships during my time there. More recently, Brasenose College appointed me as a William Golding Junior Research Fellow, a position I am told is supposed to "add to the intellectual luster of the college." I don't know if I delivered on that, but I am nevertheless extremely grateful for the convivial atmosphere and superb facilities provided by the college, which helped make my years there my most enjoyable yet. The Jeffrey Fund, administered by Brasenose, also provided invaluable financial assistance in the later stages of the project. The Hedley Bull Research Fellowship gave me the most valuable gift of all—the time to figure out exactly what this book was about and to revise it into its present form. I would therefore like to recognize the support of the Hedley Bull Memorial Fund, and to apologize to the innumerable students who assumed that referencing the English school would earn them extra credit in their weekly essays.

Beyond Oxford, I have drawn on the advice and support of a range of individuals who offered valuable comments or took time to speak with me about my work at various stages of the process. Having often joked that I am a historian masquerading as a political scientist—and lived in fear that the reverse is in fact the case—I am especially grateful to the many "proper" historians who have graciously humored my occasional references to conceptual models and causal mechanisms when my mask momentarily slipped. Among them, I thank in particular Steve Casey, who offered countless excellent suggestions to sharpen the case studies and has become an invaluable source of sage advice, having trodden a similar path once before. I also thank Andrew Preston, who probably does not realize the degree to which he influenced my career, having single-handedly ignited my interest in the history of U.S. foreign relations when I was a lowly undergraduate, and inspired me to return to academia a couple of years later. More recently, Peter Trubowitz has been a constant source of encouragement and inspiration. Jeff Friedman restored my confidence in the project and helped me distill its key contributions at a crucial moment. In addition to those already mentioned, I'd also like to thank several others for sharing their insights and helping me think through various aspects of the project, including Gareth Davies, Ben Fordham, Robin Markwica, Jeff Michaels, Phil Potter, William Quandt, Rob Schub, and Melissa Willard-Foster.

Beyond those already mentioned, I am very grateful for the generous financial assistance offered by a range of other individuals and organizations, including the Harry S. Truman Library Institute and the Economics and Social Research Council. The University of Oxford's Vice Chancellor's Fund also provided invaluable support, as did the Cyril Foster Fund at the

Department of Politics and International Relations. Finally, I was fortunate to be the recipient of the Deirdre and Paul Malone Prize in International Relations, which granted me the resources to jump-start the next stage of the project. More importantly, it afforded me an opportunity to get to know its benefactor, David Malone, who has since become a mentor and to whom I owe a debt of gratitude for his generosity and warm friendship.

A small army of individuals helped me navigate the holdings of several archives across the United States. I am particularly grateful to David Clark, Sam Rushay, Randy Sowell, and Tammy Williams at the Truman Library; Mary Burtzloff at the Eisenhower Library; John Wilson at the Johnson Library; Dorissa Martinez at the Nixon Library; Scott Gower at the National Defense University; and Jim Zobel at the MacArthur Memorial Archives. My thanks also to Conrad Crane, who introduced me to the excellent resources at the U.S. Army Heritage and Education Center, and to all the staff of the Manuscript Division at the Library of Congress, who were unfailingly helpful and efficient. I would also like to record my thanks to all those who graciously agreed to be interviewed for this project, oftentimes at considerable length. George Casey and David Petraeus kindly granted permission for me to consult their papers at the National Defense University.

At Columbia University Press, I thank Stephen Wesley both for his enthusiasm for the project and for the efficiency with which he shepherded it through to production, assisted ably by Christian Winting. Marisa Lastres made sure the ensuing process ran like clockwork, with Ryan Perks responsible for polishing the manuscript so effectively. Credit for the awesome cover design goes to Elliott Cairns. Bob Schwarz compiled the index with great skill. I am also significantly indebted to three anonymous reviewers, each of whom offered invaluable suggestions that helped fine-tune the manuscript. Ria McDonald provided research assistance at the eleventh hour, which was instrumental in getting the final manuscript across the line.

Finally, and most importantly, I thank my family, without whom none of this would have been possible. My parents, Maxine and Les, have been my earliest and strongest supporters since before I can remember. My granddad, Ernst, stoked my interest in history from a young age.

I owe the greatest debt of all to my wife, Abi, whose love and support has sustained me throughout this process. She has also read—and reread—more of my writing than is reasonable, serving as the best sounding board, proofreader, and editor in chief I could possibly have hoped for. Osi, by contrast, has not read a single word, but has nevertheless overseen much of the process while making his feelings known about the long hours spent at the computer rather than on the sofa with him. It is to them both that I dedicate this book.

Introduction

Politics and military; and politics and diplomacy; these are all interwoven.

—GENERAL WILLIAM C. WESTMORELAND

IN AUGUST 1972, President Richard Nixon met with his national security advisor in the Oval Office to chart a path forward in the ongoing war in Vietnam. He was clear-eyed about the situation. Having doubled down on his predecessor's investment of blood and treasure, the prospect of securing a meaningful form of the "peace with honor" he had promised on the campaign trail now seemed more illusory than ever. With efforts to consolidate a period of détente with the Soviet Union and improved relations with China having gathered pace earlier that year, the quagmire in Southeast Asia had long since become a strategic distraction. What was needed, he concluded, was some kind of face-saving deal that would allow the United States to withdraw its troops and rebalance its lopsided geopolitical commitments. As for the contents of the deal, Nixon encouraged Henry Kissinger to be "perfectly cold-blooded about it. . . . I think we could take, in my view, almost anything, frankly, that we can force on [South Vietnamese president Nguyen Van] Thieu. Almost anything."[1]

The catch? "We also have to realize," the president told Kissinger, "that winning an election is terribly important." Thieu was already on borrowed time, but if it looked like Nixon was responsible for pushing him over the brink, it could spell political disaster for the president. The image of North Vietnamese troops pouring into South Vietnam and a collapse of the government in Saigon before November could jeopardize Nixon's reelection hopes. "We've got to find some formula that holds the thing together a year or two," agreed Kissinger. "After a year, Mr. President, Vietnam will be a backwater. If we settle it, say, this October, by January '74 no one will give a damn."[2]

The United States would abandon its erstwhile ally in Saigon, then, but it would do so at a time of President Nixon's choosing. Given the exigencies of the domestic political calendar, this meant pressing on with a fixed timetable of troop withdrawals under a "Vietnamization" policy that the president had long ago written off. It meant continuing the bombing efforts over North Vietnam that Nixon had recently assessed to have achieved "zilch," despite ten years of total control of the skies. And it meant carrying on with negotiations to end the war, not in the expectation of securing peace, but merely in the hope of getting through the election unharmed by the political fallout associated with the fall of South Vietnam.

*　　　*　　　*

It is an inconvenient truth, rarely admitted, that leaders habitually take electoral considerations into account when making decisions about military and diplomatic strategy in war. At once commander in chief and holder of the highest elected office, presidents must balance the often competing objectives of the national interest with political self-interest when assessing alternative strategies. While arguably true of all regime types, this is especially the case in democracies like the United States, where a fixed four-year electoral cycle provides clear and periodic opportunities for voters to give their verdict on the leader's performance and hold them to account. If presidents craft policy without due regard for the anticipated reaction of public opinion, they may risk having to forfeit their political futures and the chance to achieve their particular visions for the country.

Yet while we all have some intuitive sense that elections "matter," exactly how, why, or when they do so is not well understood. Frequently invoked in an ad hoc manner to give color to historical accounts, the systematic analysis of the relationship between electoral politics and wartime decision making is a blind spot in an otherwise bountiful literature on the domestic components of U.S. foreign policy. Public opinion and congressional pressures matter, to be sure, but the relative weight accorded to them varies across the political calendar. As George W. Bush put it after winning reelection in 2004, polling day is the ultimate "accountability moment."[3] This book therefore examines the particular influence of *electoral* constraints, defined as the institutional limitations on presidential decision making imposed by the electoral cycle. In doing so, it highlights the largely under-studied and often surprising electoral face of democratic accountability in war, putting the politicians back into international politics.

There are several reasons for the "persistent lack of attention to the relationship between foreign policy and American presidential elections."[4] Firstly, scholars and commentators frequently observe that the president has a relatively free hand in foreign policy compared to domestic affairs. Most famously articulated in the "two presidencies" thesis, this received wisdom has contributed to an artificial distinction between the president's dual responsibilities as a statesman in the international sphere and an elected politician at home.[5] Successive generations of realists, of both classical and structural hues, further embedded this notion of separate spheres. International politics, they maintained, is a professional activity that is not—or should not—be responsive to the ill-informed whims of the voting public.[6] Yet while this distinction has supported the development of elegant theories of international politics, it does not accurately portray decision making at the state level.[7] In candid moments like the conversation between Nixon and Kissinger secretly recorded by the president, or in comments looking back from the more dispassionate perspective of post-presidential private life, presidents hint at a more complex and interconnected reality. "It was impossible to separate completely the pressures of an ongoing political campaign from those of managing the domestic and international affairs of the nation," recalled Jimmy Carter, whose bid for reelection in 1980 was famously sunk by the ongoing hostage crisis in Iran. "In fact, they were inextricably mixed."[8]

This book, then, explores the impact of electoral politics on presidential decision making in war. It asks how the president's dual responsibilities affect the development of military and diplomatic strategy in war. Under what conditions do electoral pressures lead incumbents to escalate or de-escalate an ongoing conflict? How does the looming presence of polling day in the United States complicate the president's ability to sue for peace? Finally, how does the strength of these constraints vary across the domestic political calendar?

To help answer these questions, the book develops a new conceptual framework, comprised of five mechanisms of electoral constraint. Taken together, these mechanisms capture the nuanced ways in which the presidents featured in this book sought to reconcile strategic and electoral pressures as they made critical decisions about the wars they oversaw. Depending on each president's assessment of the decision-making environment, electoral considerations encouraged them to *delay* making a controversial decision, to *dampen* its "noisier" aspects, or, acting as a *spur*, to dial up the aggressiveness of a proposed option. Previous elections carried *hangover* effects related to campaign pledges, and upcoming elections repeatedly *spoiled* an incumbent's ability to conduct negotiations on favorable terms.

These mechanisms are illustrated in historical case studies of the wars in Korea (1950–1953), Vietnam (1963–1973) and Iraq (2003–2011). Drawing on a wealth of original documentary sources and interviews with dozens of senior administration officials and high-ranking generals, these studies reveal the surprisingly large role played by electoral politics during some of America's costliest wars since 1945. In each case, critical decisions regarding military and diplomatic strategy were all too often taken with one eye on the domestic political calendar, sometimes with striking disregard for the national interest. At the highest level of national security policy, as one senior military officer concluded with dismay, it was "all about politics."[9]

*   *   *

In developing this argument, the book departs from existing scholarship in four important ways. First, it resolves ongoing uncertainty regarding exactly *how* elections affect decisions involving the use of force. Scholarship on democratic constraint generally presumes that elections make leaders more peaceful. This conclusion is not wrong so much as incomplete, since it fails to account for empirical evidence that leaders often act more forcefully as an election nears. While other approaches suggest that incumbents may use force in a diversionary manner to boost their reelection hopes, they rely on alternative mechanisms involving the manipulation of public opinion rather than the accommodation of voter preferences. This book reconciles this tension by modeling electoral pressures as a conditional source of constraint, which can push or pull presidents toward more belligerent or more cautious courses of action depending on their perception of the strategic and electoral dynamics at stake.

Second, the book moves away from the emphasis of much existing work that focuses more narrowly on the period directly preceding a presidential election. Treating electoral pressures in such an artificially bounded way reflects the scholar's preference for neat units of analysis over the messiness of real life. The result is a biased view of the far broader impact that electoral considerations have on decision making. Whereas most existing literature assumes that electoral pressures follow a linear pattern, increasing in strength as an election approaches, this study demonstrates how electoral constraints vary quantitatively and qualitatively across different phases of the domestic political calendar. By examining how electoral pressures wax and wane across the four-year presidential cycle, this book better captures the reality that both the anticipation of future election seasons and the memory of earlier commitments made on the campaign trail can also have substantial impact, as can congressional midterm campaigns.

Third, and critically, whereas much existing work only examines decisions to start a particular war, this book extends the analysis to encompass the full course of each conflict. To be sure, the initial decision to use force undoubtedly shapes the nature of any ensuing contest in important ways. Yet neither the duration nor the outcome of a conflict is determined at the outset of hostilities. How leaders adapt to changing political and military conditions during a war plays an important role in determining its course. It is therefore crucial to understand not simply *why* decision makers decided to go to war in the first place, but *how* they decided to fight that war and sought to bring it to a conclusion.[10] Since it seems plausible that electoral constraints do not simply dissipate once an initial decision to enter into a conflict is made, it makes sense to look beyond the moment the proverbial Rubicon is crossed and presidents find themselves actively carrying out their additional responsibilities as a wartime commander in chief.

Finally, the book unearths a plethora of new evidence detailing behind-the-scenes deliberations over wartime strategy. This kind of evidence, often subtle and tacit in nature, is not easily observable through the quantitative methods that have dominated the field.[11] Analyses of large-*n* data sets are often helpful in identifying patterns, such as the correlation between election years and the outbreak of conflict, yet statistical significance should not be equated with historical reality. Since electoral pressures may encourage presidents to act more forcefully or more timidly—and sometimes both at once—standard regression models are likely to miss the nuanced and often countervailing effects that are examined in this study. Of course, presidents understand that being seen to take their own political interests into account when making decisions about war and peace is controversial. "Smoking gun" evidence is therefore likely to be scarce and hidden from the public record. After all, as Lyndon Johnson once said, "if you have a mother-in-law with only one eye and she has it in the center of her forehead, you don't keep her in the living room."[12] It is important, therefore, not to mistake the absence of evidence for evidence of absence when it comes to substantiating the claim that electoral considerations "mattered." It is with good reason that the author of the best book-length treatment of the subject—now over two decades old—admitted that his findings were "probably just the visible tip of the iceberg."[13]

This book, then, seeks to go deeper into the empirical waters, drawing on an unusually broad range of sources to shed light on the question at hand. Diaries, personal correspondence, official memoranda, and declassified minutes of high-level meetings give deep insight into the political pressures at work in the Truman and Eisenhower administrations. The account presented here contributes to an emerging revival of interest in the conflict on the Korean Peninsula, once considered the "forgotten war." For the Vietnam case, these kinds of archival sources are supplemented by hundreds of hours of tape recordings of conversations involving Lyndon Johnson and Richard Nixon. Never originally intended for public release, the verbatim accounts relayed in this book give readers an unprecedented window into the innermost circle of decision making, unfiltered by spin doctors and stenographers. More than four decades on from the fall of Saigon, nuggets of information that have eluded past scholars continue to appear, challenging conventional narratives about wartime strategy long ago considered settled.

Far less is known about the war in Iraq, and it is here where the book's empirical contribution is the greatest. Having gained unique access to thousands of recently declassified documents, I piece together various fragments of the paper trail to describe the reality of decision making, peeling away the journalistic speculation and hyperbole that has dogged existing accounts. Dozens of personal interviews conducted with the war's leading protagonists help fill in the remaining gaps. The perspectives offered are both illuminating and varied. From General George W. Casey Jr., General David H. Petraeus, and General Raymond T. Odierno, we learn how the top commanders on the ground perceived the changing patterns of presidential engagement with military strategy across the electoral cycle. From a series of ambassadors and advisors at the State Department, we hear how parochial concerns in Washington precluded efforts to develop optimal diplomatic strategies and strike critical agreements with the Iraqi government. And we hear, in their own words, how tension between the chairman and vice chairman of the Joint Chiefs of Staff may have contributed to the decision to end U.S. involvement on the eve of the 2012 presidential election campaign.

The value of the deeply historical approach adopted in this study goes beyond these empirical and methodological advantages, however. The detailed evidence presented of the nakedly political determinants of wartime policy also raises important normative questions about democratic accountability and war. The idea of presidents risking soldiers' lives in order to enhance their electoral prospects will strike many readers as morally abhorrent. Yet time and again, this is exactly the kind of behavior we observe in the cases studies. We should not be surprised to find evidence of leaders selecting strategies in flawed ways, of course. Psychological approaches to the study of foreign policy decision making have identified manifold ways in which leaders select suboptimal courses of action, thanks to a host of cognitive and motivational biases.[14] Yet it is striking just how many decisions examined in this book involve presidents *knowingly* choosing options that violate the national interest in ways that are unusually avoidable and thus pernicious. A close examination of the available documentary record, coupled with interviews with senior officials, shed light on the apparent ease with which presidents rationalize such behaviors—both to themselves and to others—as something less normatively weighty than might be assumed. More substantively, these sources afford an important opportunity to identify a series of opportunities to limit the human and financial costs of each war, gain material advantage on the battlefield, or sue for peace, which were all missed thanks to the prevailing attention paid to the domestic political calendar.

Taken together, the evidence presented in this book also offers an opportunity to add nuance to the conventional wisdom that democracies are good at fighting and winning wars. According to this common line of argument, democratic leaders, who compared to autocrats face greater domestic political costs for public policy failures, tend to enter into wars only when highly confident of swift victory, and fight harder once engaged so as to avoid incurring punishment by voters; the result, by one account, is an impressive success rate in war of 76 percent.[15] Yet each of the wars considered here seem to deviate in important ways from this pattern. Most notably, of course, it would be difficult to claim that any of the three conflicts resulted in a clear victory for the United States, with two draws and a loss probably the most that could be awarded. Since electoral accountability is cited as a leading explanation for the *effectiveness* of democracies in fighting wars, a closer examination of how electoral constraints operated in these apparently contradictory cases may yield important implications for theories of democratic victory in war.

The United States is of course not the only state to have fought limited wars, nor is it the only democracy in which electoral pressures plausibly affect wartime decision making. Yet there remains much to be gained from a focus on the U.S. experience after 1945. Since the United States was the most powerful actor in the international system during this period, policies developed in Washington had a major and often decisive impact on the course of conflicts across the globe.[16] The war record of the United States thus carries intrinsic value as a vessel through which to examine the extent to which electoral dynamics can shape the course of some of the longest and most costly conflicts in modern history. From a methodological perspective, moreover, a single-state analysis carries further benefits. Since the institutional structure of democracies varies considerably, a series of confounding variables can make comparison between states difficult at the level of analysis required for this kind of fine-grained study of decision making.[17] In this respect, the United States' fixed four-year electoral cycle adds consistency and predictability, which ensures that audience costs vary exogenously across the political calendar, unlike in a parliamentary system, for instance, where a leader can manipulate election timing in anticipation of future events.[18]

Plan of the Book

The conceptual framework outlined in chapter 1 acts as a reference point for the historical chapters that follow, setting out how, why, and when elections mattered in each of the wars examined in the book. Drawing on studies of democratic accountability, I outline five mechanisms of electoral constraint that recur throughout the cases—*delay, dampening, spur, hangover,* and *spoiler.* Which of these mechanisms operated in any given scenario is held to have depended on the relative alignment between the president's strategic and electoral preferences, on the one hand, and the stage of the electoral cycle, on the other. This book is oriented toward explaining the key decisions concerning military and diplomatic strategy, wherever they lie in the electoral cycle, before drilling down to understand exactly how electoral pressures may (or may not) have influenced their gestation. Yet it is hoped that this framework helps the reader observe the profound extent to which wartime decision making is subject to the rhythm of the domestic political calendar more generally.

The case studies begin in chapter 2 with the Korean War. After the so-called loss of China to communism in 1949, bitter invective and partisan sniping dominated the American political landscape. A Republican Party still smarting from Harry Truman's upset victory in the 1948 election was quick to associate the outbreak of the Korean War in June 1950 with the administration's "fumbling" of policy toward the Far East. With voters' passions whipped up by red-baiters and demagogues in that fall's midterm election campaign, the chapter argues that Truman's fear of reprisal at the ballot box left him powerless to resist the hawkish recommendations of General Douglas MacArthur, the wildly popular commander of United Nations forces in Korea. Archival documents demonstrate how electoral pressures played a pivotal role in the decision to cross the 38th parallel, an action that triggered massive Chinese intervention and brought America to the precipice of defeat. In the nearly three-year stalemate that ensued, the domestic political calendar continued to thwart Truman's ability to negotiate an armistice on his preferred terms, before finally giving his successor, Dwight Eisenhower, the political space necessary to bring hostilities to a close.

Vietnam remains the classic case for any study of the domestic political determinants of U.S. foreign policy. Less understood, however, is the extent to which these pressures systematically interacted with the constraints imposed by the electoral cycle. It is an unusually rich case, covering three presidential election campaigns and supported by a documentary record that is as massive as it is revealing. Chapter 3 explores the "Americanization" of the war, comprising consequential decisions on major troop deployments and bombing offensives. Delayed by Johnson's 1964 election bid, moderated by the 1966 midterms, and fruitlessly paused at the advent of the 1968 race, the "gradual escalation" strategy pursued by the administration was in large part a product of political circumstance. Yet as Johnson found out to his cost, the electoral cycle can severely limit incumbents' room for maneuver even when their names are not on the ballot, as other candidates and actors conspired to scupper efforts to reach a negotiated settlement before Johnson's departure from office in 1969.

In his attempts to secure "peace with honor," Richard Nixon faced similar domestic constraints to those of his predecessor. At first, he delicately balanced the strategic desire to win the war through escalation with the political necessity of signaling that an end to American involvement was imminent. However, chapter 4 reveals a shift in Nixon's calculus as his reelection bid loomed. Virtually every facet of strategy from 1971 onward took into account the political realities at home. Private telephone recordings make the extent of Nixon's cynical strategy devastatingly clear, as he carefully calibrated troop withdrawals, bombing offensives, and diplomatic initiatives to deliver victory at the polls in 1972. Looking at the infamous "decent interval" strategy, this chapter makes plain how Nixon sacrificed the future stability of South Vietnam at the altar of electoral expedience.

The book brings events up to date with its discussion of the Iraq War. Going beyond the initial invasion of 2003, chapter 5 sets out the profound extent to which military and diplomatic strategy was infected by electoral considerations in the aftermath of President Bush's intervention in the Middle East. Recently declassified documents and interviews with three commanding generals, multiple ambassadors, and National Security Council representatives reveal that critical operational and strategic decisions were repeatedly deferred to satisfy the White House's electoral concerns. These episodes include the on-again, off-again assault on the "bomb factory" of Fallujah through 2004, as well as the "surge" of 2007. Only in the "lame duck" phase of his presidency, following the 2006 midterms, could George W. Bush throw the Hail Mary pass he understood to be central to any fading hope of rescuing the failing mission to bring stability to the Middle East. Then, with improvements in security finally being realized, the president entered another race against time. With the 2008 election fast approaching, decisions on troop commitments in the aftermath of the surge and the negotiation of a critical diplomatic agreement covering the United States' continued presence in Iraq were both shaped in important ways by the exigencies of the political calendar.

After grappling with the legacy of his promise to end the war within sixteen months of assuming office, Barack Obama's appetite for an extended commitment of boots on the ground in Iraq eroded as his reelection campaign approached. Rejecting the consensus in his administration regarding the strategic necessity of a follow-on force, Obama instead chose to "go to zero" in late 2011, redeeming his earlier pledge before voters as the 2012 race heated up. Chapter 6 utilizes additional interviews with four-star generals, Pentagon officials, and close presidential advisors to reveal the nakedly political origins of a decision that set Iraq on the path to renewed instability and, by the reckoning of the administration's own counterterrorism chief and CIA director, facilitated the resurgence of Islamic State forces in the region.

The conclusion brings together the main findings of the book, noting a number of patterns that endure despite the contextual differences between the cases. While the conceptual framework deployed in this study is bound to the cases examined in the foregoing analysis, this final chapter also suggests potentially fruitful ways in which this may be expanded for use in other contexts. Finally, the chapter addresses two paradoxes that arise concerning the relationship between democracy and war. First, it comments on how the effect of electoral constraints challenge the received wisdom that democracies are good at fighting and winning wars. Second, it explores the normative implications of the argument presented in the book. Responsiveness to the concerns of voters is cherished as a core principle of democracy, yet time and again it has led to ill-advised strategies on the battlefield. When it comes to high-stakes decisions concerning war and peace, then, electoral politics clearly matters, but whether it *should* is still very much open to debate.

ONE

Presidents, Politics, and War

If you're going to be involved in some type of foreign activity that is going to take resources and entail risks to forces, you need to do it in a manner that is both most practical and most effective, but at the same time try to keep your political support at home, in terms of the Congress, in terms of the American public, and with the election cycles, both midterm elections as well as presidential elections.

—JOHN BRENNAN

THIS CHAPTER INTRODUCES a new conceptual framework for understanding the influence of electoral politics on presidential decision making in war. It conceptualizes electoral pressures as a conditional source of constraint on a leader's room for maneuver, which may push or pull presidents toward more cautious or more aggressive courses of action depending on their perception of the strategic and electoral stakes. It then outlines five mechanisms that explain precisely how an incumbent's desire for reelection influences decisions concerning military and diplomatic strategy, alongside the conditions under which each mechanism might be expected to operate. While the domestic political calendar plays a crucial role in mediating the significance of electoral considerations, it does not do so in a linear fashion. Rather, the impact of electoral pressures varies quantitatively and qualitatively across the four-year cycle. By plotting these five mechanisms of constraint onto a model of the electoral cycle, the chapter illustrates how the domestic political calendar generates a rhythm of decision making that may be observed during each of the major wars examined in the remainder of the book.

Warrior Politicians

In approaching decisions about military and diplomatic strategy in war, U.S. presidents have dual responsibilities. On the one hand, they are commanders in chief, responsible for pursuing courses of action they deem to be in the national interest. On the other hand, as elected officeholders, they must ensure that any course of action they choose carries minimal electoral risk to their personal political future. In thinking about how electoral constraints affect wartime decision making, then, we can employ a useful heuristic that conceptualizes decision making as an attempt to balance two sets of preferences, as illustrated in figure 1.1.[1] This conceptualization may be considered a kind of two-level game in which the president is driven by concerns about the national interest at the international level and political self-interest at the domestic level.[2]

On one side of this balance is the *strategic preference* of the president. This refers to the course of action on the table that the president perceives to carry optimal characteristics in terms of military and diplomatic utility. The way in which this preference manifests in practice will of course vary depending on several contingent factors, including the nature of the broader war aims being pursued and the president's assessment of the relative costs and benefits of the proposed action. For the purposes of this study, however, the precise origins of a president's strategic preferences fall outside the scope of analysis. This is because the book seeks to examine how electoral constraints cause presidents to deviate from what they might otherwise have done. To do this, we need to know what leaders' preferences entail, but not necessarily where they come from.

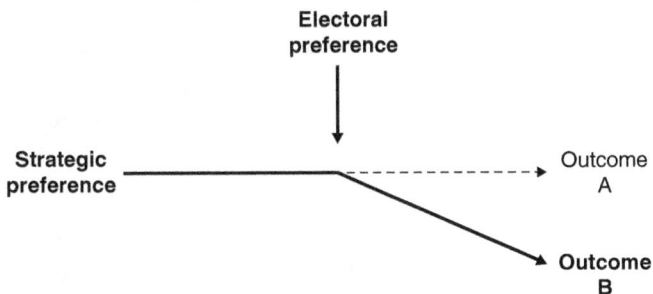

FIGURE 1.1 Presidential preference alignment. (Image by author.)

On the other side of this decision-making process is a president's *electoral preference*. This refers to the course of action the president understands to carry minimal risk to his or her electoral fortunes. Electoral pressures are conceptualized as constraints on decision making, rather than independent sources of strategic preferences. As such, they are denoted as an intervening variable in this model, acting to variously push and pull presidents away from options they deem to be strategically optimal. The precise character of this preference depends on the president's understanding of the electorate's likely reaction to a proposed course of action.

Not every decision made by a president carries electoral significance, of course. Indeed, the public is traditionally thought to know little and care less about foreign policy. Yet more recent studies of mass attitudes make clear that public attentiveness varies across issue areas, and decisions involving the commitment of military forces abroad are particularly likely to "activate" public opinion.[3] During an ongoing conflict, when the costs of military engagements are most vividly felt and placed under a spotlight by political elites and the media, many of the decisions that reach the president's desk *do* tend to garner public attention, and in ways that influence both voting patterns and turnout.[4] It is not without reason that elected officeholders worry about public appraisals of their war records. In this sense, it is not circular logic but political reality to suggest that electoral politics affect wartime decision making because wartime decision making affects electoral politics.

Nevertheless, different courses of action will vary in terms of their salience, and by extension the degree of political risk they entail. The deployment of large numbers of boots on the ground may naturally be expected to invite perhaps the greatest level of public attention, for instance, since this is the most direct and obvious way in which the costs of war may be perceived by the public. It will be particularly acute, moreover, if those troops are tasked with time- and troop-intensive missions that put soldiers directly in harm's way, as in attrition strategies, or counterinsurgency campaigns. While the average voter might not be expected to understand the intricacies of relevant military doctrine, these approaches are more likely to fail the "Dover test," whereby images of flag-draped coffins returning from overseas battlefields trigger a decline of public support for a war. Even in cases where public sensitivity to casualty rates is reduced, scrutiny from the media or political elites can provide important cues to the public in ways that raise the electoral stakes of any decision.[5] Strategies that entail less risk to U.S. forces or that may be kept secret from the public, such as those involving the use of special forces, drones, and cyber technology, might reasonably be considered less salient and therefore less electorally significant. Yet even here, ethical, moral, or legal concerns can generate politically damaging headlines. The infamous "Black Hawk Down" scenario in Mogadishu, for instance, demonstrates that even missions of relatively low human and financial cost can backfire, with political consequences that dwarf their strategic significance.[6]

Ultimately, however, this is a study of presidential decision making, not public opinion. As such, what matters in establishing the electoral preference in this model is not objective assessments of what public attitudes actually were in any given case, but rather what the president *perceived* them to be. Moreover, the president's decision-making process usually involves perceptions of latent as well as active public opinion, since presidents necessarily need to gauge the expected public reaction to a decision *before* that decision is made.[7] In coming to these judgments, presidents may use a variety of different indicators. Most academic studies of public opinion analyze mass polling data, yet while approval ratings and trends may be generally instructive for presidents, attitudes toward more specific courses of action might show up only in more sophisticated surveys.[8] Media coverage, congressional sentiment, and the views of other political elites may be monitored as alternative or additional bellwethers of the public mood on any given issue.[9] As seasoned politicians, of course, presidents may simply rely on their own political instincts to anticipate how voters might react.[10] Finally, in estimating current and especially future public opinion, it should be remembered that political leaders can be, and often are, wrong.[11] While it may still be instructive to examine opinion polls, congressional sentiment, and media coverage, then, these are not foolproof proxies for presidential perceptions of electoral risks. It is essential to strive to uncover evidence of presidents actually engaging with and speaking about their thoughts on the public mood wherever possible, as will be done in the empirical chapters that follow.[12]

In line with this book's focus on decision making *during* an ongoing conflict, the outcomes in this heuristic refer to major decisions taken by the president to escalate or de-escalate a conflict to which the United States is already committed. In the abstract, this may include a wide variety of military actions, from operational decisions (such as the authorization or cessation of bombing programs or alterations to the number of troops committed to a conflict) to broader strategic shifts (such as changes to the aims being sought through military means). In the diplomatic sphere, it could include various bargaining positions adopted during negotiations designed to bring about peace through the granting of concessions or the use of threats to generate concessions from an opponent. Yet the intended utility of this heuristic lies not in its generalizability across categories of decisions so much as its ability to provide a coherent explanation of exactly how electoral pressures mattered in the intrinsically significant cases explored in subsequent chapters. The scope of decisions to be examined is therefore limited by the actor involved and the historical context rather than some predetermined class of actions. In other words, this book is interested in the major decisions that reached the president's desk during the wars in Korea, Vietnam, and Iraq, as derived from a review of the historical literature of each conflict.

In figure 1.1, Outcome A may be considered the strategically optimal course of action, which reflects the strategic preference in any given case. If electoral considerations have no effect on decision making—akin to the null hypothesis in this analysis—we would expect to be able to observe a correlation between the strategic preference and the option ultimately chosen. If, however, as is argued here, electoral pressures do matter, we would expect the decision to look meaningfully different, with the strategic preference pushed off course by such electoral constraints, as represented by Outcome B. As the following section explores, the president may choose to adapt the proposed course of action in various ways—for instance, by altering the size of proposed troop deployments, employing alternative means of (de-)escalation, or delaying a decision altogether. The primary point, however, is that this course of action will not be predicted by an examination of the strategic preference alone.

The degree of (mis)alignment between the president's strategic and electoral preferences is an important factor determining the degree to which electoral pressures shape decision making. In general, it may be reasonably inferred that as the gap between each preference increases, so does the potential impact that electoral constraints may have, as more adjustment will be required to bring a proposed course of action to an acceptable balance. Extreme cases of near perfect alignment or near total misalignment may also be observed. In the former scenario, in which a proposed course of action is deemed both strategically optimal and of virtually no electoral risk (i.e., because overwhelming public approval is anticipated in response), electoral pressures will be pushing against an open door. More permissive than constraining in nature, they may in this situation be considered causally epiphenomenal. The latter scenario, in which presidents may struggle to find any viable course of action that sufficiently balances both their strategic and their electoral preferences, is more interesting. In this case, presidents may be forced to pick between the unpalatable choice of prioritizing *either* strategic optimality *or* political self-interest. Indeed, in the empirical part of this book, we will see instances of both the noble and cynical outcomes of this conundrum.

Go Big or Go Home: Mechanisms of (De-)escalation

Electoral pressures push and pull presidents, then, but in what direction? How might the relative alignment between preferences encourage an incumbent to double down on an ongoing conflict? What kind of balance might instead incentivize a commander in chief to climb down the ladder of escalation? In thinking about these questions, three mechanisms of electoral constraint are instructive.

Delay

When presidents perceive a clear need to increase the level of military commitment to a conflict, but fear a political backlash as an election approaches, their first preference is likely to be to *delay* making any decision until after polling day. This mechanism will be particularly prominent if the relative electoral risk of escalation strongly outweighs the strategic opportunity at stake. To take an obvious example, if on October 1 it is deemed militarily desirable to deploy a reserve battalion to shore up security in a certain position, but doing so risks the prospect of provoking an extreme political reaction at home given recent casualty trends, this course of action would be a prime candidate for the *delay* mechanism.

Even if the proposed action is deemed absolutely essential, however, the timing of that decision may be more flexible. Since the electoral risks of making unpopular changes to strategy are amplified the closer one gets to an election, the president may be willing to accept some substantive cost of postponement to avoid suffering any political fallout when it matters most.[13] For instance, if the position in question is anticipated to weaken and ultimately fall within six months unless reinforcements are sent, the president may simply wait until after the election before belatedly sending the required troops, hoping that the status quo policy could at least prevent a more serious setback in the meantime.

Similarly, this mechanism might occur even if the proposed course of action is expected to ultimately gain a significant strategic advantage or even turn the tide of the war in ways that would garner public acclaim. Both risky military gambles with potential for a tremendous political upside and slow-burning military strategies that will take time to yield visible success are usually best left until after the election. Much better to pursue such courses of action early in the following electoral period, giving them more time to succeed, or otherwise allowing political space for their failure to be forgotten by voters with notoriously short time horizons.[14] Examples here include major offensive operations or shifts to a counterinsurgency strategy.

To demonstrate the existence of this delay mechanism, there are several observable implications that the case studies presented in this book should be able to identify. First, of course, it should be possible to find evidence that a change in strategy was deemed necessary and perceived as such by the president. Indications that the president specifically favored an escalatory course of action would also ideally be identifiable. Next, we must be able to show that a decision was deferred, in the sense that viable opportunities to review the status quo strategy were not pursued. Relatedly, we must be able to show that the reason for the delay was electoral in nature. Finally, if the decision was truly delayed and not simply ignored, we should be able to find evidence of the same problem being considered in the postelection phase, likely with a degree of urgency not hitherto seen, and an escalatory decision being made very quickly.

Dampening

If the president assesses the strategic cost of delaying a decision to be more significant than the electoral risk of doing so, or if a preelection decision is made necessary by circumstances outside of the president's control (for instance, due to fixed deadlines imposed by international organizations, or immediate threats posed by other actors), political sensitivities remain a critical component of the decision-making process. Under the *dampening* mechanism, escalatory courses of action deemed to carry high utility in military and diplomatic terms will be watered down, with their most politically "noisy" aspects removed to satisfy the president's electoral preference.

There are two ways this may manifest in policy deliberations. First, the president can choose to employ a broadly similar method of escalation while scaling down its intensity. For instance, more troops may be the order of the day, but a president could send lower numbers than militarily desirable, or insist on adopting rules of engagement or a strategic approach that employs these forces in less costly ways, such as assuming active defense rather than offensive operations. Second, a president may choose to adopt a different method of escalation that carries less salience or electoral risk.[15] For instance, if it is deemed strategically optimal to destroy an enemy's military industrial base through strategic bombing operations, covert sabotage operations might plausibly be used instead to achieve some measure of the same goal.[16]

This mechanism operates in a fairly straightforward manner. In a "first cut," proposals brought to the White House must pass a test of "political acceptability."[17] If they are deemed to carry an unacceptable level of political risk, they will be rejected, often before any serious in-depth strategy review has even begun. After this initial screening, the remaining options will be assessed across a range of different metrics, of which political "noisiness" will remain an important one among many others. The remaining proposals will now likely be finessed to provide what the president perceives to be the most optimal plan in military or diplomatic terms with a sufficiently low level of political risk.

Spur

The *spur* mechanism describes a scenario in which presidents dial up the bellicosity of any option under discussion in an effort to satisfy their electoral preferences, despite such escalation not aligning with what is deemed to be the strategically optimal course of action. This is in some sense the logical mirror of the *dampening* mechanism. Typically, this would entail a president responding to concerns that a belligerent mood among voters might imperil his or her political future should a preferred course of action be branded excessively "weak" or "soft." Hence, we might expect to see decisions to send more troops than strictly needed to a conflict, or the authorization of particularly bold major operations in the run-up to an election.

To observe the existence of this mechanism, we would *not* expect to see substantial evidence of presidents expressing support for escalatory courses of action on the grounds of strategic optimality. Instead, we might find evidence of them favoring a much more constrained course of action—or, indeed, the status quo—on the grounds of military or diplomatic utility. We would then expect to uncover evidence of the president perceiving a generally hawkish existing public mood and adopting a course of action in line with these more belligerent tendencies.

*   *   *

Which of the three preceding mechanisms operate depends in part on the nature and relative alignment between a president's strategic and electoral preferences, as illustrated in figure 1.2:

1. If a president perceives an escalatory course of action to be strategically optimal, but their electoral preference points toward a de-escalatory decision as less politically risky and it is possible to leave the decision until a less politically sensitive period in the future, the *delay* mechanism is likely to be observed.
2. If a president perceives an escalatory course of action to be strategically optimal, but their electoral preference points toward a de-escalatory decision as less politically risky and it is *not* possible to delay making a decision, the *dampening* mechanism is likely to be observed.
3. When the president deems a de-escalatory course of action to be strategically optimal, while voters are perceived to favor a more escalatory approach, the *spur* mechanism is most likely to operate.
4. When the preferences are aligned, electoral constraints push against an open door and thus carry minimal causal significance.

By reconceptualizing electoral pressures as a constraint that can push or pull the president in different directions depending on their perception of the strategic and electoral stakes, it is possible to model the nuanced way in

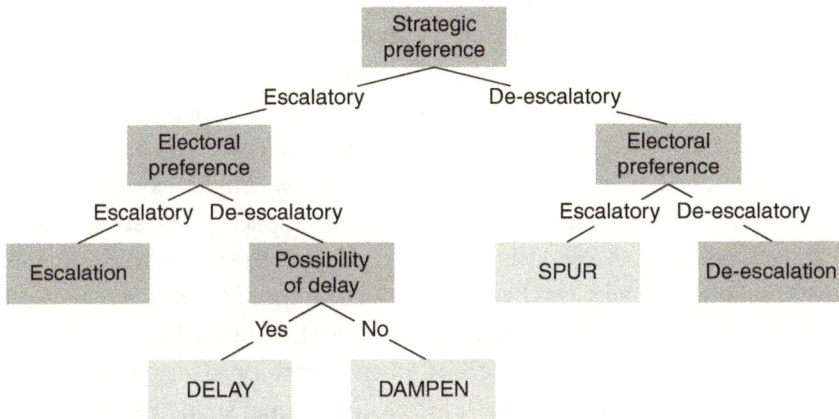

FIGURE 1.2 (De-)escalatory mechanisms of electoral constraint. (Image by author.)

which elections have a conditional impact on presidential behavior in war. The three (de-)escalatory mechanisms described in this section—*delay, dampening,* and *spur*—provide key conceptual tools through which we can identify exactly how presidents respond to the pressures generated by the ballot box.

The Rhythm of the Electoral Cycle

The relative strength of these constraints does not just vary based on the alignment of the president's preferences, however. The stage of the four-year electoral cycle is also a crucial element to take into account, since different phases will carry varying degrees of political sensitivity. Building on earlier discursive models of the impact that the American electoral cycle has on foreign policy more broadly, I begin with the general notion that the influence of electoral considerations rises with increased proximity to a presidential election.[18] Since the public tends to vote retrospectively, and discounts the significance of events as they recede into the past, it follows that the audience costs for any unpopular policy will be greatest on the eve of Election Day.[19] At root, this underpins a host of studies that find increased congruence between foreign policy choices and public preferences as an election approaches.[20] Drawing on the balancing heuristic described above, it can therefore be surmised that as an election approaches, the weight accorded to the electoral preference increases, and in cases where this misaligns with the strategic preference, we might expect particularly notable departures from the course of action originally deemed strategically optimal. By contrast, early in the electoral cycle we might expect the null hypothesis—that electoral constraints have no impact—to be supported.

The connection between the electoral cycle and the strength of electoral constraints is, however, less linear and more nuanced than this simple picture, for three reasons. First, it stands to reason that the *anticipation* of a campaign season may exert as much of an influence on decision making as being in the midst of a campaign. Electorally optimal strategies might take some time to yield success on the battlefield, while other necessary yet electorally risky strategies might be better initiated before the political spotlight is fully on. In either case, if we restrict our analysis to an election year, or the three months preceding an election, as much existing research does, we are liable to mistake absence of evidence for evidence of absence thanks to the limited time frame.

Second, and relatedly, it is not simply future elections that matter. Sensitivity to what had been promised in the *previous* election plausibly matters in decision making too, especially if a president is likely to be running for reelection in part on the basis of having demonstrated an ability to fulfill the mandate voters gave him or her the first time around. It is not axiomatic that the pressure to deliver on one's campaign pledges will be immediately felt, of course. Indeed, not having to face voters for another four years, it may be that campaign rhetoric offers only weak constraints on decision making to begin with.[21] By the time that a president begins to think about a bid for reelection, however, these earlier commitments could come back to bite. The extent to which this is the case will of course depend on how the public mood may have changed over time, but ongoing wars tend not to increase in popularity, meaning unfulfilled pledges to bring them to an end are likely to carry electoral risk as incumbents seeks to bolster their records as elected officials who do what they promised voters they would do.[22]

Third, it seems fair to argue that it is not just presidential elections that matter, but congressional ones too. Though the president's personal political survival is not directly at stake, the loss of political capital that follows a severe loss of support in Congress can jeopardize both the practical ability to pursue various policy objectives as an officeholder and of course a president's reelection prospects thereafter. Indeed, the midterms represent a moment when the balance of power in Congress can change, with a significant impact on a president's ability to push through legislative priorities for the remainder of his or her term, or indeed pursue any proposed military strategy free of congressional interference. Through its formal powers, Congress can undermine such strategies by withholding appropriations; and through its informal powers, such as in holding public hearings and providing scrutiny, it can make it hard to sustain an unpopular strategy.[23] With the president's popularity so tied to his or her party's fortunes, a similarly strong spotlight shines on the actions of the commander in chief during these electoral periods.[24] An increased sensitivity to voter opinion on wartime decisions is therefore only natural. And since the party of a newly elected president tends to suffer losses at the first set of congressional elections it faces, it is not only the voters that presidents need to worry about. In an effort to mitigate this electoral threat and preserve political capitol, a president may face incentives to appease the faction that is expected to make gains, even superficially.

The electoral cycle plays an important role in regulating the strength of the three mechanisms of escalation describe above, then. Yet electoral pressures are also qualitatively different across various phases of the four-year cycle, with the domestic political calendar itself generating constraints of its own. Two further mechanisms may now be outlined.

Hangover

Presidents are bound not only by pressures related to an upcoming election; they also face constraints that derive from what they promised to voters during the previous campaign. The *hangover* mechanism refers to the degree to which a president's strategic preference diverges from a course of action indicated in a prior campaign pledge. While this mechanism therefore operates according to a similar balancing logic as those outlined above, its retrospective character introduces several distinct features that warrant separate examination.

Campaign promises are policy prescriptions crafted in a way that aligns with a candidate's political interests in the middle of an election season. Not yet bearing the dual responsibilities as elected officeholder and commander in chief, aspiring presidents do not need to weigh the same competing priorities as incumbents. The positions they take on wartime policy need to be rhetorically appealing, but not necessarily rooted in concrete analysis of feasibility or strategic desirability. To the extent candidates do weigh such considerations when developing campaign pledges, they typically do so without access to the same range of advice and quality of information that is available to the sitting president. They may therefore simply not know that the policies they champion as a candidate may prove unworkable or inadvisable in practice. And, of course, by the time they assume office, developments on the battlefield or at the negotiating table may render those positions obsolete. For all these reasons, the strategic preferences presidents may hold once in office will not always correlate with the content of their prior campaign positions.[25]

From an electoral perspective, however, there is typically considerable pressure on a newly elected president to fulfill the promises they made to voters as a candidate. To be sure, the notion that winning candidates can be relied upon to act promptly on their campaign pledges once in office is commonly contested. As one scholar puts it, "If election promises are the benchmark, one would probably conclude that elections actually bear no relation to subsequent foreign policy."[26] From Woodrow Wilson having run on a platform of keeping the United States out of the First World War to Lyndon Johnson's infamous remark that he was "not about to send American boys nine or ten thousand miles away from home to do what Asian boys ought to be doing for themselves," it is not difficult to think of significant historical examples of presidents saying one thing on the campaign trail, only to do precisely the opposite once in office.[27] While this conventional wisdom may have a certain intuitive appeal, there is in fact a large body of evidence suggesting that democratic leaders tend to fulfill their promises more than one might assume.[28] It is in part precisely because the charge of having broken a promise carries such political significance for an incumbent's reelection prospects that U.S. presidents frequently make at least some effort to fulfill their prior pledges.

This does not mean presidents will always seek to keep their campaign promises in a consistent or timely fashion, of course. Based on the preceding analysis, this should not be surprising. Newly elected presidents enter office during something of a "honeymoon" period in which voters, the media, and congressional opponents tend to give them a degree of slack in implementing the policy agenda for which their electoral victory provided a mandate.[29] With four years until the next presidential election and with political capital at its peak, an incumbent may be able to delay the fulfillment of problematic pledges or explain away their incongruence with the policies they choose to pursue once in office. This permissive environment rarely lasts, however. In more politically sensitive phases of the electoral cycle, promises that have yet to be fulfilled will come under the political spotlight once more and add pressure to a president seeking reelection on the strength of their record.

In determining the strength of this type of electoral pressure, the specificity of a candidate's campaign pledge logically plays a critical role. On the one hand, the task of reconciling a strategic preference with a prior pledge is made much easier if the statements made on the campaign trail are broad and vague in character. On the other hand, if a campaign promise is narrow and specific, it will tend to limit the president's options once in office to a much greater degree. While a full examination of the exact drivers of campaign promises lays beyond the scope of the present analysis, it is worth noting that both approaches may carry appeal. To be sure, rhetorical ambiguity on the campaign trail is undoubtedly preferable from the perspective of seeking to preserve flexibility once in office. For certain individuals, this will be a particularly viable approach. Candidates with significant military experience, for instance, may be able to get away with a degree of rhetorical ambiguity, safe in the knowledge that a public that tends to defer to the judgment of military professionals will trust them to make the right call once in office.[30] Ambiguity might also be preferable if the electorate expresses weak or divided preferences on an issue. In such cases, it may be better to fudge and neutralize an issue, rather than alienate a significant subset of voters by articulating a clear position.[31] Nevertheless, and by equal and opposite measure, if a candidate thinks they have a winning position on an issue, it often pays to express it in a way that clearly differentiates it from that of their opponent.[32] Campaign promises that are too vague may attract charges of vacuousness.[33] And in cases where the public broadly supports a policy goal—say, ending an ongoing war—a candidate may need to be more precise in mapping out the means they will use to achieve it.

The *hangover* mechanism therefore describes a newly elected president's efforts to reconcile what they said they would do with what they now believe they should do once in office. It will be stronger in cases where the president has made narrow and specific promises to the electorate, and weaker in cases where those pledges are broad and vague. To substantiate the existence of this mechanism in practice, we would expect to find evidence of presidents choosing to reject or adapt courses of action they perceive to be strategically optimal in ways that enable them to claim they have fulfilled the terms of their promises.

Spoiler

The electoral cycle does not simply interfere with presidential decision making regarding efforts to win a war militarily. Building on the more traditional conception of a two-level game, it also presents obstacles to the president's ability to reach diplomatic agreements geared toward the peaceful de-escalation and resolution of a conflict.[34] The *spoiler* mechanism describes three ways in which an election can interfere with the bargaining positions of the president and erode his or her leverage during negotiations.

Firstly, and closely related to the underlying logic of the previous four mechanisms, a president's status as an elected officeholder generates additional political preferences beyond the national interest in any negotiation. While a deal that maximizes diplomatic utility may be desirable, it must also be "good enough" politically to allow the president to be reelected.[35] On the one hand, this may result in the granting of concessions that are strategically suboptimal because the electoral significance of reaching *a* deal may outweigh the diplomatic cost of striking a *bad* deal. On the other hand, a strategically necessary deal may prove out of reach thanks to continued stubbornness on certain red lines that, while of minimal diplomatic significance, may carry considerable political weight. Either way, presidents' political interests serve to pressure them to adopt suboptimal diplomatic positions.

Secondly, if presidents can rise above the fray of partisan politics, the challenges posed by an election campaign are compounded by the presence of other actors with competing preferences. At home, presidential challengers carry similar political incentives to the incumbent but none of the international responsibilities that come with being the nation's commander in chief. As a result, high-profile negotiations involving the United States represent opportunities for other candidates to differentiate themselves from one another and the current administration, with bold, imaginative, and sometimes downright unworkable alternative proposals. While these may be effective in garnering votes, they may also serve to weaken the incumbent administration's room for maneuver in ongoing talks. Already uncertain as to how credible any commitments made by a here-today, gone-tomorrow president may be in an election season, an opponent is incentivized to monitor the alternative positions put forward by front-runners in the presidential race and alter their bargaining position accordingly.[36]

Thirdly, the fixed nature of the electoral calendar in the United States means proximity to polling day acts as a further key constraining factor. Since there is no guarantee that the president will be able to strike a deal after the results of the election are known, there is often a structural incentive to grant additional concessions as that time horizon shrinks. This may of course be compounded by the reality that opponents will also be aware of this, so may drag out negotiations until the last moments of a campaign in order to extract as many concessions as possible, even if the sitting president already offered better terms than any other opponent. This variant of the *spoiler* mechanism will be particularly acute for those who lose their reelection bids, since their ability to credibly commit to a deal will be at its weakest during the transition to a new administration.[37]

Each of these components of the *spoiler* mechanism may again be observed through a close analysis of private meetings and memoranda involving the president in which concerns about these electoral dynamics are raised and used to justify any alterations to the president's bargaining positions. We may also see efforts by the president to convince rival candidates to keep any ongoing talks off the campaign trail or even support the incumbent administration.

*   *   *

The previous two sections have argued that the strength of electoral constraints on wartime decision making depends on the relative alignment between the president's strategic and electoral preferences as well as the phase of the electoral cycle. In turn, the exact nature of these constraints can be described using five mechanisms. When a president's strategic preference points to a more escalatory course of action than his or her electoral preference deems politically wise, he or she will *delay* making a decision if possible, or otherwise *dampen* the most unpopular aspects of the proposed action. By contrast, if the president's electoral interests suggest a more escalatory policy, this may be taken as a *spur* to a more belligerent action than perceived strategically necessary. Somewhat independent of this assessments of the public mood, the electoral cycle also creates two further limitations on presidents: they must reckon with the *hangover* effects of campaign pledges upon assuming office, and upcoming elections may also play a *spoiler* role during any negotiations with a foreign government.

By mapping these mechanisms across the domestic political calendar, it is now possible to summarize the role that electoral politics plays in presidential decisions about military and diplomatic strategy in war. As illustrated in figures 1.3 and 1.4, we can think about the relative significance of different constraints by considering when they are likely to manifest in five different phases of the electoral cycle. Taken together, these patterns reveal how presidential decision making follows a distinctive rhythm dictated by the electoral cycle.[38]

In the opening "honeymoon" phase of a president's first term, the range and intensity of electoral pressures are likely to be fairly limited. Benefiting from a boost of political capital from their recent electoral victory, a newly elected commander in chief will likely be able to hew closer to their strategic preference at this stage when making decisions about an ongoing war. Nevertheless, it is also here where the *hangover* effects of any campaign pledges may serve to limit this freedom of maneuver, depending on

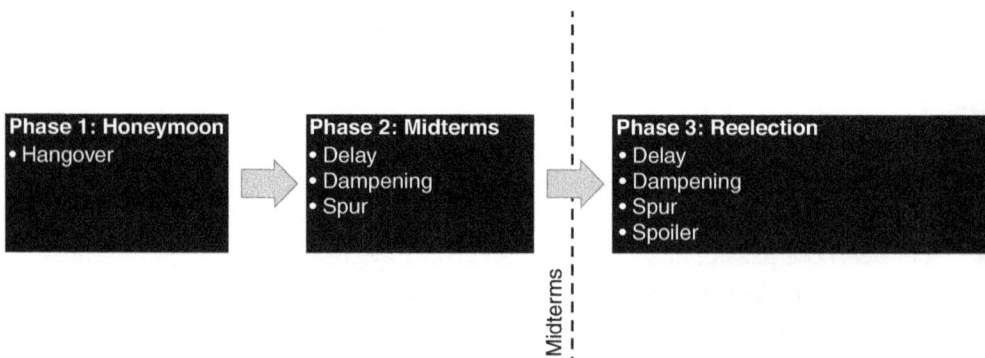

Phase 1: Honeymoon
• Hangover

Phase 2: Midterms
• Delay
• Dampening
• Spur

Phase 3: Reelection
• Delay
• Dampening
• Spur
• Spoiler

Midterms

FIGURE 1.3 First-term dynamics. (Image by author.)

the specificity of those prior commitments. Moreover, while the precise length of a president's honeymoon period varies, the goodwill offered to newly elected presidents inevitably fades over time, particularly in an era of increased polarization and media scrutiny.[39]

In the second phase, anticipation of the upcoming midterms will serve to strengthen the influence of electoral considerations on decision making. Typically, a president will seek to *delay* escalatory decisions that carry excessive risk of backlash from a conflict-averse public, or otherwise *dampen* a necessary decision's more politically controversial aspects. If the president perceives escalation instead to be electorally preferable, he or she may take this as a *spur* to action, dialing up military intervention beyond what is deemed strategically optimal.

It is in the reelection phase of the cycle, roughly from the midterms to the presidential election, that electoral constraints will have their greatest effect, however. With the president's personal future at stake, the importance of electoral preferences in the president's balancing calculus will increase significantly, and as such the *delay, dampening,* and *spur* mechanisms will be most likely to be observed as Election Day approaches. Should the United States be in the midst of negotiations, it is also here where the electoral cycle will serve to undermine the leverage afforded to the president, as the *spoiler* mechanism predicts.

Presidents who win reelection enter a decision-making environment that is generally less constrained than that of their first term—but not entirely

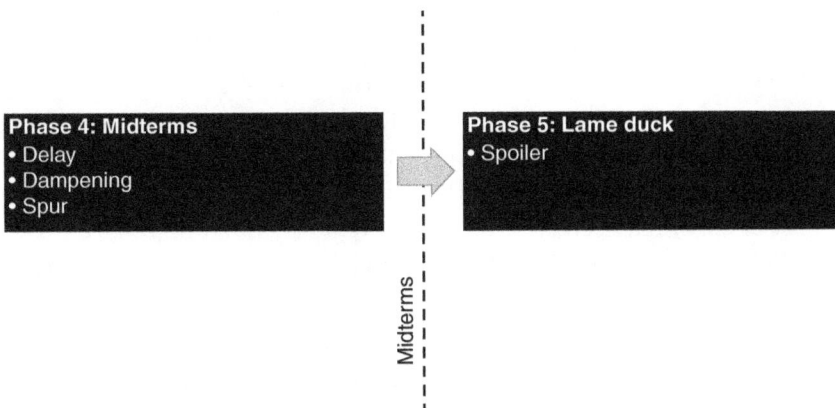

FIGURE 1.4 Second-term dynamics. (Image by author.)

so. While they may enjoy a modest increase in political capital, with a brief boost in the polls and a fresh mandate for their policies, second-term presidents tend to enjoy much shorter honeymoons.[40] As incumbents with several years of governing experience, they are simply known quantities by this stage. For similar reasons, they are much less likely than aspiring candidates to issue campaign pledges that inadvertently tie their hands to policies that are strategically incoherent. During an ongoing war, moreover, sitting presidents are unlikely to offer specific promises for how they would handle a conflict if reelected. To do so would be to admit the current course upon which they have embarked is somehow flawed, which would invite reasonable questions about why they have not yet been changed. For these reasons the *hangover* mechanism is not expected to feature in any meaningful form during this phase. Instead, the focus will likely be on implementing any policies that were delayed during the previous phase, with one eye on the implications of doing so in the context of the upcoming midterms. As those congressional races heat up, then, the *delay, dampening,* or *spur* mechanisms may be observed in a broadly similar manner as before.

After the midterms, a second-term president will enter a fifth and final "lame duck" phase. While incumbents will reach the nadir of their political power during the roughly eleven-week transition, in a country like the United States, with ever-longer campaign seasons, the slide into political impotence will realistically begin the moment the president has passed the congressional off-year elections.[41] Since the incumbent's interest in political survival is essentially removed during this phase, we should in theory see decisions being less affected by most of the mechanisms of electoral constraint offered here. Instead, with no fear of being "booted" out of office, decisions should hew closer to the president's strategic preference in any given case.

In practice, of course, the changed political environment does not entirely eliminate the relevance of the domestic political calendar, but rather alters how the president's electoral incentives are affected by it. Not facing any further set of major national elections that might otherwise impinge on his or her political capital, a president's attention will now likely shift toward concerns about legacy. Since presidents can tend to act more freely in foreign affairs than domestic affairs, it is in the international arena that they will seek to make progress. Of course, during a war, the incentive to go down in the history books as a peacemaker, or perhaps as the person who won the war, will be particularly appealing. Thus, we may see stubborn stances in negotiation, risky escalation to make one last bid for victory, or indeed constrained policies designed to preserve the president's existing reputation. The term "lame duck" is something of a misnomer for wartime presidents, then, since it is at this stage that we might expect incumbents to double down on efforts to end a war one way or the other, precisely because of the proximity of the election and their subsequent departure from office.[42]

Nevertheless, if the electoral cycle encourages presidents to be more active in foreign affairs in the twilight phases of their terms, it also typically results in any such efforts failing to achieve significant progress.[43] Lacking the ability to credibly commit the United States to a certain course of action beyond January of the following year, and lacking political capital at home, it is here where the *spoiler* mechanism may arguably be at its strongest. Even if a president's name is not on the ballot paper, the available bargaining positions are still liable to be undercut by not one but *two* presidential candidates at home, while a negotiating opponent is likely to turn its attention to the positions of the next administration. As William Quandt has rightly observed, "The idea that a president who does not have to face reelection can act free of domestic political concerns misses the point. He may be free, but he is not taken seriously as he reaches the end of his second term."[44]

If victory through decisive action on the battlefield or peace at the negotiating table is unattainable in the time an outgoing president has left in office, another way he or she may seek to protect a legacy is by trying to influence the policy of the successor. One way to do this, of course, is to take actions that help the campaign of the candidate who shares the incumbent's policy preferences. Partisan affiliation plays an important role here—by delaying an unpopular decision, for example, a sitting president may be able to shield their party's nominee from potential criticism arising from their association with the incumbent. Yet the case studies that follow also highlight interesting examples of presidents with significant reservations about the positions of their party's candidate, who in turn may have political incentives to distance themselves from an incumbent who failed to settle an unpopular ongoing war. In such cases of preference misalignment, whether exacerbated by partisan identity or not, an incumbent may prefer to adapt or self-censor actions they might otherwise take in an effort to mitigate against the possibility of a president-elect undoing their efforts during or shortly after the transition. While a presidential turnover largely involves a clean slate at the executive level, particularly in terms of personnel, incumbents know that decisions made in the twilight of their terms in office can often prove sticky, with knock-on implications for the freedom of maneuver enjoyed by the next occupant of the Oval Office. For these reasons, it is likely that the decisions of a lame duck president will still be minimally sensitive to the electoral implications they might entail for the prospects of the candidates who are running.[45]

Lame duck presidents thus serve as something of a special case. Theoretically, it is likely that few of the electoral constraints outlined earlier will operate, other than the *spoiler* mechanism, which will be particularly acute. Nevertheless, the presence of a unique political environment in which the president is no longer running adds additional complexity.

Context, Contingency, and Comparison

If presidents share an underlying interest in political survival, it does not necessarily follow that they interpret information uniformly or act perfectly alike. Rather, each individual carries various personal attributes that influence their decision-making behaviors in different ways. A leader's beliefs concerning the use of force will inevitably shape their perception of the relative strategic requirements and electoral risks in any given case.[46] A whole host of psychological biases may similarly influence a president's perception of the decision-making environment.[47] Experience matters too, both in terms of the length of time in office as president and in terms of prior background, with fresh, untested presidents as well as those with extensive prior military service being more prone to crises and the use of force than their more experienced civilian counterparts.[48] Leader attributes also interact with the preferences of the electorate in ways that make certain courses of action more politically viable for some presidents than others. Hawks, for instance, possess a domestic advantage over doves in pursuing rapprochement with a distrusted adversary, while Republicans who lose wars are punished more harshly than Democrats in similar situations.[49] As political polarization increases over time, ideological divisions among voters may also alter a president's risk calculus when considering whether to pursue victory on the battlefield or through a negotiated settlement, with liberals more likely to disapprove of an operation that incurs large numbers of casualties than conservatives.[50]

Neither do presidents make decisions in a vacuum. Wars do not follow a predictable pattern, and each one is shaped by the broader political, strategic, and social environment in which it takes place. As further detailed below, existing work highlights several contextual features that can mediate the strength of democratic constraints in any given conflict, from the relative freedom of the press and professionalization of the armed forces to the technological sophistication of military operations and ways in which a war is financed. Wars which are conducted with an all-volunteer army, supported by drones, paid for by borrowing, and with strict censorship in place are thus far less vulnerable to electoral pressures than those conducted by conscripted infantrymen, using taxes, and reported on by a free press.

In short, contextual differences undoubtedly preclude perfect comparison across cases, and the role of contingency in the messy real world of international relations renders any firm predictions questionable. The framework outlined here is thus a necessarily stylized approximation of reality. It does not seek to provide lawlike assertions, nor does it aim to predict when a need for a decision regarding military and diplomatic strategy will arise in any given conflict. Instead, it is intended to provide a rough guide to the relationship between electoral politics and presidential decision making and a set of analytical tools with which to make sense of decisions that have reached the president's desk in any given case. Above all, it should be recalled that electoral pressures are just that, *pressures*, and not deterministic phenomena forcing all presidents to act alike.

For similar reasons, it follows that the case studies presented in this book are not intended as comprehensive chronicles of historical events. Instead, they focus on aspects relevant to the framework outlined in the following chapter, which like any conceptual lens necessarily highlights certain aspects at the expense of other underlying social or political explanations of each course of action.

Public Opinion: Who Leads? Who Follows?

The framework outlined above implies that presidents seek to satisfy their electoral preference by altering the course of action deemed strategically optimal. It could reasonably be argued, however, that leaders who believe in the necessity of a politically risky decision may instead seek to bring public opinion in line with their preferences. Indeed, from the broader literature on public attitudes to war, we know that public opinion is somewhat malleable, driven at least in part by elite cues.[51] In turn, some scholars suggest that presidents not only have the power to shape and lead public attitudes, but have increasingly sought to do so.[52] While such instrumental behavior may comprise genuine attempts to educate voters on the strategic wisdom of the president's preferred policy, presidents may also use the "bully pulpit" to deceive voters about the merits and risks of proposed courses of action. By framing issues in misleading ways, cherry-picking supporting evidence, and failing to disclose more pessimistic assessments, presidents can make certain courses of action seem more palatable to voters. They might also engage in a rhetorical bait and switch, publicly describing a version of the strategy that sounds appealing, while doing something quite different in practice. "The democratic process may act as a constraint on leaders' ability to go to war," concludes John Schuessler, "but deception provides a way around that constraint."[53]

Yet while presidents may well *try* to lead public opinion, a number of studies suggest their ability to do so is rather limited in practice. Despite enjoying the supposed rhetorical advantages of the "bully pulpit," presidents are frequently unable to push the needle of public opinion to the degree they hope for.[54] Part of the reason for this, of course, is that the public is not as passive as top-down models of public opinion imply. Even if we concede that the public's views about "facts on the ground" are partly mediated by the individuals and institutions that provide such information,[55] recent work demonstrates that ordinary citizens also bring their own predispositions to the table when evaluating foreign policy issues, and may take cues from one another.[56] The effect of elite cues is also contextually contingent—varying across issues and depending on the existing distribution of mass opinion about the issue.[57] Even if the public were to simply follow the lead of elites, other actors compete with the president for the public's attention, including those from the opposing political party, the media, the military, and among the president's own inner circle of advisors.[58] As history has shown, these latter groups have often been key agents in eroding the president's traditional "power to persuade" by calling out presidential efforts to *mislead* the public, from the leak of the Pentagon Papers in the 1970s to the recent revelations in the *Washington Post*'s Afghanistan Papers. Indeed, recent experimental work demonstrates that presidents who are revealed to have misinformed the public about military operations are likely to pay a domestic political penalty, even if those operations are successful.[59] Hence, as much as some might like to, presidents cannot entirely ignore public attitudes or write themselves a blank check of support for costly military operations through a smart communications strategy. While they may have some wiggle room to influence public perceptions of their chosen course of action, the menu of feasible options open to them will usually be limited by concerns about the expected public reaction.[60]

In reality, of course, the two approaches are not mutually exclusive. Just as public opinion can both shape and be shaped by elite rhetoric, so, too, will presidents both try to lead and be bound by their perceptions of public attitudes. The more interesting question, then, is under what conditions presidents will choose to lead or follow. Douglas Foyle, for instance, argues that the president's beliefs regarding the desirability of public input into foreign policy choices are a key mediating variable in this respect.[61] Other studies explore variation across different stages of the decision-making process, with most noting that public attitudes exert more influence on decision makers in earlier phases when options are generated and policies selected compared with later implementation phases, when leaders seek to "sell" their chosen option.[62] Relatedly, given that a leader's informational advantage over the public is largest at the outset of a conflict, we might expect attempts to influence mass opinion to be more proactive (and successful) in the earlier phases of an ongoing war relative to its latter stages, when the public's perception of reality is less elastic.[63]

While this book is not a study of public opinion per se, it does partly contribute to debates concerning presidential responsiveness to mass attitudes about foreign policy. Specifically, the influence of public attitudes on wartime decision making, as filtered through the president's perception of them, are implied to vary across the electoral cycle. While this will also depend on the issue in question and the president's strategic preference in any given case, it can reasonably be inferred that presidents will tend to hew closer to their perception of the public's preference—or at least the preference of an electorally significant subset of the public—at certain sensitive points in the domestic political calendar. In the lead-up to congressional or presidential elections (in which the incumbent is running), we should therefore expect to observe evidence of the president following the voters' preferences. By contrast, after these moments of greatest political sensitivity have passed, we should expect to see far more evidence of presidents making decisions they know will fly against the grain of public opinion and seeking to lead the public in favor of their chosen course instead.

Responsiveness is just one mechanism through which the public can affect foreign policy, however. Citizens may also shape policy by selecting parties or candidates whose preferences reflect their own. Recent experimental work finds strong evidence of this kind of selection mechanism, with voters in the United States placing particularly heavy weight on the security policy positions of presidential contenders when casting ballots.[64] Jeffrey Friedman, meanwhile, argues convincingly that taking popular policy positions may matter less than taking positions that contribute to an image of foreign policy competence. Since the ability to signal an impression of leadership strength carries particularly powerful advantages on the campaign trail, candidates are incentivized to adopt hawkish foreign policy positions that voters intuitively associate with this trait.[65] Other recent work disaggregates the preferences of the electorate, notably finding that support for the use of force is lower among women and documenting how the enfranchisement of women thereby encouraged past presidential candidates to adopt more pacific stances in ongoing conflicts.[66] While elections play a critical role as the main institutional mechanism through which the public shapes foreign policy in each of these studies, they tend to focus on explaining voting behavior, campaign strategies, and electoral outcomes, often assuming or leaving implicit the process through which successful candidates deliver on the preferences of those who cast ballots in their favor. This is precisely what this book examines, adopting the lens of decision making to examine exactly how or when presidents weigh the political pressure to deliver on their campaign pledges with the strategic considerations facing them once in office.

Why Focus on Presidents?

The primary actor of interest in this study is the president. This is in line with the assumption that leaders matter when it comes to foreign policy decision making.[67] More specifically, with respect to electoral politics and wartime decision making, presidents are logically the key actors, since only they occupy such a unique position as both commander in chief and holder of the highest elected office.

In reality, of course, decisions regarding wartime strategy are not the sole preserve of political leaders. Presidents routinely delegate authority to other administration officials and the senior military leadership, and they rely heavily on the information and arguments presented by these advisors when making decisions. As a result, such figures can play an instrumental role in shaping what issues reach the Oval Office and how the president seeks to resolve them. Naturally, some bureaucratic actors will tend to be more successful than others in bringing the president's preferences closer to their own, with the result that any dialing up or down of a proposed course of action may at least in part be attributable to the influence of those advisors whom the president finds most persuasive. Officials may also be able to block or otherwise effect changes to policies they oppose through bureaucratic obstructionism. The ease with which advisors can do so also varies of course with the ways in which each president chose to structure their bureaucracies.[68] These dynamics would potentially help account for any decisions that were delayed, at least until those bureaucratic agents were removed or convinced to ease their opposition to a proposed policy. In short, to recognize that electoral pressures exert a meaningful influence on wartime decision making is not to deny the existence of alternative constraints that influence the behavior of individual leaders, and bureaucratic explanations stand out as a particularly valuable explanation for variation in outcomes over and above that which can be explained through the electoral framework.[69]

However, the role played by political and military advisors should not be viewed solely as a rival explanation to the framework offered in this book. On the contrary, insofar as presidential preferences may be profoundly shaped by the contours of internal bureaucratic debate, it is important to incorporate these dynamics in seeking to establish how the president perceived the strategic and electoral stakes of a given decision. Moreover, it may frequently be the case that it is difficult to fully disentangle the respective significance of electoral and bureaucratic factors. After all, many advisors may be indirectly influenced by electoral considerations thanks to their association with the president, without whom they very well may not be in the position that they find themselves. Since elites are often selected into foreign policy roles as much for their political experience and partisan identities as their knowledge about foreign affairs, they will be attuned to what is politically desirable for the president.[70] Even individuals who are expected to provide advice based on objective professional expertise, such as senior military officers, have institutional incentives and civic-minded reasons to recommend options that align with public preferences.[71]

These individuals also represent an important audience for a leader's foreign policy choices in their own right, particularly since high-profile advisors have the ability to influence public opinion concerning the use of force.[72] Through a variety of means, from a public statement of dissent to an anonymous leak, disgruntled advisors can raise a "fire alarm" to a wider audience, which in turn raises the specter of public opposition and ultimately electoral reprisal. Given this, it may often be easier to accommodate such individuals rather than trigger a politically costly backlash by overruling them or forcing their resignation, especially in a politically sensitive phase of the electoral cycle. Even if the official in question is not overtly partisan, the very fact of their departure may be taken as a signal of disarray in the White House and an admission of failure. This will be especially the case when it comes to the dismissal or resignation of senior military figures, to whom the public traditionally defer on assessments of the wisdom of military policy.[73] In this sense, it is to a large extent the political spillover effects of division at the elite level that make such opposition so potentially damaging, even in a bureaucratic structure in which the leader retains dominant authority to dismiss subordinates at will. Since a president's sensitivity to these political threats plausibly varies across the domestic political calendar, it stands to reason that the influence of bureaucratic pressures may be conditional on electoral politics to a degree that has yet to be fully appreciated.

Advancing the Study of Electoral Constraint

This book understands elections as a conditional source of constraint on presidential decision making. In doing so, it offers a conceptualization that is much richer than that adopted in most existing studies, which tend to presume that upcoming elections incentivize leaders to act *either* more cautiously *or* more aggressively. By contrast, the framework outlined in this chapter better captures the historical reality that electoral pressures can in fact push in either direction—and sometimes both at once—depending on the strategic and electoral context. Moreover, it shows how these pressures vary in both strength and nature across the domestic political calendar, whereas prior scholarship tends to focus on limited slices of time, notably the year leading up to Election Day. The remainder of this chapter offers a brief survey of prior work on democratic accountability in war to underline how much further this reconceptualization of electoral constraint gets us.

The Pacifying Effect of the Ballot Box

The idea that electoral politics acts as a constraint on decision making derives from the broader literature on democratic accountability and war. In its most traditional form, drawing on the ideas of Immanuel Kant, the basic logic holds that since the public bear the brunt of the human and financial costs of war, they will hold a natural aversion to conflict. In a democracy, elections are the central means through which voters can retrospectively punish decision makers for excessive belligerence. Since political leaders are at least in part motivated by the desire to remain in office, they are incentivized *ex ante* to act with a degree of caution in matters of war and peace for fear of later reprisal at the ballot box.[74] As Kant himself summarized, "If (as must inevitably be the case, given this form of constitution) the consent of the citizenry is required in order to determine whether or not there will be war, it is natural that they consider all its calamities before committing themselves to so risky a game."[75] U.S. presidents seem to intuitively understand these dynamics. As President George W. Bush quipped to troops deployed to the Middle East in 2006, "you don't run for office in a democracy and say, please vote for me, I promise you war."[76]

This central logic has informed decades of fruitful research analyzing the connection between democracy and war. At the broadest level, of course, it has animated a wealth of studies looking at institutional explanations of the democratic peace phenomenon, a core component of the liberal tradition in international relations.[77] More specifically, it spawned a profound academic interest in casualty sensitivity and public attitudes to war. Taking body counts as a proxy for the human costs of a conflict, John Mueller's pioneering study established and quantified the relationship between public support for a war and cumulative casualties.[78] More recent studies have added nuance to this finding, arguing that contextual factors mitigate this relationship, including the geographic distribution of casualties, recent trends, and how casualty figures are reported.[79] Public sensitivity to the financial costs of war may be of second-order importance compared to the more visceral impact of casualties, but a vibrant research program is emerging here too. Increased government expenditure on defense during a war has been shown to be salient to the public and negatively correlated with presidential approval ratings.[80] The most recent work suggests that the *source* of funding may be particularly critical, with voters more attentive to the direct impact of taxation than the indirect costs of deficit spending or increasing the money supply.[81]

In response to this aversion to spending blood and treasure on overseas conflicts, political leaders seek to minimize the costs of war wherever possible. Since democratic leaders are particularly susceptible to domestic political backlash if they enter into such a risky endeavor as war, they appear to be more selective about doing so in the first place. This plausibly explains why democracies tend to only enter into conflicts they are confident of winning, or where the likelihood of high casualty rates is low.[82] Once in a war, moreover, they may seek to limit losses by shifting some of the burden of fighting to coalition partners, adopting military strategies that minimize fatalities (notably, by favoring technology, speed, and mobility over manpower and attrition), or choosing to fight on battlefields far away from their civilian population.[83] Similarly, by relying on borrowing rather than taxation, successive American administrations have shielded the public from the direct financial costs of war, thereby avoiding a divisive public debate that the imposition of a dreaded "war tax" often triggers.[84] In all these behaviors designed to free leaders from domestic constraints, we find prima facie evidence that such pressures exist and materially alter the way in which democracies go to war.

This insight drives the small but growing literature examining how upcoming elections affect the foreign policy behavior of leaders. Incentivized to avoid any course of action that strays too far from their constituents' preferences as polling day approaches, elected decision makers are typically seen to adopt more peaceful choices, shielding voters from the costs of overseas conflict. The most well-known work here is Kurt Gaubatz's 1991 study, which finds that democracies tend to avoid entering into wars as an election approaches and tend to engage in conflicts more often after polling day.[85] Though some sections of the public may be in the grips of war enthusiasm, Gaubatz reasons that there will usually be a prominent antiwar voice, and when the "warmonger" label has such powerful repercussions, the prudent choice for a leader is to refrain from saber rattling at this moment of greatest political sensitivity.[86] More recent studies have supported this conclusion, pointing out that leaders are freer to use force after an election than before, because this is where audience costs and other political constraints are lowest in an electoral cycle.[87] Others argue that leaders facing reelection contests are typically less belligerent than those not due to face voters again, giving statistical credence to Alexander Hamilton's insistence that imposing tenure restrictions on U.S. presidents would cause "a diminution of the inducements to good behavior."[88]

Still further studies have suggested that presidential sensitivity to public opinion in an election year generates not just caution but inaction. Since the overwhelming preoccupation with campaigning leaves little time to embark on new ventures in foreign affairs anyway, most presidents are best advised to sit on their hands and "stick with safe themes and patriotic rhetoric."[89] This frequently makes presidents "prudent to the point of inaction during their fourth year."[90] Even if the incumbent perceives there to be long-term benefit in deploying additional troops overseas, the short-term political risks associated with the human toll of putting forces in harm's way can discourage them from doing so on the eve of an election.[91]

Challenges to the Kantian Connection

There are several problems with this pacific interpretation of elections and war, however. First, recent work on the broader phenomenon of democratic constraint suggests that both the costs of war and the public's sensitivity to them have been exaggerated. This is in part thanks to changes in mobilization practices. Since the demise of conscription and transition to an all-volunteer force in the 1970s, the share of the U.S. population with military experience has declined significantly. With less than 1 percent of Americans now on active duty, the average voter is less likely than ever to be asked to fight. This civil-military "gap" has served to insulate most citizens from the direct costs of war.[92]

Changes in the character of warfare have also eroded the strength of the Kantian connection. With battlefields increasingly occupied by drones and precision-guided munitions, rather than boots on the ground, modern forms of warfare have reduced the risk to the lives of service members. These technological shifts and doctrinal developments are an important reason why fatality rates have declined significantly over time.[93] While recent research suggests that advances in military medicine have actually *increased* the net costs of war by dramatically escalating the wounded-to-killed ratio, the public appears to be relatively insensitive to the wounded as an additional cost of war. Americans may have greater day-to-day contact with injured and disabled veterans than ever before, but there appears to be no "Walter Reed" analogue to the "Dover effect."[94] The reality of the still significant long-term human costs of war may tell a different story, then, but the *perception* of contemporary war as relatively cheap effectively loosens the public's grip over the use of force. On the financial side, Jonathan Caverley has convincingly argued that these financial burdens can be shifted toward an affluent minority, particularly in democracies with high income inequality and progressive taxation systems.[95] In short, if the price of war, measured in blood or treasure, is perceived to be falling or can otherwise be redistributed away from the average voter, it seems plausible to conclude that the Kantian constraint on the use of force is being eroded as we look ahead to an era of greater permissiveness regarding decisions to deploy military force.

A second reason why we should not always expect electoral considerations to constrain belligerent behavior stems from the reality that voters may punish leaders not only for the costs of war but also for failing to secure the outcomes they value. Studies of public opinion show that even when citizens do have "skin in the game," they may be willing to stomach a higher number of casualties than is traditionally assumed if they believe that victory is likely, or that the mission in question is sufficiently worthy.[96] If the goals of the war weigh as heavily as its costs, electoral considerations could therefore lead to escalation. Daniel Ellsberg's account of decision making during the Vietnam War, for instance, concludes that presidents faced considerable pressure not only to minimize costly escalation, but also to avoid a Communist victory before the next election.[97] These conflicting electoral pressures created what Ellsberg referred to as the "stalemate machine," incentivizing incremental escalation undertaken more to avoid defeat than in any real hope of military success. For wartime leaders, perhaps the only thing more fraught with political risk than putting troops in harm's way is being seen to "lose" an ongoing conflict.

Even in more recent cases where the public appears ambivalent, presidents are not automatically given a free pass. A large reason why successive presidents have found it so difficult to extricate the United States from the so-called forever wars in the Middle East, for example, is precisely because the public cares enough to punish leaders for appearing to "lose," but not enough to justify the commitment of sufficient resources to decisively "win." The conventional wisdom on the politics of war termination suggests that leaders who inherit conflicts should be less "culpable" for their outcomes than their predecessors.[98] Yet Democrats and Republicans alike discovered that it was far easier to promise an end to "endless" war than to actually deliver on these pledges. As Shawn Cochran has recently argued, the politics of blame are such that even leaders who cannot be held responsible for starting a war may still be vulnerable to partisan charges of "bungling" the conflict or "selling out" to reach a suboptimal outcome.[99] As a result, even those who are firmly convinced that victory is out of reach may end up prolonging or escalating a conflict to mitigate the domestic political consequences of admitting defeat. For these reasons, even in recent interventions—like in Libya and Syria, where the brunt of the fighting has been done not by large numbers of American boots on the ground but by local partners, airpower, and special forces—reduced public exposure to the costs of war does not entirely eliminate the significance of democratic constraint to decision makers. Contrary to the simple Kantian perspective, however, it is not just the costs of war that matter, but also the costs of failure.

The Diversionary Perspective

The notion that elections are sometimes a source of aggressive and conflict-prone behavior is of course no surprise to scholars of diversionary war theory. Noting the existence of a "rally" phenomenon, whereby a national crisis sparks a boost of patriotic support for the leader, this research tradition suggests that leaders may seek to artificially create a rally effect through the cynical use of force. While there are several hypothetical reasons why a leader might wish to engage in this provocative behavior, an important one concerns their desire to improve their polling ahead of an election.[100] This behavior is of course not entirely incompatible with the logic of political survival that underpins many of the studies referenced in the foregoing discussion of electoral accountability. On the contrary, when facing long odds in a tough reelection campaign, it can be perfectly rational for a democratic leader to embrace risky paths of escalation in a "gamble for resurrection."[101]

The empirical record for the diversionary hypothesis is decidedly mixed, however. Its repeated failure to show up as statistically significant in a series of studies during decades of subsequent research does not render it entirely elusive, but does suggest that it is likely the exception to the rule of caution.[102] Beyond several methodological critiques of the diversionary approach, most notably spearheaded by James Meernik and Jack Levy, there are several further logical reasons for its rarity in the empirical record.[103] First, in order to carry out a diversionary use of force, a suitable opportunity needs to be present, with a viable plan, sufficient military resources, and a would-be opponent.[104] If the need and opportunity are present, the expected electoral gain is still far from certain. Both the size of a "rally" effect and its duration can be small and dependent on factors outside the leader's control.[105] Moreover, this all assumes that the belligerent act taken will be perceived as successful and credited to the leader's own actions by the electorate. This is often not the case, particularly when partisan elites and the media seek to downplay any success of the incumbent, or in situations where the notion of success itself is ambiguous.[106]

More importantly, the mechanisms underpinning the majority of work on diversionary war theory are distinct from those explored in this book, involving the manipulation of public opinion rather than efforts to accommodate electoral pressures. Put differently, what sets diversionary behavior apart is that the electoral consequences of any chosen policy are not perceived as *risks* to be managed, but rather *incentives* to pursue. The primary objective of diversionary action is to manufacture a crisis in order to instrumentally shift public opinion in a way that favors the president's electoral prospects; any strategic benefit is of secondary importance. In the accountability approach, by contrast, the primary objective is dealing with a problem that reaches the president's desk in a manner that results in minimal electoral costs.

In thinking about how electoral politics shapes presidential decision making in war, then, it pays to begin with a more flexible conceptualization of electoral "constraint"—not as an inherent force for peace, nor as an incentive for aggression, but as a contingent pressure that may push an incumbent in either direction depending on the particular situation at hand. In line with the basic logic of democratic accountability, I use the term "constraint" to capture the way in which elected officeholders are structurally incentivized to care about public attitudes to war and act accordingly. Taking no particular stance on related academic debates regarding the determinants of those public attitudes, which may be more dovish or more hawkish under different circumstances, this study instead focuses on the underlying truth that policymakers both worry about those attitudes and act upon them. More specifically, it explores what this meant for wartime decision-making in the broader context of the American electoral cycle during some of the most significant conflicts of the post-1945 era.

*　　*　　*

This chapter has outlined a new conceptual framework for understanding the influence of electoral politics on wartime decision making. Drawing on and extending the literature on democracy and war, it reconceptualized electoral pressures as a conditional source of constraint that serves to push and pull presidents away from courses of action they perceive to be strategically optimal. Exactly *how* these constraints shaped decisions to escalate or de-escalate a conflict was suggested to depend on the relative alignment between presidential preferences and, crucially, the phase of the electoral cycle. It was argued that the pressures of democratic accountability operate according to a nonlinear pattern given by the electoral cycle, something that is missed in the majority of existing studies, which focus narrowly on the lead-up to a presidential election. The following empirical chapters apply this framework as a conceptual lens, revealing the surprising degree to which critical decisions in Korea, Vietnam, and Iraq were shaped by electoral politics.

TWO

Korea

Truman, Eisenhower, and America's First Limited War

It's a political office, and unless the President maintains his political connections, he can't remain President.

—HARRY TRUMAN

I have a mandate from the American people to stop this fighting.

—DWIGHT EISENHOWER

ON SATURDAY, JUNE 24, 1950, Harry S. Truman was at home in Independence, Missouri, when he received a call from his secretary of state. "Mr. President," said Dean Acheson, "I have very serious news. The North Koreans have invaded South Korea."[1] So began a three-year conflict, the first "hot" war involving U.S. troops during the Cold War, and one that would come to redefine the terms on which the broader superpower confrontation was fought. Closer to home, the conflict would help bring two decades of Democratic dominance in Washington to a close, elevating to power a popular general who promised to end the fighting in Korea and reverse years of "fumbling" policy in the Far East more broadly.

In deciding to meet the challenge by force, Truman initially carried the overwhelming support of the American people. In a classic example of the "rally" effect in public opinion, White House mail was running ten to one in favor of the president's actions.[2] On the Hill, even Truman's most ardent critics spoke favorably of his rapid deployment of troops.[3] Granted a degree of latitude by an electorate and legislature apparently shocked by the violation of international law on the Korean Peninsula, a confluence of other pressures all pointed toward a decision to intervene. Whether it was the strategic interest of avoiding Japan's isolation in the region, the lessons of the 1930s regarding the pitfalls of appeasing territorial aggression overseas, or concerns about the credibility of the United States' commitment to standing up to communist forces in the emerging Cold War struggle, the original decision to fight in Korea seems overdetermined.

The emphasis in this chapter, however, is on the *subsequent* decisions regarding military and diplomatic strategy that so profoundly shaped the duration, intensity, and scope of the ensuing conflict. Two episodes are explored in particular. First is the escalation of the war in the autumn of 1950, embodied primarily in the authorization granted to General Douglas MacArthur to cross the 38th parallel in pursuit of the full unification of Korea. This decision reflected a fundamental change in war aims and helped trigger a massive Chinese counteroffensive in the weeks that followed. The progress of the armistice talks that accompanied the resulting stalemate constitutes the second episode analyzed here.

In both cases, it is argued that the electoral cycle at home placed political constraints on both Harry Truman and Dwight Eisenhower as commanders in chief. While convinced of the strategic necessity of ensuring the conflict remained "limited," Truman faced an intensely partisan and belligerent atmosphere in the lead-up to the 1950 midterm elections. With public sentiment whipped up by demagogues in the wake of the "loss" of China, he understood the political price that would be paid at the ballot box if his policies could be presented to voters as "soft" on communism. As a result, through acts of both commission and omission, electoral constraints pushed the president to expand the political and military scope of the war, in a powerful example of the *spur* mechanism outlined in chapter 1.

Freed from similar political pressures following his withdrawal from the presidential race in March 1952, Truman was for a time able to pursue his preferred diplomatic course of action in the talks at Panmunjom, clinging stubbornly to the principle of "non-forcible repatriation" of POWs. As the campaign heated up, however, Truman found his bargaining leverage significantly curtailed, eventually leading him to support an India-backed United Nations cease-fire resolution that was deemed suboptimal by a majority of officials in his administration. As president-elect, Eisenhower did himself no favors during this "lame duck" phase of the electoral cycle, distancing himself from the incumbent administration's position in ways that, ironically, only further tied his hands to the Indian resolution when he took office in the New Year. Despite thereby contributing to the *spoiler* effect that an election year can have on negotiations, Eisenhower otherwise benefited from relatively weak *hangover* constraints, affording him an opportunity to threaten major escalation in a way that likely helped seal the armistice deal of July 1953.

Expanding the War

The decision to cross the 38th parallel and thereby expand the aim of intervention in Korea was made on the eve of the 1950 congressional midterms, a stage of the electoral cycle carrying high political sensitivity. As this section demonstrates, during this period there existed a strong imbalance between President Truman's strategic preference for restraint in fighting a "limited" war, and the competing escalatory pressures from a belligerent public mood. Under such conditions, according to the conceptual framework outlined in chapter 1, any salient decision regarding military strategy may be subject to the *spur* mechanism, whereby a proposed course of action is dialed up in intensity and scope in response to the electoral risks of excessive caution. In the following analysis, considerable evidence is adduced to support this hypothesis.

Containing the War

At the time of the outbreak of the Korean War, the underlying grand strategy governing American decision making was one of "containment." Starting from the realist assumption that the relative balance of power is the primary driver of change in international politics, this doctrine held that the overriding goal of national security policy should be to maintain a balance favorable to the United States. It did not dwell on the need to impress the Soviets with unlimited resolve, nor did it contemplate unqualified support for any area facing the threat of communist subversion. Instead, as articulated by George Kennan, it entailed a firm commitment to defend only those areas of concentrated military-industrial capability that could alter the overall balance of power—namely the United Kingdom, the Rhine Valley, and Japan.[4]

Though perceived as a Kremlin-supported affront to international peace, the conflict on the Korean Peninsula thus fell into the category of a proxy war, an essentially limited action designed to achieve modest Soviet objectives without implying any desire for wider escalation. While overriding political imperatives justifiably compelled an armed response to such a flagrant breach of the border between the North and South, the logic of containment implied that any resulting American action should be carefully measured, so as not to waste valuable blood and treasure on an area of minimal strategic importance.[5] In practice, noted Kennan, that meant pursuing the relatively modest objective of pushing the invading forces back to the 38th parallel, thereby restoring the status quo ante.[6]

Importantly, in the minutes of several meetings in the early days of the crisis, there is a wealth of evidence to suggest that President Truman clearly perceived this as the optimal strategy. On June 26, for instance, in waiving restrictions on naval and air operations in Korea, he was at pains to insist that "no action should be taken north of the 38th parallel." Resisting the urge to commit ground troops at that moment, he urged his Joint Chiefs to remain vigilant, adding, "I don't want to go to war."[7] Two days later, the president resisted calls from military advisors to allow U.S. planes to bomb North Korean bases across the border, flatly saying, "we were not to do it."[8] On June 29, with the situation in Korea deteriorating by the hour, Truman reversed this decision, authorizing air and sea support to South Korean troops across the parallel. He was, however, even more forceful in his insistence on utmost caution, lest the action lead to direct retaliation by Soviet forces. As the secretary of defense began reading out a draft directive implementing his latest decision, Truman interrupted to object to a paragraph that might be interpreted as more aggressive than intended. "I do not want any implication in the letter that we are going to war with Russia," ordered Truman, adding, "We must be damn careful. . . . We want to take any steps we have to push the North Koreans behind the line, but I don't want to get us over-committed." Overruling concerns from the Joint Chiefs about restrictions on bombing targets, Truman "said that he only wanted to restore order to the 38th parallel; he did not want to do anything north of it except to 'keep the North Koreans from killing the people we are trying to save.'"[9]

When the first U.S. ground units were given a green light to enter the battle the following day, there remained no doubt as to the ultimate objectives their deployment was intended to achieve. In a speech before the American Newspaper Guild on June 29, Dean Acheson publicly articulated the aims Truman had repeatedly stated that week, insisting that U.S. action in Korea was taken "solely for the purpose of restoring the Republic of Korea to its status prior to the invasion from the north."[10] As Richard Neustadt later concluded, the unification of Korea was "among the least of the objectives on [Truman's] mind."[11]

Containing the "Irreconcilables"

By the summer of 1950, a climate of fear and crisis gripped the United States. Following the recent "loss" of China, the Soviet development of atomic weapons, and the conviction of communist spy Alger Hiss, the airwaves were filled with bitter invective blaming Truman for each setback. A spirit of bipartisanship in foreign policy had given way to the shrill partisanship of a different generation of Republican senators, who turned against the "metooism" that had led to electoral defeat for the Republican presidential ticket in 1948. While Truman could still rely on an internationalist wing within the Republican Party for some support, he faced criticism from an emerging alliance between the increasingly vocal "China bloc" (led by Senators William F. Knowland and H. Alexander Smith) and an influential isolationist faction (led by Senators Robert A. Taft and Kenneth S. Wherry). Coupled with the sensational accusations of Joseph McCarthy's "Red Scare" at home, the opposition party stood primed to pounce on any chance to label the administration's policies as "soft" on communism.[12]

The Korean War was a golden opportunity for these critics. In the first days of the crisis, the president was warned by Acheson that he should "prepare for criticism and tough sledding."[13] Indeed, this Republican group, scathingly labeled the "irreconcilables" by the secretary of state, wasted little time in cultivating an alternative narrative of events in the Far East designed explicitly to reap political gains at the ballot box in November.[14] Writing to a friend in mid-July, Taft explained, "The only way we can beat the Democrats is to go after their mistakes. . . . There is no alternative except to support the war, but we can point out that it has resulted from a bungling of the Democratic administration."[15] The following month, a GOP campaign pamphlet reciting recent statements by Republican members of the Senate Foreign Relations Committee duly called on voters to hold the administration accountable for a situation of unpreparedness in the Far East and the "green light" given by Truman to the USSR to invade.[16]

Members of the more extreme "conspiracy group" went one step further, attributing the outbreak of conflict not just to fumbled policy, but conspiratorial intent as well. "It all fits into a pattern," claimed Senator George W. Malone. "We deliberately lose Manchuria, China, Korea and Berlin."[17] The similarly minded poster boy of the Republican campaign, Senator McCarthy, quickly attributed events in Korea to the actions of "a group of untouchables in the State Department." Later, he underscored the point to his constituents. "If you want more of that, keep them in office."[18]

These critics were also increasingly clear about how the conflict should be dealt with now that it was underway. Rejecting the president's limited goals in Korea, they called on him to take the fight to the enemy. "Why do we not push a more vigorous, positive policy?" asked Senator Ferguson.[19] Lest those in power fail to feel such pressure, a group of legislators—notably internationalist in composition—descended on the State Department in mid-August to make things crystal clear. Warning of "a growing disposition on the part of the American people to support the concept of preventive war," the group stressed that "this growing attitude is aired in fear, and will continue to grow in volume unless some bold alternative course of action is presented by the government."[20]

Such belligerent prescriptions were reflected in leading media publications too. "You can hear lots of 'preventive war' talk in Washington these days, and everywhere else in the country, too," reported the New Republic on August 21. "The President and his advisers," it scornfully added, "are firmly opposed to any such idea."[21] Other mainstream outlets such as Time openly advocated using the threat of atomic weapons outside Korea's borders, adding that its deterrent effect is the reason "why talk of 'preventive war' by the U.S. against the U.S.S.R. stays on the tongues of the American people."[22]

These congressional and media viewpoints were broadly accurate indicators of the wider public mood—indeed, they may well have played a key role in shaping the attitudes of ordinary citizens toward the crisis. Following Truman's July 19 speech outlining the steps taken to meet the aggression in Korea, findings from focus groups revealed that "the president was not in advance of the national mood . . . [and] if anything, the public would evidently have gone along with somewhat stronger language regarding communism." Meanwhile, other polls analyzed by the State Department revealed that "the main criticism of the administration's actions since June 25 is that the actions are inadequate." Not only was the public opposed to perceived timidity that Republican politicians had been warning them about, it was remarkably willing to pay the costs of a more forceful policy. One Gallup poll, for instance, indicated that 70 percent of Americans favored higher taxes to increase the size of the army. "Rarely has the Institute in its fifteen years of measuring public opinion," concluded Gallup, "found such heavy majorities expressing a willingness to pay more taxes for any public purpose."[23]

Importantly, Truman was aware of these sentiments spreading across the nation. Warned in a National Security Council (NSC) meeting by the vice president of "growing uneasiness in the country and the feeling that we might be pushed out of Korea," the president replied that "he was aware of this feeling."[24] He also understood that critical Republican statements like those made by prominent senators in August referring to Truman's "green light" for the invasion reflected "a purely political move and it is understood that the Republicans have been planning to make the Korean situation their leading issue in this year's congressional elections."[25]

In short, it seems clear that Truman's strategic and electoral interests pointed in opposing directions during this period. Whereas the president perceived a clear strategic danger in excessive escalation, such caution had become firmly set in Republican crosshairs in the midterm campaign. With the conditions of the *spur* mechanism in place, what role did these electoral pressures play in subsequent debates leading Truman to authorize troops to cross the 38th parallel and seek unification by force?

Crossing the 38th Parallel

That public opinion and Republican electioneering would shape internal debates about the decision to expand the Korean War was evident from early on in the deliberations. After Truman requested that a policy recommendation be prepared during a July 17 NSC meeting in the event that UN forces reached the dividing marker, the Policy Planning Staff at the State

Department quickly put pen to paper. In a series of draft memoranda, a cautious faction influenced by George Kennan spelled out the severe risks of such an escalatory step. In the first of these papers, a firm recommendation was given to avoid crossing the 38th parallel, since doing so would leave the danger of conflict with Chinese or Soviet forces "greatly increased." Notably, however, the authors also remained acutely conscious that "public and Congressional opinion in the United States might be dissatisfied with any conclusion falling short of what it would consider a 'final' settlement of the problem. Hence, a sentiment might arise favoring a continuation of military action north of the 38th parallel. The development of such a sentiment might create serious problems for the execution of United States policy."[26]

A rival group within the State Department, led by John Allison and Dean Rusk of the Bureau of Far Eastern Affairs, as well as John Foster Dulles, dissented from the conclusion of those in the Policy Planning Staff . Using strikingly similar language to that used by Republican critics in Congress, they authored a series of rebuttals, branding the recommendations "a policy of appeasement . . . a timid, half-hearted policy designed not to provoke the Soviets to war." Rejecting the significance of the 38th parallel as a meaningful division, Allison felt that the "status quo ante bellum"—the stated goal of the president of the United States—was an unacceptable war outcome. Instead, Allison advocated a policy recognizing that "he who takes the sword will perish by the sword," even if "this may mean war on a global scale."[27] Such language exasperated advisors like Kennan, who had begun to doubt whether the kind of "cool and rational analysis" he favored still had a place in the administration. "In the somewhat childish and abusive atmosphere of a democratic society already disbalanced by McCarthyism," he concluded, "there was use only for the cruder and the starker concepts."[28]

Indeed, the tenor of internal debate only moved further toward the hawkish Republican view through late July and into August. In a meeting to discuss the latest State Department draft, it was concluded that the paragraph mentioning public opinion "will be modified to indicate that U.S. public and Congressional opinion would not now be satisfied with a restoration of the status quo ante."[29] The revised memorandum noted that "a sentiment favoring a continuation of military action north of the 38th parallel *already is arising*."[30] These amendments met with the approval of advisors like Dulles, though they still considered insufficient a newly revised recommendation to adopt what was effectively a "wait-and-see" approach to the 38th parallel until circumstances made a decision necessary.[31] Instead, they turned to less equivocal recent draft memoranda prepared in the Department of Defense calling for a decision to push forward in Korea. Even there, however, public pressures loomed large in the calculations. Though a dovish faction might develop, Allison again pointed to "a growing sentiment in the United States favoring a 'final' settlement of the Korean problem and disapproving of any settlement which smacks of compromise or a 'deal.' "[32]

In other words, those tasked by the president with advising on the issue of the 38th parallel had expressly concluded that their commander in chief's strategic preference for containing the war was out of step with the public mood. It should be noted at this point that Truman himself was not directly involved in the deliberations at this stage. Had the president intervened to provide some direction to his advisors, he may well have been able to halt the drift away from his own strategic preference. That he did not do so is in one sense characteristic of the president's elusive management style, which has been appropriately described as "spasmodic rather than weak or strong."[33] Yet it is nevertheless telling that Truman would allow the debate over the central issue dividing his administration to bend further and further toward the position of hawkish Republicans like Dulles during this period. Dulles, of course, had been brought on board as consultant to the secretary of state in no small part thanks to Truman's desire to protect the political flank of his administration. That was a point of which he made no secret. "Look! You fellows don't understand politics," he told one skeptic who questioned the appointment. "Of course, John Foster Dulles is going to take time out every two years to be a Republican, but between elections we want to work with him if he's willing to work with us."[34]

In any event, the bureaucracy's incorporation of domestic political pressures into their recommendations also seemed to be in keeping with some of the White House's most urgent priorities when it did engage more directly. At an NSC meeting of August 10, for instance, the hope was expressed that the studies now underway could be "expedited," and that they "should take into consideration the possible Congressional reaction when the North Koreans have been driven back to the 38th parallel."[35] On the same day, following consultations between the president and the secretary of defense, permission was granted to General Matthew Ridgway to bomb the previously embargoed target of the city of Najin, an aggressive operational decision among several others around this time that was later attributed in part to the perceived need to counter charges that the administration was "doing nothing" and were "appeasers."[36]

As the midterm elections approached, Republicans in Congress were becoming even more specific in their criticisms of the administration's apparent timidity in Korea, calling a restoration of the status quo ante fundamentally insufficient as the objective of any strategy. "For the invaders merely to move north of the thirty-eighth parallel will not mean a great deal in the final analysis," said Senator Knowland, adding, "if the Republic of Korea, the United States, and the western world are to be living under a gun, in that aggression of the same type might take place three months from now or six months from now, a peace achieved under those circumstances would be a very uneasy one."[37] Senator Taft, perceived by Truman as a would-be candidate for president, now gained support for his belief that UN forces should "march right on over the 38th parallel and at least occupy the southern part of North Korea."[38]

Sensing the political winds, Kennan left government later in August, penning a final note of advice to the secretary of state in which he pulled no punches. "The course upon which we are today moving is one, as I see it, so little promising and so fraught with danger that I could not honestly urge you to continue to take responsibility for it," he explained. In truth, and "leaving aside for the moment our domestic political inhibitions," a unified and independent Korea was not in the core strategic interest of the United States. "A period of Russian domination, while undesirable, is preferable to continued U.S. involvement in that unhappy area," and as such a moderate policy of restraint and negotiation should follow. "So much for national interest in the abstract," Kennan nonetheless concluded, noting how "public opinion, aroused by the Korean aggression, and confused by the partisan attacks on the administration, is not prepared for this sort of a policy. I realize that an attempt to proceed along these lines would encounter, as things stand today, violent and outraged opposition both within sectors of the Executive branch and in the Congress. In particular, it would mean pouring oil on the fires already kindled by the Republican opposition in the charge that our Far Eastern policy has been over-lenient to communism and therefore neglectful of our national security."[39]

It had become an open secret within government by this point that, as the chief of staff of the army later recalled, in planning the next move in

Korea, "public opinion and political considerations had to be weighed by the President and his advisers."[40] Though Acheson later claimed that Kennan's August 23 memorandum had offered "good, even if purely negative, advice," there was little that could be done. "In view of public opinion and political pressures in the concrete," he wrote, "ideas such as these could only be kept in mind as warnings not to be drawn into quicksands."[41]

The following month, the die was cast. On September 11, President Truman approved NSC 81/1, authorizing ground operations north of the parallel, provided there was no entry into North Korea of major Soviet or Chinese forces, no announcement of intended entry, nor any threat to counter such operations militarily. This action, it was hoped, would bring about the "complete independence and unity of Korea," a political goal that up to this point had been considered separate from the military mission now being pursued.[42] A directive was duly sent on September 27 by the Joint Chiefs to General MacArthur giving as his new aim "the destruction of the North Korean armed forces."[43] As General Omar Bradley later put it, "NSC-81/1 reflected a drastic change in our concept of the Korean War. Our initial intervention had been launched as an effort to 'save' South Korea. Now we had broadened our war aims to include complete destruction of the North Korean Army and political unification of the country. This was a bold and aggressive step on the Far East stage. I might even say that, given the possibility of Chinese communist or Soviet intervention, it was an extremely dangerous step."[44] The Rubicon had well and truly been crossed.

Mission Creep? The Battle of Inchon

Since a critic might suggest that the decision to cross the 38th parallel was simply an example of "mission creep" following the success of the amphibious assault on Inchon in mid-September, two additional points are worth noting here. First is the timing of Truman's approval of NSC 81/1, which came four days *before* the Battle of Inchon commenced. Second, even if the remarkable success of that operation made an opportunistic gamble to press on with the military advance more likely, the authorization of the plan in the first place was arguably another product of the *spur* mechanism at the operational level of war.

The operation was widely acknowledged to be a gamble. "It was bold—and very risky," recalled the chairman of the Joint Chiefs, Omar Bradley, who noted that "Inchon was probably the worst possible place ever selected for an amphibious landing."[45] Indeed, thanks to the unfavorable terrain involved, an utter dependence on unpredictable climatic conditions, and a severe shortage of reserve manpower, the chiefs made several attempts to convince MacArthur to adapt or postpone his plans over the summer of 1950. They found little reassurance, however, when during one of several such efforts, they heard a briefing on the plan by Admiral James H. Doyle, the commander of U.S. Amphibious Forces in the Far East. "Though the operation was not impossible," concluded the man who would lead the assault in the event it was approved, "he did not recommend it."[46] His ultimate superior, Chief of Naval Operations Admiral Forrest P. Sherman, basically agreed, noting, "If every possible geographical and naval handicap were listed—Inchon has 'em all."[47] It remained, according to General Bradley, "the riskiest military proposal I had ever heard of," while even MacArthur admitted it was a "5,000 to 1 gamble."[48]

Truman also understood very well that Operation Chromite, as the landing was to be called, was a "bold plan" and "daring strategic conception."[49] Not only would failure at Inchon mean a great military disaster, possibly leading to total defeat in Korea, even moderate or complete operational success raised the risks of Chinese or Soviet intervention that threatened the president's conception of the war as a "limited" affair. Since Truman had been so incredibly sensitive to such risks in the fateful decision meetings of late June, it is not credible to suggest that he was ignorant of such concerns now. Indeed, it was one of the primary reasons why he sent Averell Harriman to see MacArthur in early August. While there, MacArthur assured Truman's delegation that while the Chinese would be unlikely to intervene, he would "welcome it" if they did. "I pray nightly that they will," continued MacArthur, "[I] would get down on my knees."[50] In Harriman's covering report, Truman learned of considerable unease that the commander's appreciation of the risks of escalation were not aligned with that of the president.[51]

Nevertheless, Truman appears to have been one of very few individuals in Washington willing to support MacArthur's invasion plan. Hence, on his return, Harriman was ordered by the president to immediately meet with the secretary of defense and chairman of the Joint Chiefs, with Truman adding, "I want them to act on it rapidly." By the time Harriman reached General Bradley, the president had already apparently called to press his top military advisors to formalize a recommendation for Inchon, which received his assent the following morning, August 10.[52]

Inchon was precisely the type of aggressive move that the electoral atmosphere of late 1950 called for. Besides the pressure from General MacArthur, addressed later in this chapter, what arguably swung Truman's decision in its favor was the advice of Frank E. Lowe. Probably the only person able to consider himself a mutual friend of both the president and General MacArthur, Lowe had been sent to Korea as Truman's eyes and ears. As Harriman was en route back to the United States following his visit of August 8, Lowe filed a private cable back to the president, pressing him hard to authorize additional deployments of men to Korea in order to allow Inchon to proceed. After admitting that MacArthur's request was in practice "logistically impossible," he nevertheless concluded with a clinching argument. The reinforcements, he claimed, "would permit General MacArthur to seize the initiative to an extent that would cause acclaim in the States, and register September support to you."[53]

In turn, amid the hot political environment of September 1950, the remarkable success of the Inchon operation only added fuel to growing pressure for a further expansion of the war. As the State Department's Bureau of Public Affairs noted, Inchon served "to widen and intensify the [media] demand that the UN must formulate a 'plan' for postwar Korea—that it must make decisions concerning the crossing of the thirty-eighth parallel, the occupation of North Korea, and the future government of the war-torn land."[54] Behind the scenes, as noted above, that expanded ambition had already been baked into formal orders to the commanding general. Yet it may reasonably be concluded that the momentum generated by Inchon raised the political costs that would be paid to reverse that escalatory decision.

Truman Doubles Down

Having made the pivotal move, Truman should have taken developments through October as cause for a reconsideration of the course of action now embarked upon. Indications of intended or actual intervention by the Chinese—an explicit condition of NSC 81/1's guidance—were aplenty in this period. Among the more notable warnings sent via the Indian ambassador to Beijing, K. M. Panikkar, was an explicit threat on October 3 by the Chinese foreign minister, Zhou Enlai, that while the South Korean presence in North Korea might not precipitate Chinese intervention, if *U.S.* troops crossed the parallel, such aggression would be met with outside force.[55] This seemed to support a report from the week before quoting the chief of staff of the Chinese army as warning that "China would not take such provocations lying down."[56] Mao Zedong confirmed his decision to intervene in early to mid-October, before tens of thousands of Chinese troops began crossing the Yalu on October 19.[57] Importantly, the United States picked up concrete signs of this development through the second half of the month, with a flurry of reports detailing the capture of Chinese soldiers reaching Washington.[58] By November 1, the CIA director had heard enough to author a memorandum to Truman telling the president that Chinese intervention had now been "clearly established," and while ultimate objectives were unclear, at least some fifteen thousand troops were operating in North Korea, supported by Soviet air support, with many more stationed in Manchuria.[59] "If ever there was a time for military caution," recalled the chairman of the Joint Chiefs, "it was now."[60]

Instead, Truman doubled down. In the first week of October, the United States helped draft and guide through the United Nations a new resolution authorizing steps to be taken to ensure stability *throughout* Korea.[61] The following day he approved new orders to MacArthur, authorizing him to continue operations in case of major Chinese intervention in North Korea, so long as the commander felt there to be "a reasonable chance of success."[62] Next, when MacArthur issued orders on October 24 waiving all restrictions on the use of non–Republic of Korea (ROK) forces near the borders with Manchuria and the USSR, Truman remained essentially silent. Though the commander's actions were in direct contradiction of his September 27 directive, and were known to raise risks of Chinese retaliation, Truman favored using "caution and understatement" in questioning MacArthur's actions, approving a brief note from the Joint Chiefs merely noting that the action had been a "matter of concern" in Washington.[63] Finally, on November 6, Truman permitted a request from MacArthur to bomb the bridges across the Yalu River, on the Korean border with China.[64]

There are, of course, several possible explanations for Truman's failure to backtrack as the specter of imminent outside intervention loomed large during these fateful weeks.[65] Yet while misperception and path dependencies played important roles, so, too, did the electoral landscape. If the public mood during the summer made a decision to halt at the 38th parallel politically difficult, the subsequent development of hawkish sentiment and the increasing proximity of the midterms made any subsequent reconsideration of that order unfathomable. Among the mass media, even political opposites like conservative *Life* and the liberal *New Republic* agreed that, as the latter put it, "the restoration of the status quo ante [was] no longer a matter of negotiation with the USSR."[66] Editorials in the *New York Times* agreed that the 38th parallel was a pure "fiction" and any anxiety about crossing it was thus "groundless." Reporting "an overwhelming surge of opinion and emotion that favors a free and united Korea," anything less was "to admit defeat and to invite disaster."[67] These sentiments were picked up in a State Department media survey of October 3, while among the broader public, polling indicated a more than two-to-one majority in favor of the decision to push into North Korea.[68]

It was in this political context that Truman explicitly integrated the decision to cross the 38th parallel into his campaign strategy for the upcoming midterms. The very day after MacArthur received his orders to cross the demarcation line, Truman and his advisors agreed that his party could now credibly run on a newly strengthened Democratic record in fighting communism. Acheson assured his colleagues that Korea could soon be added to the list of accomplishments touted by the administration, explaining that since "the 38th Parallel will be ignored," events on the Korean Peninsula could now "be used as a stage to prove what Western Democracy can do to help the underprivileged countries of the world."[69] A few weeks later, on October 24— the day MacArthur removed restrictions on the use of non-ROK troops— Truman proudly stated that the fighting in Korea was "nearly ended," in a speech that one White House aide had earlier advised would "permit the president, without the slightest taint of 'politicking,' to emphasize his (and the Democratic Party's) foreign-policy plank for the November elections."[70] Despite alarming signals of Chinese intervention having been received by this point, the administration felt it politically prudent not to include in the president's speech a statement of reassurance about the scope of the newly widened U.S. military activities, at least in part because it "did not want to risk a charge from his bitter Republican critics that he was attempting to appease the communists."[71]

Back to the Status Quo Ante

China's massive offensive of late November 1950 laid bare just how misplaced this apparent optimism about the course of the war was. Within weeks, UN forces were brought to the precipice of defeat, with MacArthur gloomily reporting that he now faced "an entirely new war."[72] In this transformed military context, it is perhaps not surprising that the administration quickly retreated back to the president's original strategic understanding of the conflict. Within weeks, the NSC would agree to a new policy statement favoring a negotiated cease-fire at or around the 38th parallel.[73] On December 29, MacArthur's orders were changed, with the commander now directed not to destroy the North Korean armed forces, but merely to "defend in successive positions . . . inflicting such damage to hostile forces in Korea as is possible," while making plans for a possible evacuation.[74] Despite resistance to these orders and repeated complaints about the "extraordinary limitations" placed on his command, MacArthur's alternative proposals for escalatory steps against China, including the bombing and blockading of the mainland, were left by the wayside, as the Eighth Army under the leadership of General Matthew Ridgway regained the initiative without requiring any such widening of the war.[75] In May 1951, having snatched a stalemate from the jaws of defeat, the administration formally abandoned NSC 81/1 as the document governing U.S. policy and replaced it with NSC 48/5, a broader document expressly renouncing the objective of Korean unification by military means and committing instead to a satisfactory termination of hostilities.[76]

Yet if events on the battlefield thus largely overdetermined this retreat to modest objectives in Korea, it is still instructive to highlight the president's newfound indifference to a public mood that if anything had become increasingly critical in this period, demonstrating how sensitivity to public opinion is conditional on the stage of the electoral cycle.[77] While the Republican Party did not have a consistent alternative policy proposal in this period, oscillating between calls for outright withdrawal and all-out war, Republican lawmakers all agreed that the "limited war" conception favored by Truman was intolerable.[78] Having made gains at the polls in November, the increasingly hostile GOP now set its sights on Dean Acheson as a symbol of the ills of Truman's foreign policy, something that irked the president, who later excoriated those detractors who "never stopped their partisan campaigning."[79]

Indeed, President Truman clearly heard these criticisms, referring in a November 28 meeting to a "campaign of vilification and lies in the United States," spearheaded by the adversarial Hearst and McCormick newspaper chains.[80] Many of the charges, of course, were addressed directly to him, including, for instance, a telegram from Senator McCarthy denouncing the handling of the war by a "crimson clique in the State Department," and calling for Truman's impeachment unless he fired Acheson and unleashed Chinese Nationalist forces in the fight.[81] Neither can he have failed to observe that his own approval ratings had fallen to a dismal new low of 26 percent.[82] As State Department opinion summaries reported "deepening gloom" among the broader public, polling revealed that some 66 percent of Americans now favored withdrawal from Korea, with 49 percent viewing the decision to intervene as a mistake.[83]

To the extent that Truman responded to public opinion in this phase of the electoral cycle, it was in the shape of a vigorous defense of his strategy for a "limited" war against widespread calls for its abandonment. He thus first called for a national emergency in mid-December, which, while "not technically necessary," admitted Acheson, "would show the country the general attitude the President was taking."[84] Outlining his approach to congressmen, Truman explained the "very great psychological effects on the American people" he was hoping to bring about with such a proclamation.[85] Later, in April, Truman went on the PR offensive again, articulating his strategy as the best way forward. With a clear aim of "trying to prevent a third world war," popular calls for escalation would only spread the conflict and raise the "grave risk" of catastrophic, all-out war.[86]

Instead of quietly bending his strategic preference to suit the domestic political environment, then, as had happened before November 1950, now Truman stubbornly held to his convictions, shifting from a position of broadly following public opinion to seeking to lead it. With two years until the next election campaign, the president was able to set the course of military action in Korea relatively free of the constraints that had previously proven to be so acute. For the rest of his term in office, the broad contours of military strategy in the Far East would remain unchanged, as attention shifted to efforts to conclude hostilities through diplomatic means.

"God's Righthand Man": The Political Weight of Douglas MacArthur

The figure of Douglas MacArthur looms large in the decision to escalate the Korean War. It was his soaring oratory that arguably single-handedly made the case for the Inchon operation, with bold claims like "Inchon will succeed. And it will save 100,000 lives."[87] It was his guidance that apparently convinced the president that the risks of Chinese intervention were "very little," as he put it during their one and only meeting at Wake Island in October.[88] It was MacArthur's opinion, too, that seemed to carry the argument when reports of that intervention came flooding in, with the general warning against "hasty conclusions which might be premature" in early November.[89] It was also his unilateral order of October 24 on the use of non-ROK troops, and his alarmist request for permission to bomb the Yalu bridges on November 6, that helped raise the stakes once Chinese intervention had begun.[90] In short, there is evidence to substantiate the contemporary charge made by George Kennan that, "by permitting General MacArthur to retain the wide and relatively uncontrolled latitude he has enjoyed in determining our policy in the north Asian and western Pacific areas, we are tolerating a state of affairs in which we do not really have full control over the statements that are being made—and actions taken—in our name."[91]

Yet if MacArthur was undoubtedly an incredibly powerful bureaucratic agent, the source of his influence over the president was political in nature. Truman understood that MacArthur harbored a strong ambition to replace him as commander in chief. Indeed, having flirted with a bid for the presidency in 1944, the general had actively encouraged a draft movement four years later from his headquarters in Tokyo. In the run-up to the Wisconsin primary during the 1948 race, he maintained regular contact with the head of a national MacArthur-for-president campaign, Lansing Hoyt, regularly forwarding him copies of letters he had written to supporters at home in an apparent attempt to help coordinate the ongoing efforts. In one such letter, typical of many that were notionally sent under an aide's signature, a supporter was told the general would "feel a sense of highest honor and distinction were he to be the choice of Wisconsin voters in the Republican primary," and given his "loyalty and devotion" to the state he would "unquestionably accept its mandate."[92] In Washington, it did not go unnoticed that MacArthur failed to publicly withdraw his name from the campaign until *after* the returns of the subsequent primary in Nebraska indicated his fading prospects. It was not without reason, then, that Truman would later compare MacArthur to George McClellan, President Lincoln's troublesome general who shared similar political aspirations.[93]

That the relationship between Truman and MacArthur was infused with mutual partisan skepticism and electioneering is further substantiated by reference to their first (and last) meeting at Wake Island in October 1950. The president later justified the trip in part on the grounds that he wanted his general's first-hand appraisal of the chances of Chinese intervention in Korea.[94] Yet MacArthur felt that since such assessments had been covered in detail in his regular dispatches, there must have been another reason.[95] With the midterms just two weeks away, Truman was widely accused of cynically seeking a photo opportunity with a popular general in order to help fellow Democrats ride on the coattails of the so-called sorcerer of Inchon. MacArthur and his confidants thus variously referred to the entire conference as a "political junket" and "sly political ambush," while Dean Acheson outright refused to attend a meeting he claimed constituted such a "distasteful" idea.[96] Notably, Truman's White House aides simply saw it as "good election-year stuff."[97]

One revealing facet of Truman's private conversation with MacArthur at Wake concerned the two men's political plans. MacArthur, buoyed by a recent influx of telegrams encouraging *him* to run for president again in 1952, first raised the question, asking whether Truman intended to stand for reelection.[98] The president immediately countered by asking the general if he had any ambitions along the same lines. "None whatsoever," MacArthur replied, adding that "if you have any general running against you, his name will be Eisenhower, not MacArthur."[99] Truman scribbled down notes that essentially confirm MacArthur's account of the conversation, adding that the general had also noted how "the politicians had made a 'chump' (his word) of him in 1948 and that it would not happen again."[100] There was, of course, little MacArthur could do but deny retaining any political intentions; it would be impertinent if not self-defeating to announce any such intentions to the president in person and in the middle of a war. However, coming from a man who had already run against Truman, and had hinted in June at persisting ambitions by telling a journalist, "I am ready to serve at any time, in any capacity, anywhere," the denial was not very credible.[101]

Crucially, it was precisely this perception of MacArthur as a political threat that guaranteed the general's influence over policy in the Korean War, despite the president having given repeated thought to his replacement. Most strikingly, as early as July 1, less than a week into the crisis, Truman seemed more inclined to fire MacArthur than designate him commander of UN forces in Korea. "MacArthur is a supreme egotist, who regarded himself as something of a god," felt Truman, according to a contemporary record of a private conversation written by a White House aide. Revealing "little regard or respect" for the general, Truman recounted how John Foster Dulles had advised him earlier that week to relieve MacArthur from his duties. Truman's response makes crystal clear that if MacArthur can be credited with steering decision making in 1950, this had a great deal to do with electoral politics: "The President pointed out to him that the General is involved politically in this country—where he has from time to time been mentioned as a possible Republican presidential candidate—and that he could not recall MacArthur without causing a tremendous reaction in this country where he has been built up to heroic stature."[102]

Truman had a second opportunity to dismiss MacArthur in August, when the general issued a statement to the head of the Veterans of Foreign Wars (VFW). Calling for "aggressive, resolute and dynamic leadership," MacArthur decried the notion that the defense of Taiwan against the Communist-held Chinese mainland would alienate continental Asia as a "threadbare argument" put forward by "those who advocate appeasement and defeatism."[103] Since this appeared to undermine official U.S. policy, which sought to find a political solution to the issue of Taiwan and to de-escalate tensions in the region, Truman was furious.[104] The entire episode reflected the reality that the strategic preferences of the president and his commander when it came to Korea and the Far East were fundamentally misaligned; Truman sought to avoid war with China, while MacArthur felt it necessary and perhaps even desirable.

Yet, though Truman apparently gave "serious thought" to replacing MacArthur with General Bradley at this juncture, he decided against it, and instead merely ordered the withdrawal of the offending statement. In his memoir, the president attributes this decision to his unwillingness to hurt

General MacArthur personally.[105] This is difficult to believe. To be sure, Truman took a keen interest in every facet of the general's well-being during the war, once asking Frank Lowe, a mutual acquaintance, to report back extensively on his medical records.[106] Yet the fact that Lowe was in Korea in the first place was indicative of the level of distrust Truman felt toward MacArthur. He had, of course, once griped about "Mr. Prima Donna, Brass Hat, Five Star MACARTHUR," disparagingly referring to the general as a "stuffed shirt" and "bunco man" in 1945. On the way to Wake, he sarcastically told his cousin he was on the way "to talk to God's righthand man."[107] This was not a man who cared much for the feelings of a "supreme egotist."

Instead, the primary focus of the administration's frustrations with MacArthur's VFW statement appears to have been inextricably linked to the congressional election campaign. "Everyone knew that this was going to cause a bad mess at the best," recounted Averell Harriman, in a conversation with Dean Acheson. Harriman, who had been the one to first present Truman with MacArthur's message on August 26, lamented to the secretary of state that "the MacArthur statement would plague us through the election."[108] Indeed, in a meeting of advisors to discuss the letter's significance, "It was recognized by all of us that the statement, having already been given to the press, would get into print and that action of any kind would arouse a storm of discussion and controversy, and would provide opponents of the administration with further ammunition for their campaign . . . MacArthur is regarded as a Republican and seemingly is playing the Republican line in Far Eastern and Asian policy." Lumping the recalcitrant general together with another thorn in the side of the administration, Secretary of Defense Louis Johnson, the group were well aware of the risks of dismissing both high-profile figures at such a politically sensitive time. "It was pretty well agreed," concluded his advisors, "that nothing can be done before the election."[109] This evidence would appear to corroborate Truman's later recollections of what really influenced his reaction to MacArthur's actions. "That's the day I should have fired him," admitted the president, adding that his advisors "talked me out of it. They said it would cause too much of an uproar."[110]

After the midterms, MacArthur's grip on U.S. policy in Korea rapidly diminished. Increasing numbers of restrictions placed on his command led him to publicly complain that orders from Washington provided the enemy with a "sanctuary" and placed "an enormous handicap without precedent in military history" on UN forces.[111] In turn, such comments led Truman to issue a gag order, directed at MacArthur, requiring that all public statements be cleared with Washington prior to their release.[112] Notably, MacArthur had apparently been bitterly complaining to friendly press figures like Robert McCormick and Roy Howard in a similar manner even after the VFW statement.[113] Truman, in turn, having already attributed the "campaign of vilification and lies" in the United States to McCormick's newspaper chain, continued to describe his *Washington Times-Herald* as a "sabotage sheet," yet failed to censure MacArthur's correspondence with its owner until after the midterms.[114]

More sensational still was the rebuke MacArthur received from General J. Lawton Collins on November 11 for unauthorized communications with foreign officials. Detailing intercepted reports from Brazilian and Portuguese sources, Collins, the army's chief of staff, presented MacArthur with evidence that he had spoken disparagingly about the U.S. president and decried the Wake conference as a gimmick designed to help the governor of California in the upcoming gubernatorial election. More worryingly, MacArthur had implied far more aggressive intentions than U.S. policy allowed for at the time. Insisting on the importance of a united Korea and resolute defense of Taiwan, MacArthur had let slip his view that "it would be better to face a war now than two or three years hence" with the USSR. Acknowledging that this October 21 cable was but one of many similar instances of leaks by MacArthur's intelligence unit discovered since June, Collins did not offer an explanation as to why it took Truman until four days after the congressional elections to raise his "great concern" over the matter.[115]

By contrast, when MacArthur committed similar offenses in March 1951, Truman showed little hesitation in finally and infamously dismissing the recalcitrant general. Ignoring the December 6 gag order, MacArthur released a statement that directly undermined an imminent peace offer the administration had been planning, instead threatening China with an expansion of UN military operations, which he claimed would cause the country's military collapse. Worse still was the letter he had written four days earlier to the minority leader, Joseph P. Martin, in which MacArthur advocated a similarly aggressive policy against the Chinese, insisting that "there is no substitute for victory."[116] As William Stueck has pointed out, there may have been good military reasons why Truman might now countenance the dismissal of the commanding general of UN forces. Faced with reports of a sizeable buildup of airpower in Manchuria, the Joint Chiefs had felt it militarily necessary to authorize the UN command to pursue enemy air-craft across the border to counter any stepped-up air campaign. In light of the general's recent actions, however, the senior military leadership did not feel they could trust MacArthur with such broadened authority, fearing that he might instead use it as pretext to expand the war beyond what was strictly necessary. In explaining Truman's willingness to finally overcome his reluctance to fire MacArthur at this stage, the advice of both the chair-man of the Joint Chiefs and the secretary of defense—two men who also had five stars on their shoulders—would have surely played an important contributing role.[117]

Yet it was the political significance of MacArthur's latest transgressions that appeared to rankle Truman the most. "The situation with regard to the Far Eastern General has become a political one," the president wrote in his diary on April 5, adding, "MacArthur has made himself a center of contro-versy, publicly and privately."[118] The following day, Truman bristled at the public revelation of MacArthur's letter to the minority leader, complaining that "MacArthur shoots another political bomb through Joe Martin," in an act that amounted to "rank insubordination."[119]

In explaining why this latest act of perceived insubordination led to MacArthur's dismissal while earlier instances had not, the changed politi-cal context must be properly understood. As Lawrence Freedman has argued, "the aura surrounding MacArthur had been punctured by his failures of command."[120] After experiencing a succession of setbacks on the battlefield, a record of basic errors under his leadership had developed, leaving the five-star general's image as the "sorcerer of Inchon" somewhat tarnished. Yet if MacArthur was no longer unassailable, he still remained a politically for-midable foe. Much as they had over the previous summer, a series of advi-sors and confidants—this time including Secretary Acheson and Speaker Sam Rayburn—warned Truman of the "political repercussions" that would follow MacArthur's recall, thanks to the general's status as a "popular hero," particularly among the Republican "primitives" who would help generate "the biggest fight of your administration."[121] However, now with eighteen months until the next election, and with Truman already thinking about not standing for reelection, he was better placed to ride out the political storm he had once feared.[122] Receiving "telegrams and letters of abuse by the dozens," Truman put events into context in his diary. "Quite an explo-sion," he admitted, adding that it "was expected but I had to act."[123] When

MacArthur's speech before Congress on April 11 sparked a further frenzy of partisan mudslinging, Truman brushed the furor off as "nothing but a damn bunch of bullshit."[124]

In sum, if the bureaucratic power held by General MacArthur played an important role in the decision to expand the Korean War, the strength of this influence was conditional on the stage of the electoral cycle. Prior to the 1950 midterms, the political risks of countermanding the five-star general appeared to outweigh any concern that his more aggressive conception of optimal military strategy was driving U.S. policy. Deference to MacArthur in this period might reasonably be said to approximate Truman's electoral preference, given the alignment between the commander's views and those of the president's most vocal critics. Only after the midterm elections had taken place, and with the president's own interest in reelection waning, could he summon up the courage to confront and ultimately dismiss MacArthur.

*   *   *

The decisions taken in September by Harry Truman appear to have been subjected to electoral pressures on the eve of the 1950 midterm elections. Having established a firm strategic preference for keeping the war "limited," the president nevertheless embarked on an escalatory course of action both he and his advisors understood would severely raise the risks of conflict with China and/or the Soviet Union. In dialing up the level of military intervention on the Korean Peninsula and opting not to back down when evidence of Chinese intervention became apparent, instead deferring to the hawkish demands of the commander in the field, he was responding to an increasingly belligerent public mood. Sensitive to Republican charges of timidity and "softness" at the height of the congressional election campaign, his actions bear the distinctive characteristics of the *spur* mechanism.

Seeking an Armistice

As explained in chapter 1, the electoral cycle generates pressures at all stages of a conflict, not simply affecting how a war may be fought, but also any subsequent efforts to settle it peacefully. Under the *spoiler* mechanism, the leverage afforded to the administration to pursue its preferred bargaining position may be eroded by several factors, including the president's own political preferences, the strategic calculations of other candidates and nego- tiating opponents, and the pressures related to the fixed deadline of Elec- tion Day. This section illustrates these pressures by examining the relation- ship between the 1952 campaign and the progress of ongoing armistice talks that had begun in mid-1951. It finds that the combination of Truman's "lame duck" status and other states' concerns about possible future escala- tion under President-elect Eisenhower served to generate the basis of a dip- lomatic solution to the deadlocked issue of POW repatriation. It concludes by briefly exploring how the honeymoon period of Eisenhower's presi- dency then permitted him sufficient latitude to make a deal stick in July 1953.

"Not a Point for Bargaining!": The 1952 Campaign and Interregnum

For much of the 1952 campaign season, President Truman was able to pur- sue his preferred course of action relatively free of electoral constraints. Part of the reason for this had to do with his decision, announced in March of that year, that he would not stand for reelection. This removed the core officeholding incentive that drives much of the logic of electoral account- ability. While Truman was undoubtedly keen to support the campaign of Adlai Stevenson, the eventual Democratic nominee he had all but hand- picked, such political incentives were weaker than they might have been had Truman's name been on the ballot. As it was, particularly through the first half of 1952, the president could focus on negotiating a peace on terms he felt to be in the best interests of the United States, and perhaps his own legacy in the longer term.

In practice, these circumstances help explain why Truman stubbornly maintained his principled opposition to any solution that would involve the repatriation of POWs against their will. This policy of "non-forcible repatri- ation" is widely considered to have been the primary obstacle to peace after it became the administration's firm preference in February 1952. It was also adopted in large part thanks to the president's personal advocacy of the position. While couched in moral terms, Truman knew that the sight of thou- sands of Communist troops deciding not to return home would be a great propaganda victory in the Cold War. As such, he was eager to stick to a hard-line position even as he knew that doing so would make the POW issue "the sole remaining fundamental issue in the Korean armistice negotiations," and therefore one he surmised would likely be seen as increasingly unacceptable to the U.S. public.[125] As a "lame duck" in the spring of 1952, however, he had both the time and political latitude to stick resolutely to this red line despite such anticipated pressures. "As far as I was concerned," recalled Truman later, "this was not a point for bargaining!"[126]

Truman's leverage was aided, too, by the fact that both Stevenson and Eisenhower entered the race relatively late (the former on account of inde-cision, the latter thanks to his status as a serving military officer), and nei-ther made Korea a centerpiece of their early campaign strategy. Unlike in 1950, the long-stalemated conflict in the Far East generated few headlines, drifting in and out of public consciousness, with the result that little politi-cal capital could be made.[127] Electoral constraints were shaping up to be remarkably mild, then, in what looked set to be, as one scholar has recently put it, a "confirming" campaign.[128]

This relatively permissive electoral environment began to change in the closing months of the presidential contest, however. First, public ambiva-lence gave way to increasing interest in Korea as critics in Congress stepped up their partisan sniping ahead of polling day. A new bombing campaign designed to "ginger up" the peace talks appeared to have only whetted the appetite of those calling for a MacArthur-style military solution to the con-flict, with one representative calling on the administration to "quit pussy-footing in Korea," and another insisting that "we should go all-out in Korea or get out entirely."[129] Unencumbered by the pressure to be reelected, Tru-man was largely willing and able to brush off such criticism in charting his own strategic course, but he understood that the renewed political spotlight on Korea infused any actions he might take with important political and dip-lomatic implications. When his advisors raised the prospect of building up Chinese Nationalist forces in Taiwan in an NSC meeting of September 24, for instance, Truman dismissed the idea out of hand. "We must take into con-sideration both the forthcoming U.N. meeting and the impending election," he reasoned. "Both of these make it difficult to do this without creating a political situation which might upset the whole apple-cart."[130] As he pre-pared to depart for a month-long speaking tour ahead of the election, he "jokingly" told advisors that "during the next thirty days he would not be so interested in military decisions."[131] Instead, the president authorized the UN delegation to present an ultimatum, threatening an indefinite recess to talks unless the Communist side agreed to the U.S. position on POWs. When negotiations duly stalled, it only added fuel to criticism that the administration lacked a clear plan for how to resolve the conflict. Coupled with news of intense fighting in Korea, with "bitter and costly fighting for several inconsequential hills" yielding nine thousand casualties in a single month, the salience of the war spiked just as the election campaign reached a crescendo.[132] Whereas in January 1952 just 25 percent of Americans felt the war was one of the most important issues facing the country, this figure more than doubled to 52 percent by late October.[133]

Second, and relatedly, daylight between the candidates and the administration began to emerge during the course of the campaign, with both moving to distance themselves from Truman and his policies. Stevenson's break was more subtle. While defending the decision to intervene and promising no easy solutions, the Democratic candidate nevertheless noted that "mistakes were made" in Korean policy, pointing to the lack of a security guarantee afforded to South Korea and adding that "it might well have been wiser if American forces had not crossed the 38th parallel."[134] In the context of Truman's broader dissatisfaction with how his would-be successor was running his campaign, such comments irked the president. After staffing his campaign with men carrying few connections to the White House, Stevenson had already sought to muzzle the president's public appearances, much to Truman's anger. "I have come to the conclusion that you are embarrassed by having the president of the United States in your corner in this campaign," wrote Truman in a fiery, though ultimately unsent, letter addressed to Stevenson around this time. After being rebuffed in his latest efforts to help the Stevenson campaign with strategy, he resolved to leave the Democratic nominee to it for the rest of the campaign, admitting that, "I can't stand snub after snub by you."[135] In another unsent letter, he was even less restrained, advising Stevenson to "take your crackpots, your high socialites with their noses in the air, run your campaign and win if you can."[136]

Eisenhower's rightward turn in the autumn of 1952 was more dramatic. After his initial restraint, the Republican candidate soon embraced his party's campaign strategy, which was explicitly designed to cause voters "to fear for their national security and lives" and summarized by the slogan of

"K1C2"—Korea, Communism, and Corruption.[137] Seeking to foster his image as a military hero uniquely suited to bringing the war to an end, Eisenhower increasingly spoke out against the Democratic "record of bungling that has trapped us into the Korean War" in September.[138] For similarly political reasons, Eisenhower cultivated relationships with the hyper-partisan and pro-MacArthur faction of the Republican Party, thereby seeming to tacitly endorse their scathing criticisms of Truman's Korean strategy and aggressive prescriptions. In what became known as the "surrender at Morningside," Eisenhower struck a politically expedient deal with Robert Taft, exchanging influence over future foreign and financial policy for the senator's support in key midwestern states. He compounded the move with his subsequent failure to denounce Joseph McCarthy, instead endorsing the party's chief demagogue at an October election rally in the red-baiter's home state of Wisconsin. That same month, Eisenhower sought to associate mounting casualties in Korea with Truman's short-sighted decision to enter into negotiations, claiming the president had fallen into a Communist "bear pit," while noting that if fighting was necessary, "that is a job for Koreans."[139] Finally, Eisenhower delivered the coup de grâce on Stevenson's ailing campaign by dramatically pledging on October 24 that, if elected, "I shall go to Korea."[140]

In turn, this hostile electoral environment was perceived by the president to have placed constraints on his ability to make progress in the negotiations. Recalling how "shocked and disappointed" he was "to see our foreign policy used as a political football," Truman later lambasted Eisenhower's decision to appropriate Korea for partisan purposes at such a delicate time of negotiation. Of the candidate's pledge to go to the battlefront, in particular, Truman insisted that Eisenhower "must have known that he was weakening our hand in negotiations."[141] Such a view was apparently firmly shared by General Bradley. "He knew very well that he could achieve nothing by going to Korea," he wrote, adding that "this new element could weaken our hand at the negotiating table."[142]

Though the talks at Panmunjom had already broken off by this time, Truman and Acheson specifically blamed Eisenhower's campaign statement for their inability to garner support at the United Nations for a resolution affirming support for the principle of "non-forcible repatriation." "In view of General Eisenhower's imminent trip to Korea and uncertainty in their minds as to whether he will support the position thus far taken by the United States in the armistice negotiations, many of the delegations appear reluctant to proceed with this resolution," Acheson informed Truman on November 6.[143] In fact, prior to the American election, a number of close allies refused to even come to New York until after polling day in the United States, including the British and French foreign ministers. "We had hoped for quick action on the twenty-one-nation resolution, but it was not to be," regretted Acheson later, adding, "the U.S. election was only eleven days away; my authenticity as a spokesman for the United States was at low ebb, for General Eisenhower's announcement that if elected he would go to Korea indicated that he was committing himself to nothing."[144]

Perhaps the most significant manifestation of the *spoiler* mechanism, however, came during the "interregnum" between the election and Eisenhower's inauguration. During this period, the Truman administration, weakened by its "lame duck" status, reluctantly abandoned its efforts to pursue a UN resolution affirming the principle of "non-forcible repatriation." Instead, pressured by Commonwealth countries who feared what the president-elect might do from January, the United States supported an India-sponsored proposal that contained the basic mechanism for resolving the POW issue, which would ultimately be adopted in the 1953 armistice.[145]

As Truman and Acheson had suspected, the fact that Commonwealth opposition to the U.S. resolution stemmed from anxiety about Eisenhower's future plans is quite clear from the record. In British cabinet meetings that December, fears that Eisenhower would authorize major military operations against Chinese forces in Korea or unleash Chiang Kai-Shek's Nationalist forces on the Chinese mainland were paramount, with Prime Minister Winston Churchill agreeing that "it would be a grave mistake to take any course which would widen the area of conflict in Korea." Support for the Indian resolution against American wishes was therefore essential.[146] The British ambassador to the United Nations later summed up the British position clearly: "Our immediate interest lay in the take-over of the American Administration by the Republicans—out of office for twenty years." With many within the Republican Party "intent on war with Peking," and carrying little experience in foreign affairs, "We did not look forward to this with any great enthusiasm."[147] The American administration understood as much too. In a November 20 note to the president, Acheson advised that British, Canadian, and French support for the Indian resolution stemmed from "grave apprehensions about what the new administration may do regarding Korea," meaning they shared "a desperate anxiety to exhaust all possibilities for an armistice now, however remote."[148]

American opposition to the Indian resolution was no secret to these allies either. Under the Indian proposals, the fate of POWs not wishing to return home would be decided upon by a repatriation committee, composed of four neutral nations and an "umpire" with a casting vote. Any prisoners remaining in its custody after ninety days would have their final disposition agreed at a later political conference. In a series of meetings with Commonwealth delegations over the winter, Acheson slammed these proposals as both vague and a recipe for indefinite captivity for those prisoners unwilling to return home.[149] Unless the British fell in line with the American viewpoint, threatened Acheson, "there would be no NATO, no Anglo-American friendship."[150] President Truman was kept informed of these developments, and in fact authorized Acheson to take a confrontational line in his efforts to sink the Indian proposal.[151]

Thanks to dynamics generated by the American electoral cycle, however, U.S. efforts to coerce America's allies failed. The Truman administration could not bully others into supporting its position, for with just weeks left in office, any threats of later punishment for going against the U.S. position carried little credibility. Blaming the tense situation in New York on the "inept" strategy and tactics of the American delegation, British foreign minister Anthony Eden reported to his cabinet that Acheson and others had apparently developed an "irrational dislike of any Indian proposal." The recent election results and history of partisan attacks on the U.S. secretary of state had apparently induced in him "a mild persecution complex," leading him to adopt an intransigent attitude, apparently feeling it "necessary to be more Royalist than the King." These efforts were futile, Eden recalled, since "General Eisenhower and Mr. Dulles were avoiding committing themselves publicly or privately in support of the United States Government's attitude," meaning "retreat was inevitable."[152]

This latter point was particularly crucial. As Truman understood well, Eisenhower's support for the administration's position at the United Nations was essential to the long-term credibility of the U.S. position. At Acheson's suggestion, the president made repeated attempts to secure a public statement of support from the president-elect. On November 6, for instance, Truman put the Korean resolution at the top of a list of "really fundamental things pending in the United Nations" that necessitated his input.[153] Eisenhower, however, remained "coy" in his relations with the administration, according to Truman, demurring before finally announcing Henry Cabot Lodge Jr., his erstwhile campaign manager, as liaison to the administration.[154]

When Eisenhower did finally meet with the incumbent president on November 18, Korea was again the first item on the agenda. After detailing the basis of U.S. opposition to the Indian resolution, Acheson explained that "energetic action" by the United States to defeat the proposal was required, since a "showdown" was coming. It would be of the "greatest possible assistance" to such efforts if General Eisenhower could issue a statement in support of the administration's view. Acheson then handed Senator Lodge a draft that the president-elect might wish to use. Eisenhower remained noncommittal, promising only to give the matter "careful study," while Truman privately reflected that his advice "went into one ear and out the other."[155]

Eisenhower's coolness was in fact the product of a hard-nosed political calculation. This much was made clear in an exchange between the president-elect and his Republican advisor Harold Stassen. Having received advance warning about the Truman administration's desire to obtain Eisenhower's support for its repatriation policy, Stassen warned the president-elect that agreeing to this would be a "great mistake," since it "would link your first foreign policy decision to the discredited Truman administration." Worse still, adherence to Truman's "clumsy moves" would "reduce the possible range on your future policy decisions."[156] In his response two days later, Eisenhower agreed, assuring Stassen that "I have already warned my representatives in Washington to agree to nothing that sounds like policy."[157]

Eisenhower's success in minimizing his ties to the unpopular Truman administration, in turn, helped spell doom for Truman's hopes of pursuing his preferred diplomatic course of action at the United Nations. After Soviet denunciation of the Indian resolution helped paper over the cracks in the relationship between the United States and its allies, the U.S. delegation acceded to a series of compromises in the wording of the Indian resolution, and was ultimately instructed to support it in a vote of December 1.[158] By that point, there was no time or appetite for further action of a diplomatic or military nature, as further progress toward peace was left to the Eisenhower administration.

"A Mandate from the American People"

During the opening phase of the American electoral cycle, newly elected presidents can expect to enjoy relatively permissive conditions at home when making decisions about wartime strategy. Electoral constraints will not be entirely absent, however. Under the *hangover* mechanism explored in chapter 1, we might expect to observe evidence of rhetorical commitments made during the campaign influencing decisions, depending on the specificity of the candidate's campaign pledges. The legacy of inherited policies and commitments will of course also help define the range of available policy options. This section argues that this blend of a generally favorable electoral environment, combined with mild *hangover* effects from events in 1952, played important roles in affording Eisenhower the opportunity to reach an armistice deal within seven months of taking office.

In assessing the strength of the electoral hangover with which Eisenhower had to contend, it is important to note that the statements he made about the war as a candidate were extraordinarily vague in character. This was by design. Early in the race, Eisenhower had been told by his campaign manager, Henry Cabot Lodge Jr., to stick to speeches that dealt in "generalities," referring by way of example to FDR's stirring but ultimately ambiguous one-liner, "we have nothing to fear but fear itself."[159] As mentioned in the previous section, Eisenhower addressed the war in Korea most directly in a speech on October 24, 1952. Though he pledged "to bring the Korean War to an honorable and early end," he declined to say how that would be achieved. Instead, relying on his reputation as one of the most respected senior military officers of his generation, he simply explained that a personal trip would be required to fully assess the situation and chart a way forward. As such, he had promised, "I shall go to Korea."[160] As the advisor widely credited with the idea for such a statement later explained, there was a "simple and inexorable" political logic to the pledge: "It rose from the need to say something affirmative on the sharpest issue of the day—*without* engaging in frivolous assurances and *without* binding a future administration to policies or actions fashioned in mid-campaign by any distorting temptations of domestic politics."[161] Combined with Eisenhower's aforementioned efforts to distance himself from the administration during the campaign and its aftermath, the new president had strenuously sought to keep his hand free for the future.

Once in office, Eisenhower frequently referred back to his position on the campaign trail. In doing so, he seemed to interpret his pledges as having tied him to a path that ruled out major escalation. During his visit to Korea in late November—itself an early fulfillment of his campaign pledge—the incoming president gave General Mark Clark no time to formally present his extensive plans for obtaining a military victory. "I know just how you feel, militarily," explained Eisenhower, "but I feel I have a mandate from the American people to stop this fighting."[162] While frustrated by the commander in chief's unwillingness to adhere to his prescriptions at the time, General Clark came to admire the way in which Eisenhower took his political commitments seriously, later recalling a conversation in which Eisenhower said, "I made campaign pledges, and when some of my close supporters afterwards said, 'you don't need to pay attention to them,' I said, 'those are my sacred promises and I will live up to them.'"[163] Notably, the president-elect would also hear Douglas MacArthur out on his proposals during the transition. His ideas remained substantially similar to those Truman had repeatedly rejected two years prior, but Eisenhower again made no commitment to embark on such an escalatory course.[164]

Eisenhower was not opposed in principle to the adoption of more aggressive means of waging war, however. On the contrary, Eisenhower spent much of the next several months seriously weighing the case for using nuclear weapons in Korea. For instance, in his first meeting discussing the war, held on February 11, he mulled their utility in a prospective operation aiming to destroy a buildup of enemy capabilities in the Kaesong area, saying that "somehow or other the tabu [sic] which surrounds the use of atomic weapons would have to be destroyed."[165] In a March 31 meeting, he felt the use of such weapons elsewhere would be "worth the cost" if they could help secure a victory over the enemy and an advance to the "waist" of Korea well above the 38th parallel.[166] Eisenhower again raised the possibility on May 6, declaring that "he had reached the point of being convinced that we have got to consider the atomic bomb as simply another weapon in our arsenal."[167] Told the following week that the military was "most anxious" to make use of nuclear weapons in any course of action involving operations outside of Korea, even though they were skeptical that suitable targets could be found within Korea, Eisenhower's only real issue appeared to be their excessive caution on target assessment.[168]

Eisenhower actually ended up approving a suite of aggressive measures—including air and naval attacks on Manchuria and other Chinese targets, an offensive in Korea to capture the "waist" line, and atomic weapons "on a sufficiently large scale to insure success"—as the "general guide" to follow should armistice talks break down.[169] In doing so, he benefited from a largely permissive domestic political environment, with public opinion assessed to be engaged yet ultimately malleable in the event that stronger measures were deemed necessary. The president was expected to receive "predominant public support" for adopting a more "vigorous" approach and "predominant public acceptance" for sticking with a more cautious policy.[170] Enjoying approval ratings of 70 percent and with four years until his reelection campaign, the apparent insensitivity to warnings of public "hysteria" if atomic weapons were used points toward the role that the permissive electoral environment played in shaping Eisenhower's strategy.[171]

Eisenhower's dismissal of the plans favored by Clark and MacArthur may therefore say less about how the president felt genuinely constrained by the content of his prior campaign statements, and more about his determination to preserve his flexibility to chart his own path once in office. That, of course, was why he had outlined such a vague position as a candidate in the first place. And it was why he was so irked when critics later accused him of vacillation and indecision in making progress toward a negotiated settlement in the weeks and months after he assumed office. Informed by Dulles that Democrats in Congress were in an "ugly mood" thanks in part to "our failure to have done anything on the Korean war," Eisenhower counseled patience, explaining, "all during the campaign we said there was no easy formula for solving the war."[172]

At the negotiating table, then, the key constraint on Eisenhower was thus not so much what he *had* said on the campaign trail—because he said very little that committed him one way or the other—but what he failed to say. This was because, in determining the essential basis of this negotiated solution, Eisenhower found himself effectively wedded to the terms of the Indian resolution, which as a candidate he had ironically declined to help defeat. After a March 30 proposal from Zhou Enlai to exchange sick and wounded prisoners also first signaled Chinese recognition of POW repatriation as an issue to be resolved, it appeared that talks might make rapid progress. In Washington, an alarmed Dulles expressed concern to colleagues about "the armistice agreement that we are being sucked into," before raising his proposal to renege on the deal in the NSC meeting the following day.[173] Instead, during weeks of tentative negotiations at the United Nations, the Indian mechanism for resolving the POW issue was embedded in a Brazilian-sponsored resolution and approved unanimously. As the first resolution relating to the war to carry full UN support, this procedural agreement went on to set the parameters of the discussions that would take place during renewed armistice negotiations.[174]

This was made clear in a key concession made on May 7, when China for the first time proposed a solution to the POW issue involving a repatriation commission, a time limit, and a political conference. "It had many similarities to the Indian Resolution," recalled General Clark, who, noting that the United States had supported this in December 1952, was instructed to accept the plan "as the starting point for discussion."[175] Indeed, in a May 8 meeting at the White House, Eisenhower decided that the United States "should adhere to the provisions of the Indian Resolution."[176] Again, it seems reasonable to conclude that the United States took this position reluctantly. In the minutes of a May 9 meeting between Dulles and several leading congressmen, the general feeling was recorded that "there was no liking of the situation, but a recognition that matters had gone so far through the India Resolution that there was no practical alternative."[177] A couple of weeks later, instructions came from Washington "to follow generally the terms of the Indian Resolution" in the U.S. counterproposal of May 25, as Clark recalled.[178] On the same day that the Chinese agreed to the latest iteration of the deal, President Eisenhower told Dulles to inform skeptics like Senator Knowland that their concerns were to some extent shared by the administration. As someone who had recently described Jawaharlal Nehru as a "psycho-path" who needed to "shut his mouth," Eisenhower was clearly less than comfortable with following India's prescription for an armistice in Korea.[179] "No one was happy," the president instructed his secretary of state to tell Knowland.[180]

In sum, the electoral cycle had mixed effects on Eisenhower's strategy for ending the Korean War. On the one hand, the general's perception of his own "sacred promises" made in 1952 appear to have pushed him toward a negotiated settlement as his preferred exit strategy from the Korean Peninsula, while the basis of such a settlement was to a considerable extent forced upon the administration by the lasting influence of the Indian resolution, adopted during the interregnum period. On the other hand, a permissive honeymoon period, supported by relatively mild hangover effects, thanks to Eisenhower's solid victory and vague pledges, gave him the room required to explore various escalatory contingency policies free of public and congressional constraints that might otherwise have ruled such options out as unacceptable.

*   *   *

Electoral politics played a pivotal role in shaping American strategy during the Korean War. Committed to the pursuit of the status quo ante through limited military means, Truman understood the strategic risks associated with any course of action that threatened to widen the war. However, the specter of the 1950 midterms magnified the Truman administration's susceptibility to public and congressional opinion, thereby placing a clear and imminent political price tag on any action that could be seen as timid or "soft." As a result, the president was repeatedly pushed down the escalatory path. In assenting to the bold military gamble at Inchon, approving NSC 81/1, and failing to act when it became clear that the actions of both the Chinese and his own commander in the field jeopardized his vision of a "police action," Truman succumbed to the pressure of the *spur* mechanism of electoral constraint. Only after the midterms were over could Truman renounce the expanded goal of Korean unification and dismiss the recalcitrant general who had helped lead him there.

Having contributed to the expansion of the conflict on the Korean Peninsula, the American electoral cycle then placed a series of obstacles in Harry Truman's preferred path to peace during the 1952 campaign. Able, as a "lame duck," to commit to the principle of "non-forcible repatriation," the incumbent soon perceived threats to his bargaining position from other actors with a vested interest in the outcome of the presidential race, providing evidence of the *spoiler* mechanism. By refusing to commit to the administration's position on POWs, Eisenhower's ambiguous pledges and increasing closeness to firebrand anticommunists in the party helped exacerbate fears among Commonwealth allies about future escalation. Taking advantage of the weakness of the U.S. administration during its time as a "lame duck" in the winter of 1952, these allies then forced Truman into support for the Indian resolution at the United Nations, which in turn would narrow Eisenhower's room for maneuver during the spring of 1953. Nevertheless, benefiting from a mild electoral *hangover* and taking advantage of the honeymoon phase of the electoral cycle, the newly elected president retained the political latitude at home to prepare military contingency options that he felt would secure a deal at the armistice talks in Panmunjom.

Taken together, the episodes examined here offer solid support for the conceptual framework outlined in chapter 1. While the conflict in Korea lasted only three years, it illuminates key phases of the electoral cycle that have been understudied in existing accounts of the impact of electoral politics and war—especially those relating to midterm campaigns and the "lame duck" period. That we can clearly observe evidence here that the role of electoral constraints in shaping decisions is broadly as expected should increase our confidence in the framework as a whole.

Having demonstrated that electoral politics mattered to decision makers in these key episodes, it of course does not follow that such pressures necessarily made a material difference to the course of the conflict. For this reason, it is fruitful to consider some counterfactual scenarios that shed light on the possibility that opportunities to limit the scope and duration of the Korean War were missed thanks to the pressures of the electoral cycle.

Firstly, were it not for the constraints generated by the 1950 midterm election, would there still have been an expansion of the war? In a calmer and more bipartisan climate, it is not difficult to imagine that Truman would have been able to stick closer to his strategic preference throughout the summer and autumn of 1950. Crossing the 38th parallel was understood to carry grave risks of Soviet or Chinese intervention, which went directly against the president's overriding desire to keep the war "limited." In an electoral environment in which he did not have to fear a harsh backlash from Republicans like Taft and McCarthy, it is quite easy to imagine Truman opting to follow a more cautious approach in Korea, along the lines that George Kennan had repeatedly advocated. If other bureaucratic agents like Dulles, and of course MacArthur, might still have pressed for escalatory policies, their power would be radically diminished in this apolitical counterfactual world. Indeed, as Truman came to regret later, MacArthur's message to the VFW organization had provided ample opportunity to replace him as commander, which might have permitted cooler heads to prevail in the fateful months of September and October.

In turn, if the 38th parallel had not been crossed, the chances of keeping the war contained would have risen considerably. Chinese leaders were in fact divided on whether to intervene through the month of September, and

U.S. aggression surely helped force their hand.[181] Even if events got this far, a directive countermanding MacArthur's order to waive restrictions on non-ROK troops would have given the opportunity to U.S. forces to avoid a rout and hold defensive positions when the Chinese assault began in the North. That, in turn, might have provided a better foundation for fruitful negotiations, or at least sufficient time to prepare for enemy offensives in the spring. In virtually any permutation, the United States would have been in a better political and military position than it actually was at the time of the massive Chinese counteroffensive of November 1950.

Secondly, absent the electoral pressures described in this chapter, would an armistice have been reached earlier? At a minimum, it seems highly plausible to suggest that any deal might at least look substantially different to the terms agreed in July 1953. As discussed earlier, both the genesis of the December 1952 Indian resolution at the United Nations and Commonwealth nations' ability to get it passed despite U.S. opposition owed much to electoral dynamics. Had the Truman administration not been a caretaker government, it would surely have been able to threaten its Commonwealth allies more credibly, and they in turn may well have fallen in line, as had been true for the majority of the war.[182] Since it was largely thanks to fear of Eisenhower's future plans that the resolution gained such support in the first place, moreover, it might never have come up as an issue at all. Either way, it seems likely that, absent the 1952 elections, the Truman administration might have been well-positioned to continue with its hard-line policy on "non-forcible repatriation."

Whether this would have generated an earlier peace is debatable. Acheson seemed to believe so. "It would have been better all around if the constitutional calendar had called for an election a year later than at that peculiarly critical moment," he later wrote. "With a longer life-span the existing government would have had a good chance of . . . convincing the Chinese and North Koreans to bring the Korean war to a close. The virtual interregnum of more than a year was costly."[183] More likely, however, in this scenario, was an indefinite continuation of diplomatic stalemate. The Communist delegation hardly seemed on the verge of a concession on POWs on the eve of Truman's withdrawal from the presidential race. Acheson might well have been able to strike down the Indian resolution, then, but all other things being equal, a continuation of the U.S. administration's position on POWs entailed far less chance of progress in the talks.

Relatedly, if it were not for Eisenhower's role during and after the 1952 campaign, it seems reasonable to speculate that the Chinese might not have moved toward the Indian position in the spring of 1953. Indeed, Chinese documents reveal that this crucial shift in China's bargaining position was likely a response to fears that Eisenhower would raise the costs of war through military escalation if he became president. Certainly, in the summer of 1952, Zhou Enlai instructed his Foreign Ministry to track Eisenhower's public speeches during the American election campaign. From these statements, it seemed clear to the Chinese that "Eisenhower would be more aggressive in Korea." Of particular note was the Republican candidate's promise of an "honorable peace" through "deeds" rather than "words," which Beijing took to mean a possible amphibious invasion of North Korea.[184] Observing Eisenhower's conferences with General Clark and General MacArthur, both known hawks, Chinese leaders were further convinced that, as Mao Zedong anxiously informed Joseph Stalin on December 17, Eisenhower was "currently carrying out preparations for military actions that will take place after he comes to power." That Eisenhower was in fact paying the generals' ideas no more than lip service was not known to the Chinese at the time, of course. In turn, as Elizabeth Stanley has recently argued, it was this pattern of perceptions that prompted the Chinese to quickly compromise on POWs within days of Stalin's death in March 1953.[185]

On balance, it seems fair to conclude that electoral constraints may actually have *helped* secure an armistice that otherwise might not have been expected, were such pressures not a factor. To be sure, both Truman and Eisenhower wound up with outcomes they felt were less than optimal (which is the reason we can still consider their diplomatic strategies to have been spoiled by electoral constraints), bound as they were by the terms of the Indian resolution. Yet the counterfactual alternatives did not look promising. In the end, Eisenhower's electoral victory may have been the quickest path to peace, not because of the atomic threats he later lauded, but because it indirectly (via events in the United Nations and independent Chinese concessions) led to a crucial compromise on POWs.[186] While Stalin's death remained a key final ingredient permitting the Chinese to act on their preference to settle, these electorally induced shifts may have served as catalysts for peace.

THREE

Vietnam

Lyndon Johnson and the "Americanization" of the War

> I've got to win an election . . . and then you can make a decision.
>
> —LYNDON JOHNSON, MARCH 1964

> The closer you get to the elections, the more troubles you have.
>
> —LYNDON JOHNSON, OCTOBER 1968

ON ASSUMING THE PRESIDENCY in November 1963, Lyndon Johnson inherited an increasingly acute problem in Southeast Asia, a rhetorical commitment to solving it, and yet no sure plan for achieving such a resolution. Since the defeat of French forces at Dien Bien Phu in 1954, the United States had steadily increased its share of the burden in supporting the efforts of the South Vietnamese government in combating an insurgency backed by Hanoi. Framed as a key test of the containment strategy that had dominated national security debates since the Korean War, this approach saw successive presidents pour more money and materiel into Saigon to prevent it falling into Communist hands. Under Johnson, a "gradual escalation" policy resulted in 542,000 troops being stationed in Vietnam, supported by a sustained bombing campaign of the North. It had become "LBJ's war."[1]

The aim of this chapter is not to "explain" American intervention in Vietnam, a task that has already generated something of a historiographical canon.[2] Nor is it the first word, of course, on the role of domestic politics in the Vietnam War.[3] Instead, drawing on the conceptual framework outlined in chapter 1, it seeks to explore how a focus on electoral politics can help illuminate the nature and timing of President Johnson's decisions to

"Americanize" the war. Specifically, it argues that the pressures of the 1964 election campaign compelled Johnson to *delay* escalating the conflict in Southeast Asia until after the moment of greatest political sensitivity had passed. His concern with the domestic political calendar then further contributed to the form of "gradual escalation" that ensued, with decisions on bombing operations and troop commitments taken with one eye on the upcoming midterm elections of 1966. As the 1968 presidential election approached, finding his strategic and electoral preferences to be irreconcilable, Johnson then chose to put his perception of national interest above political survival, only to find his efforts to sue for peace frustrated by the *spoiler* effect that upcoming elections have on negotiations.

"Americanizing" the War

The 1964 election was a key turning point in the history of American decision making during the Vietnam War. As this section demonstrates, electoral politics contributed to a stagnation in policy debates in the politically sensitive period between Kennedy's assassination and Johnson's election as president in his own right, with decision making profoundly influenced by the *delay* mechanism. While strategic considerations largely overdetermined the question of *whether* Johnson would increase the preexisting military commitment to a steadily deteriorating situation, electoral constraints played a crucial role in determining *when* and *how* this escalation would take place. Only under the more politically permissive environment following his electoral victory did Johnson venture farther down the fateful path into the "quagmire" in Southeast Asia.

Strategic Considerations: "We're Losing. So We Need Something New."

Upon assuming office, President Johnson quickly learned from his advisors of a dire need for a shift in strategy in Vietnam. A steady consensus had emerged in the administration concerning the deteriorating situation in Southeast Asia following the secretary of defense's visit in December 1963. Secretary of Defense Robert S. McNamara's report warned that "Current trends, unless reversed in the next 2–3 months, will lead to neutralization at best and more likely to a Communist-controlled state."[4] Through 1964, McNamara would reiterate the message. Following another trip to Vietnam with Maxwell Taylor in March, he reported back to the president that "the situation has unquestionably been growing worse, at least since September."[5] The following month, he told his colleagues in the National Security Council that the United States was "right on the margin in Vietnam and that he could not guarantee that we would still be there six months or twelve months from now."[6] By May, he was gloomier still. Rejecting mild proposals for increased financial assistance for South Vietnam, McNamara began to insist that sterner measures be considered, with the near universal support of his fellow NSC principals. The various socioeconomic plans hitherto under consideration "will not substitute for the use of force," he complained, recommending that full U.S. intervention be put on the table. "We do not have a solution and these proposals will not save us," he concluded. "The situation is still going to hell . . . Nothing we are doing now will win."[7]

While McNamara would come to be closely associated with the escalation of the war, he was not alone in his concerns at this time. The CIA director, for instance, basically agreed. "The military situation, bad in December, has worsened and the problem of reversing the trend is formidable," reported Director John McCone in an early March meeting. "A continuation of the present nature of GVN [Government of Vietnam] and U.S. military and political actions," he warned, "does not appear to me to be enough to reverse current trends toward defeat."[8] Intelligence reports were equally stark, predicting that "if the tide of deterioration has not been arrested by the end of the year, the anti-Communist position in South Vietnam is likely to become untenable."[9] Shortly thereafter, the ambassador in Saigon, Henry Cabot Lodge Jr., told McNamara frankly that "it would not be prudent for us to think that the situation in South Vietnam can be expected to improve in the near future without our introducing something new and significant into the equation." He was, of course, preaching to the choir. McNamara quickly agreed, adding that the military situation was now "approaching the hopeless category."[10] Not without good reason, then, did McNamara report back to the president in early June that "the CIA estimators, Lodge, many of the rest of us in private would say that things are not good. They've gotten worse."[11]

Most importantly, Johnson was no bystander to this debate, and appears to have agreed with such assessments. After the very first meeting to discuss Vietnam following Kennedy's death, the president gloomily remarked to an aide that "it's going to hell in a hand basket out there," and apparently accepted the ambassador's advice that "if we don't do something . . . it'll go under any day."[12] By April, he was complaining to McNamara that "We need somebody over there that can get us some better plans than we've got, because what we've got is what we've had since '54. We're not getting it done. We're losing. So we need something new." As to what exactly that looked like, Johnson's instincts were clear. "What I want," he instructed McNamara, "is somebody that can lay up some plans to trap these guys and whoop the hell out of them, kill some of them."[13] In a subsequent conversation with his mentor, Senator Richard B. Russell Jr., he tipped his hand again with a rhetorical question: "Is it more dangerous for us to let things go as they're going now, deteriorating every day . . . than it would be for us to move in?"[14]

Through 1964, Johnson had been repeatedly pressed by his advisors, and especially the Joint Chiefs of Staff, to act upon these strategic concerns. A series of studies and planning exercises had been initiated in the State and Defense Departments, at Johnson's personal request.[15] By May the main options were clear: withdrawal, escalation, and a "neutralization" agreement based on the Laos settlement of 1962. Among these options, Johnson also received a recommendation from his secretaries of state and defense that he "make a Presidential decision that the U.S. will use selected and carefully graduated military force against North Vietnam."[16] The escalatory plan they advocated envisaged the use of both air support and ground troops, foreshadowing the policy outcomes of 1965.

Perceiving a clear need to change strategy, the logic of containment and commitment to "domino theory" also pointed clearly toward greater intervention in Vietnam. As George Herring has written, "U.S. involvement in Vietnam was a logical, if not inevitable, outgrowth of a world view and a policy—the policy of containment—that Americans in and out of government accepted without serious question for more than two decades."[17] While it may seem irrational and profoundly mistaken in hindsight, evidence for the existence of this "ironbound and unshakeable dogma" is indeed omnipresent in the documentary record.[18] Littered throughout meeting minutes and recordings of telephone conversations involving the president are statements depicting Vietnam as the first in a row of dominoes. In one typical example, Johnson framed the problem in 1964 as follows: "Of course if you start running from the Communists, they may just chase you right into your own kitchen."[19] The credibility of this commitment before U.S. allies was a corollary to the argument. Johnson would often refer to the legal and moral requirement to fulfill America's international obligations, as he explained to Dick Russell: "We're in here by treaty [the Southeast Asia Collective Defense Treaty] and our national honor's at stake. And if this treaty's no good, none of 'em are any good."[20] To be sure, Johnson's assessment of the chances of success even with increased intervention was hardly rosy, informed more by hope than expectation—"he was very pessimistic about the outcome," recalled his deputy national security advisor, Francis Bator.[21] Yet, facing few good strategic choices, it is clear that the status quo was understood to be suboptimal.

But if this strategic understanding of the situation made a decision to escalate the war likely, there remain important puzzles to explain. If domino theory was an ironclad belief, why did Johnson wait so long to act, despite being warned of the dire consequences of delay? Likewise, if containment required a firm U.S. response to Communist aggression in Vietnam, why not unleash the full power of the American military to achieve those goals with more certainty and efficiency?

Electoral Preference: "Some Peace Demagoguery for the Mothers"

As concerned as Lyndon Johnson was with what was strategically beneficial, he was also acutely aware that he faced an election in November 1964. Johnson remained deeply interested in "what the average American voter is going to think about how he did in the ball game of the Cold War," as his national security advisor, McGeorge Bundy, put it. "The great Cold War championship gets played in the largest stadium in the United States and he, Lyndon Johnson, is the quarterback, and if he loses, how does he do in the next election? So don't lose . . . He's living with his own political survival every time he looks at these questions."[22] Johnson himself put it more simply: "I'd hate like hell," he frankly told McNamara just weeks after assuming office, "to be such a statesman that I didn't get elected."[23] As such, he displayed a profound sensitivity to the electoral risks of any course of action placed before him.

In the particular case of the ongoing war in Vietnam, electoral considerations appeared to push Johnson further away from de-escalatory courses of action. Much as the *dampening* mechanism predicts, an initial screening process based almost exclusively on the "political acceptability" of the options under consideration appeared to eliminate the prospect of withdrawal or "neutralization" before any significant review was undertaken. "The one we haven't been taking up for any serious study," Secretary of State Dean Rusk told the president in June 1964, "is the alternative of pulling out of Southeast Asia."[24] In the political climate of 1960s America, much as in the early 1950s, a failure to stand up to the forces of global communism would invite scathing criticism from prominent hawks, imperiling any Democrat's election prospects. Since Rusk, Bundy, and McNamara all believed the partition of Vietnam would lead to a Communist takeover, the same logic applied to neutralization. As one aide concluded, "This would have greater political liabilities than our present course. The commitment to preserve Vietnamese independence was not made by Democrats—but we are not free to abandon it."[25] Bundy put things more bluntly: neutrality for South Vietnam would be viewed as a "betrayal" that would alienate a large enough constituency "to lose us an election."[26]

The following excerpt from a call with the chairman of the *Miami Herald* in February nicely summarizes Johnson's thinking on these options:

> There's only one of three things you can do. One is run and let the dominoes start falling over. And God Almighty, what they said about us leaving China would just be warming up, compared to what they'd say now. I see Nixon's raising hell about it today. And Goldwater too. You can run, or you can fight, as we are doing, or you can sit down and agree to neutralize all of it. But nobody is going to neutralize North Vietnam, so that's totally impractical.[27]

Both withdrawal and neutralization were associated with the "loss" of Vietnam, something Johnson believed would cause such consternation at home as to make the "loss" of China by Truman mere "chickenshit."[28] The two likely critics he cites are Goldwater—his Republican opponent in the 1964 campaign—and Nixon—who had made his political name in the trial of Soviet spy Alger Hiss at the height of the McCarthy era. Having failed the "political acceptability" test, there was apparently little electoral incentive for Johnson to revisit options that, in any case, jarred with the thrust of the steady stream of broadly interventionist suggestions he had been receiving from advisors.

Yet if there were electoral risks to de-escalation, so, too, was there significant political peril associated with getting deeper into war in an election year, especially through highly salient methods involving the commitment of combat troops and the use of bombing campaigns. Indeed, Johnson's entire political campaign was to some degree premised on the idea that he was the cool-headed alternative to the ultra-hawkish Barry Goldwater. Therefore he "tried as far as possible to keep the war out of the political race," and was furious when any campaign surrogates mentioned the conflict in Vietnam.[29] After learning that Hubert Humphrey had gone on television and "blabbed everything he had heard in a briefing" about ongoing operations in Vietnam, for instance, the president was furious. "He's just got to understand that you can't talk about war plans," he complained to an advisor about Humphrey, who would become Johnson's running mate in late August. "He just ought to keep his goddamned big mouth shut on foreign affairs, at least until the election is over."[30] Similarly, when newspapers revealed information about planning for an escalation of activities, apparently leaked by the military, Johnson fumed to his national security advisor, "We've got a convention and an election going on and it's not up to the military to go talking."[31] Speaking to his secretary of state the following week, he remained determined to keep emerging plans for escalation out of the public view. "I think we [have] got to be awfully careful what we say about war in Vietnam the next short while," he told Dean Rusk, adding that "our people ought to just say, 'We haven't got any comment.' "[32]

Indeed, Johnson would often discuss the election campaign with his key national security advisors, actively encouraging them to cultivate a public image of peace. Thus Bundy, when consulting on a foreign policy speech, was advised by Johnson that "we want a little peace demagoguery for the mothers," while McNamara was instructed to ensure he associated himself with the diplomatic staff in Saigon, not simply the military, because "if you're going up in the polls now, I don't want you to be a warmonger. I want to have a peacemaker."[33] As Johnson later told a congressman in a private telephone conversation, while he may have perceived the need to escalate during 1964, he "held off as long and long as I could, because I knew the people would raise hell. I knew it didn't look good. It didn't have a peace image."[34]

In sum, it may reasonably be inferred that Johnson's perception of the electoral risks of each broad course of action available to him through 1964 both reinforced his desire not to simply cut and run and, perhaps more significantly, threw cold water on his emerging strategic preference for escalation. Given this latter misalignment of preferences, in such a sensitive phase of the electoral cycle, this study's conceptual framework strongly predicts that the *delay* and/or *dampening* mechanisms may be observed in the ensuing decision-making process.

The Slow Path to Gradual Escalation

Having already seen substantial evidence of the first two observable implications of the *delay* mechanism—the perception of a need for change, and the existence of viable opportunities to review the existing strategy—it remains to be shown that there was an electorally motivated deferral of a decision. The evidence is in fact crystal clear.

Asked why Johnson chose to wait until 1965 before acting on his emergent preference, his deputy national security advisor was adamant: "The '64 election played a very large role in that. He didn't want to engage before the election into starting a new war."[35] The documentary record supports such a claim. When Johnson was presented with a Joint Chiefs of Staff (JCS) program for selective airpower to be applied in the North, General Taylor's minutes note that "the President accepted the need for punishing Hanoi without debate, but pointed to some other practical difficulties, particularly the political ones with which he was faced. It is quite apparent that he does not want to lose South Vietnam before next November nor does he want to get the country into war."[36] Meanwhile, General Wallace Green, the commandant of the Marine Corps, said the quiet part out loud in his account of the same meeting: "He repeated again that the Congress and the country did not want war—that war at this time would have a tremendous effect on the approaching Presidential political campaign and might perhaps keep the Democrats from winning in November. He said that he thought it would be much better to keep out of any war until December; that would be after the election."[37] "I've got to win an election," Johnson told Bundy after this meeting. "And then you can make a decision. But in the meantime, let's see if we can't find enough things to do to keep them off base."[38] Bundy later agreed that at this stage Johnson's "pre-emptive concern" was to "win, win, win the election, not the war."[39] McNamara, for his part, was by

September well attuned to the president's priority, advising him that "the odds are we can squeeze through between now and the next several weeks, but it certainly is a weak situation ... After the election, we've got a real problem on our hands."[40] Thus U.S. policy remained a holding action. Roughly six months before the election, Johnson's view was clear: "I just can't believe that we can't take fifteen thousand advisers and two hundred thousand [South Vietnamese] people and maintain the status quo for six months."[41] Evidence for the *delay* mechanism cannot get much stronger than this.

If President Johnson sought to put the major strategic decisions on ice, however, the same cannot be said for officials in North Vietnam. Having made a determination in late 1963 to dramatically escalate the armed struggle in the South through "mass combat operations," Hanoi was not standing still.[42] As a result, the Johnson administration was in the position of reacting to developments on the battlefield throughout this period. To be sure, when facing significant enemy initiatives, the White House's first preference was still to look the other way until the political fallout of such developments could be more easily managed after the election. In July 1964, for instance, the American consul in Hué reported the capture of two North Vietnamese soldiers, representing the first suspected presence of North Vietnamese units in the South. A week later, a cable came back reprimanding the American official for sending telegrams to Washington, insisting that they be cleared in Saigon instead. According to one analyst in the embassy, "the reason for that was that LBJ and the people around him put out the word that we don't want any surprises. We don't want to see information coming in that suggests that the war might be escalating, because we've got a political campaign going on here ... It wasn't because they didn't want to face up to reality. They just didn't want the reality to come to the attention of the American people too soon."[43] As one scholar put it more recently, "Johnson acted like the proverbial ostrich that buries its head in the sand when it sees danger. He wanted to keep Vietnam at arm's length, to delay confronting vexing problems, and to postpone difficult decisions until after the election."[44]

Not all enemy initiatives could be so easily swept under the carpet. Insofar as there were any new policy outcomes in this period, however, they were minor, and approved more for their political acceptability than their expected strategic effectiveness, in a clear example of the *dampening* mechanism, which is to be expected when the possibility of delay is precluded.

CIA-led covert operations against North Vietnam and several socioeco-nomic programs were approved on a rolling basis through 1964 as less politically salient substitutes for the increased use of force many now felt was necessary. Strikingly, the former were expected by Rusk to address per-haps 2 percent of the problem in Vietnam, and even the CIA director warned Johnson to expect "no great results" from them.[45] The latter clashed directly with Johnson's own skepticism on "so-called social reforms," stated in his first meeting on Vietnam as president.[46]

Yet both policies were advocated by Ambassador Lodge, who, despite being renowned for his "idiotic" proposals and general incompetence ("He ain't worth a damn . . . he can't work with *anybody*," remarked Johnson), was none-theless treated as "Mister God" at Johnson's direction.[47] Why? Because he was a political threat to Johnson's electoral prospects, subject to a Lodge-for-president write-in campaign. Expecting Lodge's imminent resignation to free the Republican to run against him, Johnson sought to insulate him-self from possible future attacks by keeping him close. "I'm not gonna let him have any differences," reasoned Johnson. "I'm gonna agree with every damn thing he does. That's my strategy."[48] Minor programs in which the adminis-tration had little faith were thus fast-tracked to authorization because they could either be kept covert—McNamara notably referred to such actions as "disavowable"—or because they served some other electoral purpose.[49]

On the surface, Johnson's response to the Gulf of Tonkin attack on U.S. naval units in August 1964, entailing tit-for-tat bombing raids in the North, appears to jar with this characterization of presidential inaction during 1964. Yet a closer examination of the president's electoral preferences during this phase reveals decision-making behavior that is in fact consistent with the broader argument presented in this book. At a minimum, it is worth noting that the very fact that U.S. destroyers were in the waters off the coast of Viet-nam had a great deal to do with Johnson's aforementioned desire to find minor programs to keep the enemy "off-base" while he focused on his own election bid. The USS *Maddox* was conducting electronic surveillance and intelligence gathering on a so-called DESOTO patrol in support of the expanded program of covert action the president had recently authorized when it came under enemy fire. More broadly, what is not really in doubt is the fact that, as then national security advisor McGeorge Bundy later put it, "what really mattered to Lyndon Johnson in 1964 was the election politics of these events."[50] At stake was not the president's political survival per se.

While Johnson did receive a notable boost in the polls, he hardly needed it at this stage, leading Goldwater on the eve of the incident by twenty-eight percentage points.[51] However, Johnson remained acutely aware of his status as an "accidental" president and wanted to achieve an electoral victory large enough for him to claim his own mandate to govern. Internal polling conducted by the Johnson campaign indicated that foreign policy remained the president's primary political weakness—indeed, it was an issue that was deemed "unfavorable" in twenty-eight of fifty states, and "favorable" in none, according to a series of studies conducted by public relations firm Doyle Dane Bernbach.[52] While the public did not express a strong preference on what was still a low-salience issue, the Johnson camp worried that Goldwater might use the ongoing situation in Vietnam to exploit the president's vulnerability on international affairs more broadly. As early as May 1964, in a conversation with Senator Russell, Johnson thus predicted that "Republicans are going to make a political issue out of it [Vietnam]." His mentor agreed, observing that, "It's the only issue they've got."[53]

With prominent Republicans beginning to call out Johnson's "indecision" over the summer as an "electoral gamble that could endanger the American position in the entire Far East," the administration was eager to find some way to blunt charges of weakness and "flaccidity of determination," crucially *without* embarking on a costly course of escalation that would alienate more dovish segments of the electorate.[54] A congressional resolution authorizing the use of force in Vietnam was considered a key mechanism for achieving that goal, and indeed had been the subject of extensive discussion within the administration for months. "The resolution should be as vague in its mandate as the lawyers will permit," wrote one aide in June 1964, clarifying that, "its main purpose would be to express Congressional support for the Presidential power during the election period ahead."[55] Absent a "dramatic event in Southeast Asia" that might minimize the prospect of divisive congressional debate, however, the administration worried that the "risks of a contest at home" outweighed the benefits of pursuing a resolution.[56] The Tonkin incident changed that calculus. Presented with what was popularly understood to be an unprovoked attack, even those sections of the public generally opposed to an expansion of the U.S. commitment to the conflict favored a strong response.[57] "In a single stroke," pollster Louis Harris concluded, Johnson had "turned his greatest political vulnerability in foreign policy into one of his strongest assets."[58]

While a delay in embarking on a major course of intervention in Vietnam remained clearly in Johnson's electoral interests, anticipatory legislative preparation for that future escalation, accompanied by the limited use of force, allowed Johnson to simultaneously balance countervailing electoral pressures from hawkish Republican critics. Ironically, then, the net effect of the Gulf of Tonkin incident was to breathe life into the president's underlying approach of delay by fending off criticism of his foreign policy image. As an added bonus, Johnson now carried the authority required to escalate the U.S. involvement in Vietnam with minimal congressional scrutiny once his election had been secured.

Taking the Shotgun from the Mantel

To show that a decision was delayed, rather than simply ignored, it must also be possible to find evidence that the same problem was addressed quickly and proactively in the aftermath of Election Day. This is indeed plain to see from the documentary record, as obfuscation gave way to an eagerness to take action.

The day after the election, Johnson created an official structure, the NSC Working Group, to formalize the same basic proposals for alternative strategies that had been postponed through 1964. Having kicked the problem into the long grass repeatedly, now the president set in motion what the group's chairperson called "the most comprehensive" Vietnam policy review "of any in the Kennedy and Johnson administrations."[59] Three specific courses of action emerged: "Option A," to continue on the present course; "Option B," a "hard/fast squeeze" of systematically escalating attacks on North Vietnam; or "Option C," a "slow, controlled squeeze" of gradually escalating aerial bombardment, aiming to bring the North Vietnamese to the bargaining table.[60]

When Johnson met to discuss the recommendations in early December his tone was no longer anguished. "The day of reckoning is coming," he declared, and while willing to give diplomatic and clandestine operations one last shot, "If more of the same, then I'll be talking to you, General," gesturing toward the chairman of the JCS. A conditional plan entailing a thirty-day intensification of existing actions followed by a second stage of increasingly severe air strikes against North Vietnam was authorized two days later.[61] Operation Rolling Thunder, the sustained air bombing campaign authorized in February, was simply phase two of this earlier plan. Thus, Rolling Thunder was not solely a reaction to a February 7 attack on U.S. installations at Pleiku. Indeed, on the very day before the attack, Johnson was telling advisors that "he had kept the shotgun over the mantel and the bullets in the basement for a long time now," concluding that "cowardice has gotten us into more wars than response has."[62] What Pleiku provided, then, was a pretext for implementing a plan that had already been agreed.[63] In word and deed, preelection risk aversion and delay had given way to risk acceptance and daring action.

A similar point can be made about the decision to escalate the U.S. ground commitment. Already in December 1964 Johnson told McNamara that "appropriate military strength on the ground" was now necessary, adding, "I am ready to look with great favor on that kind of increased American effort."[64] While aware that the odds of long-term success still looked slim, he was now willing to accept such risks. "The game now is in the fourth quarter, and it's about 78 to nothing," he explained. "We've got to try to rescue something."[65] As such, a series of Marine deployments were made over the spring of 1965, newly tasked with combat missions. The rapid pace at which Washington was proposing additional troop commitments even caught the ambassador, Maxwell Taylor, who had spent much of 1964 urging bolder action, off guard. Having cabled back to urge a degree of caution in the deployments on April 14, he quickly learned that the direction had come from the highest authority. "Having crossed the Rubicon on February 7," the former chairman of the Joint Chiefs later recalled, "he was now off for Rome on the double."[66] Finally, in July, a decision to increase troop levels to 125,000 with the promise of additional forces as requested opened the proverbial floodgates of almost unending commitment to Vietnam.

To be clear, the argument here is not that these decisions were solely caused by electoral political considerations. It is claimed, instead, that such factors introduced a permissiveness that made them possible, and which was not present in 1964. Though Johnson had not served a full first term, he now entered a phase of the electoral cycle in which electoral constraints tend to be relatively weak. As an incumbent hoping to be elected president in his own right, moreover, he had staked out a position on the campaign that was ambiguous enough to preserve his room for maneuver into his second term. On the one hand, of course, he had sought to engage in the aforementioned "peace demagoguery" with a series of highly suggestive comments, which famously included his statement that "we are not about to send American boys nine or ten thousand miles to do what Asian boys ought to be doing for themselves."[67] On the other hand, as he later recalled, having repeatedly professed a continued commitment to South Vietnam, he could hardly be painted as a "peace-at-any-price" candidate.[68] In one typical interview, he said of the situation that "we must do everything we can, we must be responsible, we must stay there and help them, and that is what we are going to do."[69]

This apparent freedom from the constraints of an upcoming election might have caused a reconsideration of the escalatory path to which Johnson was binding himself. Urging Johnson to do just this, the vice president pointed out that "1965 is the year of minimum political risk for the Johnson Administration," making it more possible to cut losses in Vietnam than ever before.[70] It is not inconceivable that Johnson might have chosen this course. After all, it was not the case that he held any great degree of optimism vis-à-vis the course of action he settled on, even if he felt the costs of doing nothing were worse. In the days after taking office, he admitted to Senator Fulbright that "I'll be goddamned if I don't think it's hopeless . . . I think the whole general situation is against us, as far as real victory goes."[71] A few short weeks after authorizing Rolling Thunder, meanwhile, he told his mentor, Senator Richard Russell, that "airplanes aren't worth a *damn* . . . Bombing anything . . . that's the damndest thing I ever saw. The biggest fraud."[72] If that pointed toward the logic of committing ground troops, Johnson held similarly low expectations for that form of escalation too, lamenting to McNamara that he saw "no program from either Defense or State that gives me much hope of doing anything, except just praying and gasping to hold on during monsoon and hope they'll quit. I don't believe they're *ever* going to quit."[73]

Why, then, did Johnson not take advantage of the favorable electoral environment in 1965 to pump the brakes on the escalatory trajectory with which he was clearly uncomfortable? One powerful explanation offered by existing work highlights the role of certain advisors, such as McGeorge Bundy, who controlled the flow of information to the White House in a way that marginalized more dovish voices. In one notable example, Bundy presented Johnson in January 1965 with a memorandum declaring that the United States had reached a "fork in the road," with the only viable options on the table being two different forms of escalation.[74] For several months prior, the national security advisor had relegated the views of perhaps the sole dissenting voice left in the administration—that of Under Secretary of State George Ball—to that of a "devil's advocate."[75] Other skeptics, few and far between as they were, fared, if anything, worse than Ball in having their views presented before the president. No less than Hubert Humphrey, the vice president, was effectively banished from Vietnam discussions altogether after submitting one too many memoranda urging caution in February 1965.[76]

Yet if it is true that skeptics were shut out of the inner circle of decision making, this reflected the bureaucratic environment the president sought, in which loyalty and a conformity of views were prized. As one historian puts it, "Johnson was poorly served by his advisory system, but it was a system he in large measure created."[77] Notwithstanding his later attempts to portray his role as that of a prescient lone voice of caution fighting against a tide of hawkish momentum, Ball in truth understood and accepted his role as devil's advocate. Tellingly, he recounts in his memoirs an early conversation with the president in which Johnson teased him about this very matter. "You're like the school teacher looking for a job with a small school district in Texas," Johnson said to Ball. "When asked by the school board whether he believed that the world was flat or round, he replied, 'Oh, I can teach it either way.' " To hammer home the point, Johnson clarified, "That's you . . . You can argue like hell with me against a position, but I know outside this room you're going to support me. You can teach it flat or round."[78] It was perfectly understood that Ball was retained not to encourage meaningful challenge to prevailing assumptions, but precisely the opposite. Even Bundy understood that Ball had little other option, since "You can't organize against Lyndon Johnson without getting bombed before breakfast, because in his view that's the final and ultimate conspiracy."[79]

Even if we may still ascribe some importance to underlying bureaucratic factors in shaping Johnson's decision-making process in this period, the manifestation of such pressures appears indelibly linked to the electoral calendar. If Bundy's infamous "fork in the road" memorandum of January 1965 was as instrumental as is sometimes implied, the timing and intent of this memorandum points clearly to the underlying electoral dynamics explored in this chapter. Coming just two months after the election, Bundy later acknowledged that the memorandum was designed "to push President

Johnson out of the zone of indecision that had characterized the 1964 campaign year."[80] Similarly, it is surely notable that the sixty-seven-page-long
memorandum drafted by George Ball on October 5, 1964, the clearest and
most detailed articulation of Ball's dissenting views, would apparently not
even reach the president until late February 1965—*after* Rolling Thunder had
been authorized and *after* Ball himself came to believe that the president
"could no longer be deterred."[81] This timing was not solely down to Bundy's
role as gatekeeper; Ball, in fact, fully expected that the national security
advisor would hand the memorandum to Johnson if he had asked him to,
since "he was scrupulously fair in such matters." But Ball never followed up.
Why? "The president was then engaged in his election campaign and was
troubled with a thousand problems," he later recalled, "so I decided to wait
until I could get his full attention."[82]

If Johnson had only the war in Vietnam on his agenda, perhaps he might
have been more willing to spend political capital on a reconsideration of the
path on which his administration had embarked. As it was, the president had
his eyes set on what he considered a larger prize at home. Crucially, however, he perceived his ability to achieve his domestic policy goals as fundamentally linked to his willingness to escalate in Southeast Asia. As Bator has
argued, "I don't think one can understand Johnson's Vietnam choices in
July 1965 without taking into account that on June 30 his rent subsidy bill
for needy families was almost defeated, that the voting rights bill and legislation creating Medicare were due for conference at the end of July, that . . .
the entire Great Society agenda—[was] sitting on his desk."[83] So as not to irk
hawkish critics on the Hill, and avoid a "guns versus butter" debate that
would imperil such domestic priorities, Johnson felt forced to defer to his
generals on their escalatory proposals. Critically, the domestic political calendar added urgency to this calculation, bolstering the case for a "slow
squeeze" form of escalation. "He basically thought with the '64 election that
he had a filibuster-proof majority in the Senate to ram through the Great
Society program," recalled Bator. "He didn't think that that would last
through the midterm election in '66."[84]

There is certainly evidence to support Bator's interpretation. Bundy's
handwritten notes following the crucial July 27 NSC meeting on the eve of
the troops decision are insightful, recording his feeling "that while the
President was placing his preference . . . on international grounds, his unspoken object was to protect his legislative program."[85] More reliable evidence

comes from Johnson's own comments to Ball in July 1965, which make his conundrum clear: "The great black beast for us is the right wing. If we don't get the war over soon they'll put enormous heat on us to turn it into an Armageddon and wreck all our other programs."[86] Perhaps most colorfully, he once elaborated on his fear that, unless he escalated in Vietnam, "they won't be talking about my civil rights bill, or education or beautification. No sir, they'll push Vietnam up my ass every time. Vietnam. Vietnam. Vietnam. Right up my ass."[87] While some scholars have suggested that Johnson's concerns about a right-wing backlash were in hindsight exaggerated, this does not change the reality that the president appears to have genuinely perceived such a significant political risk at the time.[88] Here, then, we see domestic politics intersecting with the electoral calendar to create incentives for bold, aggressive outcomes, taking place after the presidential election.

* * *

In sum, the "Americanization" of the Vietnam War offers strong support for the conceptual framework outlined in chapter 1. While Johnson perceived a clear need to do something different to avert disaster early on, the electoral risks of dragging the country deeper into war on the eve of the election proved prohibitive. Instead, he chose to bury an emergent if reluctant preference for escalation as the controversial decisions to commit air and ground forces were delayed until after the voters had cast their ballots.

The Pursuit of Peace

For the remainder of Johnson's time in office, the broad underlying strategy of gradual escalation would continue, consisting of steady increases in the intensity of bombing and numbers of troops committed to Vietnam, culminating in 1968, the bloodiest year of the entire war. Throughout, however, Johnson remained engaged in a perpetual struggle to reconcile diverging strategic and electoral preferences. The following section explores how these pressures ultimately led Johnson to decide in March 1968 that, since a viable balance could no longer be struck, he had to make an unpalatable choice between what he understood to be the diplomatically optimal path to a negotiated settlement and his own political future. After withdrawing from the presidential race, he nevertheless found his bargaining position repeatedly undermined by electoral considerations over which he had little control, much as the *spoiler* mechanism holds.

Hawks, Doves, and the Disappearing Middle Ground

Having committed to the "slow squeeze" strategy of steadily increasing aerial and ground attacks on North Vietnam in 1965, Johnson spent much of the next three years monitoring and trying to adapt his policy to suit his and his fellow Democrats' political needs. As this section shows, this did not prove easy, and resulted in something akin to a Goldilocks approach to policy—neither too hawkish nor too dovish—so as to protect the Democrats' chances in the 1966 and 1968 elections.

The 1965 Christmas bombing pause offers an interesting insight into Johnson's priorities. Already by early December, Johnson was strongly resisting suggestions from his civilian advisors to temporarily halt the bombing in Vietnam as a gesture toward de-escalation. Citing concerns that hawkish sentiment would not tolerate a pause, he made his priorities crystal clear: "We've got a new election here. This is a priority problem. It comes ahead of poverty & education. It's a new ball game. 1966 election."[89] That a thirty-seven-day pause ended up being approved over the president's deep political concerns speaks to both the influence of the stage of the electoral cycle, with almost a year until the midterms still to go, and to the equally political justification used by the pause's advocates to bring their commander in chief on board. As Bundy explained to Johnson, a pause would establish the political groundwork for further escalation in January, balancing the competing political pressures from dovish and hawkish sentiment. "We are going to have to do these other tough things in January," he wrote on December 9, and "I think the peace-lovers will support our January actions a whole lot more if there has been a pause beforehand."[90]

Another memorandum to Johnson from his previous press secretary at the beginning of 1966 elaborates on the dynamics of this period remarkably well. After noting that policy debates were "being conducted in the tone of a 'hawks' and 'doves' clash," he admitted that "the current debate has ... limited the Administration's freedom of action. At the present time, the 'doves' are having their innings and therefore the Administration is being presented to the public as a 'hawk.' Somewhere along the line the 'hawks' will come up to bat and at that point the scene will shift and the Administration will look like a 'dove.' "[91] Opinion in Congress was indeed becoming polarized. Hawks like Senator Karl Mundt began decrying the self-imposed restrictions on bombing North Vietnamese cities, lobbying Johnson to begin "using our strength instead of applying our weakness."[92] On the other side, Senator J. William Fulbright's hearings, fully televised, brought the dovish critique to every home in America. In private, Johnson's mailbox testified to this sentiment. On January 21, seventy-two House members called for him to seek peace through a UN mediation effort.[93] Six days later, fifteen senators signed a letter endorsing calls by Mansfield, Aiken, and Fulbright for a complete cessation of bombing.[94] As the midterms approached, growing disillusionment with the war began to imperil Democrats in dovish areas, while criticism of excessive military limitations threatened those in hawkish districts. Of the two positions that were slowly beginning to define both public and elite opinion during this period, Johnson still assessed the hawks to be the greater threat. "The *real* pressures on me are coming from people who want me to go North, mine the harbors, bomb Hanoi, get into a war with the Chinese—they're crazies," he told Bator, who was himself a dove on the subject.[95]

The path of least political resistance thus ran to the right of the middle ground—but only just. When Johnson approved the expansion of bombing targets to include petroleum storage areas in June 1966, for example, he did so with considerable hesitation, wondering aloud whether the strategic benefits of this latest escalatory step were worth the political cost. "The Hartkes are all—they're starting their campaign tomorrow on the Senate floor," the president told McNamara in a phone call, referring to a prominent opponent of the war.[96] Just weeks earlier, Johnson had been advised by Walt Rostow, his national security advisor, that widening the bombing program to include these targets would "look like an Administration move to the hard side" and thus required "something new on the dove side to balance our account."[97] Coupled with a steady stream of reports indicating that the bombing program had largely failed to meaningfully impact North Vietnam's willingness or ability to support the insurgency in the South, this might have justified renewed consideration of a bombing pause.[98] Yet that idea was dropped soon after Rostow penned another memorandum to the president offering his "amateur political judgment: a 'pause' during the campaign, without solid evidence that a move towards peace will promptly follow, could be quite dangerous during the campaign." In the margin of this memorandum, McNamara scrawled, "I am inclined to agree that a 'pause' prior to November would be unwise."[99] Growing increasingly pessimistic in private about the prospects for meaningful success in Vietnam, he elaborated on his thinking in a subsequent phone call with the president, telling Johnson, "I myself am more and more convinced that we ought definitely to plan on termination of the bombing in the north but not until after the election."[100] The pause would indeed be implemented only in the New Year.

Instead of embarking on any serious reevaluation of a strategy with which several key advisors were growing increasingly disillusioned, Johnson seemed more interested in the optics than the efficacy of the present course. In the months prior to the midterms, for instance, the administration quietly imposed a series of constraints on military operations to minimize the salient costs of the existing strategy, including switching targets away from cities and reducing the number of daytime raids. As anticipated, these changes suppressed casualty rates during this politically sensitive period, before rising again to previous levels almost immediately after polls had closed.[101]

If this reflected a desire to reduce the number of negative headlines about the war, there were also efforts to generate more positive coverage during this period. It is in this context that we can best understand Johnson's last-minute decision to hold a conference in Manila with the leaders of South Vietnam and several other troop-contributing nations just a fortnight before the midterms. Such a summit had been proposed by a senior State Department official in late September to present a "dramatic picture of the collective support being given to South Viet-Nam."[102] While recognizing that some quarters would characterize the summit as a cynical ploy for votes, Johnson's advisors ultimately left the decision on the domestic political benefits of a pre-polling day conference to the president. Johnson signaled his desire to move fast on the initiative. And, for good measure, he made sure to build a visit to the local U.S. Air Force hospital in Cam Ranh Bay into the trip, where journalists obligingly reported back on the president's activities, which included signing the casts of the wounded and pinning Purple Hearts on their pajamas.[103] The president's speech describing his visit, reprinted in full in the *New York Times*, "broke no new policy ground," as the paper accurately noted, but rather "was an appeal to patriotic emotions."[104]

With the congressional elections over, and as public opinion continued to diverge on Vietnam, Johnson doubled down on the Goldilocks strategy through 1967. In one month the president was taking renewed interest in a peace feeler.[105] In the next, he would be authorizing Rolling Thunder targets, including many that had been proposed by the military in the fall of 1966 but deferred until after the midterms, stressing that "we ought to get every damn target we can."[106] In the end, though, the hawk-dove pressure in Congress and the wider public inhibited any radical departure from the strategy begun in 1965. As polls began to register a greater distrust of the administration, attitudes toward Vietnam became increasingly polarized. Prominent hawks like Ronald Reagan continued to deride gradual escalation, lamenting that "We have the power to wind it up fast, and I think we should use it."[107] Meanwhile, dovish senators like William Fulbright and Jacob Javits condemned the strategy as a "grievous mistake" in private, and the product of "illusions and overoptimistic predictions" in public, calling in varying degrees for immediate cease-fire and withdrawal.[108]

Policy, still broadly under the strategic conception of "gradual escalation," was constantly being adapted in response to the administration's perception of the public mood, which, as one special advisor put it, was like a "'Korean whipsaw': On Mondays, Wednesdays and Fridays, we will be the war party; on Tuesdays, Thursdays and Saturdays, the party of appeasement."[109] Indeed, this dynamic was supported by polling data, which revealed that Americans were deeply split between those favoring escalation (45 percent) and those preferring withdrawal (41 percent).[110] Thus mid-1967 saw further incremental increases in troops alongside a new negotiating position, known as the San Antonio Formula, which offered a bombing pause in return for the commencement of "serious" talks and a cessation of infiltration of men and materiel into South Vietnam.[111]

With the 1968 presidential election campaign approaching, sensitivity to public opinion increased yet further. While certain advisors had begun to shift away from advocacy of bombing operations and ever-increasing ground commitments, amid mounting evidence that such tactics were strategically futile, Johnson remained scornful of any proposal that carried excessive electoral risk. Johnson's response to McNamara's bombshell memorandum of November 1—his most forceful to date—is a good example. In it, the secretary of defense called for a policy of "stabilization" comprising a bombing halt and a cap on troop numbers, having concluded that "continuing on our present course will not bring us by the end of 1968 enough closer to success."[112] Before firing McNamara, Johnson penned a response outlining his belief that the proposals would only "encourage extreme doves," lose the support of erstwhile "friends," and not gain anything beyond a few "moderate dove" votes.[113] Johnson's advisors were also conscious of such political counterarguments. Rostow, for instance, feared that Johnson "would be pushed off the middle ground you now hold at home" by McNamara's policy, which would spark "a debate between united Republicans claiming we had gone soft and a Democratic Administration, with the JCS in disagreement if not open revolt."[114] This struck at the heart of the matter. Even if he could be convinced of the strategic necessity of a change in approach, Johnson could not at this stage authorize a major de-escalatory step without opening himself up to a slew of Republican opponents who would capitalize on perceived timidity.

Uninterested in significant strategic departures, President Johnson's attention turned instead to the question of how his administration might better explain the current course as part of an intensified public relations campaign to improve political conditions at home. The day after receiving McNamara's memorandum, Johnson sought the counsel of a group of several elders of the foreign policy establishment. Broadly united on the strategic wisdom of staying the course at this stage, the "wise men" were asked for their perspective on what "positive steps" the administration might take "to unite the people and communicate with the people better." Their responses varied in their specifics but revealed a consensus behind the need to enlighten a "confused" public on the merits of the chosen course. Above all, the administration needed to "show some progress," argued one participant, adding that this might be achieved by asking a senior official to return from Vietnam to give a report to the nation indicating that there was "light at the end of the tunnel."[115] And that is precisely what the president did, recalling Ambassador Ellsworth Bunker and General William Westmoreland to Washington to deliver upbeat reports in a number of nationwide television appearances. In his most widely reported remarks, before the National Press Club on November 21, Westmoreland assured viewers that "we have reached an important point when the end begins to come into view."[116]

The "conversation gap" between those public comments and the more measured assessments of progress revealed in the military command's private dispatches would soon transform into a more visible "credibility gap" when events on the battlefield punctured the optimistic picture that the administration had sought to project.[117] Yet even before coverage of the Tet Offensive in early 1968 triggered an acceleration of the drift in public attitudes toward either the dovish or hawkish ends of the spectrum, Johnson found it increasingly difficult to manage these countervailing domestic political pressures.[118] On authorizing new bombing targets weeks after this episode, Johnson emphasized to his national security team that "the clock is ticking . . . The bombing arouses so much opposition in this country."[119] Whereas before he could simply dismiss doves like Fulbright as "crybabies," now he would dwell on the mounting pressure they brought to bear, agonizing privately about how to respond. In one instructive example in February 1968, days after Fulbright called for televised hearings into the earlier Gulf of Tonkin incident, Johnson penned a forceful letter to the senator claiming that such an effort would serve only to fulfill Hanoi's aim of sowing discord and confusion among the American public. Yet instead of taking on one of his chief critics, Johnson tellingly chose now to suppress his anger, ordering his secretary to destroy all evidence of the draft letter. "Don't file. Tear up. Flush away," he wrote in a cover slip that remains buried among archival material. "I don't want a record of it."[120] Johnson's infamous penchant for secrecy remained intact four years into his presidency. His relative insensitivity to dovish sentiment, however, was beginning to crumble.

Indeed, after the Tet Offensive, the political threat from doves had become just as severe as that from hawks, placing Johnson in a pincer movement of constraints rendering his pursuit of reelection and peace mutually exclusive. Scenes of Vietcong forces ambushing the U.S. embassy in Saigon shocked the nation, as the number of self-described doves rose from 24 to 42 percent overnight.[121] Strikingly, this was precisely the outcome Hanoi had been hoping for. Though much has been made of the fact that North Vietnam suffered a major strategic setback during the Tet Offensive, recent scholarship points out that the Politburo had studied the dynamics of the American political system and chosen to launch a major military offensive at the start of an election year, hoping to generate a political tsunami in the United States that would pressure the president to move toward de-escalation, or else sway American opinion in favor of alternative candidates advocating a more dovish policy.[122] Indeed, when news leaked of a 206,000-strong troop request by General Westmoreland, it sparked a firestorm of protest. Chants of "Hey, hey, LBJ, how many kids did you kill today?" reached the White House from crowds at the gates, having an "enormous influence" on the president, according to Tom Johnson, a close aide.[123] Most concerning for Johnson was that such pressure was being translated into a direct threat to his renomination at the Democratic National Convention, as antiwar candidates gained traction. On March 12 Eugene McCarthy registered a stunning performance in the New Hampshire primary, and on March 16 Robert F. Kennedy announced his candidacy for the 1968 election. Ominously, the president had received polling data even *before* Kennedy announced indicating that Johnson would lose the dove vote by a ratio of over two to one.[124] The net effect was to rule out further escalation as a viable option, in a demonstration of the *dampening* mechanism.

By mid- to late March, Johnson was being pressured instead toward a proposal to halt the bombing. Redrafting an originally hawkish speech, he admitted to his new secretary of defense that while he believed that a total bombing halt was "not worth a damn," the political circumstances required some movement. "We ought to have some kind of something on peace" in the remarks, he continued, "because they're concluding . . . we are just the Goldwater of '68 and we can't take that."[125] Johnson's previous national security advisor was preaching to the converted, then, when he subsequently wrote the following to Johnson: "If we get tagged as mindless hawks, we can lose both the election and the war . . . You were dead right when you asked me to find a good left hook to go with the military right . . . the only one that the whole world—and Kennedy and McCarthy too—will call serious is a bombing halt."[126] The problem, of course, was that such a move would open Johnson to criticism from Nixon or Reagan, who had recently demanded that "the war in Vietnam must be fought through to victory."[127] Indeed, by March 26, Johnson was agonizing with his military chiefs about the way forward. "This is complicated by the fact it is an election year," he explained, adding, "We need more money in an election year, more taxes in an election year, more troops in an election year . . . We have no support for the war."[128] In short, he could no longer prosecute the war as hawks would like amid such dovish electoral pressure.

Facing stalemate in Vietnam and a failing strategy, electoral constraints put Johnson in a catch-22: escalate, and risk losing the Democratic nomination in August; de-escalate, and risk losing to hawks in November. Johnson concluded that he could not simultaneously pursue peace and run for reelection. His decision to sacrifice his political future is a good example of an extreme case of misalignment between a president's preferences.

The Pentagon Goes Soft

How much of the ebb and flow of Vietnam policy in this period, culminating in Johnson's peace overture of March 1968, can be attributed to the waning appetite for continued escalation in the Pentagon?

On the surface, McNamara's increasing disillusionment with the war, culminating in his bombshell memorandum of November 1967, may have played some role.[129] The administration did move closer to McNamara's position within weeks of his departure. Yet it would be wrong to read too much into this. Rather than have McNamara make the case for a policy of "stabilization," Johnson engineered an opportunity for him to lead the World Bank so quickly that it left McNamara wondering whether he had quit or been fired.[130] McNamara might have had a greater influence on policy had he actively resigned in protest, citing policy differences with the president. Yet he felt bound by his oath of loyalty to the commander in chief, considering such a course of action to be "a violation of my responsibility to the president."[131] Perhaps the most striking thing about the shift in McNamara's views for this study is the fact that the secretary of defense had begun articulating his views within an explicitly electoral context. It was McNamara's opinion, for instance, as told to Ambassador-at-Large Averell Harriman in September 1967, that "we must do everything possible to get negotiations going before our election in 68," otherwise Vietnam would "tear the country apart" in the campaign.[132]

McNamara was of course not the only secretary of defense during this period, and a case could be made that it was in fact his successor, Clark Clifford, who wielded more influence over policy, particularly in the lead-up to the March 31 announcement of a bombing halt. Clifford was sworn in on March 1, just days after General Westmoreland's infamous request for some 206,000 additional troops. Having been tasked with an initial review of strategy, the new secretary of defense wasted little time in challenging basic long-held assumptions about the course of the war and the most appropriate path forward. In a lengthy meeting on March 4, Clifford reported back to the president on the findings of his "task force." Papering over a wide variety of viewpoints in the administration, he nevertheless pulled few punches, speaking of the "deep-seated concern" and "grave doubts" held among Johnson's advisors about the wisdom of Westmoreland's request. With the strategic reserve already depleted, and precious little evidence that the "search and destroy" strategy currently being employed in Vietnam was making any progress, he cautioned against granting the commander's wishes. The task force recommended that Westmoreland should be given barely a tenth of his requested number of troops, with any further deployments subject to a comprehensive review of strategy.[133] In the documentary record, there is some evidence supporting Clifford's retrospective claims that his role as a relative outsider allowed him the bureaucratic power to shift the debate in a way that McNamara, as a principal architect of the existing strategy, had been largely unable to do.[134] On March 12, for instance, Johnson told advisors that while he had been inclined to give Westmoreland what he said he needed, "That Monday [March 4] session did moderate my judgment some. I do think we should evaluate our strategy. It is a good idea from time to time to have a good, sound review."[135]

Yet if it is true that Clifford played some role in pushing the president toward de-escalation, it must also be noted that the political context was rarely far from the new secretary of defense's mind, either. During a March 20 conversation with the president, for instance, Clifford responded favorably to Johnson's suggestion that some kind of dovish move would be electorally beneficial. "We have a posture now in which Kennedy and McCarthy are the peace candidates and President Johnson is the war candidate," agreed Clifford, adding, "Now we must veer away from that and we can do it."[136] And, of course, it was not just the secretary of defense who thought in these terms. On March 26, Johnson was shocked to learn that the "wise men," too, now felt that the time had come to reconsider strategy in Vietnam and pursue a negotiated settlement. In justifying this conclusion, Maxwell Taylor tellingly mentioned that "behind all this is concern about the election front which I am sure racks us all."[137]

It might be countered that these advisors were only framing their recommendations in ways they thought might appeal to the president. Yet while that fact alone would give some indication of the nakedly electoral flavor of bureaucratic politics in this period, in truth this was more than window dressing. Most intriguing in this respect are Clifford's retrospective comments on the development of the March 31 speech and the proposal to halt the bombing contained therein:

> We thought we were drafting a speech for an embattled candidate, not a man ready to sacrifice his career, in his own eyes, in pursuit of peace. We were at all times mindful of the fact that the critical primary in Wisconsin would take place two days after the speech. Had I known that the President would be a lame duck with ten months left in office, I would have argued for a full bombing cessation despite the difficulty of gaining his approval. The limited bombing halt I had supported was designed for another political scenario, and might not result in serious negotiations with Hanoi; a full bombing halt might have . . . We worked on the most important speech of the Johnson Presidency ignorant of information that would have changed at least some of our positions, and perhaps affected his own decision on the bombing.[138]

On one level, Clifford's statement reveals plainly how Johnson's advisors were crafting recommendations under the influence of electoral constraints. This in itself is powerful evidence of the interconnectedness of the electoral framework offered in this book and alternative accounts of foreign policy decision making that stress the significance of bureaucratic politics. Yet there is a cruel irony here too. It is true that Johnson's imminent withdrawal from the race would alleviate many of the electoral pressures that had restricted Vietnam policy until this point. Johnson understood this. In fact, he directly attributed his willingness to consider a bombing halt to this new electoral reality. "I was judging the possible impact of a peace move linked with an announcement of my decision to withdraw from politics at the end of my term," he later recalled. "That consideration put things in another perspective," he added. He also understood that his advisors were, apparently unlike him, "thinking of a peace move in terms of public opinion and political consequences."[139] Yet what he seemingly failed to recognize was that, by keeping his chief foreign policy advisors in the dark about his political intentions, he tacitly allowed the recommendations brought to him to continue to be constrained by electoral pressures that in truth should no longer have applied. Even if the announced policy shift approached the limits of how far Johnson was willing to go in the interest of peace, he had denied his advisors the opportunity to convince him to go further, inadvertently or otherwise. Given the lack of progress that would ensue, this was no small matter.

Monkey Wrenches in Paris

Johnson's withdrawal meant that for the remainder of the electoral period he would be rendered a "lame duck" president. Unencumbered by the need to get reelected, electoral constraints are expected to be weaker in this period. Indeed, Johnson publicly stated in his withdrawal speech that he did not feel he should devote "an hour or a day of my time to any personal partisan causes" while dedicated to the pursuit of peace in Vietnam.[140] Yet he was of course not insensitive to the reality that his ability to secure a peaceful resolution of the conflict would form a central pillar of his political legacy if honorable terms could be agreed. Moreover, as he well understood, the very presence of an upcoming election might serve to erode the bargaining leverage afforded to him even though his name would not be on the ballot. The following section thus offers an illuminating example of the *spoiler* mechanism, whereby a mixture of the president's own political preferences, the strategic calculations of other candidates and negotiating opponents, and the time pressures related to the fixed deadline of polling day conspired to render Johnson's diplomatic efforts ultimately fruitless.

In what might be termed the first phase of this episode, lasting all summer, the Johnson administration figured that Hanoi had calculated that they could reach a better deal closer to the 1968 presidential election, when the U.S. side might be more willing to stop bombing in an effort to help Hubert Humphrey's candidacy and bolster Johnson's legacy as a peacemaker. Such a calculation would have been entirely reasonable, since Johnson had spent much of the summer stubbornly rejecting proposals for a bombing halt without reciprocal concessions being made by Hanoi. As Clark Clifford subsequently complained to his fellow pause advocates, "You don't realize LBJ's mood. It's: 'I'm God-damned if I'll stop the bombing without something from the other side!' "[141] With no letup in the intensity of the ground war either, Johnson was tending toward the hard-line position associated with Richard Nixon.[142] As such, for the moment at least, little good could come of precipitous concessions on Hanoi's side. Even though Johnson was not running, this electorally informed consideration restricted his bargaining position, as he well knew. "They're waiting to see if they can have a better deal with anybody that they select," he explained to Majority Leader Everett Dirksen, adding, "They know that they can't get a better one from me. They know they can't get a better one from Nixon. So they're trying to play this other side."[143]

This logic appeared to have been validated on September 30, when the Democratic candidate publicly offered weaker terms than Johnson's. Pledging to halt the bombing "as an acceptable risk for peace," Humphrey required only good faith from the North Vietnamese and de facto evidence that they would restore the demilitarized zone between the North and the South.[144] Johnson also required firm commitments from Hanoi to accept South Vietnamese participation in negotiations and refrain from shelling South Vietnamese cities. The president understood that his bargaining leverage was significantly eroded so long as Humphrey had a chance of winning in November, as he explained to Rusk: "They're not going to do anything until after the election . . . If Humphrey's elected, they're in clover. If he's not elected, then they can look and see what they want to do between me and Nixon. So you can just forget everything until then."[145]

Johnson tried his best to preserve his leverage. This can be seen first in his attempts to destroy the dovish minority plank at the Democratic convention. In a call to Charles Murphy, an advisor, who had been working on Humphrey's platform, he made his opposition clear, flatly stating, "We do not favor any words that say 'stop the bombing.' Let's make that clear and repeat it over and over again."[146] In the end, Johnson's preferred platform defeated the weaker version. Second, throughout the campaign season, Johnson continually called the candidates to censor them on Vietnam. One such hastily arranged conference call was especially striking. Calling for a "minimum of discussion" in public speeches, he stressed that "we can get [peace] only when they understand that our position is a firm one, and we're going to stay by it. And what y'all's position will be when you get to be president, I would hope you could announce it then."[147] He then explained his predicament to them in true Johnsonian style:

> We have really this kind of a situation. If I've got a house to sell, and I put a rock bottom price of $40,000 on it, and the prospective purchaser says, "Well, that's a little high, but let me see." And he goes—starts to leave to talk to his wife about it, and Lady Bird [Johnson] whispers that, "I would let you have it for $35,000." And then he gets downstairs, and Lynda Bird [Johnson] says, "We don't like the old house anyway, you can get it for $30,000." Well, he's not likely to sign up.[148]

In case the candidates missed the point of his parable, Johnson reiterated the point later in the same call, explaining, "I think if I were in their place and I were negotiating, and I read that Ho Chi Minh was in a sick bed, and in three weeks he would be out, and there'd be a better deal awaiting me, and the new president would really do better than he's doing, I just don't think I would dash in . . . Anybody that's ever bought a cat knows that."[149] Evidently, Johnson did not need to be in the race, or even thinking in a remotely partisan manner, for his negotiating position to be affected by the U.S. election.

The next phase of the *spoiler* mechanism saw Hanoi calculate, based explicitly on its assessment of the runners and riders in the U.S. election campaign, that it was now "an opportune time" to adopt a more conciliatory approach in Paris to encourage the Johnson administration to further de-escalate the war through additional concessions.[150] Having tried and failed to gain a decisive advantage on the battlefield in major attacks in February, May, and August of 1968, North Vietnamese officials came to believe that their best chance of securing a favorable outcome may now lay at the negotiating table.[151] With time running out on his presidency, Johnson might give them a better deal now, as a lame duck wanting to be remembered as a peacemaker, rather than wait until Nixon, considered by Politburo leaders to be "obstinate," took office.[152] On October 11, strong indications were therefore sent through secret channels that North Vietnam was ready for talks, and even willing to agree to Saigon's participation, in return for a cessation of bombing, giving Johnson a reciprocal concession that he had demanded since March 31.[153] Just over a week later, Hanoi instructed its negotiators to start serious talks on a schedule designed to initiate formal talks just days before the U.S. election—the moment at which Johnson might be especially willing to bend for an electorally convenient deal.[154]

Indeed, Hanoi had good reason to think that the American delegation in Paris would jump at the chance. Lead negotiator Averell Harriman wrote in a personal memo of December 1968 that, "For several years, I have taken the position that Viet-Nam was important in U.S. policy, but that other things were more important. When asked what was more important, I always gave as my first point, not permitting it to elect Nixon as President."[155] The paper trail from his time in Paris seems to substantiate that ranking of priorities. Harriman was in almost daily contact with the Humphrey campaign, admitting to the candidate in late August that "I am torn between staying here in Paris working for a constructive break in these negotiations, and coming home to do what I can with the liberal groups to encourage them to give you their fullest support."[156] Moreover, in several phone calls with Humphrey's advisors he would offer his own advice on campaign strategy, including recommendations for staffing decisions and further promises to come home and confer with Humphrey because "I feel very strongly I can do a lot of good with some of the Kennedy people."[157] Most suggestive, though, were comments such as those shared with George Ball—another close advisor of Humphrey's—that perhaps he was best placed to help the candidate by staying in Paris because "there was always a chance we might work something out here which would have an effect on the election."[158]

"Harriman was a real partisan," recalls John Negroponte, the American delegation's language officer and liaison with the North Vietnamese at the time, adding, "he was a real Democrat."[159] Or, as Dean Rusk observed in a conversation with the president at the time, "Averell is 50 percent ambassador and 50 percent an experienced Democratic politician and . . . sometimes he gets those two hats confused."[160] There was, of course, no better judge than Johnson when it came to the identification of individuals with such an uneasy marriage of identities. Most importantly for the present discussion, however, these electoral considerations appear to have had a material impact on the negotiations. "In October I think the Vietnamese sense that there's political pressure on us to produce some results in the Paris talks for the benefit of the Democratic Party," recalls Negroponte. "Definitely the pressure of the presidential politics there pushed us to want to reach an agreement on a bombing halt before the election, both in the interest of getting something done, but also with the thought of trying to help Hubert Humphrey."[161]

Yet, though some have argued that this bombing cessation was simply a cynical attempt to swing the election to Humphrey with a bold de-escalatory move, this seems implausible.[162] On a basic level, Johnson did not change his conditions, but rather simply waited until Hanoi moved closer to his. As Johnson put it to Humphrey, "It's not new on our part. It *is* new on their part."[163] Moreover, the personal political incentives for such action in this lame duck phase were simply not sufficiently strong to warrant such a bold move. Johnson may have wanted to go down in history books as a peacemaker, but he feared that his legacy would be *weakened* if he was seen to authorize a "cheap political trick," and that was a major argument Johnson cited repeatedly *against* a bombing halt in two crucial meetings of October 14 and 27.[164] Indeed, it took strenuous lobbying by all elements of government and the military, including the head of Tactical Air Command himself, to reassure Johnson that he would be innocent of charges of electoral cynicism.[165] "You and I can't have our reputations ruined the rest of our lives trying to get Humphrey elected," he told Rusk, adding that he would "be damned if I am going to throw a peace for him."[166]Johnson of course may have intentionally downplayed his enthusiasm for a bombing halt in these discussions, preferring to let his advisors express their support for the move in a way that would insulate him from potential criticism. In doing so, however, the sincerity of his concerns about those political optics remains clear.

Neither was it the case that the desire to see his vice president elected in November compelled Johnson in this action. In fact, Clifford's contemporary view was that "I happen to *know* LBJ didn't end the bombing on 31 Oct. just to elect Humphrey because I've never believed he wanted Humphrey to win!"[167] Johnson deemed Nixon "more responsible" on Vietnam than Humphrey, and frankly told advisors that "the GOP may be of more help to us than the Democrats in the last few months."[168] According to Clifford, Johnson also openly doubted that Humphrey had the "ability to be President," and repeatedly denigrated him as "disloyal" and weak after his September speech breaking with Johnson's policy.[169] On several occasions, Johnson even called Nixon and his campaign surrogates to suggest lines of attack on Humphrey's position, even sharing classified information to bolster Nixon's case.[170] As Clifford later recalled, "What mattered to President Johnson at that moment was not who would succeed him, but what his place in history would be."[171] Intriguingly, therefore, the net result of these dynamics was that electorally motivated behaviors by Hanoi, based on what was essentially a miscalculation of Johnson's political preferences, had actually *helped* the U.S. president come closer to striking a deal, at least momentarily.

If Humphrey and Hanoi may have stood to gain from a preelection bombing halt, the problem for Johnson was that the same could not be said of Nixon and Saigon, who also had interests in seeking to influence the prospects of a diplomatic breakthrough that were similarly informed by the electoral process in the United States. Indeed, there is reasonable evidence to suggest the Nixon campaign actively sought to sabotage the peace process to gain electoral advantage. Anna Chennault, a prominent Washington hostess with links to the China lobby, had for several months been acting as an interlocutor between the Nixon campaign and Saigon's ambassador, Bui Diem. FBI wiretaps at the South Vietnamese embassy revealed that in one call between the two, Chennault offered the following message from her "boss": "hold on, we are gonna win."[172] In other words, Saigon should not participate in the Paris peace talks, which had by that stage been agreed upon by Washington and Hanoi as part of the bombing halt, because they would get a better deal from Nixon if they waited until he was elected—a clear example of the *spoiler* mechanism. Recently, evidence has been found that implicates Nixon himself, who had appointed Chennault his "sole representative" to Saigon in a July meeting. According to notes written in late October, he authorized a "monkey wrench" of the talks and ordered his team to "Keep Anna Chennault working on SVN [South Vietnam]."[173]

Proving Nixon's culpability in what one of Johnson's allies still refers to as "treason" is less important here, however, than substantiating the claim that South Vietnam acted with the U.S. election in mind.[174] When the U.S. lead negotiator, Harriman, was informed about the allegations involving Nixon a couple of months later, he wrote in a personal memorandum that "this explains what I had thought—that the Saigon Government was motivated in withholding approval of a bombing halt to attempt to avoid the election of Humphrey."[175] Framed this way, any skullduggery by Nixon would only have reinforced the logical calculation to be made by any rational South Vietnamese leader. Though hardly an impartial source, Anna Chennault's recollection that President Thieu informed her that he "would much prefer to have the peace talks after [Nixon's] election" remains a quite plausible reflection of the South Vietnamese leader's view, since Nixon's record of hard-line commitment to the war surely indicated that he would be kinder to Saigon in negotiations than Johnson would have been.[176] Just as Hanoi had calculated a better deal was more likely before the election, so Saigon deduced that waiting would better serve its interests. After Johnson finally announced a bombing halt on October 31, to be followed by serious talks with Hanoi the day after the election, Thieu promptly torpedoed the initiative by announcing that he would not send any representatives to Paris. "This is nice," commented the South Vietnamese leader in conversation with his private secretary. "Now at least we have bought ourselves some time."[177]

While his lame duck status undoubtedly afforded Johnson the political space required to pursue a diplomatic solution to the conflict, having been previously bound to a course of steadily increasing military pressure, he learned that the U.S. electoral cycle presents serious constraints on a president's room for maneuver, even when the incumbent is not running for reelection. With Johnson's hopes to have secured peace in Vietnam thus thwarted by the *spoiler* mechanism, it would be up to his successor to find a way out of the war.

*   *   *

This chapter has illuminated the considerable role played by electoral politics in Lyndon Johnson's decisions to escalate and de-escalate the war in Vietnam. Specifically, it argued that the pressures associated with the upcoming presidential election in 1964 introduced *delay* and *dampening* dynamics into the policy-making process, as Johnson sought to sweep politically toxic issues under the carpet, despite increasingly strong calls for a change of course. As expected, this resulted in an aggressive set of policy outcomes once these pressures were lifted in 1965, as Johnson sought to take advantage of the greater latitude afforded to him by his electoral victory. Such a move toward a proactive policy was also emboldened by Johnson's predisposition to protect his domestic priorities from hawks in Congress. After trying and failing to balance his strategic and electoral preferences before an increasingly frayed coalition of congressional and public support, however, Johnson belatedly sought to sacrifice his personal political survival in the hope of securing peace. Thus freed from most constraints as a lame duck, Johnson discovered that the American electoral cycle can hamstring a president's room for maneuver in negotiations, even if the incumbent is not running, in a prime example of the *spoiler* mechanism outlined in chapter 1.

Absent electoral constraints, would the course of American intervention in Vietnam under Lyndon Johnson have looked materially different? At a minimum, it seems reasonable to conclude that a decision to change course would have come in 1964 rather than in 1965. Without the need to pass the test of political acceptability, the withdrawal and neutralization options would have at least been more seriously considered, and, just possibly, approved. Yet even if this push toward greater intervention was partly over-determined by prior structural factors, or propelled by bureaucratic or psychological biases, the electorally driven delay in implementing that decision allowed the infiltration of North Vietnamese troops and materiel across the border to continue unchecked. In the long term, this made the American job harder and probably lengthened the war. Relatedly, if Johnson had not feared that the upcoming midterm campaign set a time limit on his ability to "ram through" the Great Society legislation he favored, per-haps, too, there may have been less pandering to congressional hawks in 1965. Electoral politics therefore had a strong impact on the timing of pol-icy decisions, and a plausible effect on the nature and ultimate utility of those policies.

To evaluate the impact of electoral politics in 1968, we might consider two further counterfactual questions. First, if Johnson was running for reelec-tion, would U.S. policy have been any different? The evidence above suggests that March 31 was a crucial turning point, at which constraints were lifted, or at least considerably eased, almost overnight. It seems likely that if John-son were still running, spring 1968 would have seen more of the Goldilocks policy of gradual escalation that characterized the previous three years. As the conventions approached, Johnson might have considered a dove-friendly move to lock up the nomination, before being pressured to issue further con-cessions to Hanoi in a bid to secure peace for his own benefit in November.

The second counterfactual is more fundamental: Absent a U.S. election in 1968, would there have been peace in Vietnam? The evidence above indi-cates that both the opportunity to bring Hanoi to the table and the futility of doing so given Saigon's desire to stay away from Paris were determined by electoral calculations on the part of seemingly everyone but the presi-dent. Johnson did not need to be a candidate to have his bargaining posi-tion affected by the election. At a minimum, we can conclude that he might have been able to bring about serious negotiations earlier had the *spoiler* mechanism not been in operation. There remained no guarantee of peace, of course. A meaningful negotiation requires the commitment of two will-ing parties, and Hanoi had shown little evidence of any desire to settle the war through diplomatic means throughout some two hundred peace initia-tives that had been attempted in this period. Yet we have seen that Hanoi's decision making was also shaped in important ways by calculations related to the U.S. electoral cycle. Getting all sides to the negotiating table would have offered at least a glimmer of hope. As it was, with South Vietnam con-tinuing to stall, it was quite literally the shape of the table itself that was under debate as Johnson left office.

FOUR

Vietnam

Richard Nixon and the "Vietnamization" of the War

It seems vitally important to me at this time that we increase as much as we possibly can the military pressure on the enemy in South Vietnam.

—RICHARD NIXON, FEBRUARY 1969

I'm afraid we have too many chips on South Vietnam. And if my re-election is important, let's remember, I've got to get this off our plate.

—RICHARD NIXON, MARCH 1971

IN SEEKING TO CRAFT a way forward in Vietnam, Richard Nixon faced the same fundamental dilemma that had doomed the political fortunes of his predecessor. After years of fighting, there remained no clear path to military victory, and support was dwindling at home for the level of commitment required to sustain a conflict that had long since become a stalemate. The essential task before the president, then, was to find some way of reaching a negotiated settlement on terms that were favorable enough for him to be able to say he had delivered on his pledge to secure "peace with honor." Having expected to reach such an agreement within months, it would instead take another four years before a peace treaty would be signed. As this chapter demonstrates, electoral constraints played an increasingly important role in shaping this outcome. Nixon's selection of the military and diplomatic tools he would use to end U.S. involvement in the war, as well as the manner in which he would apply them, owed a great deal to pressures associated with the domestic political calendar.

In the opening phase of his presidency, Nixon sought to balance his strategic preference for inducing concessions from Hanoi at the negotiating table through increased military and diplomatic pressure with the need to limit the intensity and duration of these escalatory steps to account for political conditions at home. Over time, however, growing unrest and mounting congressional opposition in the aftermath of controversial operations in Laos and Cambodia served to narrow the president's room for maneuver. After the midterms of 1970, Nixon recalibrated his approach. Having become fatalistic about the utility of his "Vietnamization" plan to turn the fighting over to local forces, the president nonetheless doubled down on it, manufacturing a series of staggered troop withdrawals that would defer South Vietnam's collapse until after Election Day 1972. In the meantime, Henry Kissinger was dispatched to pursue the diplomatic side of this electorally motivated plan, signaling to Hanoi, Moscow, and Beijing that the U.S. president was prepared to sacrifice Saigon's future to ensure his personal political survival. When Hanoi threatened this overarching plan with its Easter Offensive of 1972, Nixon's response was carefully designed to protect the president's electoral prospects in a manner that illustrates the *spur* mechanism. As the presidential election approached, *spoiler* dynamics threatened to further unpick Nixon's plans, recalling markedly similar events of four years prior. Yet the president was ultimately able to ride out the prospect of a damaging split with Saigon long enough to secure his reelection. A peace agreement would be signed then and only then, albeit on terms that had been on the table in the weeks prior to a blistering final rally of bombing raids.

Seeking "Peace with Honor"

Nixon had been elected in large part because voters expected him to be able to bring the war in Vietnam to an "honorable" end. In determining exactly how he would go about doing so, he had given himself a degree of flexibility, thanks to the deliberately vague character of his campaign statements on the issue. Knowing both that the hawkish vote was safe in Republican hands and that his advantage over Humphrey had more to do with the vice president's image problem—as a candidate tied to Johnson's unpopular handling of the war—rather than an alternative set of policy proposals, Nixon had been satisfied to convey the impression that he had a "secret plan" for winning the war without detailing precisely what that meant.[1] Moreover, having been Eisenhower's running mate in 1952, Nixon grasped well how a protracted and bloody conflict overseas might be exploited for partisan gain without tying oneself to any particular course. Indeed, Nixon had not been shy in invoking the Korean analogy on the campaign trail as a model of how peace might be achieved, though what that meant beyond ambiguous allusions to the importance of projecting military and diplomatic strength remained unclear.[2]

If the *hangover* mechanism might therefore have been modest in theory, in practice the legacy of antiwar dissent Nixon inherited loomed large as a significant constraint on his policy choices. The new president understood that his honeymoon period with voters would not likely be a particularly long-lasting one unless he was seen to make material progress toward the goal of ending the war. And unlike President Johnson, who at least had a modest window of political opportunity before the midterms, Nixon was faced with a Congress controlled by the opposing party and with a predisposition to look unfavorably upon any expansion of the war. The formula Nixon ultimately settled on reflected an uneasy balance between intertwined strategic and political considerations. As he later reflected in a handwritten note scrawled on a yellow legal pad, there were two ways he could gain leverage over Hanoi: "Give them a jolt & they'll talk," or "Stop U.S. dissent and they'll talk."[3]

That Nixon's strategic preference rested more with the former path, that of escalatory steps on the battlefield, is made plainly apparent by the president's own words to Kissinger less than two weeks after assuming office. "It seems vitally important to me at this time," he explained, "that we increase as much as we possibly can the military pressure on the enemy in South Vietnam."[4] His comments echoed those expressed in an NSC meeting a week earlier. "I think we will need about six months of strong military action," the new president told advisors. "I feel we must not lose our nerve on this one. We should buy time with negotiations and continue to punish the enemy."[5] Outside of the formal NSC setting, Nixon stated his views more colorfully. "I call it the Madman Theory, Bob," he confided to his chief of staff, explaining, "I want the North Vietnamese to believe I've reached the point where I might do anything to stop the war. We'll just slip the word to them that, 'for God's sake, you know Nixon is obsessed about communism. We can't restrain him when he's angry—and he has his hand on the nuclear button' and Ho Chi Minh himself will be in Paris in two days begging for peace."[6] Evidently, Nixon felt that Hanoi had a breaking point that could only be reached through the application of a sufficient degree of military force.

The bombing of Cambodian sanctuaries, authorized in March 1969 in Operation Menu, was the first practical manifestation of this preference. Designed at least in part to signal to Hanoi that Nixon was willing to take actions that his predecessor was not, the measure was certainly aggressive in nature. Over the next fourteen months, some 3,360 B-52 raids would be unleashed in the skies over Cambodia. Yet the fact that Nixon opted for a covert method of escalation was telling. While he understood that the stage of the electoral cycle gave him some latitude, he was equally aware that carpet bombing a neutral country was a sure way to end his honeymoon with the American people. "My administration was only two months old," he later explained, "and I wanted to provoke as little public outcry as possible at the outset."[7] Indeed, Nixon would have preferred to resume bombing over North Vietnam, but concern over the protests that such a move would engender put paid to that more visible proposal. Those political instincts were essentially borne out by the vociferous backlash in May after U.S. forces suffered significant losses taking and then abandoning what was presented by critics as an inconsequential position in Vietnam, dubbed "Hamburger Hill." Nixon viewed scathing comments by leading politicians like Edward Kennedy as the opening salvo of the 1972 campaign, but clearly recognized the very real constraints they placed on the intensity of the "jolt" he was able to apply to the enemy. After publicly insisting that commanders had been instructed to conduct the war with a minimum of American casualties, Nixon quietly authorized a shift in military emphasis away from operations involving large commitments of ground troops and toward the use of artillery and airpower as part of a focus on "protective reaction."[8]

A similar set of countervailing pressures may also be observed on the diplomatic side of Nixon's approach to the war. Convinced that the USSR was capable of pressuring Hanoi into making concessions, Nixon dispatched Kissinger to meet with the Soviet ambassador in a series of secret talks through 1969. In an early form of "linkage" diplomacy, Kissinger suggested that Soviet assistance in bringing about an acceptable settlement to the conflict in Vietnam might unlock progress on other issues of great significance to U.S.-Soviet relations, including arms control and the Middle East. American patience was not unlimited, however. The president was willing to consider taking "other measures" to conclude the war "by unilateral means" if a reasonable settlement could not soon be reached. While Kissinger declined to elaborate on the specifics, he underlined the seriousness of the message by sharing ominously worded talking points bearing the president's initials. "In dealing with the president," he added, "it was well to remember that he always did more than he threatened and that he never threatened idly."[9] Kissinger then upped the ante in the fall by issuing Hanoi with an ultimatum, warning of "measures of the greatest consequences" if no progress was made by November 1.[10] As planning continued for an extraordinarily aggressive program of bombing and mining operations, code-named "Duck Hook," Kissinger again sought to convince Moscow to help break the impasse with Hanoi before those contingency plans would be implemented, warning Ambassador Dobrynin that "the train had just left the station and was now headed down the track."[11] As the moment of decision drew closer, however, Nixon grew increasingly uncomfortable with the severity of the proposed escalation amid mounting antiwar sentiment across the country. In a meeting called to evaluate options to increase military pressure on October 11, the president repeatedly referred to "the very grave political problem" he faced, with massive nationwide protests planned for the following week and a growing chorus of opposition in Congress.[12] Kissinger's plans may have struck a chord with Nixon's strategic preference, but, as the president's chief of staff put it, they didn't "include the domestic factor."[13] Nixon ultimately shelved the proposals, authorizing instead a secret nuclear alert that increased the operational readiness of the American nuclear arsenal so as to be detected by foreign intelligence but not by the U.S. public.[14]

With plans for further military escalation thus reduced to a bluff thanks to concerns about political conditions at home, Nixon mounted a public relations offensive instead. In a major nationwide address on November 3, the president offered the clearest articulation yet of his plan to "Vietnamize" the war in a bid to blunt the impact of the antiwar movement and rally the "great silent majority" behind his handling of the conflict. By focusing more on strengthening local forces, he explained, the responsibility for security in South Vietnam could be transferred away from U.S. troops while negotiations for a peaceful settlement continued.[15] The policy was consistent with the Nixon Doctrine, announced in July, which declared that problems like Vietnam "will be increasingly handled by, and the responsibility for it taken by, the Asian nations themselves."[16] Yet the underlying concept of "de-Americanizing" the war was not new. In fact, it had roots in the Johnson administration.[17] Under Nixon, the authorization of a concrete plan of phased troop withdrawals owed much to the "enthusiastic advocacy" of the secretary of defense, Melvin Laird.[18] Following a trip to Vietnam in March, Laird initially recommended the redeployment of fifty to seventy thousand troops in 1969 alone, and was soon thereafter granted principal responsibility for the overall planning and implementation of a longer-term glide path of redeployments.[19]

Vietnamization was not part of Nixon's preferred plan to win the war. Far from it. Indeed, less than a week before a crucial March 28 NSC meeting in which the term "Vietnamization" was coined and further studies commissioned, the national security apparatus had unanimously concluded that "The RVNAF [Republic of Vietnam Air Force] alone cannot now, or in the foreseeable future, stand up to both the VC [Viet Cong] and sizable North Vietnamese forces."[20] This was not an aberrational assessment. Though Secretary of Defense Laird remained optimistic, Kissinger wasted few opportunities to point out how tall an order it would be to address the myriad issues affecting the capacity of South Vietnamese forces on anything like an acceptable time line. He also felt that the maintenance of a U.S. troop presence represented the principal bargaining chip available to him in ongoing peace talks, which should not simply be given away without a quid pro quo. On the eve of a critical September NSC meeting in which he expected the long-term future of Vietnamization to be decided, Kissinger wrote several background memoranda to the president expressing his skepticism. After informing the president that he had become "deeply concerned about our present course on Vietnam," Kissinger cast doubt on the capacity of South Vietnamese armed forces to assume the burden of fighting quickly enough and warned that redeployments may in fact be counterproductive to the war effort. Among several "serious problems" the administration would encounter in pursuing its path of Vietnamization were the domestic effects. "Withdrawal of U.S. troops will become like salted peanuts to the American public," he explained. "The more U.S. troops come home, the more will be demanded."[21]

Nixon understood the politics of the situation differently. If Kissinger's views turned out to be prescient, Vietnamization was for Nixon a necessary evil. He did not really think of it in terms of its expected military utility. Instead, it was a kind of lid he could slowly lift to keep the pressure cooker of public opinion from spilling over and spoiling his preferred course of action. He was transparent on this point from the outset. As early as January 25, he explained that unilateral troop withdrawals were but a "ploy for more time domestically, while we continue to press at the negotiating table for a military settlement."[22] Kissinger may have been Nixon's most trusted advisor on national security issues, but on this occasion the president sided with Laird—a veteran political operator with nine terms of congressional experience—and did so explicitly on the grounds of political exigency. Casting Kissinger's concerns aside, the president explained to advisors in the September NSC meeting that they were really fighting "three wars—on the battlefield, the Saigon political war, and U.S. politics." Vietnamization, he made clear, was not his preferred strategy for winning the war as a whole, so much as his preferred method of fighting a rearguard action on the domestic political front. "At home here it would be great to lower the level of forces and reduce casualties," he said, emphasizing that "We buy time with troop withdrawals."[23] In short, as the most recent study on this topic aptly notes, "Vietnamization was not a strategy for defeating Hanoi militarily or for aiding Saigon in pacification efforts in the RVN [i.e., South Vietnam]. It was a politically driven initiative to lessen domestic political opposition to the administration."[24]

Strikingly, it was not just public opinion in the abstract that Nixon was concerned with. Repeatedly, he made clear that the electoral calendar played a critical role in his calculations. "If we had no elections, it would be fine," he stated when weighing Laird's initial recommendations back in March. "We cannot sustain this at current rates for two years. The reality is that we are working against a time clock."[25] He made no secret of this even in private discussions with the South Vietnamese president. In a meeting on Midway Island on June 8, after which Nixon would publicly announce the withdrawal of twenty-five thousand troops, the American president expressed his appreciation for Thieu's understanding of the "difficult political problem in the U.S." Stressing "the importance of the 1970 elections," Nixon told Thieu that "the U.S. domestic situation is a weapon in the war."[26]

With the public relations plan in place, Nixon did indeed press on with escalation, launching a joint U.S.–South Vietnam ground incursion of Cambodia in the spring of 1970. The operation was designed to cut off supply routes to North Vietnamese forces in the latest attempt to compel Hanoi into making concessions at the negotiating table. Like Operation Menu, the ongoing bombing of the country authorized in 1969, Nixon anticipated administering such a "jolt" with great aggression and enthusiasm. "We are going to kick the shit out of them," he told Kissinger, "everything short of nuclear

weapons."[27] Yet, again, he was acutely aware that he faced significant risks at home in authorizing such a step. As his chief of staff, H. R. Haldeman, recorded in a diary entry at the time, the president "realizes he's treading on the brink of major problems as he escalates the war there," and expected a "monumental squawk from the Hill" as a result.[28] Hoping to "drop a bombshell on the gathering spring storm of antiwar protest," Nixon thus preceded the Cambodian action with the announcement that some 150,000 additional troops would be withdrawn by the following year.[29] Summarizing well both Nixon's approach to the Cambodian operation and the war as a whole, Haldeman noted how the president "still feels he can get it wound up this year if we keep enough pressure on and don't crumble at home."[30]

The opening stage of Nixon's first term thus leaves a complex record of escalatory strategic instincts tempered by political conditions at home. To be sure, the vague nature of the president's campaign pledges on Vietnam gave him some flexibility, as did the relative permissiveness of this phase of the electoral cycle. Nixon felt that Hanoi had misjudged him for this precise reason, privately remarking to a British counterinsurgency expert that the enemy "had caught him in the beginning of his term with three years more to run."[31] Nevertheless, in the covert nature of Operation Menu, the shift away from casualty-intensive ground operations, the shelving of Duck Hook, and most notably the initiation of a steady withdrawal program to offset criticism of his chosen escalatory steps, there is clear evidence that residual discontent at home placed meaningful limits on Nixon's ability to pursue his preferred path to peace.

Hysterical People and Diplomatic Duds

In the lead-up to the 1970 midterm elections, decision making concerning Vietnam entered a period of relative stasis. Nixon's strategic preferences do not appear to have materially changed, yet his ability to act on them became increasingly bound by domestic political concerns, particularly after the backlash to the Cambodian incursion. Though Nixon disparagingly referred to the thousands of antiwar protestors as "the hysterical people," he was in private deeply affected by unrest in the aftermath of the invasion.[32] After four student protestors were shot dead at Kent State by the National Guard,

Nixon became "very disturbed," according to Haldeman, and was "afraid his decision set it off."[33]

Chief among Nixon's concerns was the congressional response to his latest escalatory step. The president understood early on how precarious his support in the legislative branch was. "In 1969 I still had a congressional majority on war-related votes and questions," he later recalled, "but it was a bare one at best."[34] In the aftermath of Cambodia, Congress now began to exercise its oversight over presidential war powers, swiftly acting to try to cut off all funding to the Cambodian campaign by passing the Cooper-Church Amendment in the Senate. While the amendment failed in the House, this unprecedented flexing of congressional war powers in the aftermath of Cambodia did in effect force Nixon to limit the campaign to a duration of sixty days and precluded any further efforts to apply serious military pressure across the border. Besides the moral condemnation any action would spark, Nixon could not expect this Congress to give him the necessary funds. In this respect, it is instructive to note that when the commander in chief of Pacific forces requested an additional supplemental budget to support the resupply of arms to noncommunist forces in Cambodia, he was told "the White House has decided to delay it until after the election."[35]

It was a similar story on the diplomatic front. Throughout 1970, Nixon continued to hold private misgivings about the likelihood that negotiations would yield any meaningful progress. "I don't know what these clowns want to talk about," he said scornfully to Kissinger in a phone call in January. "The line we take," he explained, "is either they talk or we are going to sit it out. I don't feel this is any time for concession."[36] The president did ultimately permit Kissinger to press on with secret talks with North Vietnamese officials through the remainder of the year, but he remained clear-eyed about things. Detailing Nixon's skepticism about the talks, Kissinger recalled that he "never went into a negotiation without a written or oral injunction to hang tough and some expression that Nixon did not really expect success."[37] While this may in part be attributable to the president's anticipatory efforts to ease the emotional pain of being rebuffed, it is also consistent with his belief that Hanoi would only settle on agreeable terms after it suffered a major military setback. With that more aggressive strategic inclination kept in check, it is perhaps no surprise that no major diplomatic effort was attempted in this period.

Moreover, when the president in late 1970 *did* appear to engage with the diplomatic track with any degree of enthusiasm, it turned out to be the exception that proved the rule, with the president's interest a clear function of electoral politics. In a televised address at the White House on October 7, Nixon announced a "major new initiative for peace," made possible by the "remarkable success" of the Vietnamization plan. At the core of this initiative was a proposal for a cease-fire-in-place, to cover all actions including "bombing and acts of terror," and to apply not just to Vietnam but also Cambodia and Laos.[38] If this seemed to some antiwar critics at home to be too good to be true, frankly, it was. What Nixon had failed to mention in his speech was the fact that Kissinger had proposed such a move precisely a month earlier, in a September 7 meeting in Paris, only for Hanoi to flatly reject it. Even that outcome was wholly expected inside the administration. In an NSC meeting on July 21, it was not the diplomatic value of a proposed cease-fire-in-place that was really in contention—all present appeared to agree that Hanoi would not accept it—but rather the timing. The secretary of defense first suggested that "we begin the talks in August and then reveal a proposal in September for domestic impact." This logic appealed to the president, who agreed that "if we don't believe the enemy will take it, the timing relates to the effects here. It would be better to be more deliberate." Announcing a peace initiative would rally public support in his favor, he calculated, but if it came too early, its demonstrable failure would erode any political benefit too soon to have any impact at the ballot box. "It will have an effect on American opinion," clarified Nixon. "I don't want to have a dud fall on the schools and bring down public opinion."[39]

With congressional pressures beginning to bite, Nixon's Vietnam decisions of mid- to late 1970 were premised on the need to regain congressional support in the November elections. This meant avoiding the types of escalatory strategies in Vietnam that had aroused such opposition until then, and urging negotiators to keep a low profile in Paris before announcing an "October surprise" peace initiative in which no one had any faith. "Vietnamization" continued apace, but few held any illusions about the capacity of South Vietnamese forces to shoulder more of the burden anytime soon. As we shall see, after the Democrats held their Senate majority in the midterm elections—and picked up twelve seats in the House—Nixon proceeded to engage in a more fundamental rethink of strategy, with the 1972 presidential election front and center in his mind.

Seeking Reelection

It is in the second half of a president's term that we might expect the relative importance of electoral pressures to rise in the wartime decision-making process. As will be demonstrated, the case of Nixon and Vietnam is a perfect illustration of these dynamics. Having become pessimistic about the viability of continued U.S. engagement in Southeast Asia, Nixon increasingly allowed electoral considerations to permeate all discussion of strategy, as he prioritized his own political self-interest over concerns related to strategic optimality. At the broadest level, this profoundly shaped what came to be known as the "decent interval" strategy that he and Kissinger now adopted, which sought extrication from Vietnam on an electorally friendly timetable, whatever the cost to South Vietnam. After exploring the development of this cynical strategy, this section goes on to argue that decision making around major bombing offensives—Linebacker I and II—were subject to the *spur* and *delay* mechanisms predicted by the conceptual framework outlined in chapter 1. It also examines how the *spoiler* mechanism further frustrated any remaining hope for the kind of "peace with honor" that Nixon had once promised.

The "Decent Interval" Strategy

The abject failure of the South Vietnamese–led ground invasion of Laos in April 1971 marked a key turning point in the administration's handling of the war.[40] Framed as a test of the "Vietnamization" policy, which neither Nixon nor Kissinger really placed much hope in to begin with, the outcome of the operation was a chaotic retreat by the South Vietnamese armed forces (Army of the Republic of Vietnam, or ARVN), with estimated casualty rates as high as 50 percent. "Henry, I have become completely fatalistic about the goddamn thing," Nixon lamented in the aftermath. "I don't think they're up to it." Though "we've given them a hell of a chance," the fact of the matter was that the South Vietnamese "aren't as good as we thought." Both Nixon and Kissinger had of course harbored serious doubts about the strategic merits of Vietnamization from the outset, but this latest setback removed any lingering uncertainty. With congressional opposition effectively foreclosing the possibility of further escalatory steps involving U.S. forces, the president's conclusion was simple: "we've been heroes long enough." Unable to "jolt" Hanoi through increased military pressure, and with South Vietnamese forces incapable of picking up the strain, the president weighed a new approach to the war. "If they're not up to it," he concluded, "we're going to get the hell out and hope and pray that nothing happens before 1972." Why this timing? "Above all," explained Kissinger, "your re-election is really important." Nixon agreed, adding, "if my re-election is important, let's remember, I've got to get this off our plate."[41]

Indeed, the failure of the Laos campaign was significant not only because it demonstrated the hollowness of Vietnamization as a strategic concept, but also because of the political fallout. Whereas Nixon's "silent majority" speech had successfully framed the antiwar movement as a fringe position back in November 1969, the president's optimistic spin in public could only do so much to offset the souring of wider public attitudes toward a war that seemed far from over. "The people are sick of it," lamented Nixon, in a telling conversation with Kissinger in April 1971. Reciting the polling history of the operation apparently from memory, the president complained that his various efforts at damage limitation still left him ten points down. "Everything has to be played in terms of how we survive," he therefore instructed Kissinger.[42] If there was a precise period in which the balance between strategic and electoral preferences shifted decisively in favor of the latter, the spring of 1971 was very likely it.

Kissinger had just the plan to meet the president's revised preferences. In the ensuing months, Kissinger would try to reach a deal with Hanoi that traded a cease-fire and the release of American POWs for an American unilateral withdrawal timed to keep South Vietnam on life support through 1972. He had in fact been thinking along these lines pretty much ever since the midterms. According to Haldeman's December 1970 account, the national security advisor was wary of the president's initial inclination to make a speech in April 1971 in which he would effectively declare victory and bring all U.S. troops home: "He thinks that any pullout next year would be a serious mistake because the adverse reaction to it could set in well before the '72 elections. He favors, instead, a continued winding down and then a pullout right at the fall of '72, so that if any bad results follow they will be too late to affect the election."[43] Kissinger had also already hinted to Hanoi at the formula that might be employed to achieve his preferred outcome. To North Vietnamese negotiators in September 1970, he hypothesized that "if we withdraw our troops unconditionally and quickly what happens in

Saigon is *your* problem."[44] To Dobrynin in January 1971 he was more explicit, suggesting that, as U.S. troops left, "the North Vietnamese should undertake to respect a ceasefire during the U.S. withdrawal plus a certain period of time, not too long, after the U.S. withdrawal," and "if thereafter, war breaks out again between North and South Vietnam, that conflict will no longer be an American affair."[45]

This, in effect, was the "decent interval" strategy, whereby the United States would agree to withdraw unilaterally in return for a promise from Hanoi not to overrun South Vietnam until a sufficient time after the 1972 U.S. election. This would enable Nixon to declare he had won "peace with honor," guaranteeing his election, and make plausible the claim that Saigon's inevitable fall did not occur on his watch. In the wake of the Laotian operation, the president was eager to put the Vietnam war in the rearview mirror, relishing the day when he could "announce the whole damn thing. And that's that. And then the war's dead as an issue. [Snaps his fingers.] Like that. Out!"[46] Kissinger felt similarly, but again reminded the president of the need to factor in the decent interval part of the plan too, because "if we get out after all the suffering we've gone through . . . we can't have it knocked over, brutally—to put it brutally—before the election." Nixon agreed, "That's why this strategy works pretty well, doesn't it?"[47]

A month after these discussions, the "decent interval" was made a realistic prospect by Kissinger in the ongoing peace talks in Paris. Dropping his long-held demand for mutual withdrawal, Kissinger effectively signaled that the United States would unilaterally withdraw. In return, a cease-fire-in-place, which allowed Vietcong forces to remain in South Vietnam, would simply mortgage Saigon's future for a short-term truce.[48] "That's important, because we don't want South Vietnam to fall," Nixon clarified in a briefing with Kissinger two days prior. At least not before November, anyway, since "our major goal is to get our ground forces the hell out of there long before the elections." Kissinger then clarified the purpose of the deal:

KISSINGER: So we get through '72. I'm being perfectly cynical about this, Mr. President.

NIXON: Christ, yes.

KISSINGER: If we can, in October '72, go around the country saying, "We ended the war and the Democrats wanted to turn it over to the Communists"—

NIXON: That's right.

KISSINGER: —then we're in great shape.

After the election, Saigon's survival was less critical:

KISSINGER: If it's got to go to the Communists, it'd be better to have it happen in the first six months of the new term than have it go on and on.[49]

This is not merely straw-in-the-wind evidence. The desire to craft a settlement that minimized any negative electoral fallout featured prominently in many other private discussions during this period.[50] Throughout these conversations, there is precious little mention of the need to guarantee the survival of President Thieu in Saigon's government, which Nixon later claimed, and which Kissinger still maintains to this day, was a red line.[51] In fact, the president explicitly dismissed the fate of the South Vietnamese president as a valid concern. "Without question we are gonna get out—cut off this fucker," he told Kissinger, reminding his top national security aide that "everything is domestic politics from now on."[52] As such, Nixon insisted that Kissinger needed only "get them to consider a POW/ceasefire/withdrawal agreement. That's all. Those three things."[53] Nor was there meaningful mention by Kissinger of his previously held and publicly declared beliefs about the deep flaws of a cease-fire-in-place, other than the frank acknowledgement, shared by the president, that it would be difficult to enforce any condition that prohibited the continued infiltration of outside forces across the border.[54]

Kissinger went on to broach the subject formally with Beijing and Moscow. According to minutes of Kissinger's July 1971 meetings with Chinese premier Zhou Enlai, the May 31 "POW/ceasefire/withdrawal" deal was outlined and guarantees given that the United States would not re-intervene should the South Vietnamese regime be toppled after a certain "transition period." "If it is overthrown after we withdraw," Kissinger promised, "we will not intervene."[55] Kissinger's handwritten comments on his briefing document read, "We want a decent interval. You have our assurance."[56] Though Kissinger has since distanced himself from supposedly inconsequential scribbles, his former advisor, John Negroponte, recalls distinctly a moment after a meeting with Zhou Enlai when Kissinger leaned across the table and said, "we do not want to be reading battlefield reports in the morning after the next election."[57] The following year, Beijing passed the repeated request for a "reasonable interval" on to Hanoi.[58] In the meantime, Kissinger had also asked Soviet Foreign Minister Andrei Gromyko to lobby Hanoi, admitting, "We will not leave in such a way that a Communist victory is guaranteed. However, we are prepared to leave so that a Communist victory is not excluded."[59]

With the "decent interval" strategy now in play, Nixon and Kissinger sought to carefully calibrate a complementary troop withdrawal schedule. Being able to declare "peace with honor" necessitated a domestic signal of total disengagement by November 1972. Since total withdrawal also spelled doom for South Vietnam, it could not occur too early for fear that Saigon's collapse would occur too close to the election. The net result was a series of staggered drawdowns. Three announcements between April 1971 and January 1972 saw troop numbers incrementally drop to 69,000 by May 1972. Though he publicly stated that AVRN improvements made these drawdowns viable, privately Nixon knew the opposite was true. Indeed, as mentioned above, he concluded that the South Vietnamese forces were not up to scratch as early as March 1971, after the botched invasion of Laos, which itself was, according to the second-in-command in Vietnam, an "unmitigated disaster" motivated by Nixon's desire to give superficial credibility to the "Vietnamization" plan and was questioned even by the South Vietnamese.[60] Indeed, the former commander of U.S. forces in Vietnam and chief of staff of the army under Nixon, General Westmoreland, was clear on this point. "They withdrew on a straight-line basis, regardless of the justification. I mean it was just a withdrawal, a planned withdrawal regardless of other factors. It was all tied into the forthcoming elections. In other words, over a 4-year period they were going 'to get the hell out of there.' It was just that simple." For Westmoreland, "it was all politics."[61]

And of course, Nixon said as much in his own words. As he weighed a further withdrawal in the spring of 1972, the president made clear that any announcement had to come before the Democratic National Convention, when his political opponents would try to make an issue of Vietnam. "We mustn't give them that issue," he told Kissinger. "We've got to defuse it to the point where it's a nothing issue politically." As for the exact numbers of any redeployment, added Kissinger, "the only thing we have to balance is not to let the thing unravel before November." The president agreed. "Nothing is to be done at the cost of unraveling," he confirmed, before returning to the importance of depriving antiwar candidates of political capital. "We must not look at the merits," he concluded, "we must look to the politics of it."[62]

In effect, Nixon's electorally timed withdrawal schedule gave a steadily deflating life buoy to a drowning man. Saigon's long-term future was mortgaged to the short-term goal of Nixon's reelection, as the president sought to delay South Vietnam's expected fall. Alexander Butterfield, his deputy assistant, acknowledges this, recalling rumors "that we were biding our time to end the war the last week before the election or two weeks before the election . . . Yeah, we were aware that that was the case. It *was* the case . . . and as we dragged our heels on this thing, more and more people were being killed. Needlessly, you could say."[63]

While the precise timing of Nixon's strategy would be the matter of further debate throughout 1972, as explored below, the evidence presented here demonstrates that already by early 1971, Nixon's decision making on Vietnam had become driven almost entirely by his electoral preference. This clearly supports this study's claim that electoral politics do not only matter in an election year. Further, it offers a powerful example of a case when the balancing process between strategic and electoral preferences yields no satisfactory course of action, forcing the president to choose between incompatible priorities. In Nixon's case, he chose to sacrifice the future of South Vietnam at the altar of electoral expediency.

"Playing a Much Bigger Game": Nixon's Response to the Easter Offensive

By the spring of 1972, all the elements of Nixon's revised strategy were in place. However, as was so often the case in each of the wars examined in this book, there was only so much the U.S. president could do to orchestrate events to fully suit his preferred timetable. When Hanoi mounted an all-out offensive aiming to deliver a decisive blow to South Vietnamese forces and force a final withdrawal of U.S. troops, Nixon's "decent interval" strategy was placed in jeopardy. In going for broke, the North Vietnamese Politburo had apparently counted on Nixon being relatively restrained in his response to the attack, bound by election-year pressures in much the same way his predecessor had been.[64] Yet, as they would soon find out, electoral constraints do not operate in a uniformly pacific manner. Calculating that his political interests were best served by dialing up the aggressiveness of the military response, Nixon authorized a massive bombing and mining campaign over Hanoi and Haiphong, in an action illustrative of the *spur* mechanism.

Nixon's response to the North Vietnamese assault was not entirely without strategic logic. On a basic level, the Easter Offensive posed a serious threat and required a firm response. "All the chips are on the line," Nixon would comment privately. "They weren't in Cambodia, and they weren't in Laos . . . Now it's win or lose."[65] The campaign Nixon ordered to address this threat began as an interdiction exercise, designed to cut off lines of communication and supplies running across the border. It developed into a strategic bombing campaign, focusing on critical infrastructure targets in the North. On both counts, U.S. forces exacted a heavy toll on the enemy. By early July, some 7,600 air attacks had been carried out over the North Vietnamese panhandle, while the destruction of 125 rail bridges and 270 highway bridges seriously disrupted the movement of supplies. Naval traffic entering and leaving Haiphong Harbor was stopped altogether after 11,603 mines were laid in North Vietnamese coastal waters and ports. The North's industrial base, meanwhile, was virtually eliminated, with 70 percent of its electrical capacity wiped out in the first two months of bombing alone.[66] Perhaps even more than its military value, Nixon valued the psychological shock that the use of B-52 bombers would inflict. By signaling to Hanoi and its allies just how far he was willing to go in defending South Vietnam, he hoped to use the attacks to coerce them into concessions.

The military power Nixon committed in these operations did not constitute an entirely effective solution to the precise challenge posed by the Easter Offensive, however. To be sure, a large-scale air offensive in the North might have been useful in blunting the earlier buildup of enemy forces prior to the assault beginning. Indeed, General Creighton Abrams had requested authority to do just that in March, only for his proposals to be watered down considerably by officials more concerned about the impact of such a move on the fledgling diplomatic rapprochement with Beijing then underway.[67] By April, however, the military situation had been transformed. As General Abrams repeatedly insisted, the immediate danger now lay in the fact that almost the entire complement of North Vietnam's fourteen active army divisions were already operating across the border. Cutting supply lines might have a useful downstream effect if the South survived the assault, but that situation remained hypothetical unless airpower could first be directed toward targets of more pressing significance below the border. Abrams would later complain bitterly that Nixon sent the B-52s "away hunting rabbits while the backyard filled with lions."[68] And he was not alone in his opposition. "Raids could have some impact on operations a few months hence," argued Winston Lord, a member of Kissinger's NSC staff, in a memorandum of May 1, "but they take away assets from more urgent and lucrative targets in the battle zone."[69] The secretary of defense agreed, insisting that the battle in South Vietnam would be decided on the ground, after telling Kissinger that sending more B-52s in theater was "just crazy."[70] The CIA director, meanwhile, presciently argued that Hanoi would simply circumvent any blockade created by naval mining by reorienting its logistics from ships to railroad from China.[71]

In explaining both the character and intensity of Nixon's response to the Easter Offensive, it pays to examine some of his first reactions as he realized the full scale of the North Vietnamese attack on April 3:

KISSINGER: If the ARVN collapses, we've done everything we can, Mr. President—

NIXON: We lose if the ARVN collapses. Don't say—that's just a, that's a—that's a question that we can't even think about. If the ARVN collapses a lot of other things will collapse around here. If they were going to collapse, they had to do it a year ago. We can't do it this year, Henry.

KISSINGER: Right. They're not going to collapse. I know—

NIXON: You see what I mean? We can't take it.

KISSINGER: I agree. That's why we've got to blast—

NIXON: That's right.

KISSINGER: —the living bejeezus out of North Vietnam. We will gain nothing for restraint . . .

NIXON: Like I say, let's don't talk about, "Well, if the ARVN collapses we've done everything we can." Yeah, that's fine with regard to this, but we're playing a much bigger game. We're playing a Russian game, a Chinese game, an election game.[72]

At some level, of course, this conversation indicates yet again that Nixon was not concerned about the long-term future of South Vietnam per se. As he would remind Kissinger three days before authorizing the Operation Linebacker raids in early May, so long as there was a "decent interval," he could live with the South's potential collapse. "If we could survive past the election, Henry, and then Vietnam goes down the tubes, it really doesn't make any difference."[73] Nixon's instincts were to hit back hard in response to the Easter Offensive to keep Saigon afloat, but he was under no illusions that such measures would provide only temporary relief. "In terms of domestic public opinion," he told Kissinger, "the most important thing is when they are kicking us we have got to be kicking them or we look bad."[74]

The conversation also underscores the reality that, in making decisions about Vietnam, the president's menu of considerations went well beyond those of the commanders on the battlefield.[75] Indeed, Nixon's policy choices in Vietnam must properly be viewed in an international context, as one piece in a broader jigsaw and therefore inseparable from parallel efforts to achieve détente with Moscow and Beijing. Each action was a "carrot" or "stick" designed to send a message to the Communist superpowers, as Vietnam became a chip in Kissinger's "linkage" politics. This dynamic was clear in Nixon's early attempts to pressure the Soviets into using their perceived influence over Hanoi in 1969. It was implicit, too, in Kissinger's enlisting of both Moscow and Beijing as intermediaries in his secret talks. And as the Easter Offensive wore on, so it became increasingly clear that Nixon's choice of response had significant implications for his ability to strike a range of diplomatic agreements with the Soviets. The most notable potential casualty of any heavy military response was the upcoming summit in Moscow, at which Nixon hoped to finalize the Strategic Arms Limitation Treaty. The prospect of losing the summit was a source of severe political anxiety for Nixon, rekindling dark memories from 1960, when Nikita Khrushchev's cancellation of a summit with Eisenhower had cast a shadow over Nixon's first presidential bid. "If the Russians cancel the summit," he warned Kissinger in mid-April, "we are virtually assuring the certainty of a Democratic win."[76]

That Nixon went ahead with the aerial bombardment of North Vietnam anyway demonstrated that in his hierarchy of perceived electoral risks, the prospect of Saigon collapsing ranked higher than the cancellation of the summit. He was in fact quite transparent on this point. "We won't lose the country if we lose the Summit meeting," he explained, "but we will lose the country if we lose the war."[77] In coming to this revised conclusion, he was apparently convinced by the counsel of John Connally, whom Kissinger later described as "the Cabinet officer generally believed to have the best political brain in the Administration."[78] Having spent several weeks toying with the idea of preemptively cancelling the summit to avoid the humiliation of having the Soviets take the initiative, Nixon lauded Connally's "animal-like decisiveness," in a taped conversation with Kissinger on May 5. "If you're going to put first things first," the president said Connally had told him, "you've got to remember: you can do without the summit, but you cannot live with defeat in Vietnam." With it far from certain that the Soviets would in fact cancel, Nixon was convinced that demonstrating strength in Vietnam was the greater priority. "Everything's got to be measured against what wins or loses in Vietnam," he concluded.[79] When he addressed a final NSC meeting called to debate the proposed operations in Hanoi and Haiphong, Nixon's mind was made up. "If South Vietnam goes, as far as the political situation is concerned we are done. What is on the line is an election."[80]

Contrary to Hanoi's belief that Nixon would be measured in his response to the Easter Offensive, the aggressive character of the operation the president authorized on May 8 had in fact been poll tested. Sitting in the president's desk was a 1969 poll commissioned by the Republican National Committee reporting that 66 percent of Americans favored an end to the war brought about by a six-month bombing and blockade campaign of the North's harbors.[81] As Nixon weighed his options, he gleefully reported to Kissinger that "this gives us one hell of an opportunity, an opportunity to really clobber them, something we've been wanting to do . . . and now, by God, they have walked into it."[82] As plans dating back to the aborted Duck Hook operation were dusted off in early April, Nixon told Kissinger that "we must right now do things there for public opinion. It will be there, if we act strongly."[83] The next day he concluded, "the main thing is to rally our people."[84] As planning crystallized around bombing and mining operations over Hanoi and Haiphong, Nixon repeatedly requested that Haldeman run further surveys to check how the public would respond to the various measures under consideration.[85] And when Kissinger suggested postponing bombing raids, Nixon refused, insisting that "we'll lose public opinion if we delay the raids: it's the raids that they want, not the talks."[86] Indeed, the exact timing of the operation was wholly bound up with similar considerations. Not wanting to strike too close to the Moscow summit or in the lead-up to the Democratic National Convention in June, and expecting a loss of congressional and public support thereafter, the time for action was now. "Unless we hit the Hanoi-Haiphong complex this weekend, we probably are not going to be able to hit it at all before the election," Nixon wrote in an April 30 memorandum to

Kissinger.[87] As the most authoritative account of this period concludes, "the timing of the conventions and the electoral campaign imposed urgency on aggressive action that might not otherwise have existed."[88]

Throughout this episode, it was not the case that Nixon was particularly optimistic about the military utility of bombing the North. Handwritten comments on a January 1972 memorandum from Kissinger, found recently among boxes of papers taken home by Butterfield, reveal the president's thoughts on the matter: "We have had 10 years of *total* control of the air in Laos and V.Nam. The result=Zilch."[89] Even as Nixon was personally directing the military to flood the theater of operations with B-52 bombers, he expressed his "grave doubts" about the utility of airpower to a close aide.[90] Yet Nixon repeatedly insisted that bombing levels be increased, not because his advisors felt it militarily necessary, but "for American public opinion."[91] Bombing, explains Butterfield, "had been, over the years, ineffective . . . There was never any great breakthrough or victory and the bombing was not helping and certainly didn't ever stem the tide of things coming down the Ho Chi Minh trail. And what does he do? He doubles down." Asked why Nixon ignored the advice of much of his national security team, or indeed his own intuition, Butterfield is clear: "No, the only thing that affected him, really, was the popularity polls. You know, he was thinking of the election."[92]

Nixon's political instincts were right. While criticism from Congress and in the media was fierce, polls reported that 59 percent of the public approved of the mining of North Vietnamese harbors.[93] Though CIA estimates calculated that Hanoi could still generate a surplus of war supplies for another two years if the U.S. bombing levels were maintained, the destruction wrought by the aerial assault, combined with Abrams's efforts in the South, enabled Nixon to successfully repel the Easter Offensive.[94] And in doing so in the brutal way that he did, his electoral gamble paid off. While riding high in the polls in mid-October, Kissinger congratulated him for the action: "I think you won the election on May 8th."[95]

Déjà vu? Politics and the Paris Peace Talks

This electoral period also contains a prime example of the *spoiler* mechanism, where the president's diplomatic strategy and leverage in negotiations were affected by electoral considerations. We can distill the complex negotiations in Paris into three such calculations.

First, until October 1972, Nixon figured a better deal might be possible *after* the election. A diary entry reveals his logic:

> I am inclined to think that the better bargaining time for us would be immediately after the election rather than before. Before the election the enemy can still figure there is an outside chance their man [George McGovern] can win or at least that he could come closer and that we, therefore, would be under pressure to have a settlement.
>
> Immediately after the election we will have an enormous mandate, we hope, for bringing the war to a successful conclusion, and the enemy then either has to settle or face the consequences of what we could do to them.[96]

Just as important was Nixon's calculation that he did not *need* a deal before the election. Enjoying a large polling lead over his opponent going into the final stretch of the campaign, the president had apparently succeeded in convincing the electorate that "peace with honor" was nigh. "We don't need it. We're going to win without it, and very heavily," he confidently told Kissinger.[97] The net effect of Nixon's reasoning was that he instructed Kissinger in August in effect to "sit tight" in Paris, refuse to grant further concessions, and generally "put the whole negotiating process on ice until after the election."[98] A series of meetings in Paris beginning in June 1972 did indeed result in successive impasses.

The second key calculation was Hanoi's. In autumn, their chief negotiators requested permission from the Politburo to take a "reasonable position" in Paris, owing to their judgment that "we should not pin too much hope on McGovern," who was offering much softer terms than Nixon, but also hopelessly lagging in the polls.[99] Hanoi agreed, having gauged Nixon's game plan with remarkable accuracy: "We should endeavor to end the war before the U.S. election, to foil Nixon's scheme to prolong the negotiations and to win the election, to continue Vietnamization, and to negotiate from a position of strength."[100]

Losing faith in McGovern, just as they did with Humphrey in 1968, Hanoi apparently made a tactical decision to capitulate in Paris, agreeing to a cease-fire and cessation of further infiltration of the South in return for a U.S. withdrawal, while dropping demands for a change of administration in

Saigon. As Kissinger recalled, this was in essence "the basic program we had offered and insisted was essential since May 1971."[101] Aware of the American desire for a "decent interval," the North Vietnamese were comfortable with a deal to get the Americans out for now, confident "that after some time the hostilities will resume" and they could achieve their war aims without American intervention.[102] "They wanted to give us something in October," recalls Negroponte wryly, who was by that point the Vietnam director on Kissinger's NSC and a leading member of the U.S. delegation, "and it's an interesting coincidence, coming in the context of our upcoming elections."[103] Indeed, in his recollection, the North Vietnamese lead negotiator, Le Duc Tho, matter-of-factly came to the October meeting, following four years of deadlock, and "with our election obviously in mind" handed over the terms they knew would appeal, adding, "You are in a hurry aren't you . . . If you are, here it is."[104]

The third critical electoral calculation came after South Vietnam signaled great discomfort with the deal brokered in Paris, before rejecting it altogether on October 22, in a rerun of 1968. This altered Nixon's calculus. Though he still did not *need* a preelection deal for his own political benefit, he did not want to take a PR hit should Hanoi go public with the fact that he was wriggling away from conditions he had offered. More fundamentally, he could not afford a public fallout with Saigon. He and advisors like Alexander Haig, the deputy national security advisor, now feared that a preelection settlement with a resistant Thieu was "going to be messy," and in electoral terms "it couldn't help, it could only hurt."[105] In practical terms, the policy outcome of these considerations was that successive envoys would be sent to Thieu, armed with the deal and letters from Nixon, to "cram it down his throat."[106] Failing that, Nixon ordered Kissinger to continue to stall in Paris, hoping that the inevitable break with Saigon could come after his victory was assured. "The real basic problem," recalled Haldeman, summarizing a conversation with the president on October 12, "boils down to the question of whether Thieu can be sold on it . . . and if he doesn't buy it, there's no option but to flush him, because we can't turn down the offer . . . It's too good to turn down and get away with it in this country, because they'd release it."[107] Or, in Nixon's words, "the more we can stagger past the election the better. I don't want it before the election with a Thieu blowup. It's going to hurt us very badly."[108] As Negroponte recalls, Nixon then sent instructions to Kissinger to avoid traveling to Hanoi to wrap up the deal without Saigon's blessing, as he had been planning: "Nixon said no, you better come home. You can't go on to Hanoi now. We can't be seen to be jamming Thieu just before our election because it'll be interpreted as us sacrificing Saigon in order to get elected."[109] This, of course, was precisely what Nixon had been doing for two years with his broader strategy, but the repercussions of that becoming public knowledge now would be far too damaging.

The unspoken reality contained in this calculation, which made a consensual agreement with Thieu impossible, was what Haig later called the "self-evident truth that Thieu's regime could not survive" under the terms of the deal, which left hundreds of thousands of Communist troops in the South.[110] Kissinger recounted Thieu's opposition to Nixon, saying, "these proposals keep him going, but somewhere down the road he'll have no choice except to commit suicide. And he's probably right . . . our terms will eventually destroy him." This much Nixon knew; the May 31 terms, upon which the October deal was based, was designed to secure a "decent interval," *not* South Vietnam's future. Indeed, when Kissinger predicted that South Vietnam would likely collapse after a full U.S. withdrawal even with six months of additional military support, Nixon was unfazed. "Well, if they're that collapsible, maybe they just have to be collapsed," he concluded. "We've got to remember, we cannot keep this child sucking at the tit when the child is four years old."[111] A few weeks later, he spoke with similar frankness. "We don't care about Thieu," he said on October 27, "nobody cares about that."[112] Indeed, by this point Kissinger was openly considering a bilateral agreement with Hanoi.[113] The sticking point, as ever, was timing. The deal that Nixon had successfully crafted to get him reelected was so obviously rotten for Saigon that he needed to push it beyond Election Day before abandoning Thieu. Kissinger tactfully manufactured several scheduling delays to bring the required deferment about.[114]

The progress of the talks in Paris through 1972 was driven to a significant degree by the electoral environment in the United States, then. On seemingly all sides—Washington, Hanoi, and Saigon—negotiating positions were altered in light of the expected outcome of the presidential election, with the net effect being a continued impasse on the eve of Election Day, consistent with the *spoiler* mechanism.

"School's Out": Operation Linebacker II

Just over two months after the election, the Paris Peace Accords would be signed, but not before Nixon had chance to reprise his "madman" strategy of intense military pressure, unleashing a fierce final bombing campaign over North Vietnam, which had been explicitly delayed until the president found himself free of the electoral constraints that otherwise inhibited such escalation.

That Nixon both intended to launch such an operation and deferred it for electoral reasons is straightforward to demonstrate. Nixon said as much on a number of occasions. As early as a whole year before the presidential election, it was on his mind: "If we win the election, the day after, we say, 'All right, we give you 30 days.' . . . I really would. I'd finish off the goddamn place. Bomb Haiphong. You know, the whole thing. I would put a crippling blow on it. Go on for 60 days of bombing. Just knock the shit out of them."[115] The thought remained with him through August of 1972: "If we win, after November 7, school's out . . . We're going to take out the heart of the installations in Hanoi. We're going to take out the whole goddamn dock area, ships or no ships."[116] That such a course of action would be electorally unpalatable was self-evident, after years of growing disillusionment with the war. Unlike the spring bombing raids, this would be a belligerent strategy launched without major military provocation, which even the "silent majority" would surely find hard to stomach. Indeed, on the eve of the election, Kissinger had declared in a press conference that "peace is at hand," raising expectations of a deal, not a renewed aerial assault.

Yet Nixon deemed it the best way to convince Hanoi to finally accede to the terms on the table. Though these terms were essentially the same as those previously agreed, there was some need to convince Hanoi to accept a series of additional amendments that had been designed to reassure President Thieu in the South. Safely reelected in a historic landslide—losing only one state in the 1972 election—Nixon was now newly released from electoral constraints. Apparently buoyed by this position, he unleashed twenty thousand tons of bombs on Hanoi to bring them around. "Well, the election is over," he reasoned, "[so] we must not stop bombing the North until we get a settlement." Repeatedly he intervened in military operations to ensure they were sufficiently strong, at one point fuming that he had been unable to get the message through the JCS chairman's "goddamn thick head" after he had presented him "some half-assed little thing."[117]

Critics have understandably characterized this campaign as nothing more than an attempt to improve the optics of the "decent interval" plan, making it appear more like a military victory by distracting the public from the hollowness of the agreement.[118] This bombing campaign would simply be the way to retain American "honor." Kissinger reassured Nixon that he had a mandate to do this: "they didn't vote for you as a bleeding heart."[119] For Negroponte, it was reflective of Nixon's desire to get Vietnam off his plate as he began his second term: "he was fed up, didn't want to have anything more to do with this damn war, and sort of said, 'Let's get it over with before the second inauguration.' "[120] Whatever the real reason, it seems quite clear that this final military episode in the war was profoundly shaped by the *delay* mechanism, whereby Nixon's strategic preference for escalation, barbaric and bloody as it was, had been rendered politically unacceptable until after his reelection.

*   *   *

The evidence presented in this chapter offers strong support for the electoral framework laid out in chapter 1. In the opening stages of his first term, Nixon sought to force Hanoi into meaningful concessions at the negotiating table through the application of increased military pressure, tempered in form and intensity by the legacy of antiwar sentiment that he had inherited from his predecessor. After the midterms, a changed evaluation of the strategic realities on the battlefield and the looming prospect of his reelection campaign forced the president to look to alternative strategies for achieving an outcome he could credibly describe as "peace with honor." After settling on a plan to secure only a "decent interval" before Saigon's expected defeat, electoral political considerations took on seismic importance in the decision-making process. Nixon's response to the Easter Offensive of 1972 was at least consistent with this approach, and in its aggressive character bore many of the hallmarks of the *spur* mechanism. The negotiations through to Election Day 1972, meanwhile, were dominated by calculations representative of the *spoiler* mechanism. Once reelected, Nixon used his electoral mandate to reprise his early escalatory strategy and finally settle on terms that had been available prior to unleashing this final rally of intense bombing raids.

Absent the election process, would things have followed the same course? While the strategic viability of "Vietnamization" remains a matter of scholarly debate, it seems unlikely that Nixon would have embraced it in the first place.[121] While Nixon periodically expressed hopes that the South Vietnamese would pick up the burden of fighting, he had been quite transparent with advisors about the domestic political ends to which the troop withdrawal program was principally directed. Recall his aforementioned comments in the crucial NSC meeting of March 28, 1969, in which the term "Vietnamization" was coined: "We need a plan. If we had no elections, it would be fine . . . The reality is that we are working against a time clock."[122] In the counterfactual scenario he envisaged, logically there would be no need for such a plan at all. Instead, it seems reasonable to speculate that Nixon would have continued to prosecute the war in line with his strategic preference, relying on a course of escalation designed to force Hanoi into concessions at the negotiating table.

Whether or not this alternative—a more sustained level of military pressure *without* corollary troop withdrawals—would have led to the kind of result Nixon anticipated is, of course, up for debate. Officials in Hanoi rarely displayed any desire to offer meaningful concessions in the ongoing talks. What can be said with a degree of certainty, however, is that it would at least have made Kissinger's task in Paris easier. In comments made at the time and since, the national security advisor was essentially correct to note that the unilateral withdrawal of troops embodied in Nixon's "Vietnamization" policy severely undercut his bargaining leverage in Paris. Pleading with the president in a memorandum of early 1969, he wrote that the presence of U.S. troops was "our main asset," and that "Hanoi has no hope of attaining its objective of controlling the South unless it can get us to withdraw our forces."[123] He later recalled that with every successive withdrawal announcement, the administration risked "throwing away our position in a series of unreciprocated concessions."[124] This was perfectly reasonable. It was implausible to think that any rational adversary would agree to reciprocal troop withdrawals, on which Kissinger had for years been insisting, while the United States continued to embark on what appeared to be an irreversible and wholly unilateral program of reductions. While there was no guarantee that the continued presence of U.S. forces would induce concessions in Paris, the politically motivated drawdown plans undoubtedly robbed Kissinger of significant leverage to seriously test that proposition.[125]

Furthermore, if increased military pressure ultimately still failed to break Hanoi's intransigence, an absence of electoral constraints would have made it more likely that Nixon may have called time on the American misadventure in Southeast Asia altogether. After all, he had at least toyed with a "bugout" option in spring 1971, after the failure of the Laos operation. By that time, Nixon's interest in the war had undoubtedly sapped, as he sought to devote more time and energy to what he saw as the bigger prize of resetting relations with the Soviet Union and China. Indeed, the main reason he did not announce a full U.S. withdrawal at that time was because Kissinger managed to convince him of the damage it would do to his electoral prospects. If Nixon did not have to fear for his political future, he could arguably have accepted this public policy failure. He did, after all, sign a deal that broadly reflected terms he had offered in May 1971. Most historians have argued that the eventual settlement of the war was not substantially different from what Nixon might have achieved had he agreed to a negotiated withdrawal upon taking office.[126] A little spin from Haldeman's PR team would have enabled him to overcome concerns about American credibility at a time when even the most ardent hawks were losing enthusiasm for such arguments.[127] Strikingly, Nixon privately expressed such a line of thought. As late as October 1969, he remarked in a meeting that "it would have been a popular move for him to say on the day that he came in, or even nine months later, that the Vietnam situation had been badly mismanaged by the previous Administration, and that while we had tried to handle it, it was such a mess that we felt we had to get out. The people would have been relieved."[128]

Of course, if Nixon had announced this option even in the spring of 1971, the Easter Offensive would surely not have occurred; Hanoi could have simply waited until the Americans left before moving in. Even if it did, Nixon's response might have been different. With no need to dial up the aggressiveness of the bombing "for public opinion," it is likely Nixon would have gone with the broad consensus of his national security team; airpower resources would be sent to support the counteroffensive in the South, rather than diverted North for bombing raids that Nixon perceived to be ineffective. If the war still had not ended by October, Nixon would surely have taken a deal after Hanoi acceded to terms. The only reason he did not was because of the electoral consequences of "flushing" Thieu. Absent an election, those concerns would again disappear. In short, without electoral constraints, U.S.

involvement in Vietnam could have ended on at least two earlier occasions, and thousands of civilians in Hanoi and Haiphong would have been spared.

On signing the accords on January 27, 1973, Kissinger was jubilant, telling the president that "it's the greatest diplomatic feat . . . in American history." "Well," replied Nixon, "we'll see how long it works." The answer? Eight hundred and twenty-three days. The "decent interval" having lapsed, on April 30, 1975, North Vietnamese troops overran Saigon, storming the U.S. embassy and bringing America's long entanglement in Vietnam to an ignoble end.

FIVE

Iraq

George W. Bush and the Decision to Double Down

A U.S. president must face public opinion and the consequences that come
with elections. . . . These were practical checks we all needed to keep in
mind.

—DONALD RUMSFELD

GEORGE W. BUSH was an unlikely wartime president. By most accounts,
he had little interest in foreign policy, and even less expertise. "I don't have
any idea about foreign affairs," he once admitted to Condoleezza Rice in the
lead-up to his first campaign.[1] Running instead on a platform to reduce the
size of the federal government, Bush rarely spoke of foreign lands or leaders whose names he notoriously found difficult to pronounce. To the extent
that he did signal any strong preference when it came to foreign policy, it
boiled down to an aversion to "nation building," reacting to the perceived
excesses of President Bill Clinton's interventions in Somalia and Haiti.
"If we don't stop extending our troops all around the world, and nation-
building missions, then we're going to have a serious problem coming down
the road," Bush explained in one 2000 campaign debate. He made his views
clear: "I'm going to prevent that."[2]

The events of September 11, 2001, changed all this. "You can't understand
anything about Iraq without understanding 9/11. That was Bush's presidential moment," says James Jeffrey, a career diplomat who would play a leading role in shaping strategy in Iraq. Indeed, the terror attacks fundamentally shifted the threat perception of the Bush administration, setting it on
a collision course with Saddam Hussein's Iraq. After first intervening in
Afghanistan, a long-standing desire for regime change in Iraq acquired
greater urgency and was subsumed into the broader project of the global war

on terror. "It was the soul of his presidency," as Jeffrey puts it, "a transcendental project to change the nature of a Middle East that had produced 9/11."[3]

The origins and legacy of the decision to invade Iraq in 2003 continue to attract the lion's share of scholarly attention about the war.[4] This chapter, however, focuses instead on the aftermath of the invasion, and especially the subsequent escalation of the conflict.[5] First, it assesses the electoral dynamics of the bloodiest operation of the entire war—the on-again, off-again attempts to secure the city of Fallujah in 2004. Second, it examines the development and implementation of the surge, arguably the biggest strategic shift of the war, whereby almost thirty thousand additional troops were sent to Iraq under a new, population-centric counterinsurgency strategy. While Bush's commitment to the conflict in Iraq was clear throughout, it does not sufficiently explain the character of his administration's intervention into operational matters in 2004, nor does it fully explain the nature or timing of his decision to double down in 2007. Instead, it is shown here that President Bush's decision making during these critical episodes was profoundly conditioned by the constraints of the electoral cycle.

Taking Fallujah

In March 2004, gruesome images of the charred bodies of four private military contractors who had been ambushed by Iraqi insurgents in Fallujah sparked outrage and a thirst for revenge in the White House. Conscious of the explosive optics of the attack in an election year, President Bush ordered an immediate assault on the city. "Kick ass!" he instructed Lieutenant General Ricardo Sanchez, the top commander in Iraq.[6] Yet, when it became clear that the military solution might turn out to be politically counterproductive, both in terms of incurring significant casualties and in threatening an all-important timetable for the transfer of sovereignty, the administration suddenly called a halt to the operation. What followed was a protracted period of inaction in dealing with a growing hotbed of violence. The Second Battle of Fallujah, which would turn out to be the bloodiest battle of the entire war, would only take place in November, just days after the U.S. presidential election. Taken together, the on-again, off-again nature of decision making concerning the Fallujah operation, and the White House's interest in it, reveal compelling evidence of the *delay* mechanism in practice.[7]

The First Battle: Transferring Sovereignty Under Fire

The need to take action to clear the city of Fallujah of insurgents was widely appreciated by the spring of 2004. "Security in Fallujah was steadily going to hell," recalled L. Paul "Jerry" Bremer, who served as the top civilian administrator in Iraq at the time. Having been underwhelmed by the 82nd Airborne's attempts to establish security in Anbar Province, Bremer remembers taking his concerns to Sanchez. "The situation is *not* going to improve until we clean out Fallujah," he stated flatly.[8] Though the pair saw eye-to-eye on very little, Sanchez agreed that the contractor incident had generated a "consensus across the board" on the need to respond forcefully. While he suspected that the administration's appetite stemmed from a desire to avoid appearing "weak" in an election year, Sanchez nevertheless felt that the attack had "opened up an opportunity for us to eliminate some of the threats posed by Fallujah, which had been used as an IED-production sanctuary and was a known safe haven for insurgents."[9]

It was a source of great frustration to those on the ground, then, when an order to cease offensive operations came down after just three days of fighting. As videos and pictures emerged of what local reporters portrayed as unarmed civilian casualties, the heavy fighting in Fallujah had swiftly transformed into a political liability for the administration. This was a risk that General John P. Abizaid, the commander of U.S. Central Command (CENTCOM) had essentially foreseen on the eve of the battle. "We will be the focal point for bad news in Iraq between now and November," he wrote in a summary of recent meetings he had attended in Washington issued as guidance to his staff on April 2. "We are not here to get the President re-elected or Senator Kerry elected," he emphasized, adding that a careful approach would be required to ensure "we don't inadvertently create a political dynamic."[10] Yet if Abizaid may therefore have been somewhat braced for the negative headlines coming out of Fallujah, the officers tasked with carrying out the operation were less than impressed to learn of the decision to stop the attack. To be sure, the Marines on the ground had not been enthusiastic about the knee-jerk manner in which the administration had ordered them into battle. Nevertheless, once committed, they, too, were eager to see the job through. Upon learning of the decision to suspend the operation, the division commander leading the assault—a certain Major General James Mattis—did not mince his words. "First we're ordered to attack, and now we're ordered to halt," he told Abizaid, who had flown to Iraq to deliver the news. "If you're going to take Vienna," he continued, channeling Napoleon, "take fucking Vienna."[11]

In Iraq, the blowback generated by this coverage threatened the fragile political process that had been designed to restore sovereignty to Iraqi hands. Under the terms of a compromise agreement struck on November 15, 2003, between Bremer and senior representatives on the Iraqi Governing Council—a provisional government appointed by U.S. officials during the transition period—full authority was to be handed back to Iraqis at the end of June 2004. Upon hearing news of the U.S. assault, however, Sunni representatives threatened to resign in protest over what they perceived to be collective punishment of the people of Fallujah. According to Bremer, the collapse of the Governing Council was a serious possibility. Should that happen, the United Nations might also withdraw its support, and, with the November 15 agreement already hanging by a thread, the whole endeavor could quickly fall apart. As Bremer later explained, "To lose both the Governing Council and the UN would mean losing the June 30 date, with no clear way to get a credible political process revived and no idea of how long that would require."[12] Importantly, Bremer claims that President Bush's support for his recommendation to halt the operation was driven by these concerns. In the crucial April 9 NSC meeting, the president reportedly expressed his concern "that if the political situation were to fall apart, we'd have nobody to transfer sovereignty to in June. He ended the meeting with a firm statement that we would stick to the June 30 date."[13]

To understand why this date was considered sacrosanct, however, the electoral significance of this time line must also be properly appreciated. Bremer, convinced that the establishment of effective political institutions in Iraq required considerable time to develop, favored a much slower transition process. Yet, after the publication of a seven-step program in the pages of the *Washington Post* triggered considerable anxiety around the administration, Bremer found himself under pressure to expedite the process. Around the secretary of defense, for instance, a group of current and former officials met in late September 2003 to propose an expedited time line for the transfer of sovereignty, convinced that Bush was "not going to get reelected unless we get this thing straightened out."[14] Days later, Rumsfeld encouraged Bremer to take some "interim steps" to "migrate" political authority to the Iraqis. The Pentagon chief sounded more impatient than usual. "The conflict in Iraq had come to a political boil in Washington—the presidential election was only a year off—and the Secretary of Defense was no doubt feeling the heat," surmised Bremer.[15] Elsewhere in the administration, Condoleezza Rice actually sympathized with Bremer's plan, later admitting that "it didn't seem like a bad road map for the way ahead."[16] The issue, however, was one of viability. "I don't think the political situation in Washington will support another year of the current status," she warned Bremer, urging him to consider a faster alternative. "Can we put together some kind of provisional government?"[17] Not wanting to overrule Bremer herself, Rice dispatched Robert Blackwill to try to elicit a quicker timetable and generally keep tabs on the free-wheeling administrator.

The U.S. effort to calibrate the transfer of sovereignty according to the political exigencies at home—and to ensure that military operations did not jeopardize that time line—was something of an open secret in Iraq. Sanchez later recalled that Blackwill had been quite candid in explaining that he had been dispatched both to protect the time line and to "prevent any military strikes, political activity, or comments in the press that might have a negative impact on opinion polls back in the United States." He would even at times say things like, "you can't do that, because it won't look good on CNN."[18] On the time line more specifically, Blackwill openly proposed alternative plans for the path to sovereignty with foreign allies, foreseeing a transfer by October 2004, just a month before American voters went to the polls. "He indicated that the time-line for a political transition would have to take account of the US election calendar," recalled Jeremy Greenstock, the leading British envoy in Iraq at the time. When Vice President Dick Cheney outlined a tentative proposal to transfer by October 2004, echoing what Greenstock had been hearing from Blackwill beforehand, it only reinforced the British diplomat's "sense that the American side was becoming more concerned about timing than principles." In a subsequent meeting with the U.K. foreign secretary, Condoleezza Rice outlined a further rough plan and "sought our agreement for a transfer of power to an interim Iraqi government as early as 1 July 2004 in order to move it well clear of the Presidential election campaign." As to how to elect the interim government—via caucuses or elections—there were some difficulties discussed, but "Rice's response showed that the calendar was the administration's most important concern."[19]

Taken together, it seems clear that if the transfer of sovereignty played a key role in the White House's decision making in Fallujah, the timing of that political process itself was also to a large degree a function of electoral politics. After initially supporting Bremer's view that democratic legitimacy was the priority, the White House ended up fast-forwarding the plan. In June, the Coalition Provisional Authority would dissolve and a largely dysfunctional group of appointed Iraqi politicians would take over. As Sanchez concludes,

> I realized that the decision to transfer sovereignty to Iraq by July 1, 2004, amounted to a calculated political decision. The Bush administration knew that things were going poorly in Iraq and were sure to get worse. . . . The administration knew something had to be done immediately so that the November 2004 presidential election would not be impacted. Giving Iraq sovereignty by the first of July would create the illusion that significant progress was being made. It would also provide a full four months for voters to be convinced through the media that America's mission in Iraq had been a success. If things got worse in the interim, the administration could simply blame it on the Iraqis and a bit of bumpy transitioning. The politics of a presidential year were beginning to unfold. It was all about winning the presidential election and maintaining power.[20]

"Avoid Rocking the Boat": The Second Battle of Fallujah

Despite wide awareness of the continued need to finish the job in clearing Fallujah, no renewed offensive would take place for almost seven months following the initial cessation of hostilities in April. This section presents the case for an electorally motivated *delay* mechanism having constrained the implementation of the long-awaited Second Battle of Fallujah. Specifically, in accordance with the observable implications of this mechanism, it acknowledges a perception of the need for action; the existence of a viable plan to initiate such action; evidence that the operation was deferred for electoral reasons; and the fact that the plan was implemented almost immediately after the period of electoral sensitivity.

Right from the start, even the architects of the cease-fire in Fallujah were clear-eyed about the fact that the halt was only a temporary measure. Bremer, for instance, while understanding the political necessity of halting operations in April, nonetheless admitted in a call to Condoleezza Rice on April 21 that "sooner or later, we've got to go back in there and get those guys."[21] To Blackwill he admitted, "We'll have to fight again in Fallujah."[22]

After the transfer of sovereignty took place in late June, the incoming diplomatic and military team in Iraq were even more aware of the need to act. "I didn't think that we could allow a sort of gaping wound like that in the middle of the Iraqi body politic to persist," recalls John Negroponte, the new ambassador.[23] From July, "things started getting progressively worse in Fallujah. We were getting more and more reports of sharia law, kangaroo courts, public executions, so on and so forth, and Fallujah was sort of a bomb factory. They were sending garages full of car bombs."[24]

In August, the Fallujah Brigade, an armed group notionally supportive of the coalition that had been tasked with assuming the burden of reestablishing security in the city, was deemed to have been essentially complicit in the kidnapping and murder of two Iraqis with whom the Americans had been working. With the president having been advised by the new commanding general in Iraq, General George W. Casey Jr., that some 70 percent of the brigade were now part of the resistance, the military were clear-eyed about what needed to be done. "There's only one way to disarm the Fallujah Brigade," said Mattis. "Kill it." Yet, once again, word came from higher authorities that the time was not right for precipitating a full-scale assault: "Keep the noise down," the Marines were told.[25] Mattis would later complain of the "maddening situation" in which American policy makers had left the military "playing defense" through ill-advised restrictions on "necessary tactical actions."[26]

By mid- to late August, a viable plan for the much-needed action was being finessed. It was part of a wider effort by Multi-National Force—Iraq (MNF-I) to improve security ahead of the January 2005 elections. "We became convinced that having a terrorist safe haven within 30 miles of the capital presented an unacceptable risk to the conduct of the upcoming election," recalled General Casey.[27] With the experience of the first battle in April in hand, it did not take long to tweak the plan, which aimed for the same objectives, albeit with slightly different tactics and resources applied this time around. Already in the first week of September a briefing was delivered to military figures referring to the pending task of "Fallujah Clearing Operations," and an initial concept paper was drafted the following week.[28] The available documentary record suggests that President Bush was updated on the operation and a decision briefing held on September 29, with subsequent email traffic suggesting that the plan received the president's blessing. The timing, however, was notable: "We have a decision to be ready to go by early November."[29]

On the ground, the Marines were itching to get started. "There was pressure from some of my subordinate commanders, and some of the young Marines too," recalls Lieutenant General John Sattler, who was charged with leading the renewed assault. Indeed, Sattler himself had received intelligence reports in September stating that the insurgents were expecting a U.S. offensive to begin and had begun fortifying their defenses in preparation. "So yes, that was always kind of looming there: 'Let's go now, before they get any stronger.' "[30]

If all agreed that the operation was critical from a strategic standpoint, why, then, was it delayed further? The looming presidential elections do appear to have affected the timetable, at least indirectly. According to the reporting of Tom Ricks, "By late summer, when it became clear that it would take a major battle to pacify the city, the Marines pulled back and waited for the U.S. presidential election campaign to conclude. They were determined not to fight half a battle again, and some in the military thought the next round would be so ugly that it shouldn't be waged until after the election was past."[31] While the military may not have shared the politicized preferences of the administration, their experience from the First Battle of Fallujah offered a stark lesson in how operations could be hamstrung by such considerations. Casey acknowledged in general that "the other thing that always casts a shadow on that second Fallujah was the first one. I was determined that if we started this, we were going to finish it."[32] Much better to initiate the operation after the election, then, when there would be far less prospect of Washington interfering mid-operation. This would seem to explain why the operational order issued in September, which could plausibly have been implemented in a couple of weeks, would actually only receive final authorization five days after the U.S. election.[33]

More importantly, it is a view directly supported by the then ambassador, John Negroponte: "It took us awhile to prepare for it. Our elections were going on in November of that year. I am not saying that President Bush didn't want the invasion of Fallujah to happen before the elections but I have been around him long enough and in Vietnam and elsewhere to know presidents tend to avoid rocking the boat just before a presidential election."[34]

Indeed, as strategically necessary as the operation was, drawing attention to a flash point of anti-American hostility at a time when the administration was resisting even the use of the term "insurgency" did not make for good political optics in an election year widely seen as a referendum on the Iraq War. Even less so when one considers, as Democrats no doubt would have pointed out, that this reality was largely a product of the administration's own making after the botched operation in April. As it was, Bush reportedly had tunnel vision through 2004 when it came to Iraq, which was constantly and solely viewed through the prism of the election campaign, according to Robert Blackwill, who was selected to accompany Bush on the campaign bus that year. As reported by Bob Woodward, "Blackwill was struck that there was never any real time to discuss policy. In between the stops in the air, whenever Iraq came up, it was always through the prism of the campaign. What had the Democratic nominee . . . said that day about Iraq? What had happened on the ground in Iraq that might impact the president's bid for reelection?" Blackwill, of course, had been on the ground in Iraq with Bremer for the previous several months. "But he was with the campaign only as part of the politics of reelection. Not once did Bush ask Blackwill what things were like in Iraq, what he had seen, or what should be done. Blackwill was astonished at the round-the-clock, all-consuming focus on winning the election. Nothing else came close."[35]

Perhaps most striking of all is the fact that when the operation did finally receive the green light, it was just five days after the presidential election. When it came, it was if anything far bolder and more aggressive than the first offensive. Using a supply model that amassed as much firepower as possible in an "iron mountain," some eight battalions were ordered into battle. Accompanied by three times as many air strikes as in the first battle, the Marines destroyed up to 10,000 of the 50,000 residencies in Fallujah, killing over 2,000 insurgents. One army lieutenant recalls, "You sometimes wonder what the appropriate use of force is, but Fallujah was just a joke as far as the amount of force we could use . . . There seemed to be no limit on main gun or .50-cal [ammunition], so we were hitting every house we were taking contact from with main gun rounds."[36] It also took more coalition casualties; some 70 Marines were killed and over 650 wounded. And yet, strikingly, there was no politically necessitated compromise this time around in response. Indeed, after the moment of greatest political sensitivity, the White House's interest in the operation was in fact minimal. Sattler recalls how he "completely operated as I pleased," free of interference from political entities.[37]

In Fallujah, then, we find a striking example of the *delay* mechanism, with evidence available for all observable implications. After a knee-jerk reaction to the murder of four American contractors ended in a wholly unsatisfactory bottom-up compromise, the specter of further U.S. casualties served to apply pressure on the military to hold their fire until after the 2004 presidential election. When that moment of political sensitivity passed, the Marines were finally permitted to deal with the "gaping wound" absent political interference, in the bloodiest battle fought by the U.S. military since the Vietnam War.

The Surge

In a prime-time televised address of January 10, 2007, President Bush announced the most significant shift in strategy of the Iraq War, officially named "The New Way Forward."[38] The revised plan would see almost thirty thousand additional troops head to the Middle East in an attempt to boost security amid spiraling sectarian violence. Whereas the existing strategy sought to transition security responsibility to Iraqi forces, the surge instead shifted the focus to a more population-centric counterinsurgency strategy with U.S. forces in the lead.

The decision was a long time coming. The following discussion demonstrates that key components of the national security bureaucracy, including Bush himself, perceived a need to try something different in Iraq through the spring and summer of 2006. Yet because admitting the existing strategy was failing was politically unwise, and switching to a casualty-intensive alternative at a time of growing public disillusionment with the war was even less palatable, a course correction was deferred. It was only after the midterm elections that a formal review process was launched, and a presidential decision quickly reached, in a classic illustration of the *delay* mechanism.

The Need for Change: "It's Hell, Mr. President"

The evidence is abundant that a steadily growing consensus emerged in the Bush administration on the need for a change in strategy from as early as the winter of 2004, substantiating the first observable implication of the *delay* mechanism. A series of advisors in the national security team, as well as the president himself, understood that the status quo was strategically suboptimal.

Some of the first observers to perceive the need to rethink the United States' Iraq strategy were senior officials in the State Department. As State Department counselor, Philip Zelikow began to worry during a fact-finding mission to Iraq in February 2005. Perceiving a huge inconsistency in the military activity conducted in Iraq, Zelikow concluded that "there really was no strategy."[39] His observations fueled great consternation in Washington: "By the summer of '05 and certainly into the fall of '05, the whole circle around the secretary of state were seething with frustration about the Iraq situation. We could feel it killing the administration."[40]

While chargé d'affaires in Baghdad in 2004, James Jeffrey sensed Secretary of State Condoleezza Rice's growing pessimism. "By the fall of 2004," he explains, "Rice was growing far more skeptical about the Iraq adventure. . . . Despite all of the money, and all of the committees we had in Washington and at the embassy, and the military running around, not a lot was getting done." By the time Jeffrey returned to Washington in 2005, Rice "was probably the most skeptical of any of the officials." From here, matters only deteriorated further. "There was a tremendous frustration below the scenes that things weren't working," recounts Jeffrey, who at this point had become Rice's Iraq coordinator. "Things by the spring of 2006 were pretty grim."[41] Rice admitted as much in her memoir: "It was becoming painfully obvious that we had neither the right military strategy in Iraq nor enough forces to carry out the flawed one that we were pursuing. . . . Maintaining the status quo was not an option."[42]

Among the NSC staff, concerns were born during the process of writing the National Strategy for Victory in Iraq in late 2005. "During that effort it became clear that there were large disagreements within the administration about what the strategy should be and what the strategy was," recalls Meghan O'Sullivan, deputy national security advisor for Iraq and Afghanistan, adding, "that whole effort made me uncomfortable about exactly where we were." After the bombing of the al-Askari Shrine in Samarra in February 2006, those initial niggling concerns had transformed into worry about the fundamentals of the course of action in which the United States was engaged in Iraq. "These disconnects were hamstringing our strategy. This became really evident in the early part of 2006," recalls O'Sullivan. "I went out to Iraq in early spring . . . and it became very obvious to me that our strategy and the realities on the ground were totally out of line with one another."[43] O'Sullivan's colleague on the NSC, Peter Feaver, similarly recounts that "over 2006 the Iraqi situation slowly deteriorated to the point where it came to correspond to the seemingly hopeless situation that critics had long claimed it to be. . . . Senior civilians on the National Security Council . . . (myself included) believed the situation warranted launching a top-to-bottom reassessment of the strategy by late May 2006."[44] On her return to Washington, O'Sullivan and like-minded colleagues began seeking to bring about precisely that outcome, beginning with a memorandum to her boss, Stephen Hadley, in which O'Sullivan all but begged for a strategy review, concluding in bold text, "We are executing a plan based on assumptions that are no longer valid."[45] When the president pulled her aside after a meeting and asked what it was like on the ground, O'Sullivan did not sugar-coat her assessment, replying, "It's hell, Mr. President."[46]

The intelligence community, meanwhile, was soon issuing similarly dark forecasts. In his summary report offered to President Bush in June 2006, Director of National Intelligence John Negroponte noted the ever-growing violence metrics, which had reached an all-time high. The report zeroed in on the sectarian dynamics now at play, pointing out that vast swaths of dis-affected Sunnis were siding with al-Qaeda in Iraq (AQI) "not because they find the message appealing, but because they feel that AQI can protect them against Shia militias and the Iraqi Security Forces."[47] By implication, the existing transition strategy was arming and equipping Iraqi forces that were in many cases complicit in the violence. Looking back, Negroponte confirms the gravity of the problem. "It had plunged into a very severe situation. . . . We were losing it."[48] With many CIA analysts believing Iraq to be in a state of civil war, Bush received an intelligence update on July 20. "The deterio-rating security situation is outpacing the Iraqi government's ability to respond," it read. "Violence has acquired a momentum of its own and is now self-sustaining."[49]

Among the uniformed military, there was also skepticism. "We all knew it wasn't going well," admits Michael Mullen, then chief of naval operations, speaking of the views of the JCS. "Quite frankly, there was no strategy. That's what drove us crazy."[50] Even General Casey understood that the nature and scale of the challenge before him fundamentally changed during 2006. "The sectarian violence really began in April or May of '05," he later recalled, yet "after Samarra it was a fundamentally different tone."[51] Although he still ultimately believed in the fundamentals of the underlying transition con-cept, the threat posed to this plan by worsening sectarian violence and a lack of political reconciliation was plain to see, particularly after the "Together Forward" operation in June 2006 failed to decisively stem the tide of bloodshed in Baghdad. The evolving complexity of the threat was something he had tried to brief in his video teleconferences with superiors that summer, emphasizing how the conflict in Iraq was transitioning from an insurgency against the coalition to a struggle for the division of political and economic power among Iraqis. Notably, the reaction in Washington was muted. "I was saying all the words," recalls Casey, "but it wasn't connecting."[52]

Most important of all, President Bush was aware of a need for change, and by the spring of 2006 began to count himself among the doubters of the current U.S. military strategy. Although a model of sunny optimism in public, in private "the president became very depressed about it," according to Negroponte.[53] "This is a daily conversation in the White House," adds O'Sullivan. "It was very clear that he was concerned about the situation, worried that it was going in the wrong direction."[54] Indeed, Bush tells us as much in his own words: "In the months after the Samarra bombing, I had started to question whether our approach matched the reality on the ground." By spring, he had come to a conclusion, telling National Security Advisor Hadley, "This is not working. . . . We need to take another look at the whole strategy. I need to see some new options."[55]

At this stage of the analysis, then, we can rule out the alternative argument that Bush did not make a decision sooner in 2006 because he or his national security team were not aware of the need for a change in strategy. The strategic preference through 2006 was clearly to change the status quo; a clear body of opinion in the administration felt events were spiraling out of control and that something different was needed.

*　　*　　*

While a firm determination of precisely what strategy should replace the current one required a full review, there are several signs suggesting that the balance of opinion in the administration, and most importantly for the president, pointed toward greater intervention.

At the State Department, the articulation of a strategy of "clear, hold, and build" in the fall of 2005 was perceived by its authors as "the first big effort to tear up and change the strategy." At a minimum, argued Zelikow, "We needed a story. And finally, by golly, at least we're going to offer a story. Since no one else went out to do it. And maybe that will spur others."[56] A short-hand for classic counterinsurgency principles, "clear, hold, and build" was hardly a groundbreaking concept, but key elements of the approach were not being implemented with consistency on the ground, according to Zelikow. While coalition forces were effective at clearing areas of insurgents, lasting progress too often proved elusive, with troops leaving areas before a robust set of governmental institutions and security provisions were in place. "We were building and investing too early," agreed Raymond Odierno, who accompanied Zelikow on the trip as a three-star liaison officer at the State Department. "We were spending a lot of money. We were building things. But frankly, they weren't doing much good because we had not yet established the groundwork where it could be fully integrated into the societal norms inside of the country."[57]

Enthusiasm for such an approach continued at the State Department into 2006, when, sensing a new appetite for a fresh look among NSC staffers like O'Sullivan, Secretary Rice asked Zelikow and Jeffrey to put pen to paper on a new proposal for a full military campaign plan. The recommended "selective counterinsurgency" strategy, outlined in a June 5 memorandum, called for a focus on securing and holding several key areas in Iraq, necessitating "some additional infusion of American forces in the short term."[58] It was simply the latest manifestation of a long-standing view in the State Department that "you should actually do a goddamn counterinsurgency. That is, you do something like the surge."[59]

This aligned with work being done in Baghdad too. Having himself concluded that that "our strategies to date had not worked," the new ambassador, Zalmay Khalilzad, commissioned a red team study in Iraq, which concluded that the plan devised by the commanding general of coalition forces was badly off course.[60] Instead, the report advocated the adoption of an "ink-spot" strategy, based on classic population-centric counterinsurgency principles. Around the same time, in November 2005, the Iraqi national security advisor wrote to the American team in Baghdad calling for essentially the same type of strategy, backing the view of experts that the military should shift its focus "away from hunting down and killing insurgents, emphasizing instead an effort to better protect the population."[61]

In military circles, a series of strategic thinkers were inclined to a similar position. Out in Fort Leavenworth, Kansas, Lieutenant General David H. Petraeus was busy overseeing development of the U.S. Army and Marine

Corps counterinsurgency manual, which provided the doctrinal foundation of the concepts of the strategy pursued during the surge in Iraq. Petraeus, who had been told that there was a strong possibility he would return to Iraq in 2007, was determined to get the manual written and published by the end of 2006 because he felt "we did not have an adequate doctrinal manual to guide what we were doing in Iraq and Afghanistan," and desperately needed "an intellectual foundation for those operations."[62] Indeed, while designed for much broader application, the manual's lead author admits that "Petraeus saw this as a tool for Iraq. . . . It was very obvious to me by the time we got to the late summer that this was going to Iraq and he was going to use it in Iraq, and that's what he was shaping it for."[63] The manual in essence called for a standardization of the strategy employed by H. R. McMaster in Tal Afar—the same operation used as a model for the State Department's "clear, hold, and build" formulation—and included a specific force-ratio requirement for such counterinsurgency practices that was insisted on by Petraeus "because it was the justification for the troops for the surge."[64] These ideas filtered through to the White House through direct informal channels of communication Petraeus maintained with key aides like Meghan O'Sullivan.

President Bush, while crucially stopping short of authorizing any action on such proposals, seemed intellectually sympathetic to their nature. He kept a "close eye" on Petraeus's proposals, using their troop-intensive logic to query whether Casey could carry out a "clear, hold, and build" strategy, and telling key aides to read the manual as soon as it was ready, in a "sign of where the president's thinking was."[65] According to his chief of staff, Joshua Bolten, the president made up his mind in a way that was likely "ahead of the process." Even before the fall of 2006, he recalls, Bush "was coming around to the view that of the options, the only one that had a reasonable prospect of the kind of success that the US needed from this, in this situation, was something like the surge."[66] Karl Rove agrees, adding that, "I think the president's mind, by the summer of '06, is already that the answer to this is that security must come first. That would require surging additional troops to reestablish security."[67] Indeed, over the summer Bush recalls reading a series of articles from colonels and one-star generals whose perspective jarred with those of Casey and Abizaid, noting that "many of those closest to the fight thought we needed more troops."[68] Whether or not Bush actually understood the intricacies of counterinsurgency doctrine as much as he later implied, he does appear to have believed that more troops were preferable than fewer. In this respect, it is instructive to note General Casey's perception from his weekly interactions with Bush: "I did have a sense all along that the president had a more conventional focus to what we were doing, and the more firepower he applied, the more successful he'd be."[69]

Indeed, even earlier, when his doubts about the existing strategy emerged in the spring of 2006, Bush's instinctive diagnosis had been that the "sectarian violence had not erupted because our footprint was too big," which in turn pointed to an escalatory prescription, since, "with the Iraqis struggling to stand up, it didn't seem possible for us to stand down."[70] More explicit were his subsequent comments in an August 17 meeting in which he began to vocalize his concerns with the existing strategy. In Bush's recollection, he tried to send a "signal" to his team that he was thinking differently. "We must succeed," he reports having said, adding, "If [the Iraqis] can't do it, we will. If the bicycle teeters, we're going to put the hand back on. We have to make damn sure we do not fail."[71]

If Bush's strategic preference alone drove his decision making on Iraq during this period, then we should expect to have seen a change in strategy to rescue a deteriorating situation by the spring or summer of 2006 at the latest, and likely one that doubled down on the commitment to the war through further escalation. Instead, the decision to surge would be taken in the New Year, after a protracted delay in the initiation of a strategy review. As the next section argues, the reason for this delay owes much to the president's electoral preference, which pointed to the excessive political risks that such a course presented prior to the midterms.

Electoral Risks: "The Most Unpopular Decision of My Presidency"

From an electoral perspective, the 2006 congressional midterms looked set to be a referendum on Bush's handling of the Iraq War. As such, there was intense political sensitivity associated with any potential course correction, and indeed much evidence to suggest that the public mood was set firmly against the kind of escalatory steps Bush seemed to be moving toward.

After Congressman Jack Murtha's powerful demand for an immediate withdrawal in late 2005, the center of gravity in the Democratic Party was by the following summer firmly in favor of a scaling down of the U.S. military presence in Iraq, with a dozen senior figures writing a scathing open letter to Bush on July 30 calling for a shift to a "more limited mission focused on counterterrorism, training and logistical support of Iraqi security forces."[72] Even senior Republicans, including the chairman of the Senate Armed Services Committee, John Warner, were busy writing anxious memoranda outlining their concerns with any hint in the rumor mill that additional forces were being readied for deployment.[73] In September, meanwhile, Senator Mitch McConnell pleaded with the president to withdraw some troops from Iraq at least as a political token—such were the concerns about the increasingly de-escalatory preferences of the electorate ahead of the midterms.[74] Among the public at large, appetite for something like the surge was in fact vanishingly small. In June 2006, just 6 percent of Americans favored an increase in troop levels. While the public disagreed on the speed with which troops should return from Iraq—some favoring either an immediate or scheduled withdrawal and others preferring a conditions-based drawdown—the overwhelming public demand, representing some 89 percent of Americans, was for fewer troops, not more.[75]

The president and key advisors privately understood that any possible escalation would arouse a firestorm of public criticism. "The surge option brought risks of its own," recalls Bush. "Increasing our troop level would be deeply unpopular at home. The fighting would be tough, and casualties could be high."[76] In response to McConnell's plea, meanwhile, he later admitted that it was apparent that opting to increase, not decrease, troop levels would be "the most unpopular decision of my presidency."[77] O'Sullivan, one of the chief advocates of the surge in Bush's inner circle, acknowledges the situation as follows: "Initial opposition to the idea of the surge was virtually uniform. With a few notable exceptions, such as [Senator] John McCain, members of Congress from both parties argued strongly against it. Public opinion was firmly in the camp of bringing troops home. Even many senior members of President Bush's own administration were, throughout much of the process, arguing against the surge."[78] Even in Baghdad, the constraints the political leadership were under could be sensed, with one of General Casey's aides later recalling, "I guess the read of domestic public opinion at the time, or even looking back on it, I don't thing [sic] the people would have supported an increase in forces, it had to wait until after the election."[79]

Not only would the initial decision to escalate have been unpopular, but, from a communications perspective, such a strategy would only make things worse before they got better. The population-centric COIN (counterinsurgency) approach, which according to multiple sources caught Bush's eye through the summer of 2006, was almost by definition a casualty-intensive military strategy.[80] "We understood the inherent violence in a counterinsurgency," notes Conrad Crane, the lead author of the army's doctrinal manual, adding, "we use the word 'kill' like seventy times."[81] If the experts could effectively guarantee the president that such a strategy would incur more casualties in an election year, what they could not do was offer any real hope that conclusive results would be seen in the short term. "We were pretty honest in the manual: it was going to take a lot of killing, a lot of violence, it's going to take a lot of time," says Crane.[82]

At a phase of the electoral cycle in which a president is likely to be casualty sensitive and time poor, then, the emerging strategic preference was known to carry a high cost, both in human and temporal terms. With the midterms looming, how did George Bush respond to the imbalance between his strategic and electoral concerns?

"It's a Bust": Missed Opportunities to Course Correct

If the lack of a change in strategy through most of 2006 was not for want of an awareness of the need for one, neither was it down to a shortage of attempts to spark such a process. In fact, a series of largely independent efforts were launched in the year leading up to November 2006, each of which fizzled out in the face of presidential inaction, providing plenty of evidence for the second observable implication of the *delay* mechanism.

First, the State Department's "clear, hold, and build" approach of late 2005 failed to go any further than a public relations effort to repackage the existing strategy. What was known as the National Strategy for Victory in Iraq was considered ultimately insufficient for achieving the real change some inside the administration were seeking. "Except for at the level of rhetoric," regrets Zelikow, "it's a bust."[83] As for the State Department's later proposal for a "selective counterinsurgency," there had been greater hopes for substantive change, since it had been fed into planning for a "war council" summit held at Camp David in June, widely expected to be a warts-and-all review of strategy, where the president and his advisors were "really going to have the blunt, all-out conversation that they have long needed to have so this strategy can be pulled up and thoroughly re-examined," as Zelikow puts it.[84] Again, though, "that turned out to be a bust."[85] Indeed, President Bush left halfway through the set of scheduled meetings, using the get-together as a cover for a secret trip to Iraq for a photo opportunity with Prime Minister Nouri al-Maliki. "What I thought would have started a zero-base review of the strategy miscarries back into debates about implementation on the margins," recalled Feaver.[86]

By August, Bush had begun vocalizing his concerns to his inner circle. Yet if he held an emerging preference for escalation, he still held it close enough to his chest at that stage as to inhibit any actual follow-up by those leading the military mission in Iraq. Indeed, it seems that Bush's memory may have embellished the strength of the signal he sent in the August 17 meeting. General Casey, for instance, still felt that he had the support of the president, which was reasonable to think given that he had been asked to stay on for another year in Iraq a few months prior, and following Camp David, where Casey's update on the existing strategy was approved.[87] "And then I read in President Bush's book that August was the worst month of his presidency," the general recalls, "and I'm going, *What?*"[88] The August meeting was "weird," admits Zelikow, who was there representing the secretary of state. While he sensed the ice beginning to break, he concedes that he may have picked up on Bush's signals because he was already thinking along those lines. "What Bush says is true," he explains, "but to be fair to Casey, it's not like anyone at this meeting triple underscored the point."[89]

Between the August 17 meeting and the November 2006 elections, the number of closely held studies looking at Iraq strategy proliferated among the various skeptical groups. Yet the establishment of a full interagency review, which was critical in bringing about real change, was again deferred. An internal NSC effort to consider alternatives was held very closely, and only gradually opened up to State Department officials on a strictly informal basis. Unsurprisingly, perhaps, the importance of having military representatives in the room quickly became apparent. "We can only go so far," explained David Satterfield, the State Department's coordinator for Iraq. "We can't make judgments about military force capabilities, about readiness capabilities. . . . It's the chiefs, J-3 and J-5"—the directors of operations and of plans and policy, respectively—who could say "what exists out there."[90]

In military circles, several studies were underway, none of which were formally connected to the other, let alone to the efforts of the NSC and State

Department. By early November, the stark assessment of the "Council of Colonels" group, established in the fall at the chairman's request, had reached the JCS: "We are not winning, so we are losing."[91] While Petraeus continued to lay the intellectual foundations of the surge in Fort Leavenworth, the officer who would later implement the new approach at the operational level, Odierno, was busy making trips to Iraq and speaking to a slew of experts and fellow officers who had served in Iraq to solicit ideas. "If we continue to do [things] the way we're doing it now, it's not going to work," he concluded, adding that, given the inability of Iraqi forces to hold areas and maintain security, additional forces were necessary.[92] Further outside of the chain of command, meanwhile, retired general Jack Keane had begun leading a "cabal" aiming to trigger a shift toward a similar more troop-intensive COIN strategy, briefing Secretary of Defense Donald Rumsfeld—and indeed anyone who would listen—on the need to send additional troops in support of a revised plan.[93]

Had each of these disparate studies and reviews been formally brought together earlier, a full airing of views might have led to a change in strategy much earlier than it ultimately did. In a normal interagency review process, explains Zelikow, "the first thing you do is run a subcabinet process that elicits papers and arguments about strategy from State, Defense, JCS, maybe convened under the deputies and J. D. Crouch. J. D. Crouch never ran such a meeting until like the end of November. Not one."[94] As a result, dissatisfaction with the existing strategy remained isolated among disparate silos in the bureaucracy, without constructive interagency analysis and input that would help move the concerns toward a solution. Before November, adds Zelikow, "that just simply never happened. These papers don't exist. At no point before the end of November of 2006 did I ever see a paper and an interagency process in which DoD [Department of Defense] or the command are being forced to engage in the arguments about their strategy." The net effect of the White House's failure to launch a formal strategy review, then, was the deferral of any real decision on a new strategy. "Everything that happened then could have happened more than a year earlier, or two years earlier," regrets Zelikow.[95]

The persistent failure of the Bush administration to launch a full strategy review despite all the strong indications of a need for one and efforts by senior officials to instigate such a process is fully consistent with the second observable implication of the *delay* mechanism. We can therefore rule out the alternative explanation that the failure to make a decision to change strategy through 2006 was the result of a lack of viable opportunities to establish a normal interagency review process. There was clearly something else pressuring the White House not to act upon its strategic preference to instigate a change in strategy.

"I Decided to Wait"

Some of the best evidence that the delay in authorizing a formal review was caused by electoral constraints appears in Bush's own memoirs. In a key passage explaining his thinking in the fall of 2006, he wrote, "I decided a change in strategy was needed. To be credible to the American people, it would have to be accompanied by changes in personnel.... [But] with the 2006 midterm elections approaching, the rhetoric on Iraq was hot.... I decided to wait until after the elections to announce any policy or personnel changes. I didn't want the American people to think I was making national security decisions for political reasons."[96] Putting aside the somewhat troubling assertion that timing critical decisions on strategy based on the domestic political calendar was somehow an example of keeping national security policy free of political considerations, this statement alone is highly suggestive of the *delay* mechanism.

Secretary of State Rice, meanwhile, though convinced of the need to change strategy, reportedly said at the time that she was not willing "to do anything that would be above the radar screen in the heavy political breathing of the November elections," because the last thing the administration needed was "a hothouse story" that revealed that things were so bad in Iraq that the administration was looking for alternative approaches.[97] Hadley agreed, telling her in October 2006 that discussions between the NSC and State Department concerning the situation had to remain informal: "We've got to do it under the radar screen because the electoral season is so hot."[98] Earlier that summer, Hadley reportedly elaborated on his thinking: "I've got to help this President get through what is going to be a really rugged three years. And if the Democrats take over the House and the Senate it's going to be unbelievable after 2006." If there was a "raging debate" over Bush's war record, with people arguing "we have no choice but to throw the Republicans out and bring the troops home . . . this is really going to be awful."[99]

Looking back, O'Sullivan acknowledges that an important factor behind her inability to spark a formal review process was the fact that "this is the summer before the midterm elections. And I think that it would have been potentially awkward for there to be a strategic review of our Iraq strategy publicly out there in the run-up to the elections."[100]

Colonel Peter Mansoor, meanwhile, explains why the Council of Colonels on which he sat was prevented from discussing their deliberations with NSC or State Department officials as follows: "It was unstated but clear that the administration did not want a leak to the press that it was rethinking the strategy for the Iraq War, because that would be a tacit admission that the current strategy was failing. Such an admission would have an impact on public opinion and hasten the calls for US departure from Iraq."[101] "With the midterm elections less than three months away," he wrote elsewhere, "any hint that the administration was having second doubts about Iraq was politically radioactive." Fearing the explosive fallout of any leaks from a full review, "serious debate on changing course would have to wait until the voters had had their say."[102]

This was certainly a perception shared by others in the uniformed military. In Baghdad, for instance, there was apparently a sense that requests for additional troops during an election season would be unwelcome in Washington. In an after-action review, General Casey played devil's advocate and asked his advisors if he should have changed strategy and asked for more troops over the summer of 2006. Ed Donnelly, then the chief of Casey's internal think tank in Baghdad, pointed out that "domestic public opinion at that time was all focused on the elections, and at least our read of it from OSD [Office of the Secretary of Defense] was 'get the numbers down so that we can show progress.'"[103]

Instead of pursuing alternative approaches, the administration acted as one might expect in the lead-up to an election by diverting greater attention toward the minimization of casualties associated with the existing plan. This, indeed, is one of the aspects General Casey sensed in his interactions with Washington. In handwritten notes of one such call, the commander listed a series of questions he had been asked: "Can we shift weight away from activities that cause casualties?" "What are the risks of going to a lower visibility posture now/6mos/12mos?" "Less troops = less casualties?"[104] Secretary of Defense Rumsfeld had, of course, always believed in pushing the responsibility for security onto the Iraqis; yet in the summer of 2006, his concerns seemed to have also been driven by concerns about congressional reaction to the continued exposure of U.S. troops to violence in Iraq. Hence, when General Casey reluctantly decided to extend the tours of the 172nd Stryker Brigade to shore up security in the short term, Rumsfeld fired off a note lamenting the move as "unfortunate," as the administration was now "facing some difficulties in Alaska and Congress because of it."[105]

The impact of casualties on other senior officials' concerns was also significant. Looking back at 2006, Rice remembers how "each morning I opened the *Washington Post* to 'Faces of the Fallen.' The *Post* had begun the series in 2003 to memorialize Americans killed in the war. I made myself look at every one of the photos—a harsh reminder of the costs of the war."[106] Explaining why she began to reconsider her earlier proposals for a better-resourced COIN plan during the summer, she notes that her growing concern was that putting more troops in harm's way "would only result in more casualties."[107] The problem with "clear, hold, and build," agreed Abizaid, was that the "build" component "was going to cause casualties to increase, not decrease." At a time when the administration—from the president on down—was sending instructions to commanders to "minimize our casualties," this appeared to jar with the overriding priorities of the civilian leadership.[108] Rice's new proposal—threatening to withdraw U.S. support—might not work, she admitted, but "at least this way, fewer Americans would die."[109] As Casey himself later lamented, speaking of the views of political leaders in Washington, "Over time, casualties and violence became the de facto measure of strategic progress in Iraq."[110] Such heightened sensitivity to casualties during an election season is exactly what theories of democratic constraint predict, as the administration seeks to minimize the prospect of public backlash on the eve of Election Day.

Bureaucratic Bottlenecks?

The two most commonly cited alternative explanations for the delay described in the previous section are wholly interconnected with related electoral concerns. The first is nicely illustrated by Zelikow's judgment that "Don Rumsfeld did more than any other single person to destroy the Bush presidency."[111] For James Jeffrey, Rumsfeld was "the eight-hundred-pound gorilla" who blocked all efforts to change strategy, on the basis of his view that "shit happens. Chill out. We've got a plan, which is to build up the Iraqi army [and] get out of there."[112] When fellow members of the administration challenged the commanders working on Iraq at weekly videoconferences, Rumsfeld would often stand in the way of attempts to elicit a full discussion of views, on one occasion even writing a follow-up memorandum threatening that "If NSC meetings are going to have the tone of the last one, I am going to have Abizaid and Casey not on the meetings."[113] For good reason, then, when the State Department was developing its own "selective counterinsurgency" proposal, Zelikow recalls admitting to Rice, "The strategy we have in mind, we will not be able to execute this with Don Rumsfeld as the secretary of defense. . . . It's just not going to happen."[114]

Yet, if Rumsfeld alone was the cause of the bureaucratic bottleneck, Bush, despite having a number of prior opportunities, waited until the day after the midterm elections to dismiss him, suggesting political timing was wholly interrelated in the matter. "He had been skeptical for [the] better part of a year," notes Jeffrey, "but [he was] not willing until after [the] elections to take on Rumsfeld and Cheney."[115] Rumsfeld had offered to resign on a number of occasions before this time, including March 2006, a month after the Samarra bombing. With Rove advising that firing Rumsfeld would place an albatross around the necks of Republicans in the congressional elections, from a political perspective the safer thing to do was to wait it out, thereby lengthening Rumsfeld's grip on Iraq strategy.[116] As emphatic as Jeffrey is about the detrimental role that Rumsfeld played in this decision-making process, he concludes that "this all broke because of the election. The election was a seminal event."[117]

Another alternative hypothesis identifies the source of the delay as Bush's fear of overruling the uniformed military, who remained fairly solidly against a troop increase, at least within the formal chain of command. Admiral Mullen understood the problem as follows: "As powerful as presidents can be, they know the importance of having the military on board. By on board, I don't mean actively espousing policy. Military leaders shouldn't do that. But it does help inoculate the president from criticism if he can say he has consulted the Pentagon and his commanders helped inform the policy and are comfortable carrying it out. I think President Bush understood this dynamic well and did not want to get himself into a position where people could accuse him of bullying the chiefs or pulling us through a knot hole to get our support."[118] With his vantage point at the NSC, Feaver speculates that the delay may well have come down to a "respect and fear" of opposing General Casey, or concerns about a "revolt of the generals" among the JCS. This was why Bush turned to studies by retired senior military officers, outside the formal channels, using the ideas contained therein "as stalking horses to elicit JCS views gradually," rather than confronting the set of four-star generals with his own views outright.[119]

Yet, again, this explanation cannot be disentangled from the electoral context. On the most basic level, if the risk of upsetting the generals was political in nature, as Mullen notes, then it is logical for the president to have waited until after the period of heightened political sensitivity—during election season—before going up against the grain of military opinion. As President Harry Truman found out after firing Douglas MacArthur, the widely popular general, in 1951, having a vocal critic with a litany of stars on his shoulders may prove politically disastrous. Furthermore, Bush's narrative of a slow, gentle process of consensus building among the military does not fit with the recollection of the key generals involved. Having been excluded from all of the informal reviews, General Casey identified the November elections as a crucial turning point in Bush's appetite for something new: "It was the first videotelecon we did after the midterms. It was noticeable because he was always very ebullient. And he wasn't. He was just very direct and matter-of-fact. That was when I first kind of said, 'OK, there's something up here.' It was November, right in that early part of November. . . . I honestly didn't perceive any change in his attitude until after that midterm election."[120]

A similar point could be made about the perspective of the JCS. As stated earlier, they had not been made aware of Bush's doubts through the spring and summer of 2006, nor the informal studies undertaken into the fall. Indeed, the Council of Colonels was an independent review running on parallel tracks to the concerns of the NSC or the State Department. Both within that review, and among the JCS more generally, there was limited appetite for sending additional brigades. "We thought," says Mullen, "just from a readiness standpoint, the shape the army was in, that two [brigades] was about max."[121] The five-brigade option that was chosen came from outside the chain of command, and was "180 degrees out of sync with the uniformed military's view of things," recalls Lieutenant General Douglas Lute, then director of operations on the Joint Staff. "There was no appetite to surge among the JCS or the operational commanders," he confirms, adding, "it was imposed by the president."[122] This was not a story of a president gently bringing his chiefs along, but rather a president confronting them with a fait accompli after waiting until a politically sensitive context had passed after the election.

Finally, instead of a long period of gentle persuasion, it appears that the enticement that actually brought the chiefs on board was Bush's promise in a meeting of December 13, 2006, of more resources for the U.S. Army and Marines. The pledge to pump resources into the depleted forces did not only placate the Joint Chiefs, who were responsible for allocating those resources, but it also served to further mollify the opposition of the commanding general. When Casey drafted a memorandum for the president, stating his objections to the proposed surge strategy, Abizaid advised him to scrap the letter, explaining that it was a done deal. "Look, this is all tied to decisions about increasing the size of the army and the Marine Corps," Abizaid told Casey. "It's done, get out of the way."[123] What, one might reasonably ask, stopped the president from offering these before this point? Lieutenant General John Sattler, at that time the director for strategy, plans and policy on the Joint Staff, admits that "had we decided to grow the army and the Marine Corps earlier, then that may have been a more viable option earlier than it was."[124] Absent Bush's caution regarding the political fallout of countermanding the JCS, then, there was a plausible route to overcome their objections much earlier than was the case. That Bush waited until after Election Day points decisively to the existence of the *delay* mechanism.

Opening the Windows

Election Day 2006 acted as a turning point, giving way to decisive and bold decision-making behavior by President Bush. Although the decision to surge U.S. troops was announced in early January, the record indicates that it had effectively been made by the time Bush visited the JCS on December 13, just five weeks after the congressional elections.

On November 10, three days on from the midterms, and two days after firing Rumsfeld, Bush appointed J. D. Crouch to lead a full review of strategy in Iraq. A flurry of interagency meetings subsequently took place, finally bringing together several of the informal efforts and injecting them with a sense of urgency not hitherto seen—Bush wanted a report in only sixteen days. "Basically the day after the election. . . . it's as if all of a sudden the windows had been opened and fresh air is coming in," recalls Zelikow.[125] Having been largely deferential on questions of military strategy up to this point, Bush was suddenly front and center of the deliberations. During the initial stages of the review, this was manifested through Hadley, who, at Bush's behest, intervened on one of the first meetings to instruct the participants that, whatever their own proposals were, "you have got to give the president the option of a surge in forces. He will want to see it, and he'll want to know what it means. You all can take your positions for or against or in between, but you have to present him that as an option."[126]

By the time the review made it beyond the deputies to the cabinet level, the key follow-up meeting minutes reveal a president eager to push ahead with bold steps. On December 8, for instance, Crouch had barely begun his presentation on the propositions under discussion before Bush challenged his suggestions, asking, "What is different from now? Don't see anything different?"[127] Rejecting the State Department's new plan to step back and let the violence burn itself out as at best an abdication of responsibility, Bush turned to Casey, who reiterated the intention to press on with the transition of security responsibilities to the Iraqis, as agreed with Prime Minister Maliki and foreshadowing key tenets of the "Accelerated Transition" plan he was scheduled to formally brief a few days later.[128] "So six months more of the same stuff?" asked a seemingly incredulous Bush, before showing his own hand by asking, "Does this argue for more US forces as a bridge?"[129] Casey later conceded that, "our life changed after those election[s]. . . . It was clear to me that the President was out of patience with the Iraqis to do anything, and we needed to focus on securing Baghdad."[130] Although Casey briefed his subordinate commander in Baghdad to think creatively on strategy, it soon became clear that the president "was already doing it."[131]

Referencing the late-2006 report of the Iraq Study Group, which effectively supported the central tenets of the existing strategy, Bush, on December 9, spoke of the "radical action we will take [to] achieve victory," imploring his team to "understand that Baker-Hamilton [is] not setting orders. I am running this show."[132] Then, over Casey's objections, he questioned whether the Iraqi Security Forces could assume responsibility as early as proposed. "If forces [are] unreliable to protect Baghdad," he said, it would amount to "a lot of wasted effort." Instead, he thought aloud, it "seems [we] should move more resources into Baghdad. . . . Do we need more troops?" Bush made plain his state of mind: "People concerned US not engaged. Think about symbols. Show muscle. . . . Most important is put us in position where can win. Want to win. No mistake. Victory. Surge important."[133]

It is not just the speed or decisiveness with which Bush reached a decision that is notable, but also the bold and risky nature of the surge option, which was selected over an overwhelming level of opposition. Having now passed the moment of highest political sensitivity, there was no reason to resort to half-hearted measures. "It's a Hail Mary pass," says Zelikow, "because he's throwing the ball at a time where he doesn't really have a play, where he's got the receiver in mind. . . . It was really up to Petraeus and Odierno to figure out how to deal with it and make it work."[134] Yet, as Petraeus's executive officer, Peter Mansoor, admits, "We did not know whether the surge would work; indeed, the odds were stacked against us."[135] Even the architects of the new COIN doctrine underpinning the surge had their doubts. "Baghdad was a mess," admits Crane, adding, "I thought you had to consider the possibility of failure."[136]

This is arguably what explains the determination to go with a five-brigade option, rather than the two that the chiefs said was the most they could accommodate. While the incoming commander had told the White House through back-channel communications in late 2006 that he would need "everything you can get your hands on," this was far from a consensus view in Iraq.[137] Lieutenant General Martin Dempsey, the three-star officer in charge of efforts to train the Iraqi Security Forces at MNSTC-I (Multi-National Security Transition Command—Iraq), felt additional forces were the "wrong answer" to the ongoing challenges in Iraq, something that risked a loss of momentum on progress toward increasing Iraqi capabilities.[138] General Casey, meanwhile, stands accused by his successor of repeatedly obstructing efforts to secure the additional forces required. "I had to insist on several occasions subsequent to my nomination to be COMMNF-I [i.e., commander of MNF-I] that we get all 5 Army BCTs [Brigade Combat Teams] and 2 Marine battalions plus the MEU [Marine Expeditionary Unit] that I had been told to expect," recalls Petraeus, "as Gen. Casey kept telling the CJCS [chairman of the JCS] I did not need all five, or that I should have to request 3, 4, and 5, etc."[139] Yet each of these skeptics were overruled. Why? According to senior officials in the White House, the logic that compelled a president who had heretofore been deeply resistant to countermand his senior military advisors was simple: "We're going to get one shot at this. It's going to be politically tough in any case, so we're not going to get multiple bites at this apple. Do it properly: send in five."[140] Or, as J. D. Crouch reportedly told Stephen Hadley at the time, "We've decided to be a bear . . . So let's be a grizzly bear."[141]

Indeed, in choosing the "all-in," full-throated gamble that the surge represented, Bush also demonstrated a newfound willingness to overrule virtually his entire national security team, in another sign that the lifting of electoral constraints had a real impact on his decision-making behavior.[142] In addition to the aforementioned opposition from the chiefs and the State Department, it was clear that the combatant commander was briefing a plan diametrically opposed to that which Bush had in mind. During his meeting with the president on December 12, Casey made clear that additional U.S. troops would at best have "a temporary, local effect" in reducing violence, would not be decisive absent progress on political reconciliation on the part of the Iraqis, and, in the meantime, would result in additional casualties and extend the time it took to pass on security responsibilities. In short, he was "adamantly opposed" to the plan favored by the president.[143] Furthermore, the record shows that Donald Rumsfeld was fully in tune with Casey at the time of the formal strategy review. In a videoconference with his commander, the secretary of defense addressed the prospect of sending more troops, simply stating, "Doesn't help. Feeding alligator. They will just want more. We do not want to give more troops."[144] Before long, both Rumsfeld and Casey would be gone—dismissed and "kicked upstairs," respectively, by a president apparently intent on implementing a clean sweep of senior positions associated with the war.

Bush's overruling of the State Department is perhaps even more striking. At Foggy Bottom, concerns about the deteriorating state of public support for the war by this point had actually led key figures to retreat altogether from their earlier advocacy of a better-resourced counterinsurgency plan. "My concern, which led me and others around Rice to become skeptical of our own recommendations," recalls Jeffrey, "was based on rapidly fading domestic support. . . . We were all growing skeptical that we would have the public support for anything."[145] Indeed, for this reason, Rice defended a proposal that contemplated the withdrawal of U.S. troops to the outskirts of the cities in Iraq and intervention only in cases of uncontrollable, near-genocidal violence. Why? Because "we lost the US people when we got into a one thousand year blood feud. They understood going after al Qaeda; understood Sadaa[m]ists; understood all of that. Do not understand this blood feud. Must . . . realize our limitations."[146] The reality that Bush would now reject such a plan, breaking openly with his loyal secretary of state in so doing, points decisively to the president's newfound freedom from the constraints of public opinion in this final electoral stage.

There is even some question as to whether Prime Minister Maliki supported the proposed surge. Bush states that he secured Maliki's blessing during a November 30 meeting in Amman, Jordan.[147] Yet the main subject of these discussions was a new Baghdad security plan, a strategic concept created by the Iraqis that would see the Iraqi Security Forces take over increasing security functions from the United States. Maliki's response to Bush's offer of additional troops was negative. "I don't need your forces," he said. "We can do it ourselves. We should do it ourselves."[148] The record shows that the Iraqis had been eager for a U.S. withdrawal to begin as soon as possible, with rough timetables for such an eventuality being proposed by August 2006.[149] According to the minutes of several key NSC meetings held in mid-December, however, the president's reaction to his Iraqi counterpart's response was one of significant frustration. Expressing concern at Maliki's apparent reticence in confronting the threat posed by sectarian militias, Bush had raised the idea of introducing more U.S. forces to offset a lack of military readiness among their Iraqi counterparts. Warned by General Casey against a unilateral imposition of troops without a request for help from the Iraqi prime minister, Bush emphasized the "need to get moving. He cannot be the roadblock." Complaining that it was "Ironic that this guy [Maliki] can determine how we move forward," the president repeatedly brought up the possibility of bypassing or even replacing the Iraqi prime minister. "He's gotta know he's got us in a bind. If he can't hack it, find someone who can," said Bush, before concluding that "[we] cannot let Maliki decide if we surge."[150] The following day the president again wondered aloud if it was "time to choose somebody else," before walking the statement back somewhat and instructing his advisors not to leak any suggestion that he was considering replacing the Iraqi prime minister. He was merely "Looking at options," he explained.[151] Yet, just two days later, the thought again crossed his mind during another discussion about the possibility of adding troops. "If he's not [the] guy, then we've got to make [a] change."[152]

*   *   *

The election was thus a key turning point in the decision-making process on Iraq. Yet it was not the case that Bush was now inclined to simply reflect the concerns of the electorate, who had signaled their dissatisfaction with the president's war record by handing Democrats sweeping gains in the midterms. If keen to respond to public wishes in this way, Bush would presumably have opted to embrace some elements of the Baker-Hamilton report, which enjoyed solid, bipartisan support from the public.[153] He certainly would not have embraced something like the surge given that public appetite in December remained dead set against it, with just 12 percent favoring sending more troops, versus a 52 percent majority in favor of a fixed withdrawal time line.[154] On the contrary, the real significance of the election as a turning point lay in the reality that neither Bush nor his party had to face the verdict of voters again. "After the Republican defeat in the mid-term elections," recalls Colonel Mansoor, "the president no longer had to veil his actions; in that sense he was liberated to replace the Secretary of Defense, the commander of US Central Command, the commander in Iraq, and announce a change in strategy in the Iraq War."[155] Only at this stage of the electoral cycle, newly freed of electoral constraints, could this lame duck president make what he understood to be "the most unpopular decision of my presidency."[156]

Indeed, much evidence exists to suggest that Bush's bold gamble of January 2007 was further propelled by concerns about his own legacy, as he entered the final two years of his presidency. In Casey's notes of a December 15 meeting, for instance, the president stressed the need to "make sure [the] next administration cannot undo" the strategy being put in place.[157] Similarly, in Peter Feaver's insider account of deliberations, the surge—or the "bridge," as it was notably referred to internally—was explicitly designed with the presidential calendar in mind. From the moment he and others in the NSC began to think about a surge, "it was painfully obvious to everyone involved that the only decisive outcome that could be achieved during President Bush's tenure was the triumph of our enemies, America's withdrawal, and Iraq's descent into a hellish chaos as yet undreamed of. . . . The challenge, therefore, was to develop and implement a workable strategy that could be handed over to Bush's successor."[158] This, in turn, gives credence to General Casey's hypothesis that "once they lost both houses, he was faced with the possibility of losing the White House in two more years to save his legacy and set the Republicans up for the next election, and the only question that had never been answered was, 'Do we have enough troops?' . . . If you're a political guy, your horizons are a year, not ten years. I don't mean to be crude, but it's always someone else's problem."[159]

Bush's legacy was, after all, intertwined with Iraq. It was, as James Jeffrey put it, "the soul of his presidency."[160] Faced with the prospect of failure, Bush knew his place in the history books depended on turning things around. "The Iraq War is the giant millstone," Zelikow notes. "It's the giant thing, like Vietnam is for the legacy of LBJ."[161] That Bush would allow the mess in Iraq to drag on for months through 2006 despite such consciousness of the stakes only serves to underline how powerful an effect electoral constraints had on presidential decision making in the war up to this point.

Two Clocks and a SOFA

Having escalated the war despite overwhelming political opposition, President Bush now faced the challenge of managing the aftermath of the surge so as to lock in its perceived strategic gains. This section demonstrates that Bush's status as a lame duck did not entirely free him from electoral constraints, but instead added both urgency and political risk to his decision-making process. Since Bush was now incentivized by concerns for his legacy, rather than a desire for reelection, a series of decisions regarding the pace of troop withdrawals were significantly shaped by the domestic political calendar. In turn, Bush's efforts to tie his successor's hands to his preferred strategic vision for a continued engagement in Iraq were hamstrung by anticipation of the 2008 election. As such, this section offers strong evidence that even incumbents who do not have to face voters again are still required to balance competing strategic and electoral preferences. Further, by exploring how the upcoming 2008 election eroded Bush's leverage during negotiations over a status of forces agreement, or SOFA, this section offers support for the claim that the *spoiler* mechanism can still constrain presidential decision making even when the incumbent is not running for reelection.

Clock-Watching: The Drawdown of the Surge

From a strictly military perspective, a conditions-based drawdown of troops in Iraq was widely perceived to be strategically optimal. Inherent in the original decision to surge was the idea that improvements in security were a prerequisite for political reconciliation. This causal relationship, taken "almost as a matter of faith" among proponents of the new strategy, implied that troops should be withdrawn as violence metrics declined, acting as a "return on success."[162] How, exactly, "success" would be measured Bush would leave up to Petraeus, but it was quite clear that his strategic preference did not include any fixed or politically predetermined schedule for redeployments. As he later put it, "we were keeping as many troops in Iraq as our commanders needed, for as long as they needed them."[163]

In turn, the commanders on the ground understood that establishing a minimum level of security in what had essentially become a civil war would take time, and as such were evidently geared toward a long-term commitment to Iraq. This was crystal clear to Petraeus's second-in-command, Lieutenant General Raymond Odierno, who wrote in an August 2007 memorandum of the myriad challenges that still faced the U.S. mission in Iraq, from the continuing threat from al-Qaeda and Shia extremists to the fragile progress toward political reconciliation and training of the Iraqi Security Forces. The memorandum, designed to inform Petraeus's upcoming recommendations to the White House on future adaptations to the strategy, pulled few punches. Having created many of the problems now afflicting Iraq, the United States had "a moral responsibility as well as a national security responsibility to continue to assist" the country. As such, while "resource and political constraints" required some rebalancing of security responsibilities now, "the impact of a rapid withdrawal of troops would be devastating." In truth, the United States needed to be thinking in terms of a ten-year strategy, drawing on all elements of national power. "Iraqis think in weeks, months, and years," Odierno concluded, "while we think in seconds, minutes and hours."[164] In truth, Odierno was preaching to the choir. According to Stephen Biddle, an external advisor during this period, "Petraeus is not remotely interested in drawdowns during 2007. He knows he's in the fight of his life, this is all hanging in the balance, and he wants every soldier he can get. . . . Petraeus's understanding of the situation was that U.S. troops were helping not hurting."[165] A series of eighteen benchmarks were established against which progress could be assessed and recommendations about withdrawals made, but there was no illusion that Jeffersonian democracy would suddenly emerge out of the ashes of violent sectarian conflict, having failed to do so for the past four years.

From an electoral perspective, by contrast, Bush was keenly aware that the domestic political landscape placed limits on his ability to pursue a conditions-based drawdown. In the short term, the previous midterm elections saw a vocal group of skeptical Democrats elevated to power, and they threatened to use their newly won full control of Congress to mandate a fixed and early withdrawal. In the longer term, meanwhile, there was a real possibility that such an atmosphere would lead Democrats to nominate a rigidly antiwar candidate for the 2008 election campaign. Since it was understood that the deep-rooted challenges in Iraq would not be resolved quickly, Bush needed some way to ensure a degree of continuity in strategy after his term in office ended. Or, in the words of James Jeffrey, who served as deputy national security advisor for Iraq and Afghanistan during this period, "Bush knew that we had the 2008 elections coming up, and by this time it was obvious from the polls and everything else that we weren't going to convince the American public of this, and he was afraid that the Democrats would run against the war and win. He didn't want the Democrats to win because he figured they would just screw it all up. So how do you save your project?"[166]

The challenge presented by this imbalance between Bush's strategic and electoral preferences was conceptualized at the time by a metaphor involving two clocks. While the president himself recalls being struck by Petraeus's comment that "the Washington clock is ticking a lot faster than the Baghdad clock," the clearest articulation of the task ahead comes from the secretary of defense, Robert Gates:

My enemy was time. There was a Washington "clock" and a Baghdad "clock," and the two moved at very different speeds. Our forces needed time to make the surge and our broader plan work, and the Iraqis needed time for political reconciliation, but much of Congress, most of the media, and a growing majority of Americans had lost patience with the war in Iraq. . . . My role was to figure out how to buy time, how to slow down the Washington clock, and how to speed up the Baghdad clock.[167]

In other words, what the administration needed to do was temper the desire to pursue the strategically optimal plan of a slow, conditions-based drawdown, with a politically pragmatic approach that protected the strategy from the electoral ramifications of the "bugout" fever so prevalent in Congress and among the wider voting public.

The domestic political calendar played a crucial role in efforts to address this challenge. For starters, electoral realities were used to try to speed up the Baghdad clock by providing the United States with leverage over Iraqi officials. In December 2007, for instance, Secretary Gates invoked Bush's situation to pressure Prime Minister Maliki to make progress on a backlog of legislation. "I told Maliki there is no longer a Baghdad clock or a Washington clock," recalled Gates, "there is only a George Bush clock. You need to move and get things done while your best friend is still in the White House."[168] In Baghdad, Petraeus and the team around him attempted a similar strategy. "I do think there was some leverage from explaining to our Iraqi counterparts that the unqualified support that we enjoyed from President Bush during his final years might not continue into the next administration," he recalls, "and that the Iraqis needed to come to grips with some of the difficult Iraqi political and, ultimately, legislative issues that would demonstrate to the US Congress and the US people that they were making progress in resolving their own issues and thus merited continued support."[169] A similar strategy was reportedly employed from the bottom up too, as U.S. Marines began warning Sunni leaders that the departure of U.S. forces would leave them exposed to al-Qaeda and Iranian-backed Shia militias, from whom they had hitherto been protected. As such, it was in their interests to work with U.S. forces while they were still there to counter these threats, while brokering a series of local political agreements. "We are leaving," the Americans would reportedly say to Sunni sheikhs. "We don't know when we are leaving, but we don't have much time, so you better get after this."[170]

In order to slow down the Washington "clock," meanwhile, the president adopted an approach to troop withdrawals that carefully calibrated the desire for a long-term presence in Iraq with the electoral realities at home. Though Bush publicly maintained that all decisions regarding the pace of the drawdown were based purely on the guidance of the commanders in the field, this obscures the reality that those recommendations were in turn subject to repeated direct and indirect pressures from Washington to remain sensitive to the domestic political calendar.

The basic problem was framed well by Gates in a meeting with the president on March 30, 2007, in which the secretary of defense recalls explaining to Bush how he "needed to get the issue of Iraq off the front burner politically by the presidential primaries in February 2008 so that the Democratic candidates did not lock themselves into public positions that might preclude their later support for sustaining a sizeable military presence in Iraq for 'years to come.'"[171] Prior to General Petraeus's scheduled testimony before Congress in September, Gates sought to stave off these risks by repeatedly hinting that the public could expect the commander to recommend withdrawing units sooner rather than later, while pressuring the general behind closed doors to deliver a politically realistic plan. As violence in Iraq continued to spike despite the earlier influx of troops, Petraeus reluctantly stomached the operational costs of strategically premature redeployments. Shortly after May, the bloodiest month of the entire war, he outlined a program that would bring a brigade home roughly every six weeks starting that autumn, with an ambition to have all surge units out of Iraq by the summer of 2008, conveniently just as the presidential campaign would reach its peak.[172]

By September, with violence metrics in Iraq finally beginning to fall, and Petraeus's appearance on Capitol Hill having punctured the Democrats' efforts to defund the war, the administration redoubled its efforts to finesse a drawdown schedule so as to avoid a precipitate withdrawal. Again, Gates articulates the challenge clearly, writing that the key objective "was to make the continuing reduction in our combat forces in Iraq unmistakable, in an attempt to keep Iraq from being a central issue in the presidential election. It would also provide the new president with political cover for a longer troop presence and a sustainable U.S. role in Iraq's future for the long term."[173] Importantly, he recalls explaining his logic to a receptive president in a meeting of January 29, 2008. While noting that the time line he had in mind "may be too aggressive," he stressed that any decision to keep troops on for longer, however strategically desirable, "could have a potentially significant impact on the campaign debate in the United States and decisions after January 20, 2009. . . . No additional drawdowns would make it more likely that troop levels would fall off a cliff on January 20 if a Democrat was elected."[174] The net effect of another series of meetings and videoconferences including

Bush and Petraeus was indeed an electorally friendly program involving the redeployment of two further brigades before Bush's last day in office, with the promise of a further shortly after Inauguration Day.

Petraeus understood that it was not sustainable to maintain such a large troop presence in perpetuity. "I strongly believed that US troops were part of the solution, not part of the problem," he recalled, "but not forever." In particular, he knew that what he called "armies of liberation" have half-lives. "Over time, ours would gradually run out, as the accumulation of inevitable mistakes, missteps, and inability to achieve all that the local population sought (including jobs for all!) chipped away at the credits we had earned."[175] In making recommendations to Gates and the White House on the pace of future drawdowns, moreover, he employed the same approach he had outlined to the president in the past: "I will *base* my advice and recommendations on the mission you have given us and facts on the ground, on the military situation—*informed* by an awareness of the issues beyond my purview that you nonetheless must consider (e.g. strain on the force, budget deficits, the opportunity cost of forces in Iraq or Afghanistan, domestic politics, congressional politics, etc., etc.)—but, in the end, *driven* by the facts on the ground."[176]

Yet if it was surely the case that Petraeus's recommendations factored in a wide variety of strategic and operational considerations, the role of the political environment back home is particularly notable for the present study. "I always sought to maintain an understanding of Washington politics," recalls Petraeus, "as well as politics in London and other capitals, including Baghdad, not to mention political sentiment more broadly in each country."[177] And as observers of and advisors to the general note, these factors included precisely the kinds of pressures Gates had been emphasizing. "Petraeus understood that there was political pressure to bring troops home, and didn't want to bring troops home," argues Stephen Biddle, adding that, "to an unusual degree, Petraeus was trying to be attentive to Washington politics. . . . He was willing to send more troops home than he thought was a good idea, because that seemed like the alternative to having them all pulled out. Left to his own devices, I suspected he would have left them there a lot longer if not indefinitely. But he felt pulled by Washington and made concessions as necessary."[178] Similarly, Colonel Peter Mansoor admits that while Petraeus was primarily concerned with balancing the security requirements in Iraq with the need to ease the strain on the force, he was "certainly aware of the domestic political context of the surge and its aftermath," and "the interface of politics and military operations was never far from General Petraeus's mind."[179]

If this balance of priorities drove the decision-making process in 2007 and 2008, to what extent was Bush engaged in the process? In describing some criticism of his May 2007 Senate appearance, in which he indicated the possibility of further troop reductions, Bob Gates revealingly notes that "this was what the president, Condi, Steve Hadley, Pace, I, and the commanders had been working on for weeks. . . . Most outside observers and 'military experts'—even the vice president—seemed to have no idea of how thin a thread the entire operation hung by in Congress through the spring and summer. George W. Bush understood."[180] Indeed, the White House's deep level of engagement with military strategy in 2007 and 2008 was a far cry from the deference and delegation witnessed in the early years of the war. "In truth, in many respects there were two George W. Bushes," says General Petraeus, who would hold weekly videoconferences with the president during his time as commander. "There was the one who, until November 2006, largely allowed the SecDef to run the war in Iraq (albeit with increasing involvement), and the one after that, who very much took control of the war himself and directly oversaw its conduct." In short, the president "was very deeply engaged in understanding what we were doing."[181] Moreover, the fact that Bush would no longer be in office after January 2009 had a "dramatic impact" on the atmosphere in the White House, with amenability to Gates's approach the result of the fact that "all eyes were now on legacy, history, and unfinished business, above all, on Iraq."[182]

In short, it seems fair to conclude that the decisions made regarding the drawdown of U.S. forces after the surge reflected at least in part a compromise between the militarily optimal strategy (one based on conditions in Iraq) and one that carried the least electoral risk (one based on perceptions of the political landscape at home). Notably, however, the object here was not to protect the incumbent's electoral prospects per se. Instead, the conscious objective was to find some way to preserve Bush's preferred strategy beyond the lifetime of his administration, and thus protect his legacy. Even during Bush's time as a lame duck, the American electoral cycle exerted a strong influence on the nature and timing of military strategy in Iraq.

Deadlines and Red Lines: The 2008 Status of Forces Agreement

With the military strategy in place and finally starting to show signs of progress, the final task for the outgoing administration was finding a way to secure the legal basis for the continued presence of U.S. troops in Iraq. Up to now, the United Nations Security Council had provided cover for the occupation through year-to-year resolutions granting such authority. In 2007, however, Iraqi leaders, anxious to reassert their own sovereignty, had made clear that any subsequent provisions would only be agreed through a bilateral agreement between the United States and Iraq. A SOFA would eventually be signed in the aftermath of the 2008 presidential election, but the negotiation that led up to it offers an illuminating example of the *spoiler* mechanism. Even though Bush was not running for reelection, the political calendar at home set a fixed deadline that limited his ability to secure the terms of a flexible yet enduring strategic partnership agreement with Iraq. After initially adopting a hard-line stance with the Iraqis, the necessity of striking a deal before Bush left office compelled the administration to make concession after concession as November approached. The end result was a deal much closer to the preferences of Prime Minister Maliki and Barack Obama than those of President Bush.

At the broadest level, President Bush clearly understood the SOFA to be a mechanism for protecting his preferred vision of the future relationship between Iraq and the United States, and thereby bolstering his legacy as a president who brought not just war but stability to a post-Saddam Iraq. Acutely aware that his successor might choose instead to rapidly disengage, the underlying purpose of a deal was to tie the hands of whoever took over from him. According to Meghan O'Sullivan, whom Bush drafted back into the administration to work on the negotiations, the president's limited time left in office was a "big driver" of the process, adding that, "whether it was Obama or McCain—though obviously we were more worried about Obama—we wanted to put this relationship on some kind of track that could be continued. We didn't want to leave all these big open questions."[183] Similarly, Douglas Lute, whom Bush appointed "war czar" on the NSC, readily acknowledges that "it was pretty clear that broader politics, no matter who was to be elected, would push the president toward eventually leaving Iraq." In the meantime, therefore, "Bush effectively read the politics and said, 'Look, the surge seems to be having an effect. How could one cement the results of the surge, and provide some degree of predictability across this presidential transition?' "[184] In short, if Iraqi public opinion and concerns about sovereignty compelled the original legal need for a bilateral agreement, it was nevertheless viewed in the White House overwhelmingly as a means by which Bush could manage the electoral realities at home in this twilight phase of his term.

To hammer out the details of a deal, Bush appeared initially content to let a team of professional SOFA negotiators led by Robert Loftis pursue a traditional long-term basing agreement deemed to carry optimal diplomatic characteristics. Among the red lines expected to provoke tension were the insistence that the United States retain legal jurisdiction over any American personnel in Iraq, and that there was to be no taxation of U.S. activity in the country. Further, any discussion of a quid pro quo involving a fixed time line for the withdrawal of U.S. troops, something long considered anathema by President Bush, at least in public, was not on the table.[185]

Before long, advisors close to Bush grew anxious about the approach Loftis was taking. "Our original document was really long," admits Loftis. "That actually caused certain people to think that I was trying to sabotage the agreement by making it too complicated."[186] Indeed, some administration officials began questioning whether the agreement could be quickly put together in the form of a three- to four-page "diplomatic note." This irked Loftis, who insisted that such an agreement "doesn't cover 80 percent of what you need it to cover if you were going to be there on a permanent basis."[187]

By early spring, progress in the talks themselves began to stall. While the Iraqi prime minister privately indicated much interest in a deal, Iraqi public opinion nevertheless made things difficult. Eager to exert their sovereignty after years of American occupation, several groups, notably including many members of the Shia community in Maliki's political coalition, pressed the prime minister to take a harder line, particularly if the deal was expected to be ratified in the Iraqi Parliament. "Extending the presence of U.S. forces was existential for Maliki," explains Douglas Lute. "He knew he was in no position with his forces in 2008 to just say goodbye to the Americans. He couldn't have controlled the situation. So he knew he needed us. But politically—as the first Shia majority leader of Iraq, which is struggling to find its feet in a true parliamentary system and with a key partner in Iran—he couldn't admit that."[188]

Propelled by his own domestic politics, Maliki demanded movement on two of the American red lines. First, he insisted that Iraqi courts should command jurisdiction over American forces, and personally intervened when his negotiators did not get their way. Loftis would not budge, however, on his most important red line. The United States would not accept any proposal that gave Iraqi courts authority to rule over American personnel. Maliki's second demand was arguably even more fundamental: he wanted a firm commitment detailing when U.S. forces would leave Iraq.

Crucially, the response of the Bush administration to this impasse reflected its perception that, while Loftis's approach might well be optimal in strictly diplomatic terms, it did not align with the electoral situation in which the Bush administration found itself. The key players in fact tell us as much in their own words. "We spent some weeks, maybe even a couple of months . . . just approaching this in a classic way," regrets Lute. "It became pretty obvious that this wasn't going to go anywhere, and it was not going to produce on the time line that we had, which was the November election." Taking a hard line in negotiations, trying to extract every single concession possible to favor the United States might work well in other cases. But what Loftis failed to recognize, argues Lute, was that "we were not in the strongest bargaining position." Loftis's laundry list of demands would not play well with an Iraqi leadership keen to exert their own sovereignty, "and it especially didn't play so well given the deadline of the election."[189] Indeed, at the most senior levels in Baghdad, it was understood that the Bush administration had a limited time before its leverage to strike a deal reached its lowest ebb. "The deadline was the need to have a SOFA in place before the Bush Administration became a lame duck presidency," recalls General Petraeus, who, as commanding general, had personal representatives on the negotiating team.[190]

Bush, feeling the heat from the electoral clock, was thus more sympathetic to Maliki's concerns than Loftis had been, telling his top advisors that "this SOFA is not like the others" and that it was important to give the Iraqis a "win."[191] In fact, Bush gave his counterpart several "wins" in quick succession. First, Loftis was replaced as lead negotiator by Brett McGurk and David Satterfield, two men who had been advocates of the "fast" option of a "diplomatic note" agreement. Second, on jurisdictions, the United States would no longer insist on legal immunities for private contractors. Third, and crucially, the Americans were willing to discuss time lines for an American withdrawal, albeit in vague terms such as "time horizons" and "aspirational goals."[192] Bush told Maliki that any drawdown must be conditions based, as he had long insisted, but by placing withdrawal on the table, Pandora's box had been opened.

A second observable implication of the *spoiler* mechanism concerns the role played by other candidates and negotiating opponents in exacerbating the pressures generated by the electoral cycle. In the case of the SOFA, there is strong evidence to suggest that Maliki—knowingly or otherwise—acted in ways that further eroded the president's ability to pursue a robust, long-term commitment he felt was diplomatically optimal. Shortly after Bush's above-mentioned concessions, for instance, the Iraqi prime minister conducted an interview with the German magazine *Der Spiegel* in which he effectively endorsed a key campaign pledge recently made by Obama, then the newly crowned Democratic nominee. "U.S. presidential candidate Barack Obama talks about 16 months," noted Maliki, referring to the drawdown plan recently touted by the candidate, before affirming it to be "the right timeframe for a withdrawal."[193] Notably, this was just two days after the video teleconference with Bush in which he signed up to the incumbent's conditions-based, "aspirational" terminology. Maliki's intervention was slammed by General Petraeus in a private letter to the secretary of defense as "improper and an intrusion into domestic US politics," but it made perfect sense in the context of the campaign.[194] With Obama's opponent, Republican nominee John McCain, still avowedly opposed to any such timetable, it was strategically beneficial to use Obama's position as leverage with Bush now, rather than risk ending up dealing with McCain in 2009.

As the summer wore on, Maliki continued to use Obama's position as a wedge to extract further concessions for the incumbent U.S. president. Before the month of July was over, Maliki debated the question of time lines further with President Bush, with the latter reluctantly conceding more ground. American troops would be out of Iraqi towns and cities by mid-2009, they agreed, with the end of 2011 settled as the goal for a full withdrawal of forces. The 2011 date was a compromise between the mid-2010 target Maliki had wanted and the 2015 "aspiration" Bush was initially prepared to offer. While American negotiators would hold the line on jurisdictions and steered clear of naming a specific withdrawal date, still insisting on a conditions-based drawdown, the steady march toward folding on consecutive elements of the negotiation proceeded unabated, and in lockstep with the electoral cycle in the United States. As negotiations entered a "treading water" phase, with Prime Minister Maliki getting "cold feet," according to Petraeus, concerns grew that it might be the U.S. side that buckled first.[195] So keen was Bush to secure his legacy before the election, some thought, that there was a real chance that the negotiators would "give away the farm," endangering the entire mission.[196]

"Giving Away the Farm"

After a brief recess in late August to reassess the negotiating strategy for the home stretch, McGurk and Satterfield returned to Baghdad armed with the first of two major concessions. To overcome the ongoing impasse over jurisdictions, the American side would propose a mechanism whereby the Iraqis would be given the illusion of judicial authority. In reality, however, the U.S. military would retain custody of any soldier accused of impropriety, and, says Douglas Lute, "if the U.S. commander feared the outcome of the jurisdiction conversation, he would just put the accused on a plane and get him out of Iraq."[197] Possession being nine-tenths of the law, the military could cope with the ambiguity on paper. As the chairman of the JCS recalls, "the real risk was relatively low, and it was also done in a way for each of those specifics that potentially put our troops in jeopardy, it was very clear to the Iraqi government that we would not tolerate that in any way, shape, or form."[198] "I felt comfortable with that," agreed Odierno, for whom the SOFA represented the biggest unresolved issue as he assumed command of MNF-I in August.[199]

The mechanism may well have worked in keeping de facto control as the Americans wanted, but from a broader diplomatic perspective, it was a short-sighted move reflecting the reality that, given the precious little time remaining in 2008, a bad deal was fast becoming preferable to no deal. Crucially, it lacked forethought when considering the administration's overall ambition to establish a long-term strategic partnership with Iraq. As Emma Sky notes, the Americans came up with this fudge believing it to be a stepping stone to a more comprehensive and permanent agreement in the future. "They believed that this is all we can get now, for political reasons, but the Iraqis will renegotiate to keep us there. They were all absolutely, 100 percent convinced that the Iraqis would negotiate to extend this."[200] That being the case, dangling the illusion of control now only set up a fight over every single issue that arose and encouraged the Iraqis to want the jurisdictional authorities for real when any prospective renewal came about. "My view on negotiations is you don't borrow trouble in advance," concludes Loftis, "and this is exactly what we were doing."[201]

Why would the Americans sign up to such a short-term deal? Again, the domestic political calendar had a lot to do with matters. Explains Douglas Lute, "you get into the fall, and now it becomes clear that Obama is an increasingly promising Democratic candidate, and McCain is someone who was associated with Iraq, and defended it during the campaign, that the political winds here are just not blowing in a positive direction. So the deadline of the election and the transition . . . was leverage on us."[202] Indeed, the level of urgency and interest from the White House picked up exponentially. According to Emma Sky, General Odierno's representative in the talks, "Every week, even every day, Washington wanted to know, 'Are we nearly there yet?' It was *constantly* going back and forth."[203]

The biggest concessions of all would come in the final days before the election. The Iraqi delegation, timing its demands expertly, first secured an agreement from Bush to include the words "withdrawal" and "temporary presence" in the title of the SOFA. During the NSC meeting at which this change was discussed, some objected to the insertion of the word "withdrawal," but the president pressed forward. Bush, as a lame duck was less concerned with the impact of the specific terms of the SOFA on the election than the need to get any sort of deal by that time. "That was a signal that we *need* this agreement," confirms Lute, adding that "here is a case where he really did have a strategic horizon that was based on a specific time line. He knew what the milestones were in the calendar, and he drove us."[204]

A few days later, Maliki informed the American ambassador, Ryan Crocker, that he would agree to a deal only if a specific date for the final American departure was contained in the document. Lute took the request to the president, explaining how this crossed one of Bush's final red lines. A date would mean "it's not going to look conditions based," said Lute. "There is going to be a date and we've said all along that we are not going to put the commanders on a timeline."[205] Bush knew this was suboptimal, later recalling how "for years, I had refused to set an arbitrary timetable for leaving Iraq [and] I was still hesitant to commit to a date."[206]

Yet the president was also acutely aware of the electoral realities facing him. "The president ultimately agreed to a 2011 withdrawal date," recalls Deputy Secretary of State John Negroponte, "because he was concerned that if Mrs. Clinton or Mr. Obama got elected, they might end our presence in Iraq sooner. He wanted to influence the actions of the successor government [and] was guarding against the advent of a Democratic president committed to complete withdrawal earlier. Definitely—I mean, he told me that."[207] "He knew that 2011 would be around another election," agrees Admiral Mullen. "The reason he picked 2011 was he wanted to give the next president, whoever it was going to be, time to really look at it and make a decision about what happens after 2011."[208] So, believing a specific date to be diplomatically and militarily suboptimal, Bush nonetheless gave the green light to a December 31, 2011, deadline, his hand having been forced by the pressures of the American electoral cycle. "If this is what we need to get an agreement," Bush told Lute, "this is what we'll do."[209] Much to the incredulity of Lute and Crocker, the withdrawal of U.S. troops was thus enshrined in the text of the diplomatic accord. This, along with no less than 120 further Iraqi amendments, were agreed by Bush on November 3, the day before the 2008 presidential election. "To 'buy' a SOFA," admits James Jeffrey, "we needed to give a 'leave by' date."[210] Once more, then, it was a case of a bad deal over no deal, given the electoral bind in which Bush found himself.

It was not just a worse deal. These concessions, made necessary by the pressures of the electoral calendar, changed the entire *nature* of the deal. At the beginning of this process, notes Loftis, "there was a genuine thought that Iraq would become this Western bastion," with talk of a permanent basing arrangement akin to the U.S. presence in South Korea or postwar West Germany. "But as the negotiations wore on," he continues, "as we became closer and closer to the election . . . it became clear that wasn't going to happen." By the time the deal was signed, it was something fundamentally different. John Negroponte, whose office had started the entire negotiation process back in late 2008, is quite clear on what Bush ended up with: "it's a withdrawal agreement."[211] "The entire purpose had changed," agreed Loftis, affirming that "the reality was that the 2008 agreement was an agreement for the withdrawal of American forces, totally."[212]

With the Bush administration having capitulated in the face of virtually all the key demands the Iraqis made, the deal now also looked much more like what Obama had been offering through the summer. As such, the Democrat's campaign stayed relatively silent on the matter in October and November, figuring that, in the words of Obama's advisor on Iraq, Colin Kahl, "the SOFA as such would probably be OK; it would include a time line for our departure, which creates co-ownership so that, in essence, Obama's not on the political hook." Recommending that the campaign should essentially "keep our powder dry" in a memorandum at the time, Kahl cautioned against "a hard line trashing the SOFA."[213] Unlike in July, when Maliki took advantage of the distance between the Bush and Obama positions to extract more concessions from the incumbent, by the time Obama was elected, there was in fact surprisingly little daylight between the two camps, making any further delay in sending the deal for ratification in Baghdad largely pointless. The deal was duly agreed upon by Maliki's cabinet on November 16, before final ratification in parliament on November 27.

From start to finish, then, the negotiation of the 2008 SOFA was clearly subject to the *spoiler* mechanism outlined in chapter 1. Though President Bush was not running in the upcoming presidential election, his ability to forge a diplomatic agreement, even with an ally, was severely limited by electoral constraints. A lame duck, keen to secure his legacy and lock in his preferred vision of a continued American presence in Iraq, Bush hoped to sign a deal that codified a long-term, strategic partnership between the two countries. Instead, compelled by a ticking clock, and Maliki's interventions in the American political race, Bush rowed back on virtually every red line he and his diplomats had once asserted, most notably on the issues of jurisdictions and time lines. "The role of public opinion and domestic politics is quite clear in the SOFA decision," argues Douglas Lute. "With election politics breathing down, I think it was absolutely dominant. [Bush] was not in a rush in '07 to sign a SOFA. He was in 2008. What's different?" Along with the surge he concludes, "these are your classic example of vignettes, case studies, of the impact of public opinion and domestic politics. Without question."[214]

*   *   *

This chapter has demonstrated the significant degree to which President Bush's decision making vis-à-vis the war in Iraq was shaped by pressures that had more to with electoral conditions at home than the strategic exigencies on the ground. In Fallujah, a major operation designed to secure the city and weaken the growing insurgency was postponed so as to avoid "rocking the boat" ahead of the 2004 election. As security in Iraq declined further in the subsequent two years, Bush's response was similarly marked by a proclivity to *delay* politically controversial decisions. Though he felt that the existing transition strategy was failing, he nevertheless deferred a full consideration of alternatives until after the congressional elections, whereupon he suddenly sprang into action, forcefully pushing a bold and risky counterinsurgency plan against considerable opposition. Then, in orchestrating a drawdown schedule of this increase in troops, he followed a plan devised by his secretary of defense that repeatedly tempered the conditions-based preference of his commander in favor of a plan that better reflected electoral realities, mitigating against the possibility of a Democratic platform that might consign Bush's signature foreign policy shift of his second term to the dustbin of history. Finally, the *spoiler* mechanism has been demonstrated to have been in full force in the negotiation of the 2008 SOFA, whereby Bush's leverage steadily eroded as the November elections drew closer, pushing the president away from a diplomatically optimal deal with strong terms on jurisdictions and conditions-based drawdown time lines, and toward a withdrawal agreement, the terms of which increasingly came to reflect the preferences of Prime Minister Maliki and Barack Obama.

How might things have turned out were it not for electoral pressures? First, it seems reasonable to suggest that the operation in Fallujah might have been conducted differently, both in terms of its timing and nature. In line with the pattern of presidential deference to the uniformed military, which had characterized the president's engagement with military operations until that point, the absence of electoral pressure would likely have resulted in the Marines on the ground being able to define the terms of their own battle plan. As Jim Mattis has recently written, this had in fact been planned out. "It didn't take us more than fifteen minutes to decide on a low-key, three-step approach," he recalls, emphasizing how the forces under his command would seek to avoid sparking further outbursts of violence, hold a steady course, and deliver justice through the discriminate use of force. "I knew what to do and how to do it," he adds, stressing that his superiors had also agreed with his plan.[215] As it was, of course, the military was overruled, with the views of the commanders on the ground not even solicited, let alone heeded, once the assault began. The military's later claims that the operation could have succeeded within a week were it not for the White House getting cold feet may of course be colored by a degree of hindsight bias. Yet even so, we might at least permit the notion that a renewed assault would have come sooner than November were it not for the pressures—direct or indirect in nature—associated with the domestic political calendar. Instead, Fallujah was left as a festering sore, allowing the insurgency to grow, and making the eventual task of retaking the city more costly.

The opportunity costs of the on-again, off-again approach to Fallujah may have been more significant still than the immediate issues concerning the insurgency inside the city. First, senior leaders of terrorist groups were effectively provided a safe haven. These included those who played a key role in frustrating U.S. policy in Iraq at the time, such as Abu Musab al-Zarqawi, the founder of AQI, as well as those who would emerge as even bigger scourges in the future, such as Abu Bakr al-Baghdadi, who would emerge as the leader of the Islamic State a decade later. While the jury remains out on the strategic value of decapitating terrorist organizations, arguably even more crucial was the damage the Fallujah episode wrought to the credibility of the American commitment to the security of Sunni communities across Anbar Province and Iraq more broadly.[216] While the relative improvements in security witnessed in 2007 are often attributed to the influx of additional troops, an important contributing factor was undoubtedly the Sunni "Awakening." While the effort to engage with Sunni sheiks predated General Petraeus's time at MNF-I, a series of agreements struck between the Iraqi government and Anbari leaders on multimillion-dollar investments in economic aid for the province, opportunities for Anbaris to serve in the Iraqi Security Forces, and prisoner releases collectively failed to achieve the kind of progress seen in the years that followed. "Nothing happens quickly in places like that," admits General Casey.[217] While it remains speculative, a case has been made that these efforts might have made more progress than they did were it not for the lack of resolve demonstrated in 2004.[218]

As for the surge, absent the presence of the 2006 midterms, it seems fair to speculate that President Bush might have opted to launch a strategy review at least six months before he did. As skepticism about the existing strategy crystallized in the aftermath of the Samarra bombing, an interagency consensus could have been established between the NSC and the State Department, which may in turn have elicited alliances with the doubters in the intelligence community and the uniformed military. Even if the bureaucracy remained ambivalent, the decisiveness that Bush showed after the election, and indeed his willingness to overrule a firm majority of dissenters, could well have resulted in a decision to shift toward a population-centric counterinsurgency plan much earlier than was the case.

While the jury is still out on the extent to which the surge contributed to the turnaround in security in 2007, the general consensus is that it represented at least a tactical military success, helping to reduce violence metrics to manageable levels by the fall of 2007, enabling the development and spread of the so-called Sunni Awakening, and opening up space for political reconciliation to occur.[219] Without discrediting much essential groundwork for such success being completed by General Petraeus's predecessors, an earlier influx of troops and change of mission might have resulted in similar progress much sooner. Critics of the surge point out that improved security is an insufficient ingredient for political stability, but it might reasonably be countered that it is at least necessary.[220] By waiting to make the change in strategy, then, Bush "clearly made a bad situation worse," notes James Jeffrey, pointing to the "further discombobulation of Iraq" that took place, especially after February 2006.[221] An earlier decision, unencumbered by electoral pressures, could have at least saved countless Iraqi and American lives, and may ultimately have shortened the war.

On the pace of the drawdown, it seems likely that Bush may have given General Petraeus greater latitude to keep a full complement of forces in Iraq for longer. Given that violence metrics did indeed fall dramatically from late 2007 through 2008, it seems reasonable to conclude that additional troops were not essential by this stage; the missing piece of the puzzle was now political in nature, and political reconciliation in Baghdad was unlikely to be significantly affected by an additional one or two brigades. What might well have happened, however, was what Gates had in fact been warning against: without throwing a bone to the "bugout" fever at home, the Democrats might have ended up with a much more dovish platform on Iraq, which in turn could have forced a precipitate withdrawal. Whether or not one agrees with the wisdom of a continued U.S. presence in Iraq, the administration's electorally informed approach in this closing phase of the Bush presidency seems in fact to have been a rational one, given the president's interest in forestalling a radical departure in military strategy in the Middle East.

Regarding the SOFA, given the unpredictable and fractious nature of Iraqi politics at this time, it would be foolish to place too much faith in any counterfactual deal. Bush would likely have held out for longer on jurisdictions and a withdrawal time line, closer to the preferences of the expert diplomats who began this process. "He would have rather not agreed anything," agrees Negroponte, adding, "he would have rather strung out the negotiation."[222] Yet, against this, one must admit the possibility that the Iraqis may just as likely have walked away from such a deal, with untold consequences for security and political stability. It suffices to note, however, that the SOFA was a critical juncture in signaling the beginning of the end of formal American intervention in Iraq, and, absent the electoral pressures discussed here, it seems likely that both the negotiation process and the deal itself would have looked markedly different.

SIX

Iraq

Barack Obama and the Endgame

Throughout this process [Obama] was weighing a number of factors and considerations, not just in terms of security requirements, but also some of those political dimensions, as it got closer to the elections.

—JOHN BRENNAN

BY THE TIME Barack Obama took office in 2009, the U.S. intervention in Iraq had already been set on a de-escalatory path. Following the surge of 2007, George W. Bush bequeathed to his successor a conflict in which a degree of stability had finally been reached. Almost six years after Saddam Hussein's removal from power, a fully sovereign Iraq could now look forward to the departure of U.S. troops by the end of 2011, under the terms of a SOFA signed in the final days of the Bush administration. As senior Obama advisors therefore understood, the range of possible courses of action open to the forty-fourth president were significantly circumscribed. "President Bush had already put us on a withdrawal time line by having reached an agreement to withdraw U.S. forces by the end of 2011," explains Tony Blinken, then national security advisor to the vice president. "So the question really was the pace and means of that drawdown."[1] "Because the *fundamental* shift of strategy had already happened under Bush's watch," clarifies Michèle Flournoy, Obama's under secretary of defense for policy, "it was really a question, for Obama, of do I continue on this path, do I tweak it in some way, or do I abandon it?"[2]

Obama's decision making regarding the pace and finality of the drawdown in Iraq is the object of analysis in this chapter. Specifically, it first explores the development of Obama's strategy for ending the war in Iraq, announced in February 2009, which put U.S. forces on an expedited withdrawal time-table. Secondly, it examines the subsequent debate over the size of a residual force that was widely expected to remain in Iraq after the 2008 SOFA expired, culminating instead in an October 2011 decision to pull the plug on American involvement entirely. Taken together, these episodes serve as a relatively "hard" case for the overall claim that presidential decision making is constrained by electoral pressures, partly due to the nature of Obama's inheritance. With the major muscle movements of the war having already taken place, Obama's decisions concerning troop commitments might be considered relatively minor adjustments to military strategy. As such, amid growing concerns about the onset of a global recession, the salience of Obama's choices in Iraq were relatively low. Furthermore, unlike Eisenhower and Nixon, President Obama had consistently opposed American intervention in the war he now inherited, and as a result was arguably less susceptible to domestic political punishment for its outcome. Having argued against what in his 2002 Senate campaign he once called the "dumb war," his antiwar credentials were the centerpiece of his political rise thereafter, becoming a wedge issue with Hilary Clinton, who had voted for the war, and a further point of contrast with John McCain, an unreconstructed "surgionista." Of course, as this chapter will demonstrate, Obama would be held accountable for delivering on his promise of ending the war, yet the potential audience costs he faced in handling a conflict everyone knew he considered wrong-headed from the outset were surely lower than those of his forebears, who had variously promised the more challenging goal of "peace" in ongoing conflicts in Korea and Vietnam.

Nevertheless, this chapter offers striking evidence for a number of causal mechanisms outlined earlier in the book. First, the extent to which the nature of Obama's plan was shaped by the specific pledges he made on the campaign trail is highly suggestive of the *hangover* mechanism. Second, in deferring consideration of a prospective follow-on force so as not to have Iraq be a "political football" in the congressional elections, the *delay* mechanism can be observed. Finally, and most importantly, in steadily eroding proposals for that residual force, we see clear evidence of the *dampening* mechanism. As this chapter concludes, the net effect of these electoral pressures ultimately served to push Obama toward the abandonment of Iraq in late 2011, with serious consequences for the future stability of the country.

Ending the War Responsibly

On February 27, 2009, just five weeks after becoming president, Barack Obama announced the results of a thirty-day strategic review of the war in Iraq. The withdrawal of U.S. troops was to be placed on an expedited timetable, he said, with all "combat" forces out by August 31, 2010, to be followed by all remaining troops by the end of 2011.[3] Promising to bring the war to an end "responsibly," Obama based his plan on the expectation that the Iraqis would once more pick up the burden of providing security in their own country, as the new administration sought to shift the character of U.S. engagement in the Middle East. As this section will show, this revised plan represented an explicit compromise between what Obama had promised on the campaign trail and what he now understood to be strategically optimal. As such, it is an excellent example of how the *hangover* mechanism places constraints on the development of military strategy even in an otherwise permissive phase of the electoral cycle.

The Search for a "Sweet Spot"

Barack Obama's opposition to the war in Iraq was well-known by the time he assumed office. During the 2008 presidential campaign, he had staked out a clear position on how he would manage the closing stages of the conflict if elected. In a *New York Times* op-ed published in July 2008, he advocated a sixteen-month withdrawal timetable that would see all combat brigades out of Iraq by the summer of 2010.[4] Compared to Eisenhower's pledge to simply "go to Korea," or Nixon's "secret plan" in Vietnam, his was a highly specific and unambiguous pledge for which he could be held accountable.

It did not take long, however, for Obama to realize that the position he had crafted to appeal to voters jarred with what the military considered to be in the best interests of the mission in Iraq. General Petraeus had in fact told him as much in a tense two-hour meeting in Baghdad just one week after Obama's *New York Times* opinion piece had been published. "I was concerned that the 16-month pledge would box the president into a drawdown plan that would prove unwise in terms of maintaining the security gains of the surge," recalls Petraeus.[5] While Petraeus was somewhat reassured by Obama's professed willingness to be flexible in a subsequent private meeting, his successor, General Raymond Odierno, shared similar concerns. A sixteen-month time frame would "substantially increase risk" to a level that would "most likely keep us from meeting our refined realistic objectives," he wrote in a memorandum written during the presidential transition.[6] Sensing the way the political winds were blowing, Odierno went into "full bore planning mode on what we were going to present to the president."[7] In a three-hour videoconference on Obama's first day in office, the commander noted the "significant risk" associated with troop withdrawals. Tasked with preparing a formal options paper, Odierno subsequently set out three alternatives, including Obama's sixteen-month time line, which was said to carry an "extremely high" level of risk. If the president was set on expediting Bush's timetable, he recommended drawing down over twenty-three months. As to how they got there, a linear staircase reduction of a brigade a month would be more drastic than conditions could permit. Odierno pressed instead for authority to stagger the pace of the withdrawal, so as to keep as many troops in Iraq for as long as was feasible.[8]

Presented with such contrary counsel on the strategic wisdom of the course he had outlined on the campaign trail, Obama was now willing to show some flexibility, so long as any revised plan stayed within the parameters of the SOFA. As he later conceded, his prior statements "had been from the cheap seats, before I had hundreds of thousands of troops and a sprawling national security infrastructure under my command." As the sitting president, rather than simply aspirant to that office, Obama understood that any terrorist attacks or significant casualties would now occur on his watch. "These were my wars now," he recalled. With so much riding on the stability of Iraq, he conceded that "commanders who were knee-deep in the fighting deserved some deference when it came to tactical decisions."[9]

The task at hand, as he told his advisors quite explicitly, was to find a "sweet spot" between his campaign pledge and the recommendations of the commander in the field.[10] In doing so, the administration had some leeway during this honeymoon phase of the electoral cycle. Yet this was understood to be temporally bound. As Vice President Joe Biden had reportedly told the military on a trip to Baghdad during the transition, "the incoming administration had about a year to show progress before the far left in the Democratic party called for the soldiers to be withdrawn."[11]

Squaring the Political Circle

The first step in this process entailed some semantic sleight of hand. Noticing that Obama's speeches during the campaign had left more "rhetorical wiggle room" than had been anticipated, the campaign's Iraq specialist, Colin Kahl, wrote an anonymous memorandum to the transition team setting out ways the plan could be repackaged to assuage the military's concerns. Most notably, every time Obama spoke about getting troops out, he mentioned "combat" troops. He had also on occasion spoken on the possible need to leave behind a follow-on force of unspecified size, who would be tasked with a series of "residual missions," including training and small-scale counterterrorism operations. "That gives you some space," argued Kahl, who would shortly assume duties as the Pentagon's working lead on the strategic review, explaining that "the only thing that had to change was the 'combat' modifier." To ease things further, Kahl noted that Obama had offered a caveat during 2008 that he would retain an openness to listening to the commanders in the field and making any necessary adjustments as appropriate within the overall objective of withdrawing "responsibly."[12]

Over the next couple of weeks, the idea of introducing an additional milestone into the Iraq drawdown process was debated and adopted. A midpoint—serving as "a political marker"—between the start of the drawdown and the 2008 SOFA–mandated December 2011 deadline for total withdrawal would be set, whereby the "combat phase" of the American military's commitment to Iraq would end. After this point, all remaining troops would be given new "advise and assist" missions. The composition of these forces would be notionally altered, with a few more engineers, training specialists, and civil affairs personnel, but, importantly, these would be additional to the existing standard brigade combat team. As Odierno's political advisor approvingly notes, "it's the same soldiers. Same guys, different mission."[13]

Exactly when the "combat" phase would end was in theory more problematic, since the 16-month promise was both explicit and oft-repeated. Again, however, there was some rhetorical wiggle room Obama could take advantage of. Namely, on the campaign website, the 16-month pledge was not given a specific start date. The natural assumption would be that this meant 16 months from Obama's inauguration. Yet the White House press team could simply say he meant 16 months from the date on which the strategy review was concluded, giving an additional month to play with. The military's 23-month recommendation remained a stretch, yet an intervention from Secretary Gates managed to bring Odierno around to a compromise suggestion of 19 months. "This is the best thing for us to do," explained Gates, who, in Odierno's view, "understood Washington better than anybody I ever knew." While 19 months might be difficult, it was "still much better than what the president had campaigned on."[14] With Odierno sold, the compromise position was quickly embraced by the administration. "I'm okay with that," Obama told Gates, adding, "It's also good politically."[15] As Derek Chollet, a senior national security aide, recalled, "Obama accepted this counsel, settling on a compromise that allowed him to stay true to his campaign commitments."[16] By the time the month-long strategy review was completed, the 19 would become 18, and that could be—and was—skated over very quickly in Obama's speech.

As for the pace of the drawdown within this concept, the Obama administration displayed a further willingness to bend. Not only could the military keep hold of much of their resources beyond the 16-month time frame, but Washington would let the commanders on the ground decide how to get to this new milestone. More interested in massaging the nuances of the headline commitment to leave Iraq—the main headline that voters cared about—Obama was wedded less to his original idea of a linear staircase reduction in troops as the means to do it. General Odierno requested and received authority to retain the majority of his forces until after the Iraqi elections of spring 2010, a period he assessed to be the "window of highest risk," before a sharp drawdown leading up to the change of mission.[17]

The final piece of the puzzle was the size of the residual force that would remain after the change of mission. Odierno's paper had originally proposed a figure of 50,000–55,000 but allowed for a bare-bones option of 35,000. Any lower would be a "red line" for Odierno, who would prefer to cut losses and withdraw virtually all troops than to go any lower.[18] Much to the military's surprise, Obama endorsed this position with an intention to leave a "transitional" force of between 35,000 and 50,000 troops after the end of the "combat" phase.[19] In doing so, the president was taking on political risk, with co-partisans in Congress expressing dismay at the concession. Yet Obama did so knowingly, according to Kahl, conscious that he had enough "political capital" to do so at this stage.[20]

The 2009 plan for "responsibly ending the war in Iraq" offers a compelling example of how positions taken during a prior election campaign may constrain the development of military strategy once a president takes office. "What this set of compromises allowed us to do," summarizes Kahl, "was essentially take Obama's campaign pledge to be all out over the course of 16 months, to reducing from 14 brigades to 6 with a different mission over 18 months. And it could be argued that it wasn't a violation of anything he said during the campaign, because he said there would be a residual force, they would have these missions, and he'd listen to his commanders. So that seemed to kind of square the political circle."[21]

Looking back, Obama remembers that arriving at a plan that would leave troops behind in Iraq was "relatively straightforward." Having become convinced that the United States had a strategic and humanitarian interest in Iraq's stability, he was receptive to Odierno's warnings about the fragility of the Iraqi government, the weaknesses of its security forces, the still active presence of al-Qaeda in Iraq and the worrying levels of sectarian hostility across the country. Indeed, it was for these reasons that he agreed to Odierno's recommendation to leave a residual force behind "as a kind of insurance policy against a return to chaos."[22] When the renewal for that policy became due, however, things would not prove so simple.

"Going to Zero"

On December 15, 2011, a military ceremony was held in Baghdad bringing the formal U.S. mission in Iraq to a close. Though technically the Americans were fulfilling the terms of President Bush's SOFA, it did not have to be this way. In fact, between late 2010 and October 2011 there was an intense debate within the Obama administration about how many troops would be left in Iraq on residual missions of training the Iraqi Security Forces and counter-terrorism operations. That Obama would "go to zero" in October was not by any means foreordained. "I always thought it was going to be a question of how much or how little would remain," recalls John Brennan. "I was, frankly, surprised, when it went from a discussion of how many troops to just pulling out. I didn't see that coming."[23]

Drawing on the insights of those directly involved, this section demonstrates how the electoral cycle played a key role in conditioning the Obama administration's willingness to leave a residual force and negotiate a renewed SOFA. Having *delayed* taking up the issue until after the 2010 midterms, the White House belatedly picked up the question of a follow-on force over the winter. Then, as the 2012 campaign season drew nearer, the political optics of leaving troops in theater began to outweigh the perceived benefits to the administration. As such, a series of proposals related to the size of the follow-on force were rejected, in an iterative process typical of the *dampening* mechanism. The administration's appetite for retaining "boots on the ground" diminished over time until finally, and against the preferences of a strong majority of national security officials, Obama decided the effort of pushing through even a small residual force was not worth the political backlash it might engender.

Should I Stay or Should I Go?

Throughout this period, there was broad consensus within the Obama administration and senior military leadership that the strategically optimal course of action entailed the retention of a significant component of troops in Iraq after December 2011. As we will see, some, including General Lloyd Austin and Admiral Michael Mullen, were more bullish than others on exactly how many troops would be required. Yet even those with more modest recommendations were clear that "going to zero" was suboptimal. For the vice chairman of the Joint Chiefs, for instance, even in a downsized capacity, the role of special forces, air support, and intelligence was deemed critical as an "enabler" for local security forces. While many took issue with his top-line figures and manner of briefing them, there was little debate about the importance of retaining at least these functions. "I got really no pushback on the tailoring side of this question," recalls General James "Hoss" Cartwright.[24] The president's chief counterterrorism advisor similarly cautioned against a full withdrawal: "I was a supporter of maintaining a presence, mainly to enable the Iraqi forces to be able to transition to full time and complete responsibility on the counterterrorism front," recalls Brennan. "I was in favor of the train and advise/assist mission continuing."[25]

To these voices one might add both of the secretaries of defense who served in this period, as well as many other Pentagon officials. Gates records his belief, for instance, that "a substantial U.S. military presence was needed post-2011 to help keep Iraq stabilized, to continue training and supporting their security forces, and to signal our friends in the region—and Iran—that we weren't abandoning the field."[26] His successor, Leon Panetta, advocated a similar position, believing that "withdrawing all our forces would endanger the fragile stability then barely holding Iraq together."[27] As under secretary of defense for policy, Michèle Flournoy worked similarly hard behind closed doors on proposals to shape a follow-on force because "I thought it was going to be very critical to our ability to continue to have leverage to shape Iraqi politics."[28] Within the chain of command, additional voices shared such views. Over dinner with Vice President Biden in Iraq shortly after the change of command in mid-2010, General Mattis, then CENTCOM commander, made clear that any progress made to date was "reversible" and could be lost if the United States pulled out too early.[29]

Importantly, the White House seemed to agree that some sort of residual ground commitment was strategically optimal. "I thought that [Obama] was open to a follow-on agreement and leaving a residual force," recalls Flournoy.[30] Indeed, according to those closest to the White House, such as Blinken, "the president really was open to this smaller footprint in terms of a follow-on force." As national security advisor to the vice president, who had been delegated responsibility for Iraq policy by Obama, Blinken is certain on what the administration saw as the strategic necessity: "making sure that we continued to have some forces on the ground that could work with the Iraqis, to continue to train them, to prosecute the counterterrorism mission."[31] Perhaps even stronger proof, in hindsight, is the fact that, as explored below, Obama himself eventually chaired a series of NSC meetings through the spring of 2011, the net result of which was an approval on May 19 of a provisional plan to leave ten thousand troops in Iraq.

From an electoral perspective, however, there was a clear political risk associated with such a course of action. Having pledged to extricate U.S. forces in Iraq in his 2008 campaign, and having already compromised on the pace of the drawdown, Obama understood that he would be held accountable by voters for any failure to abide by his earlier promise. Indeed, looking back, some former administration officials feel that the strength of Obama's electoral preference was transparent from the start. "Look at what he said in the campaign," argues Lute, who was retained as "war czar" on the NSC by Obama, noting that "presidents tend to do what they said."[32] For Admiral Mullen, similarly, "it was very clear: you go back to his campaign promise, and it was going to be zero, it's just this question of how we were going to get there."[33] The campaign pledge to end the war in Iraq served, as Brennan puts it, as "a backdrop against anything that his administration might decide to do."[34]

Faced with such a clear imbalance between strategic and electoral preferences, how did Obama respond? With political pressure pointing toward disengagement, while the logic of strategic necessity pointed toward continued engagement, *delay* or *dampening* mechanisms may be observed, as the weight accorded to Obama's electoral preference rose and fell depending on the stage of the electoral cycle.

Kicking the "Political Football" Down the Road

When faced with a clear need to take a politically controversial decision, a president is likely to defer incurring the associated political costs until a less sensitive phase of the electoral cycle. In mid-2010, when senior military figures and officials in the Department of Defense pressed the White House to engage in a discussion regarding an extension of American intervention in Iraq, something that went against Obama's electoral preference, the decision was indeed kicked into the long grass until after the midterm campaign, in a classic example of the *delay* mechanism.

The first observable implication of this mechanism—evidence that a decision was deemed necessary—is simple enough to demonstrate. Given the existing December 2011 deadline, a decision regarding what came after was time-sensitive, as the uniformed military understood. If they were really headed for a full withdrawal, then the final decisions about closing up bases and processing redeployments were needed well in advance of that deadline. "If the military's going to get out," agrees Flournoy, "it's a major, major operation."[35] For this reason, then, as Kahl acknowledges, "the real deadline was the fall of 2011."[36] Even more time-sensitive, however, was the diplomatic side of the coin. If troops were to remain, a new SOFA would need to be negotiated with the Iraqi government. It took almost two years to agree the last one, and with Iraqi public opinion increasingly agitated about the continued presence of U.S. troops, it was likely to be a complicated process once more. A decision on the post-2011 U.S. commitment to Iraq was necessary because of the ultimate 2011 deadline, then, and for reasons of military logistics and diplomatic process it was a case of the sooner, the better.

Secondly, that attempts were made to spark this discussion is also apparent. "It was very clear to us," recalls Kahl, "we were having quiet conversations about what a follow-on force would look like in 2010. Every time I went to Iraq, I would sit down with General Austin, we talked about these things."[37] Flournoy, Kahl's boss at the time, agrees, admitting that the combatant commanders in Iraq "put this on the table pretty early on"—as soon as the "combat" troops left in August 2010, and even before, Generals Odierno and Austin repeatedly stressed that "we're going to have to start thinking about this, we're going to have to start deciding."[38] It remained clear to the civilian leadership where the military stood. "It was my opinion that we should keep people on the ground for the foreseeable future," recalled General Odierno. "I was very adamant about twenty-five thousand."[39] Any failure to take up the debate in late 2010 was not caused by a lack of understanding of the criticality of making a decision.

The electoral calculation behind the White House's deferral of active discussion on the issue through much of 2010 is quite clear. The continued deployment of thousands of U.S. forces in wars overseas "cast a pall over the midterms," as Obama later recalled.[40] Having laid dormant as a political issue for the majority of his term in office, reports of ongoing violence and a protracted struggle to form a government after the Iraqi parliamentary elections in March 2010 made the war in Iraq front-page news once more by the summer.[41] In such a context, the White House was simply not inclined to open a debate that was likely to become divisive on the eve of the congressional elections. "It was very clear that the system was to have no discussions of a follow-on force until the Iraqi government was formed and we got past the midterm elections, our own midterm elections, so that politics didn't enter into the equation," recalls Kahl. "We didn't want this to become a political football in the midterm elections and [therefore] we weren't going to talk about it right on the eve of our midterm elections."[42] This is consistent with the recollection of Flournoy, who agrees that "it took a while to get folks really focused and engaged," and that until that point, "this was *not* a major public discussion" outside of the Pentagon.[43]

The administration was not entirely disengaged from events in Iraq during this period. On the contrary, the vice president was dispatched to

Baghdad during the summer in an effort to break the deadlock between the competing parties vying to form a government. Yet senior officials on the ground felt that the White House's intervention said more about its desire to put a stop to the negative headlines generated by the ongoing impasse than any deep commitment to upholding key democratic principles that were at stake. "At that point," worried one senior military officer, "it was kind of like, is this going to be all about politics?"[44] Indeed, according to General Odierno's political advisor, Emma Sky, the vice president was quite transparent about this in a meeting held on July 4 to discuss the way forward. "The president has said, 'I need a government in place before our mid-term elections in November,'" Biden explained.[45] "The way things worked, if you're six months out from an election, everything is a possible threat," recalls James Jeffrey, who would shortly thereafter assume the post of ambassador to Iraq. "There are two dozen things you worry about and your job is to worry about them and take care of them. So I'm sure, to check that box, it was to form a government."[46] Though the administration initially gave the ambassador some room to try to resolve the situation through a variety of mechanisms, they ultimately endorsed a version of a "partnership" concept favored by his predecessor. The plan essentially recognized the incumbent prime minister, Nouri al-Maliki, as the only candidate able to muster a large enough bloc of support to form a government, despite having won fewer seats than his opponent, Ayad Allawi.[47] "They basically felt Maliki was the horse we know, and they didn't want a lot of trouble," concludes Jeffrey.[48] To the surprise of virtually no one in Baghdad, however, the coalition agreement fell apart almost immediately, leaving Maliki free to purge the government of rivals in ways that laid the seeds of considerable instability in the years that followed.

Electoral pressures, then, created something of a moratorium on discussions about the future U.S. military footprint in Iraq, a matter all agreed was time-sensitive. By delaying the real start of the interagency discussion until the New Year, "we were already on the clock," admits Kahl, who acknowledges that the electorally induced delay made everything that followed harder to achieve from the outset.[49] In the meantime, the White House's intervention in Iraqi politics, also shaped at least in part by a desire to keep Iraq out of the political spotlight ahead of the midterms, had the net effect of setting in motion a series of events that, as discussed later, came back to bite when U.S. troops did eventually leave.

Withdrawal by a Thousand Cuts

After the midterms, the administration could finally begin discussions of the politically sensitive issue of whether to keep troops on in Iraq. Unlike Bush, however, who entered a lame duck period after the 2006 midterms, Obama still had to face the voters in a reelection campaign in two years' time, so electoral constraints did not simply dissipate. Instead, the reference point changed. Now looking ahead to the 2012 presidential race, Obama needed to approach the decision at hand with a keen eye on minimizing the electoral risk of any proposed course of action. In practice, this manifested in a waning appetite for a follow-on force as the 2012 campaign approached, substantiating the claim that the influence of electoral pressures increases as an election approaches, as well as, more specifically, the *dampening* mechanism.

That Obama was now willing to engage in a discussion of the post-2011 commitment is on one level reflective of the release of electoral constraints that had suppressed such a dialogue in 2010. Now looking ahead, a follow-on force initially had some appeal. Having already agreed to leave troops behind after the end of the combat mission in Iraq as an "insurance policy against a return to chaos," Obama now weighed the renewal of that policy.[50] James Jeffrey, the U.S. ambassador to Iraq during this period, captures the logic as follows:

> It's late 2010, you're going to be running for reelection in 2012. . . . The main way you think about it is not what great things you can do for the American people . . . [but] what can screw this thing up, where can I trip up and fall? And that's foreign policy. That's Harry Truman in 1952. That's LBJ in 1968. . . . Foreign policy really can blow up your presidency. Knowing that . . . he was like, "I don't want anything to go wrong that I can be blamed for having been the cause of it. Iraq seems to be going well. Why not try to keep troops on, so that the troops might be able to fix something that starts going wrong?"[51]

Yet if Obama, a president whose political career rested in large part on opposition to the Iraq War, was now willing to accept some troop presence after 2011, he was not about to write a blank check to the military. Indeed, in the year that followed the November 2010 elections, proposals would be screened for their political acceptability, with troop numbers repeatedly cut in a manner correlating well with the increasing proximity of the 2012 campaign and resurgent political sensitivity that came with it.

When the military first briefed concrete proposals in December 2010, for instance, they rang alarm bells among the more politically aware civilian leadership. When General Austin, commander of all U.S. forces in Iraq, first recommended a twenty- to twenty-four-thousand-strong residual force, Pentagon officials, conscious of the likely reaction of the White House, were alarmed. In Kahl's telling, as soon as Austin mentioned the headline figure, Kahl's boss intervened and said words to the effect of, "Lloyd, this isn't going to work. A president who campaigned on not leaving a Korea-style presence in perpetuity in Iraq is not going to leave a Korea-style presence in Iraq. That's not going to happen. This is dead on arrival and it's actually going to hurt you in the White House."[52] Indeed, Flournoy recalls that "it was just not even in the ballpark from a White House perspective. . . . The initial number that CENTCOM put forward was way beyond what they were expecting, so DoD was asked to go back to the drawing board and massage the tasks and the role of a follow-on force, and redo the troop-to-task analysis, to try to come up with something that was more modest but would still fulfill the mission objectives."[53] The military's first proposal, then, had categorically failed the screening test of political acceptability before even reaching the president's desk, as the *dampening* mechanism would suggest, and the search for ever lower numbers began in earnest.

In the following weeks, Austin presented a revised set of options, stating his preference for 19,000 troops, a minimum acceptable option of 16,000, and a bare bones proposal of 10,000. The White House, however, recoiled at what it still perceived to be excessively high numbers. Within a few weeks, the proposals on the table at an NSC meeting on April 29, 2011, had shrunk again as low as 8,000, with a ceiling of 16,000.[54] The apparent allergy to the military's recommendations prompted Admiral Mullen, now chairman of the JCS, to author a rare memorandum laying out his concerns. Mullen was, as he recalls, squarely behind Austin's prior assessment: "Basically the ten [thousand] was equal to zero. You can put the ten thousand there, but we can't accomplish the mission with that. That was the floor. This was an important part of the process: each time the number got smaller, I pushed hard to say, 'OK, you've got to tell me what the mission is here, because if it is twenty-eight or twenty-five, that mission is different from fifteen or sixteen, and basically from ten on down, the mission assigned could not be achieved.' It's a physics problem at that point, pure and simple. And it would have been irresponsible, if in fact dangerous, for me not to say so."[55] The memorandum was as unwelcome as Austin's own recommendations, landing at the Oval Office with "a thud; they didn't want to hear it."[56] As some would later claim, the president's national security advisor, Thomas Donilon, felt "the military was boxing in the White House and creating a potentially political liability. Imagine if it leaked! . . . The White House did not like it when the military delivered PowerPoint briefs with 'high risk' stamped in red on the low troop options, and Donilon liked Mullen's letter even less."[57]

To some extent, it might be conceded that bureaucratic resistance from the uniformed military laid behind Obama's slow, iterative march toward lower numbers. President Obama's relationship with his top generals was indeed notoriously poor. The 2009 debate over the Afghanistan "surge" was central in determining the civil-military dynamics that would subsequently infect major debates, including those over Iraq, for the remainder of Obama's first term. All three senior officials at the core of those debates—General Petraeus, Admiral Mullen, and General McChrystal—were of course leading figures in the debates on both wars. According to Petraeus, Obama "clearly felt that the three of us had gotten too visible and become celebrity generals." Indeed, as Secretary Gates told him on one occasion, "there's room inside the beltway for one superstar, and it's not going to be you."[58] Having lost out in the turf wars over the Afghanistan surge decision in 2009, the White House may well have been keen to avoid a repeat of that melodrama. "The problem was they were being squeezed by the military," notes Jeffrey, adding that "the chairman wanted to keep troops on, and they did not want to take on the military."[59] Arguably, the White House resorted to salami slicing tactics in fighting this bureaucratic battle with the military, steadily cutting proposals in an attempt to avoid a sharp split with the generals.

Yet, if this is a part of the story, as in 2006 or even 1950, any kind of presidential inhibition that might stem from overruling the top military leadership cannot be disconnected from the political fallout that would undoubtedly follow. The reaction to Admiral Mullen's memorandum in early 2011 was a case in point. "They believed—incorrectly, I might add—that the chiefs were going to somehow make it more difficult politically for them because critics in Congress would use the memo to attack their policies," he recalls. "That wasn't the purpose of the memo, and it certainly didn't cross my mind when I submitted it that it would be used as some sort of political football.

It was my best military advice, period. I was surprised and disappointed that anyone thought different of my motives. That's the thud. And it bothered me. This goes to my general point on politicals. They would like the military to be as malleable as possible. They didn't like my independence, and they wanted to hear more and more of what I was supposed to deduce they wanted to hear, and I just wasn't willing to do that."[60]

Fortunately for Donilon and his colleagues, there was a black sheep among the military prepared to speak up for the politically appealing lower figures the White House was hoping for. General Cartwright wrote a dissent from Mullen's letter and, in a series of briefings with White House representatives, including the vice president, proceeded to explore several options that went down as low as three thousand, or even one thousand, with additional forces just outside theater in Kuwait. This idea of a rapid reaction force based just across the border captivated Donilon, ever conscious of the political realities, even though it was later denigrated by Mullen as a "half-baked idea" that was "blind to reality."[61] Indeed, according to Cartwright himself, "my position was not well received by the military . . . it was just heresy, and remained so."[62] Still, the headline figures were lower, and as such Cartwright's proposals got traction among the political types. Having a four-star general endorse smaller force structures was critical in legitimating the White House's embrace of numbers lower than the rest of the military was comfortable with. In a May 19 meeting, President Obama signaled he was happy to proceed with a proposal of up to ten thousand troops.

With several U.S. delegations now authorized to begin discussions with the Iraqis about a renewed SOFA, important political and military figures in both the United States and Iraq remained convinced of the strategic logic of a sizable residual force. During the spring and summer, the chief of staff of the Iraqi army and commanding general of Iraqi special operations forces publicly spoke of the need for continued U.S. presence, even until as late as 2020.[63] Senior civilian figures, including Iraq's foreign minister, had also relayed to the U.S. ambassador that they had been clear with the prime minister that Iraq "needs the United States to stay," and that, in turn, Maliki had responded, "of course we need them to stay." General Austin was similarly inclined, and so delayed the beginning of the drawdown, keeping almost fifty thousand troops in theater as late as August 2011 so as to provide "flexibility" for the prospect of a bigger follow-on force.[64] The need to stick at least to the latest iteration of the plan was underscored in a U.S. military report of July, which noted that the previous quarter ended with the highest number of combat deaths in three years, concluding "that the conflict in Iraq is not yet over."[65]

Yet congressional pressure to reduce government spending amid a spiraling budget deficit soon began to cause the administration to become uncomfortable with the financial and, by extension, political cost associated with keeping ten thousand troops in theater. In his memoirs, Leon Panetta laments how war-weary Democrats and small-government Tea Party Republicans united on the desire to reduce the "staggering investment" of men and materiel in Iraq as a way to make overall budgetary savings. "In a town where the two parties agreed on almost nothing," Panetta wrote, "they suddenly settled on the consensus that we could dramatically cut defense spending during wartime."[66] It was in this context that Tony Blinken and Denis McDonough took a tour of Iraq, meeting commanders and exploring options for alternative force commitments. According to Blinken, "We came back with the conclusion that the initial footprint that we were looking at was probably larger than the Iraqis could digest, and we wanted to get to yes with them."[67] Former U.S. ambassador Jeffrey accepts that on one level, this is fair (notwithstanding the important point that privately "the Iraqis didn't give a shit about the numbers," and were prepared to have as many as twenty thousand if they could get it through their parliament). All the same, for Jeffrey, "they were the skeptics," who, faced with the task of justifying lower numbers to the majority of the uniformed military who were opposed to them, were only really in Iraq "looking for reasons."[68] Perhaps unsurprisingly, they found them. Blinken and McDonough argued that if the U.S. military footprint around checkpoints in the North could be scaled back, the residual troop presence could go as low as thirty-five hundred, with an additional rotating component of fifteen hundred. Obama endorsed these proposals in a meeting of August 13, 2011.

Pulling the Plug

On October 21, 2011, President Obama and Prime Minister Maliki concluded that negotiations over a renewed SOFA were at a dead end, and since the

Pentagon's lawyers deemed it essential to have a parliamentary approved agreement, the formal American military commitment to Iraq would cease at the end of the year. For some administration officials, it was indeed the political climate in Iraq that ultimately settled the question that had dragged on throughout 2011. "The president really was open to this smaller footprint in terms of a follow-on force," recalls Blinken, "but the caveat was that this had to be something that the Iraqis embraced politically, because we didn't want to put our forces where they really weren't welcome."[69] With Maliki insisting that he would not be able to get U.S. demands on legal immunities through Parliament, Blinken saw this as indicative of a broader sense among Iraqi public opinion that a continued U.S. presence was unwelcome. Lute, who was instrumental in negotiating the original SOFA, paraphrased the Iraqi view in blunter terms as akin to saying, "You know, we can argue about this, but you guys need to start packing your stuff."[70]

Yet if Obama simply underestimated the difficulty of reaching a deal, there were other ways to obtain one without parliamentary approval, which was, after all, a U.S. demand. Maliki, for instance, was willing to consider signing an executive memorandum of understanding governing the U.S. troop presence, something supported by a senior member of the American delegation, Brett McGurk, as well as other former officials involved in the original SOFA.[71] As Flournoy recalls, while the lawyers had valid points, "it's hard to count the number of places where we've accepted a degree of ambiguity or just a complete absence of an agreement to do what we thought was necessary for our mission."[72] One of those places, of course, is in fact Iraq, where thousands of troops have been stationed without formal legal protections since being sent back by Obama to confront ISIS in 2014. "What I came to believe," continues Flournoy, "when 25,000 was too much, 20,000 was too much, 15,000 was too much, 10,000 was too much—was to realize that the president had made up his mind and he didn't want to have any U.S. troops remain in Iraq. And though I certainly believe that it's critical for U.S. forces to have legal protections anywhere we are, we have had many, many exceptions to that rule, where we have deployed forces without a SOFA in place. So that ended up being an excuse, or a public explanation, for what I believe was a policy choice."[73] General Odierno, who had overseen efforts to finalize the 2008 SOFA, viewed the administration's justifications in a similar light. "I absolutely reject that," said the four-star general who served at the time as chief of staff of the army. "That was just an excuse to pull them out, and a very bad one, in my opinion."[74]

The decision to "go to zero" in October 2011 seems to have been the final point of a process that sought to balance the strategic benefit of a residual presence with the electoral risk of doing so. By late 2011, things in Iraq looked more or less stable. Indeed, in assessments provided by the intelligence community at the time, Obama was advised that Iraq was unlikely to descend back into 2006-style violence anytime soon, absent some exogenous shock or significant sectarian shift in Baghdad.[75] With the 2012 campaign season looming, forcing through a renewed SOFA was for Obama not worth the political capital at such a sensitive time in the electoral cycle. In this sense, the electoral calculus had changed. In the winter of 2010–2011, the risk of things "going south" and distance to the 2012 elections permitted some modest appetite for a follow-on force. By October, "they were nine months closer to the election [and] they didn't need as much of an insurance policy with Iraq."[76] Instead, the political damage that leaving troops could do to Obama's reelection campaign was now the more potent risk to be mitigated against, which in turn led Obama to "go to zero."

Perhaps most telling in this respect was Obama's public comments during the third presidential debate of the 2012 campaign, when he denied ever having tried to attempt such a negotiation in the first place. When Mitt Romney agreed with the president's earlier ambition of reaching an agreement on a renewed SOFA, Obama quickly intervened, saying, "That is not true. . . . What I would not have done is left 10,000 troops in Iraq that would tie us down. That certainly would not help us in the Middle East."[77] In fact, as we have seen, this was precisely the policy Obama pursued between May and August of 2011. Walking back from this position in 2012 would seem to validate the view that as the 2012 election drew closer, the idea of remaining in Iraq became a political liability as the candidate ran on a platform that reified his extrication of U.S. forces from Iraq.

In both the decision to "go to zero," then, and the manner of reaching that decision in such an iterative fashion, electoral pressures loom large. John Brennan articulates a central argument made in this book by describing this decision-making pattern as a "balancing process" on the part of the president, throughout which "he was weighing a number of factors and considerations, not just in terms of security requirements, but also some of those political dimensions, as it got closer to the elections."[78]

*   *   *

This chapter has demonstrated how a focus on the U.S. electoral cycle can enrich our understanding of the Obama administration's decisions concerning the pace and finality of the U.S. troop presence in Iraq. The expedited timetable for the drawdown of combat troops, announced in early 2009, offers a compelling illustration of the *hangover* mechanism, whereby Obama's prior statements on the campaign trail served as a key reference point for internal debate, limiting the room available to the president in meeting the operational requirements of the commanders on the ground. The true significance of Obama's pledge to withdraw from Iraq, however, was arguably felt much later, as a looming constraint in deliberations over the prospect of leaving a follow-on force in place after 2011. Though never a supporter of the war in Iraq, Obama did signal a clear willingness to keep troops on, in line with the views of the overwhelming majority of his advisors. The electoral costs of doing so, however, would have been significant. As such, the administration initially *delayed* the consideration of such a course until the 2010 midterms had passed. Then, through 2011, proposals were repeatedly screened for their political acceptability in a search for ever lower numbers, in line with the *dampening* mechanism. With the 2012 campaign around the corner, the electoral preference eventually won out altogether, pulling the president away from efforts to keep any troops in Iraq at all.

Since Obama's inheritance and his own broader beliefs about the wisdom of the Iraq War already pointed toward a policy of disengagement, it may be reasonable to ask whether electoral considerations made any *real* difference to U.S. policy in Iraq during this period. The remainder of this chapter argues that if electoral constraints had only marginal substantive influence in this period, in the long run it was arguably the margins that mattered to the long-term stability of Iraq.

Had Obama not been bound at least in part by his own campaign pledge to withdraw within sixteen months of his election, for instance, it seems reasonable to speculate that the pace of the drawdown in Iraq could have been driven to a much greater extent by conditions on the ground. According to the vast majority of the uniformed military, such a course of action presented much lower risk, since it avoided advertising intentions to opponents who might simply wait until the Americans had left before stepping up their activities. "It had to be conditions based," stressed General Casey, who served as chief of staff of the army at the time of the policy's announcement, adding that even if you had some internal deadlines, "you definitely don't have to go out and make it a public statement of policy."[79] In retrospect, of course, security in Iraq did not significantly diminish during this period, and the compromise struck with General Odierno on the nonlinear nature of the drawdown mitigated much of the risk he had identified. Still, the political commitments Obama had to contend with did arguably create more risk in military terms.

The "what ifs" of the decision to effectively back Maliki after the 2010 Iraqi elections and the 2011 decision to "go to zero" are arguably more significant, in light of the subsequent spread of the Islamic State across the border between Iraq and Syria from 2014. While it is hard to imagine Obama opting to embrace the open-ended commitment of twenty-four thousand troops favored initially by General Austin, given his long-standing opposition to the war, it *is* certainly plausible to think that he may have opted for one of the in-between options discussed above, be it ten thousand or even the thirty-five hundred agreed upon in August. Absent the pressures of the political spotlight, we have already seen that mechanisms were available, in the shape of an executive memorandum of understanding, and private willingness in Baghdad was sufficient to allow for such an option to be pursued. Moreover, a redesigned force structure focused on limited missions—as had been fleshed out extensively by the Pentagon—was fully consistent with Obama's broader shift toward a counterterrorism strategy in the Middle East. As one senior official at the time recalls, "there were various ways that we might have kept a better 'footprint' in Iraq that would have enabled a much more rapid response when ISIS was so threatening in Iraq."[80]

A skeptic might argue that the capacity of a few thousand U.S. troops to forestall the expansion of such a complex and diffuse threat was significantly limited. While this is to some extent true, it misses the broader military and political utility of a continued troop presence.[81] On the former, it is important to note that the carefully tailored makeup of the residual force was designed to function as an enabler for the Iraqi Security Forces to stand up on its own, not as an alternative to those Iraqi units. Rather than simply additional "boots on the ground," the remaining troops would comprise special forces, intelligence units, and air support—three areas in which Iraqi forces were sorely lacking in capability. If the Pentagon-approved ten-thousand-strong force had been approved, according to Flournoy, "that was a force that could do real things."[82] Even with smaller numbers, a counterterrorism cell could be maintained in Iraq, providing the expertise and logistical infrastructure that Brennan explains was key in pursuing an effective counterterrorism strategy. Though he argues that the U.S. departure was one of many factors behind the explosive spread of the Islamic State in 2014, he admits that a residual force "could have slowed some of the growth of ISIS."[83] If nothing else, the situational awareness afforded by even a modest presence would have enabled the administration to detect the emergence of the threat earlier, giving advance warning and time to consider additional options for addressing it before it became an existential threat to the Iraqi state in 2014.

On the political side of the ledger, a continued presence might have helped ensure that permissive conditions for the rapid spread of ISIS did not exist in the first place. U.S. forces had played an important role in brokering political compromises between different factions during the surge, acting as a relatively neutral outside actor to mediate disputes. Even if a few thousand troops would be too thinly spread to reprise that role, however, a modest residual presence might have been sufficient to keep the sectarian excesses of the Iraqi prime minister in check. The backing of Maliki in 2010 was "a huge mistake on our part," admitted Odierno, but "the only reason he was able to work with the Sunnis he did was because we were there—because we were there to oversee that and help them."[84] So long as the Iraqi prime minister was convinced that the Americans would underwrite his government, he would continue to at least pay lip service to the calls for him to run a government of national unity and refrain from the increased sectarian excess that characterized his administration after 2011.

As it was, Maliki was left feeling vulnerable after the U.S. withdrawal. Apparently paranoid about a coup against him, he placed repeated calls to the newly established Office of Security Cooperation, asking for personal protection from U.S. forces, only to be told that no resources could be made available. Many senior officials and commentators mark this as the moment when Maliki lurched toward consolidation of his Shia base, to the exclusion and resentment of the Sunni community. For Flournoy, "I do think that that had a very real impact, and had we had ten thousand or twelve thousand troops there that turning point for Maliki might not have been there. And then you might not have had the re-marginalization of the Sunnis, and then you might not have had Anbar and Mosul become fertile ground for ISIS, and and and and and and . . ."[85] The ambassador at the time agrees with this point: "One of the reasons for why Iraq went downhill after 2012 . . . really *was* the withdrawal of troops. But not because they could have intervened, or overthrown Maliki, or anything like it. It was because they provided Maliki with a security blanket. Now he had to rely on an army he didn't trust, that still had many senior Sunni commanders, and more importantly, most of the senior Shia commanders were also former Baathists, they had been generals in the Saddamist army. So he was very, very suspicious about them."[86] Other figures are less circumspect. Asked about the consequences of the 2011 withdrawal decision several years later, as U.S. forces remained deeply engaged in a global coalition to defeat ISIS, Admiral Mullen's view was clear: "We're living with it. Look at where Iraq is."[87]

Conclusion

RICHARD NIXON WAS RIGHT. When it comes to wartime decision making, "winning an election is terribly important."[1] Faced with critical decisions concerning the escalation or de-escalation of an ongoing conflict, U.S. presidents must weigh the strategic utility of any proposed policy alongside the risks it poses to their personal political futures. This book conceptualized electoral pressures as a conditional source of constraint, which may push or pull the president away from a course of action otherwise deemed to carry optimal strategic characteristics. In doing so, it demonstrated how the impact of electoral politics on the nature and timing of decisions of crucial military and diplomatic significance is at once deeper and more nuanced than conventional wisdom implies.

More specifically, the book explained how, why, and when electoral politics mattered in three of America's costliest wars since 1945. It did so with reference to five key mechanisms. An upcoming election may encourage the president to *delay* making a controversial decision, *dampen* its "noisier" aspects, or act as a *spur* to dial up the aggressiveness of a proposed course of action. In addition, a president may have to contend with the *hangover* effects of commitments made in a previous campaign, and will face an erosion of leverage in bargaining situations thanks to the *spoiler* effect that an election can have on negotiations. Which of these mechanisms operate in any given case was argued to depend on the relative alignment between a president's strategic and electoral preference and the phase of the electoral cycle. Taken together, they can be mapped across the four-year political calendar, yielding a new conceptual framework that captures the systematic influence that electoral considerations have on wartime decision making.

In making these arguments, this study has gone beyond the existing literature's focus on cases of conflict initiation, showing how electoral pressures continue to shape how a war is fought after the Rubicon has been crossed. With rich historical case studies of key decisions made during the wars in Korea, Vietnam, and Iraq, it has brought a much-needed qualitative approach to a problem that has typically been addressed using quantitative methods. In so doing, it offers a far more nuanced account of the ways in which electoral considerations influence decision making in a nonlinear fashion across the domestic political calendar, avoiding the existing myopia that results from a narrower focus on presidential election years. Further, it has identified a series of opportunities to limit the costs of war, sue for peace, or gain advantage on the battlefield that were missed thanks to the prevailing attention paid by presidents to the exigencies of the electoral cycle. In short, this book has made several important contributions of a conceptual, methodological, and empirical nature.

The remainder of this concluding chapter draws together the main findings of the case studies, comparing the extent to which they offer support for the study's conceptual framework. It then sketches several ways in which future research might build on these findings, before offering some concluding reflections on wider theoretical and normative implications for the study of democracy and war.

Reviewing the Evidence

This section assesses the degree to which the evidence adduced in each of the case studies explored in this book aligns with the conceptual framework outlined in chapter 1. The central elements of that framework, illustrated in chapter 1 (figures 1.3 and 1.4), capture the ways in which the relative significance of different mechanisms of electoral constraint vary according to a distinctive rhythm associated with the domestic political calendar. In table C.1, the major decisions examined in each of the empirical chapters are mapped across these electoral phases, offering a useful point of reference for weighing the validity of these claims.

TABLE C.1
Key Decision-Making Episodes Across the Electoral Cycle

	PHASE 1: HONEYMOON	PHASES 2/4: MIDTERMS	PHASE 3: REELECTION	PHASE 5: LAME DUCK
Korea	*Hangover* "I shall go to Korea" (1953)	*Spur* Crossing the 38th parallel (1950)	N/A	*Spoiler* Seeking an armistice (1952)
Vietnam	*Hangover* "Peace with honor" (1969)	*Delay/Dampening/ Spur* Gradual escalation (1965–1966)	*Delay/Dampening* "Americanizing" the war (1964)	*Spoiler* Paris peace talks (1968)
			Delay The "decent interval" strategy (1971–1972)	
			Spur Responding to the Easter Offensive (1972)	
			Delay Operation Linebacker II (1972)	
			Spoiler Paris peace talks (1972)	
Iraq	*Hangover* "Responsibly ending the war in Iraq" (2009)	*Delay* The "surge" (2006)	*Delay* Taking Fallujah (2004)	*Spoiler* SOFA negotiations (2008)
		Dampening "Going to zero" (2010)	*Dampening* "Going to zero" (2011)	

In the opening phase of a president's first term, the so-called honeymoon, electoral pressures were expected to be relatively mild. With four years until their personal political survival is once again at stake, newly elected leaders can generally hew closer to their strategic preference in weighing decisions about military and diplomatic strategy. They are not entirely unconstrained, however. It is in this period that the *hangover* mechanism may limit presidents' room for maneuver by forcing them to reconcile what they promised voters on the previous campaign trail with what they now believe to be in the nation's best interest. This pressure was suggested to be stronger in cases where these prior campaign statements were narrow and specific in nature and weaker in cases in where they were broad and vague.

The empirical chapters offered solid support for these claims. On the one hand, the vague promises to "go to Korea" and win "peace with honor," made respectively by Dwight Eisenhower and Richard Nixon, granted each president a large degree of latitude in selecting their strategies for ending hostilities. While Nixon would interpret his mandate somewhat more broadly, taking another four years to sign a peace agreement after initial spasms of escalatory bombing, even Eisenhower felt free to seriously consider the use of atomic weapons to bring about an armistice. On the other hand, having offered a highly specific timetable for a sixteen-month drawdown in Iraq, the development of Barack Obama's "responsible plan" to end the war required a series of explicit compromises to be struck between those promises and the strategic realities he faced once in office.

As the midterms approach, presidents enter a more constrained phase in which the relative weight afforded to their electoral preferences is expected to rise. Due to the peculiarities of certain cases examined in this book, it is not always easy to determine which phase applies to a given episode. Lyndon Johnson, for example, was already in his second term by the time he faced his first congressional election campaign as sitting president. Nevertheless, since the expectations are broadly similar in terms of the range and intensity of electoral constraints in both the second and fourth phases of the cycle, it suffices to consider them together. In doing so, it becomes clear that each of the three primary (de-)escalatory mechanisms begin to operate in this period.

Specifically, in cases where the commander in chief favors an escalatory course of action but fears that a political backlash will result, this was argued to lead to a *delay* in the selection of such a strategy, or the *dampening* of its more controversial elements. This was observed most notably with Bush's determination to stick with a suboptimal transition strategy in Iraq until the 2006 midterms and to focus instead on minimizing casualties, before swiftly announcing the surge, which he well understood would be the most unpopular decision of his presidency. It also characterized the Obama administration's initial decision to defer serious consideration of whether to leave a follow-on force in Iraq beyond 2011. The *spur* mechanism describes a contrasting dynamic, whereby a president chooses to dial up the aggressiveness of a proposed course of action for fear of appearing weak. Harry Truman's expansion of the Korean War in 1950 was a particularly striking example of this mechanism, when fierce criticism from hyper-partisan opponents and a wider public mood inclined to favor escalation placed significant limits on the president's ability to restrain the hawkish instincts of the field commander. Lyndon Johnson's Goldilocks approach to managing gradual escalation in Vietnam, meanwhile, characterized by a series of attempts to offset competing pressures and protect his domestic legislative priorities at home, also offers plausible evidence of the heightened political sensitivity of this phase more generally. In short, there is a wealth of empirical evidence to suggest that congressional elections generate important constraints on decision making, a point that is often missed in existing studies that focus only on presidential races.

Given that the president's interest in political survival is more directly at stake in a presidential election contest, it is in the third phase of the cycle that electoral constraints were naturally expected to be strongest. Importantly, however, it was argued in chapter 1 that the *anticipation* of a campaign may be almost as significant as being in the midst of one. Indeed, in the cases under study here, this has been repeatedly demonstrated. Already by the spring of 1971, for instance, Richard Nixon had devised the so-called decent interval strategy, which effectively made his reelection, not the stability of South Vietnam, the primary object of policy decisions. In 2011, moreover, it was the *future* optics of reneging on a campaign pledge as the 2012 election season approached that in part led Obama to "go to zero" in Iraq. These findings add further weight to the importance of looking across the entire cycle for evidence of electoral constraints materially affecting wartime decision making.

In an election year itself, the *delay, dampening,* and *spur* mechanisms are likely to operate most strongly, as a president's attention turns increasingly toward managing the electoral risks of any proposed course of action. Arguably the classic illustration of these dynamics came with Lyndon Johnson's explicit deferral of a decision to increase the U.S. commitment to Vietnam until after the 1964 election, and reliance on less controversial yet largely ineffective policies in the meantime. While he evidently perceived a clear need to change strategy as early as the spring, the major decisions to initiate a sustained bombing program and commit tens of thousands of combat troops to Southeast Asia would come only after his reelection was secured. Eight years later, in 1972, President Nixon's approach to bombing operations in Vietnam also reflected his increased sensitivity to electoral politics, albeit in different ways. In the spring, for instance, he welcomed the opportunity to unleash a barrage of aerial bombardment upon the North, figuring that voters might reward an aggressive response to the enemy's Easter Offensive, even as he and several advisors began to doubt the utility of such bombing operations. He saved the heaviest bombing campaign until after his reelection had been secured, however, delaying what would become Operation Linebacker II until a less politically sensitive phase.

In other ways, however, the tension between a president's strategic and electoral preferences was perceived to be irreconcilable, forcing the incumbent to sacrifice one for the other. Accepting the need to cut losses and withdraw from Vietnam, for instance, Nixon instead chose to prioritize his own political career in 1972, keeping Saigon afloat until his reelection was secure through staggered troop withdrawals and periodic bombing offensives that he knew to be strategically ineffective. In almost equal and opposite manner, Lyndon Johnson had four years earlier concluded that his vision of a negotiated peace could not be pursued while remaining a candidate for reelection, choosing to announce his own withdrawal and a peace overture to Hanoi in the very same speech of March 1968.

Lame ducks were treated as a special case in this study's conceptual framework. Theoretically separated from the logic of electoral accountability by virtue of their ineligibility for reelection, such presidents were suggested to experience relative freedom from most of the mechanisms of electoral constraint explored in this book. There is a good degree of support for this in the three cases studied here. Certainly, Truman's refusal to take the gloves off in Korea in 1952—at least to the extent that his Republican critics demanded—suggests a relative insensitivity to public opinion, at least compared with his earlier decision to expand the war in late 1950. More directly, both Lyndon Johnson and George W. Bush implemented major shifts in their wartime strategy, one toward de-escalation and the other toward escalation, at almost the precise moment at which they entered the twilight phase of their terms.

Instead of the typical electoral constraints observed elsewhere, concerns about legacy do appear to have shaped how these lame duck presidents sought to implement their preferred strategies. Hence, while Truman and Johnson wanted to reach a deal to end hostilities in Korea and Vietnam, both stuck stubbornly to their red lines in negotiations concerning POWs and cease-fire conditions, apparently believing that no deal was better than a bad deal that might mark them as "peace at any price" presidents in the history books. Interestingly, and perhaps because his successor was more clearly dovish on the war than Eisenhower or Nixon had been, Bush proved more willing to compromise on his strategic preference for a conditions-based drawdown so as to ensure that he could lock in his vision of continued engagement in Iraq before his time in office expired.

Finally, the *spoiler* mechanism was shown to play an important role in eroding the president's bargaining position during negotiations to de-escalate and conclude a war. The significance of this mechanism was particularly pronounced in an election year and applied both to presidents seeking reelection and those in a lame duck phase. It operated in three main ways. First, the political survival incentive was shown to encourage presidents who were still up for reelection to grant concessions in pursuit of a deal that would boost their electoral fortunes. Nixon's desire for a "decent interval" and disregard for South Vietnam's future during the peace talks in Paris through 1972 serve as particularly explicit evidence for this. Second, even if the incumbent was not running, the actions of other candidates and negotiating opponents were shown to repeatedly undermine the president's leverage. Vietnam is again the classic example here, with the progress of talks in both 1968 and 1972 subject to deadlocks as well as breakthroughs resulting from each party's assessment of the likely results of the upcoming presidential election. In Iraq, however, the positions adopted by Prime Minister Maliki and Barack Obama in the summer of 2008 appear to have also restricted Bush's room for maneuver in the SOFA negotiations, while Harry Truman was not without reason in lamenting Eisenhower's criticism of his administration's policy and subsequent refusal to wholeheartedly support it during the transition. Finally, and relatedly, the fixed nature of the electoral calendar undoubtedly created constraints that made it difficult for the incumbents to strike agreements on their preferred terms. In Korea, the Truman administration's lame duck status, particularly during the interregnum, created conditions in which it became difficult to resist pressure from allies to support an India-backed UN resolution, which would ultimately help define the formula upon which an armistice agreement would be reached. In Iraq, there is credible evidence to suggest that the ticking clock associated with Bush's final months in office led the administration to row back with increasing speed on a series of red lines during the SOFA negotiations, notably ending up with a surprising decision to agree to a final withdrawal date.

In sum, the cases offered broad support for the conceptual framework outlined in chapter 1. For all the contextual variation among cases, there does seem to be an identifiable pattern to the operation of electoral constraints and their impact on wartime decision making. The logic of democratic accountability has been shown to apply beyond the point of conflict initiation, with presidential decisions to escalate and de-escalate an ongoing war subject to pressures generated by the electoral cycle. These pressures do not act in a simple or linear manner, but instead push and pull presidents in different directions at varying stages of the electoral cycle. Neither inherently a force for aggression nor an inducement to caution, the relationship between electoral politics and wartime decision making is best understood with due attention paid to the rhythm of the electoral cycle.

Future Research Directions

While this book made no strong claim of generalizability, its findings are nevertheless suggestive of the influence that electoral politics might have on foreign policy more broadly. As such, future research might build on this study through four potentially fruitful avenues.

Other Use-of-Force Decisions

While this study has focused primarily on decisions to escalate and de-escalate an ongoing conflict, further work might explore the degree to which the framework developed in this book travels to different kinds of decisions involving the use of force. For instance, while a full assessment would require an additional volume to unpack in comparable detail, the logic underpinning each of the five mechanisms plausibly also applies to initial decisions to enter a war.

To be sure, in cases like Korea, where a decision to intervene followed an act of unprovoked aggression, which in turn sparked considerable support at home for a robust response, a president's strategic and electoral preferences are likely to be closely aligned. In wars like Vietnam, by contrast, where the scale of initial intervention increased in a much more gradual fashion, there is perhaps more room for electoral constraints to have played a role. Whether John F. Kennedy would have escalated U.S. involvement in the way his successor did remains one of history's great unknowns. Yet it is nevertheless instructive to note that electoral considerations played an important role in several accounts suggesting he was planning to de-escalate. Consistent with the general logic of the *delay* mechanism, Kennedy reportedly told at least three of his colleagues that he planned to de-escalate, but only after the 1964 election. As he explained in 1963, "I can't give up territory like that to the Communists and then get the American people to reelect me!"[2]

The anecdotal evidence indicating that the planning of the 2003 invasion of Iraq was bound up with concerns about upcoming elections is even more suggestive. Certainly, such considerations occupied the minds of several top presidential aides. At a minimum, it seems plausible that the administration intentionally tabled a congressional resolution authorizing the use of force in Iraq on the eve of the 2002 midterms to put maximum pressure on representatives to vote in favor. Having already suggested in one planning meeting that the invasion itself be timed with the off-year elections in mind, the president's chief of staff was later reported to have explained why the resolution wasn't put forward sooner as a function of "marketing" considerations, claiming that "you don't introduce new products in August."[3] As for the invasion itself, the deputy secretary of state explained that "[Secretary of State] Powell and I did not object to the prospect of taking out Saddam Hussein, but we had real questions about timing," adding that "the thinking I had in mind was January 2005—win the election and then that would be a good time to begin the attack."[4] In the event, of course, it was those who wished to accelerate the onset of war who won the argument, and they did so in part for equal and opposite reasons. As Karl Rove explained to the British ambassador as the quest to secure a second UN resolution dragged on, the White House could not wait indefinitely. "Otherwise," said Bush's top political advisor, "we will get embroiled in the presidential election campaign and the President will be accused of using the war to win an election."[5]

The significance of electoral constraints on presidential decision making also plausibly applies in cases altogether unlike those examined in this book, however. Having criticized the administration of George H. W. Bush on the 1992 campaign trail for vacillating as civil conflict broke out in Bosnia, for instance, Bill Clinton spent much of his first year in office struggling to reconcile his pledges for firmer action with the limited strategic utility of the options available to him. If *hangover* dynamics may therefore have applied early on, Clinton's eventual shift toward a more energetic policy in 1995 might represent an example of the *spur* mechanism in operation. As Republican critics began to see opportunity in the ongoing crisis, political advisors warned the White House that if the conflict was not settled, "Clinton's reelection might be in peril."[6] With favorable electoral conditions for intervention further boosted in the aftermath of the Srebrenica massacre, however, the ensuing campaign of air strikes and reinvigorated diplomacy swiftly turned a political liability into an asset on the eve of the 1996 campaign. And, of course, this was not the only humanitarian crisis with which Clinton had to contend on a timeline dictated by the political calendar at home. President Bush's defeat at the polls in 1992 had liberated him from political concerns he may have had in weighing a decision to intervene in Somalia. In opting to send thousands of U.S. troops to guarantee the delivery of food and other aid supplies within weeks of the election, he was apparently motivated at least in part "to spare President-elect Clinton from having to immediately confront a messy problem needing military action."[7] This action is consistent with the evidence presented in this book suggesting that presidents tend to wait until moments of reduced political sensitivity before launching potentially costly operations.

Finally, and by contrast, just as electoral considerations play a role in initial decisions to use force, so, too, might they plausibly affect decisions *not* to authorize direct military involvement in a new overseas conflict. During his final year in office, for example, President Eisenhower was alarmed by the deterioration of the situation in Laos, where Communist forces were threatening to topple the government. The administration had in fact spent considerable time weighing its options at a series of NSC meetings throughout the year, with senior officials variously warning that a "miracle" would almost be required to hold on; that "strong action" would be required to address the situation since the administration "could not let it drift"; and that "all-out support" might be in order.[8] Believing Laos to be "key to the entire area of South East Asia," Eisenhower had even told President-elect Kennedy in a meeting held during the transition that he would be willing to intervene unilaterally if necessary.[9] He did not do so, of course, and instead left the decision to his successor, who chose instead to seek a cease-fire and Laos's neutralization. Yet Eisenhower's decision-making behaviors in this episode are striking insofar as they otherwise bear all the hallmarks of the *delay* mechanism. It is unlikely to have been the only intervention that might have eventually taken place had the incumbent served longer in office.

Other Policy Issues

Future studies might also examine the extent to which electoral constraints might operate in other areas of policy. Issues involving the use of force tend to be the traditional focus of related examinations of the influence of public opinion on decision making, primarily because it is only when the costs of foreign policy are brought vividly home to voters that their attention is "activated," and there is little comparable to the image of body bags mounting to focus the mind of the average voter.[10] It follows that many other issues, like trade or aid policy, might not be sufficiently salient to generate any real electoral risks for decision makers; or, as Lyndon Johnson colorfully put it, "Everybody worries about war and peace. Everything else is chickenshit."[11] Recent events suggest that this may not be universally true, however, with Donald Trump having been peculiarly effective at articulating the alleged costs of supposed trade imbalances between the United States and China to his political base. In June 2019, according to then national security advisor John Bolton, Trump actively sought Xi Jinping's help in securing reelection during ongoing trade negotiations, directly asking the Chinese president to cut a deal including increased exports of American soybeans and wheat so as to favor a core constituency of Trump's base of support.[12] Moreover, recent analysis of U.S. relations with Iran—another bête noire of Bolton's—suggests that the electoral cycle can play an important role in shaping the contours of a long-term diplomatic relationship, even if the mutual hostility between each side stops short of breaking into sustained conflict.[13] The wartime context explored in this book may therefore be the explosive component of a much larger phenomenon shaping U.S. foreign policy.

Beyond the United States

Since the underlying logic of electoral accountability is of course not exclusive to the United States, additional studies might also usefully explore the impact of electoral politics on wartime decision making in other states. Building on recent efforts to examine how public opinion affects foreign policy differently across democracies, this might shed light on how variation in institutional structure may leave decision makers more or less susceptible to electoral pressures.[14] Parliamentary systems of course vary in myriad ways to presidential systems, and it stands to reason that the diversity seen in the relationship between the executive and legislative branches, term limits, and election timing might all affect the way in which electoral constraints operate.[15] Anecdotally, one needs only point to Margaret Thatcher's handling of the dispute over the Falkland Islands in 1982 to illustrate how the ability of some prime ministers to call a snap election at a time of their choosing may leave them less constrained and more prone to diversionary action. Relatedly, the length of a campaign might mediate the influence that electoral politics has on decision makers. Many states, for instance, have tight limits on what candidates and the media can do and say during a legally defined campaign period. Might this cause incumbents to be less sensitive to electoral considerations compared to their counterparts in the United States, where campaign length is both unregulated and exceptionally long?[16] It is not without reason that some have written of a "permanent campaign" in the United States, and some comparative analysis may indeed mark it out as an important yet exceptional case.[17]

Relatedly, one might reasonably expect there to be a spectrum of sensitivity to electoral constraints depending not simply on what *type* of democracy a state is, but just *how* democratic it is. For instance, the size and nature of the franchise and the relative freedom afforded to the press in a state might be hugely significant, especially since we know that leaders who require the support of fewer individuals to remain in power are more insulated from the constraints of public opinion, as are those who have greater control of the information made available to voters.[18] Recent work demonstrating that the enfranchisement of women is associated with more pacific behavior among democratic states charts a particularly important path for further studies of the fine-grained decision-making processes and political behaviors that yield such patterns.[19] Interesting comparisons might also be made with authoritarian states in which elections of questionable impartiality are held. To what extent do "sham" elections still incentivize certain types of behavior from autocrats wishing to bolster their own legitimacy?[20] Even autocracies without an electoral process might help illuminate electoral accountability by way of comparison. For example, would it be reasonable to expect democratic lame ducks to behave in similar ways to these autocratic leaders during a war?[21]

Strategic Implications for Allies and Adversaries

Finally, additional work might explore in more depth what opportunities for strategic interaction between states may be generated by the patterns observed in this book. While the *spoiler* mechanism here emphasized the impact of electoral politics on U.S. presidents' bargaining positions, there was much to suggest that other states' consciousness of the pressures generated by the U.S. electoral cycle may have led to shifts in *their* diplomatic strategy too. This applies not only to adversaries but also allies, to whom the United States has time and again proven to be an unreliable coalition partner, prone to abandonment when its own domestic political conditions compel a downscaling of the U.S. commitment to a given conflict. A multistate analysis might yield important additional insights into how both friends and foes are affected by and respond to the patterns of American behavior shaped by the U.S. electoral cycle.

Going beyond negotiations, if it can be demonstrated that democracies tend to be more cautious or belligerent at certain points of the electoral cycle, how might this affect the conflict behavior of their opponents? Certainly, during the Vietnam War, it appears to have been the case that Hanoi timed its major offensive moves calculating that each successive U.S. administration's election-year sensitivity to public opinion might work to its advantage.[22] Just as potential victims of diversionary behavior have been shown to be able to identify troubling conditions and conciliate a would-be aggressor, so, too, may it be the case that the "rhythm" of the electoral cycle gives enemies of the United States a guide for when and how to confront it by force.[23] Electorally timed shifts in policy can also complicate things for coalition partners fighting alongside the United States. In Iraq, for instance, the abrupt escalation of the U.S. commitment to the war caught the British by surprise. Unable and unwilling to follow the U.S. lead, the junior partner found itself stranded and hamstrung by a lack of common purpose.[24]

Democracy and War

Beyond the conceptual, methodological, and empirical contributions addressed in the preceding sections, the findings of this study also carry wider implications for the study of democracy and war. This section explores these through two key questions.

Are Democracies Good at Fighting Wars?

Drawing on the liberal tradition in international relations theory, many scholars identify electoral accountability as a critical explanation of the superior war records held by democracies.[25] Since they can be more easily removed from office than their nondemocratic counterparts, elected leaders are acutely sensitive to the domestic political costs associated with defeat. As a result, they tend to enter into wars only when highly confident of victory, and go on to commit more resources to a conflict once engaged to avoid losing, typically resulting in relatively short wars.[26] In doing so, democratic decision makers also benefit from a series of other sources of comparative advantage in war, including superior information; better prospects for joining powerful coalitions; and better morale, initiative, and leadership among their armed forces.[27]

The cases and evidence presented in this book appear to challenge such accounts of democratic exceptionalism in war. Instead, the U.S. experience in Korea, Vietnam, and Iraq lends support for an equally strongly held belief among strategic thinkers that powerful democracies are peculiarly bad at fighting small wars.[28] U.S. participation in these "limited" conflicts has been characterized by long, protracted struggles that sap morale and ultimately result in a draw at best, if not outright defeat. The reasons for such surprisingly poor military performance are no secret. When engaged in asymmetrical conflicts, wealthy and industrialized democracies too often rely on firepower and technological superiority to overcome weak opponents, who often employ unconventional tactics to frustrate their more powerful foes.[29] Surprisingly, democratic leaders often appear to select these ill-suited strategies consciously and fail to adapt or learn from such mistakes over time.[30]

This presents a puzzle. If democratic leaders are structurally incentivized to fight hard to avoid politically costly defeat, why would they not choose courses of action with the best prospect of ultimate success? Indeed, if war outcomes are so intimately tied to an elected leader's political survival, why would presidents systematically select policies they often *know* to be suboptimal? By excluding or downplaying these deviant cases from the study of democracy and war, many scholars have failed to address why some of the most significant conflicts of the twentieth century appear not to adhere to these theoretical expectations.[31]

This study helps resolve this issue by reorienting studies of democratic success in war toward the operation of electoral accountability *during* a war itself. While it is undoubtedly true that war outcomes matter for a democratic leader's political survival, this study demonstrates that it is not just winning or losing but also *how* a president chooses to fight that matters. Unless a war can be concluded relatively quickly—and this is unlikely in the types of war considered here, since the brutality required to do so is often prohibited by the likely moral outrage it would spark—it is highly probable that voters will cast their ballots based not only on the ultimate chances of success, but also on their assessment of how an ongoing war is being conducted.[32] Knowing this, presidents are incentivized to remain acutely sensitive to the likely reaction of voters to major decisions, especially those that significantly escalate or de-escalate a conflict, as this book has shown. Since winning a war might require the adoption of some politically controversial courses of action, it follows that electoral considerations during a war may in the short term incentivize suboptimal strategies that make victory harder to achieve in the long run, however essential that victory might be to a president's eventual political fortunes.[33]

Further, the nature of these wars makes presidents peculiarly susceptible to electoral pressures. First, they tend to last a long time, with recent estimates suggesting that the average counterinsurgency campaign takes more than eleven years.[34] Second, the type of strategies most experts deem to be effective tend to be very troop-intensive and involve a great deal of violence. Given the temporal constraints of the four-year electoral cycle in the United States, and the still prevalent belief that the voting public is casualty-averse, presidents are far more likely to embrace alternative strategies prioritizing firepower over manpower, even as these are precisely the courses criticized by strategic thinkers as suboptimal.[35] Third, because these are nonexistential "wars of choice," public tolerance for poor performance or unpopular strategies is likely to be much weaker than in "wars of necessity," where a public might give a leader more slack with which to conduct a war as he or she saw fit. Victory still matters politically for the incumbent, but since defeat will probably not change the life of the average voter, the electorate may be less forgiving when it comes to how a small war is fought.[36]

While electoral accountability may partially account for overall democratic success in war, then, this study demonstrates that, when viewed through the prism of the U.S. electoral cycle, these political pressures can often cause presidents, both through acts of commission and omission, to consciously pursue strategies they perceive to be suboptimal. In turn, electoral constraints on wartime decision making help explain why democracies find it more difficult to win small wars than their preponderant capabilities would suggest, adding nuance to a central claim of liberal theories of international relations.

Is Electoral Accountability Bad?

While the primary aim of this book was to explore *how*, *why*, and *when* electoral politics affect wartime decision making, the evidence adduced raises a further related question: *Should it?*

The findings in this book certainly raise troubling questions about political representation in the United States. We know that voters essentially delegate foreign policy to elites, and that doing so is rational for ordinary citizens who have neither the time nor interest in gathering information about the complexities of international politics.[37] In placing decision-making power in the hands of elected officials, voters implicitly assume that those leaders will act in their best interests, either directly by enacting specific policy preferences favored by the public, or indirectly by relying on superior expertise and information to make decisions on their behalf. Yet throughout this book we find extensive evidence of presidents making decisions involving the use of force in ways that satisfy concerns not just about the national interest, but also their own political self-interest. Not only did the leaders examined in this study routinely select strategically flawed courses of action, they did so knowingly and in ways that were uniquely avoidable. Worse still, the very institution designed to keep such behavior in check—the electoral process—was the source of such behavior. While the degree to which foreign policy elites are deemed to be out of touch with the preferences of ordinary voters is a common complaint among many scholars,[38] this book shows the extent to which this "disconnect" stems not just from divergent beliefs or experience, but from an incentive structure that is baked into the democratic form of government.

These more philosophical concerns may be coupled with substantive observations about the strategic cost of electoral accountability. If the pressures generated by the electoral cycle systematically push presidents away from strategies they deem to be optimal, such apparent deviations from the national interest may reasonably be considered highly damaging. On the one hand, recurrent patterns of cost-aversion and excessive caution witnessed during sensitive phases of the political calendar have contributed directly to the selection and persistence of flawed strategies and missed opportunities on the battlefield. On the other, electoral pressures resulting in futile or needlessly risky operations may well have caused incalculable bloodshed and courted strategic disaster in the name of electoral expedience. Either way, there is plenty of evidence to support the traditional view held by many realists and policy makers alike that the influence of public opinion on foreign policy is a wholly regrettable feature of the democratic system. "That the four-year election process has a pernicious influence on foreign policy is evident," Zbigniew Brzezinski once noted, lamenting nevertheless that "it is also clear that this structural handicap is not likely to be undone."[39]

This study stops short of endorsing such a blanket assertion, however. There are at least two more pragmatic reasons why the influence of electoral politics on decision making may not be uniformly detrimental. First, to make such a claim assumes that, absent the pressure of electoral constraints, a president's pursuit of a given strategic preference would align with the objective national interest. Yet since the strategic preference refers to the president's *perception* of the option that carries optimal characteristics, it does not necessarily follow that this assessment will always be an accurate reflection of the course that really did carry the greatest utility. Though presidents have access to a range of experts to help inform their choices, the frequency with which scholars and analysts disagree about the wisdom of different policies should leave us with no illusions about an elected official's capacity to identify the "correct" course. In reality, what constitutes the national interest has always been contingent and highly contested, and for a wide variety of reasons.[40] While this book has offered several powerful examples of instances in which the president's deviation from his strategic preference has incurred major opportunity costs and needless bloodshed, then, it pays to recognize that alternative options not favored by the president might have been more advantageous still.

The surge offers a plausible example of this dynamic. Had President Bush not needed to worry about the "hot" political environment in the lead-up to the midterms, he may well have changed strategy and very likely escalated the military commitment to Iraq sooner than he did. This plausibly may have led far more quickly to the improvements in security that were seen through 2007 and 2008, saving untold scores of lives. Nevertheless, in hindsight, it could equally be argued that escalating in Iraq was ultimately futile, because the idea that improved security would inevitably lead to political reconciliation was a fallacy. The truth may have been that no amount of military force could resolve the deep sectarian tensions splitting Iraq apart. If so, the transition concept advocated by General Casey might well have been in the broader U.S. interest after all. Viewed in this light, it might be said that the influence of electoral constraints was somewhat beneficial, since it pushed the president to continue with a policy that, while still undoubtedly costly in the short term, might in the long term have been better from a U.S. perspective than going deeper into the conflict. This book takes no position on this debate, which remains very much live among scholars of the war, but its existence serves to illustrate how assessments of the impact of electoral constraints are partly contingent on a scholar's assessment of the strategic instincts of the president, which vary from case to case. In an era in which the constitutional checks on presidential power in foreign affairs seem to be eroding, observers of all political stripes will likely be able to find other cases in which a president's concerns about public opinion had a salutary effect on U.S. foreign policy by reining in the wrongheaded impulses of a commander in chief otherwise vested with considerable unilateral power.[41]

Second, there may also be cases in which the broader national interest is actually best served by a president's willingness to compromise on a strategic preference for the sake of protecting his or her electoral prospects. If the incumbent really does have better ideas on how to handle an ongoing war than other rival candidates, it may be reasonable to adopt some electorally friendly yet strategically suboptimal policy in order to guarantee reelection, rather than risk having to hand over to a less experienced commander in chief. As disastrous as Lyndon Johnson's management of the war in Vietnam was, for instance, it might plausibly be considered the lesser of two evils, when one thinks of an alternative world in which the ultra-hawkish Barry Goldwater was left to decide how far to escalate in Vietnam. More controversially, one might see at least some rationality in Richard Nixon's apparent belief that his election was more important than the future of South Vietnam, since his ability to achieve a rapprochement with China and détente in the Cold War more generally was conditional on his victory in 1972, and that these undoubtedly important outcomes might not have been witnessed under a President Humphrey. Even the "decent interval," as morally distasteful as it appears on the surface, might in retrospect have had some redeeming strategic value, particularly if the lens is widened beyond Vietnam to the broader Cold War conflict. As Robert Jervis suggested, the delay Nixon engineered may have been critical in minimizing the broader diplomatic and geopolitical fallout of defeat in Vietnam. Whereas a U.S. withdrawal in 1969 may well have spooked allies at a time when U.S. relations with the Soviet Union were bad and those with China nonexistent, by 1973 the development of détente had done much to calm Cold War tensions and the concomitant fears of some kind of "domino effect."[42] In an ideal world, of course, the candidates with the best ideas would be able to run and win election on the merits of their policy proposals, and would therefore not need to engage in any trade-off that compromises the effectiveness of those positions. Yet, since the strategic value of wartime policy is not always matched in terms of its political attractiveness, this behavior may in some cases be defensible, if not entirely desirable.

Whether or not they can be rationally justified, admitting that decisions about military and diplomatic strategy may be taken with one eye on the domestic political calendar is an unwise move for any elected official seeking to retain office, preserve political capital and build a legacy. To be accused of playing politics with war is one of the most serious charges a sitting president can face. Confronted, therefore, with considerable incentives to downplay or obscure the significance of electoral politics as a meaningful component of a president's balancing calculus, this behavior is something that is too often simply assumed to happen, without a full understanding of exactly how, why, or when. By applying a deeply historical approach to the study of presidential decision making, this book has shed considerable light on these questions. Yet, if the available record leaves this many clues about a practice that is generally considered so distasteful, it stands to reason that this remains the visible tip of a much larger iceberg.

Notes

Introduction

Source for chapter epigraph: William C. Westmoreland, November 9–15, 1999, Senior Officer Oral History Program, USAHEC.

1. Nixon and Kissinger, August 3, 1972, 8:28 a.m., Conversation 760-006, WHT, RNL.
2. Nixon and Kissinger, August 3, 1972, 8:28 a.m., Conversation 760-006, WHT, RNL.
3. Quoted in Jim VandeHei and Michael A. Fletcher, "Bush Says Election Ratified Iraq Policy," *Washington Post*, January 16, 2005.
4. Andrew Johnstone and Andrew Priest, *US Presidential Elections and Foreign Policy: Candidates, Campaigns, and Global Politics from FDR to Bill Clinton* (Lexington: University Press of Kentucky, 2017), 1.
5. Aaron Wildavsky, "The Two Presidencies," *Trans-action* 4 (1966): 7–14.
6. See Miroslav Nincic, *Democracy and Foreign Policy: The Fallacy of Political Realism* (New York: Columbia University Press, 1992), 5–21; Ole R. Holsti, *Public Opinion and American Foreign Policy* (Ann Arbor: University of Michigan Press, 2004), 1–40.
7. For competing perspectives, see Kenneth N. Waltz, "International Politics Is Not Foreign Policy," *Security Studies* 6, no. 1 (1996): 54–57, and Juliet Kaarbo, "A Foreign Policy Analysis Perspective on the Domestic Politics Turn in IR Theory," *International Studies Review* 17, no. 2 (2015): 189–216.
8. Jimmy Carter, *White House Diary* (New York: Farrar, Straus and Giroux, 2010), 436.
9. Author interview with senior military officer, March 2018.
10. For a similar approach, see James H. Lebovic, *Planning to Fail: The US Wars in Vietnam, Iraq, and Afghanistan* (New York: Oxford University Press, 2019).
11. Historians have generally paid greater attention to domestic politics—see, for instance, Lawrence Freedman, *Command: The Politics of Military Operations* (New

York: Oxford University Press, 2022); Julian E. Zelizer, *Arsenal of Democracy: The Politics of National Security—from World War II to the War on Terrorism* (New York: Basic Books, 2010); Campbell Craig and Fredrik Logevall, *America's Cold War: The Politics of Insecurity* (Cambridge, MA: Harvard University Press, 2009); Melvin Small, *Democracy and Diplomacy: The Impact of Domestic Politics in US Foreign Policy, 1789-1994* (Baltimore: Johns Hopkins University Press, 1996). The study of specifically electoral politics and foreign policy, however, has attracted less attention. Notable recent exceptions include Johnstone and Priest, *US Presidential Elections*; Andrew Preston, "Beyond the Water's Edge: Foreign Policy and Electoral Politics," in *America at the Ballot Box*, ed. Gareth Davies and Julian E. Zelizer (Philadelphia: University of Pennsylvania Press, 2015), 219-237; Thomas Alan Schwartz, "'Henry, . . . Winning an Election Is Terribly Important': Partisan Politics in the History of US Foreign Relations," *Diplomatic History* 33, no. 2 (2009): 173-190; and for an earlier perspective, Robert A. Divine, *Foreign Policy and US Presidential Elections* (New York: New Viewpoints, 1974). Former policy makers have also written of the influence of electoral pressure in ways that have shaped the development of the framework I offer in chapter 1. Most notably, see Michael H. Armacost, *Ballots, Bullets, and Bargains: American Foreign Policy and Presidential Elections* (New York: Columbia University Press, 2015), and William B. Quandt, "The Electoral Cycle and the Conduct of Foreign Policy," *Political Science Quarterly* 101, no. 5 (1986): 825–837.

12. Quoted in David Halberstam, *The Best and the Brightest* (New York: Random House, 1972), 424.

13. Kurt Taylor Gaubatz, *Elections and War: The Electoral Incentive in the Democratic Politics of War and Peace* (Stanford, CA: Stanford University Press, 1999), 86.

14. For a recent overview, see Emilie M. Hafner-Burton et al., "The Behavioral Revolution and International Relations," *International Organization* 71, no. S1 (2017): S1–S31.

15. Dan Reiter and Allan C. Stam, *Democracies at War* (Princeton, NJ: Princeton University Press, 2002), 28–33.

16. See Daniel Bessner and Fredrik Logevall, "Recentering the United States in the Historiography of American Foreign Relations," *Texas National Security Review* 3, no. 2 (2020): 38–55.

17. A notable exception is David P. Auerswald, *Disarmed Democracies: Domestic Institutions and the Use of Force* (Ann Arbor: University of Michigan Press, 2000). Other excellent studies have employed statistical methods to yield insight into how democratic constraints vary across different systems. See, for example, Matthew A. Baum and Philip B. K. Potter, *War and Democratic Constraint: How the Public Influences Foreign Policy* (Princeton, NJ: Princeton University Press, 2015); David H. Clark and Timothy Nordstrom, "Democratic Variants and Democratic Variance: How Domestic Constraints Shape Interstate Conflict," *Journal of Politics* 67, no. 1 (2005): 250–270; Paul K. Huth and Todd L. Allee, "Domestic Political Accountability and the Escalation and Settlement of International Disputes," *Journal of Conflict Resolution* 46, no. 6 (2002): 754–790; and Dan Reiter and Erik R. Tillman, "Public, Legislative, and Executive Constraints on the Democratic Initiation of Conflict," *Journal of Politics* 64, no. 3 (2002): 810–826.

18. Giacomo Chiozza, "Presidents on the Cycle: Elections, Audience Costs, and Coercive Diplomacy," *Conflict Management and Peace Science* 34, no. 1 (2017): 4. See also Alistair Smith, "Diversionary Foreign Policy in Democratic Systems," *International Studies Quarterly* 40, no. 1 (1996): 133–153, and Laron K. Williams, "Flexible Election Timing and International Conflict," *International Studies Quarterly* 57, no. 3 (2013): 449–461.

1. Presidents, Politics, and War

Source for chapter epigraph: author interview with John O. Brennan, telephone, July 19, 2018.

1. As with any heuristic, this of course does not perfectly approximate reality; decision makers will not always consider these preferences in a discrete two-step process. Moreover, an awareness of the broader political environment may form an important component of effective strategy. For the purposes of conceptual clarity, however, it is useful to separate out specifically *electoral* considerations from assessments of strategy based on their military and diplomatic utility.

2. For a similar approach examining presidential decisions about grand strategy, see Peter Trubowitz, *Politics and Strategy: Partisan Ambition and American Statecraft* (Princeton, NJ: Princeton University Press, 2011). See also Bruce Bueno de Mesquita and James L. Ray, "The National Interest Versus Individual Political Ambition," in *The Scourge of War: New Extensions on an Old Problem*, ed. Paul F. Diehl (Ann Arbor: University of Michigan Press, 2004); Bruce Bueno de Mesquita et al., *The Logic of Political Survival* (Cambridge, MA: MIT Press, 2003), chap. 6. For a recent perspective examining a broader context, see Peter Trubowitz and Brian Burgoon, *Geopolitics and Democracy: The Western Liberal Order from Foundation to Fracture* (New York: Oxford University Press, 2023).

3. Philip J. Powlick and Andrew Z. Katz, "Defining the American Public Opinion/ Foreign Policy Nexus," *Mershon International Studies Review* 42, no. 1 (1998): 29–61; Thomas Knecht and M. Stephen Weatherford, "Public Opinion and Foreign Policy: The Stages of Presidential Decision Making," *International Studies Quarterly* 50, no. 3 (2006): 705–727; Thomas Knecht, *Paying Attention to Foreign Affairs: How Public Opinion Affects Presidential Decision Making* (University Park: Pennsylvania State University Press, 2010); Alexandra Guisinger and Elizabeth N. Saunders, "Mapping the Boundaries of Elite Cues: How Elites Shape Mass Opinion Across International Issues," *International Studies Quarterly* 61, no. 2 (2017): 425–442.

4. John H. Aldrich, John L. Sullivan, and Eugene Borgida, "Foreign Affairs and Issue Voting: Do Presidential Candidates 'Waltz Before a Blind Audience?,'" *American Political Science Review* 83, no. 1 (1989): 123–141; John H. Aldrich et al., "Foreign Policy and the Electoral Connection," *Annual Review of Political Science* 9 (2006): 477–502; Shana K. Gadarian, "Foreign Policy at the Ballot Box: How Citizens Use Foreign Policy to Judge and Choose Candidates," *Journal of Politics* 72, no. 4 (2010):

1046–1062; Michael T. Koch and Stephen P. Nicholson, "Death and Turnout: The Human Costs of War and Voter Participation in Democracies," *American Journal of Political Science* 60, no. 4 (October 2016): 932–946; Scott Sigmund Gartner and Gary M. Segura, *Costly Calculations: A Theory of War, Casualties, and Politics* (Cambridge: Cambridge University Press, 2021), chap. 7. Studies examining public attentiveness during recent conflicts include Gary C. Jacobson, "George W. Bush, the Iraq War, and the Election of Barack Obama," *Presidential Studies Quarterly* 40, no. 2 (2010): 207–224; David Karol and Edward Miguel, "The Electoral Cost of War: Iraq Casualties and the 2004 US Presidential Election," *Journal of Politics* 69, no. 3 (2007): 633–648; and Christopher Gelpi, Peter D. Feaver, and Jason Reifler, *Paying the Human Costs of War: American Public Opinion and Casualties in Military Conflicts* (Princeton, NJ: Princeton University Press, 2009).

5. Matthew Baum and Phillip B. K. Potter, "The Relationships Between Mass Media, Public Opinion, and Foreign Policy: Toward a Theoretical Synthesis," *Annual Review of Political Science* 11 (2008): 39–65; Adam J. Berinsky, *In Time of War: Understanding American Public Opinion from World War II to Iraq* (Chicago: University of Chicago Press, 2009).

6. Dominic D. P. Johnson and Dominic Tierney, *Failing to Win: Perceptions of Victory and Defeat in International Politics* (Cambridge, MA: Harvard University Press, 2006), 205–241.

7. Powlick and Katz, "Defining the American Public Opinion/Foreign Policy Nexus," 33; Knecht and Weatherford, "Public Opinion and Foreign Policy," 708. See also V. O. Key, *Public Opinion and American Democracy* (New York: Knopf, 1961), 263–287.

8. Ronald H. Hinckley, *People, Polls and Policy Makers: American Public Opinion and National Security* (New York: Free Press, 1992); James N. Druckman and Lawrence R. Jacobs, "Lumpers and Splitters: The Public Opinion Information that Politicians Collect and Use," *International Journal of Public Opinion Quarterly* 70, no. 4 (2006): 453–476. For excellent in-depth examples of specific presidents who did keenly engage with opinion polls, see Steven Casey, *Cautious Crusade: Franklin D. Roosevelt, American Public Opinion, and the War Against Nazi Germany* (New York: Oxford University Press, 2001); Andrew Z. Katz, "Public Opinion and Foreign Policy: The Nixon Administration and the Pursuit of Peace with Honor in Vietnam," *Presidential Studies Quarterly* 27, no. 3 (1997): 496–513; and James N. Druckman and Lawrence R. Jacobs, *Who Governs? Presidents, Public Opinion, and Manipulation* (Chicago: University of Chicago Press, 2015).

9. Philip J. Powlick, "The Sources of Public Opinion for American Foreign Policy Officials," *International Studies Quarterly* 39, no. 4 (1995): 427–451. See also Bernard C. Cohen, *The Public's Impact on Foreign Policy* (Boston: Little Brown, 1973).

10. Powlick and Katz, "Defining the American Public Opinion/Foreign Policy Nexus," 45. See also Douglas C. Foyle, *Counting the Public In: Presidents, Public Opinion, and Foreign Policy* (New York: Columbia University Press, 1999); Philip J. Powlick, "The Attitudinal Bases for Responsiveness to Public Opinion Among American Foreign Policy Officials," *Journal of Conflict Resolution* 35, no. 4 (1991): 611–641.

11. Joshua D. Kertzer et al., "Elite Misperceptions and the Domestic Politics of Conflict," working paper, January 21, 2022, https://jkertzer.sites.fas.harvard.edu/Research_files/NATO-Misperceptions-Web.pdf; Steven Kull, I. M. Destler, and Clay Ramsay, *The Foreign Policy Gap: How Policymakers Misread the Public* (College Park: Center for International and Security Studies at the University of Maryland, 1997); Steven Kull and Clay Ramsay, "How Policymakers Misperceive US Public Opinion on Foreign Policy," in *Navigating Public Opinion: Polls, Policy and the Future of American Democracy*, ed. Jeff Manza et al. (New York: Oxford University Press, 2002), 201–218. See also Thomas Gift and Jonathan Monten, "Who's Out of Touch? Media Misperception of Public Opinion on US Foreign Policy," *Foreign Policy Analysis* 17, no. 1 (January 2021): oraa015, https://doi.org/10.1093/fpa/oraa015.

12. Some recent studies fruitfully employ experimental methods to assess leaders' responses to public opinion about foreign policy. For two excellent examples, see Michael Tomz, Jessica L. P. Weeks, and Keren Yarhi-Milo, "Public Opinion and Decisions About Military Force in Democracies," *International Organization* 74, no. 1 (2020): 119–143, and Kertzer et al., "Elite Misperceptions."

13. This applies Gaubatz's logic regarding conflict initiation to wartime decision making. See Gaubatz, *Elections and War*. See also Armacost, *Ballots, Bullets, and Bargains*, 65–74.

14. See Chiozza, "Presidents on the Cycle."

15. This draws on the logic of "substitutability" in foreign policy, whereby leaders can use different policy instruments to achieve the same goals. See Benjamin A. Most and Harvey Starr, "International Relations Theory, Foreign Policy Substitutability, and 'Nice' Laws," *World Politics* 36, no. 3 (1984): 383–406. Of particular interest here are decisions to use different "tools" based on the domestic politics associated with them. See Helen V. Milner and Dustin Tingley, *Sailing the Water's Edge: The Domestic Politics of American Foreign Policy* (Princeton, NJ: Princeton University Press, 2015); Chiozza, "Presidents on the Cycle."

16. See Reiter and Stam, *Democracies at War*, 159–162. On the use of covert operations to limit escalation and avoid domestic criticism from hawks, see also Austin Carson, *Secret Wars: Covert Conflict in International Politics* (Princeton, NJ: Princeton University Press, 2018).

17. See Barbara Farnham, "Impact of the Political Context on Foreign Policy Decision-Making," *Political Psychology* 25, no. 3 (2004): 441–463; Douglas C. Foyle, "Public Opinion and Foreign Policy: Elite Beliefs as a Mediating Variable," *International Studies Quarterly* 41, no. 1 (1997): 146. This dynamic also aligns with the non-compensatory principle advanced by poliheuristic theory. See Alex Mintz, "How Do Leaders Make Decisions? A Poliheuristic Perspective," *Journal of Conflict Resolution* 48, no. 1 (2004): 3–13.

18. Nincic, *Democracy and Foreign Policy*; Quandt, "The Electoral Cycle."

19. Morris P. Fiorina, *Retrospective Voting in American National Elections* (New Haven, CT: Yale University Press, 1981); Chiozza, "Presidents on the Cycle."

20. Brandice Canes-Wrone, *Who Leads Whom? Presidents, Policy, and the Public* (Chicago: University of Chicago Press, 2006); Lawrence R. Jacobs and Robert Y. Shapiro, *Politicians Don't Pander: Political Manipulation and the Loss of Democratic*

Responsiveness (Chicago: University of Chicago Press, 2000); Foyle, *Counting the Public In*; Gaubatz, *Elections and War*.

21. This relative insulation from political pressures following a recent election may also be a function of the increased power available to newly (re)elected presidents, especially in cases where their margin of victory was significant. See Philip B. K. Potter, "Electoral Margins and American Foreign Policy," *International Studies Quarterly* 57, no. 3 (2013): 505–518.

22. Andrew Payne, "Bringing the Boys Back Home: Campaign Promises and U.S. Decision-Making in Iraq and Vietnam," *Politics* 41, no. 1 (February 2021): 95–110.

23. Douglas L. Kriner, *After the Rubicon: Congress, Presidents, and the Politics of Waging War* (Chicago: University of Chicago Press, 2010); William G. Howell and Jon C. Pevehouse, *While Dangers Gather: Congressional Checks on Presidential War Powers* (Princeton, NJ: Princeton University Press, 2007).

24. Preston, "Beyond the Water's Edge," 231–234; Gary C. Jacobson, "The President's Effect on Partisan Attitudes," *Presidential Studies Quarterly* 42, no. 4 (2012): 683–718.

25. On these challenges, see Kurt M. Campbell and James B. Steinberg, *Difficult Transitions: Foreign Policy Troubles at the Outset of Presidential Power* (Washington, DC: Brookings Institution Press, 2009), chap. 4.

26. Preston, "Beyond the Water's Edge," 234–235. See also Armacost, *Ballots, Bullets, and Bargains*, 110–116.

27. Quoted in Preston, "Beyond the Water's Edge," 235. On presidential efforts to deceive the public, see John M. Schuessler, *Deceit on the Road to War: Presidents, Politics and American Democracy* (Ithaca, NY: Cornell University Press, 2015).

28. Jeff Fishel, *Presidents and Promises: From Campaign Pledge to Presidential Performance* (Washington, DC: CQ Press, 1985); Ezra Klein, "Presidents Keep Their Campaign Promises," *Washington Post*, January 20, 2012; Jonathan Bernstein, "Campaign Promises," *Washington Monthly*, January/February 2012; Jonathan Bernstein, "Has Trump Kept His Promises?" *New York Times*, August 22, 2019; Andrew Payne, "Trump Just De-escalated in the Middle East. Here's Why We Shouldn't Be Surprised," *Washington Post*, January 11, 2020; Robert Thomson et al., "The Fulfillment of Parties' Election Pledges," *American Journal of Political Science* 61, no. 3 (2017): 527–542; Colton Heffington, "Do Hawks and Doves Deliver? The Words and Deeds of Foreign Policy in Democracies," *Foreign Policy Analysis* 14, no. 1 (January 2018): 64–85. See also discussion in Jeffrey A. Friedman, *The Commander-in-Chief Test: How the Politics of Image-Making Shapes U.S. Foreign Policy* (unpublished book manuscript, July 2022), 15–16.

29. See Richard Brody, *Assessing the President: The Media, Elite Opinion, and Public Support* (Stanford, CA: Stanford University Press, 1991), chap. 2; Potter, "Electoral Margins."

30. See Jim Golby, Lindsay P. Cohn, and Peter D. Feaver, "Thanks for Your Service: Civilian and Veteran Attitudes After Fifteen Years of War," in *Warriors and Citizens: American Views of Our Military*, ed. Kori Schake and Jim Mattis (Stanford, CA: Hoover Institution Press, 2016), 97–141; Ronald R. Krebs, Robert Ralston, and Aaron Rapport, "No Right to Be Wrong: What Americans Think About Civil-Military Relations," *Perspectives on Politics*, March 11, 2021, doi:10.1017/S15375 92721000013.

31. On ambiguity as a winning electoral strategy, see Michael Tomz and Robert P. Van Houweling, "The Electoral Implications of Candidate Ambiguity," *American Political Science Review* 103, no. 1 (February 2009): 83–98.

32. See Aldrich, Sulliivan, and Borgida, "Foreign Affairs and Issue Voting."

33. Hence the following line in a certain Broadway show: "If you stand for nothing, Burr, what'll you fall for?"

34. Robert D. Putnam, "Diplomacy and Domestic Politics: The Logic of Two-Level Games," *International Organization* 42, no. 3 (1988): 427–460. See also Armacost, *Ballots, Bullets, and Bargains*, 87–92, for some instructive examples.

35. Bueno de Mesquita et al., *The Logic of Political Survival*, 249–250; James D. Morrow, "Electoral and Congressional Incentives and Arms Control," *Journal of Conflict Resolution* 35, no. 2 (1991): 245–265.

36. This condition necessarily gives rise to consideration of other actors' preferences beyond those of the president. Since the focus here remains on the impact of electoral pressures on presidential decision making, however, the strategic behavior of other actors is considered only to the extent that it helps shed light on how the president's ability to pursue a preferred diplomatic strategy is affected.

37. On foreign affairs challenges during transitions more generally, see Frederick C. Mosher, W. David Clinton, and Daniel George Lang, *Presidential Transitions and Foreign Affairs* (Baton Rouge: Louisiana State University Press, 1987); Campbell and Steinberg, *Difficult Transitions*; Jeffrey H. Michaels and Andrew Payne, "One President at a Time? How the President-Elect Shapes US Foreign Policy During the Transition," *Presidential Studies Quarterly* 52, no. 4 (2022): 730–758.

38. This builds on an excellent earlier discursive model of the broad relationship between the electoral cycle and foreign policy decision making in Quandt, "The Electoral Cycle." For applications to decisions outside of a wartime context, see Miroslav Nincic, "US Soviet Policy and the Electoral Connection," *World Politics* 42, no. 3 (1990): 370–396; Nincic, *Democracy and Foreign Policy*; Bruce M. Russett, *Controlling the Sword: The Democratic Governance of National Security* (Cambridge, MA: Harvard University Press, 1990), 12–14; and Louise Fawcett and Andrew Payne, "Stuck on a Hostile Path? US Policy Towards Iran Since the Revolution," *Contemporary Politics* 29, no. 1 (February 2023): 1–21.

39. See Jeffrey M. Jones, "Obama Honeymoon Continues; 7 Months Is Recent Average," Gallup, July 3, 2009, https://news.gallup.com/poll/121391/obama-honeymoon-continues-months-recent-average.aspx.

40. Nate Silver, "For Second-Term Presidents, a Shorter Honeymoon," *Washington Post*, January 19, 2013.

41. See Colleen J. Shogan, "The Contemporary Presidency: The Sixth Year Curse," *Presidential Studies Quarterly* 36, no. 1 (2006): 89–101.

42. See also Philip B. K. Potter, "Lame-Duck Foreign Policy," *Presidential Studies Quarterly* 46, no. 4 (December 2016): 849–867, in which a statistically significant increase in foreign policy activity is observed in this period of the cycle, including actions involving the use of force.

43. See Potter, "Lame-Duck Foreign Policy"; David Hastings Dunn, " 'Quacking Like a Duck?' Bush II and Presidential Power in the Second Term," *International Affairs* 82, no. 1 (2006): 95–120; Shogan, "The Contemporary Presidency."

44. Quandt, "The Electoral Cycle," 833. See also Kyle Haynes, "Lame Ducks and Coercive Diplomacy: Do Executive Term Limits Reduce the Effectiveness of Democratic Threats?," *Journal of Conflict Resolution* 56, no. 5 (2012): 771–798.

45. See Fawcett and Payne, "Stuck on a Hostile Path?"; Michaels and Payne, "One President at a Time?," 14–20.

46. Elizabeth N. Saunders, *Leaders at War: How Presidents Shape Military Interventions* (New York: Cornell University Press, 2011); Rachel E. Whitlark, *All Options on the Table: Leaders, Preventive War, and Nuclear Proliferation* (Ithaca, NY: Cornell University Press, 2021).

47. Hafner-Burton et al., "The Behavioral Revolution."

48. Philip B. K. Potter, "Does Experience Matter? American Presidential Experience, Age, and International Conflict," *Journal of Conflict Resolution* 51, no. 3 (2007): 351–378; Elizabeth N. Saunders, "No Substitute for Experience: Presidents, Advisers, and Information in Group Decision Making," *International Organization* 71, Supplement S1 (2017): S219–S247; Michael C. Horowitz, Allan C. Stam, and Cali M. Ellis, *Why Leaders Fight* (Cambridge: Cambridge University Press, 2015).

49. Michaela Mattes and Jessica L. P. Weeks, "Hawks, Doves, and Peace: An Experimental Approach," *American Journal of Political Science* 63, no. 1 (January 2019): 53–66; Robert F. Trager and Lynn Vavreck, "The Political Costs of Crisis Bargaining Rhetoric and the Role of Party," *American Journal of Political Science* 55, no. 3 (July 2011): 526–545. On these and related debates, see also Sarah E. Kreps et al., "The Ratification Premium: Hawks, Doves, and Arms Control," *World Politics* 70, no. 4 (October 2018): 479–514; Michael Colaresi, "When Doves Cry: International Rivalry, Unreciprocated Cooperation, and Leadership Turnover," *American Journal of Political Science* 48, no. 3 (July 2004): 555–570; Kenneth A. Schultz, "The Politics of Risking Peace: Do Hawks or Doves Deliver the Olive Branch?," *International Organization* 59, no. 1 (Winter 2005): 1–38.

50. Carrie A. Lee, "Polarization, Casualty Sensitivity, and Military Operations: Evidence from a Survey Experiment," *International Politics* 59 (2022): 981–1003. See also Gordon M. Friedrichs and Jordan Tama, "Polarization and US Foreign Policy: Key Debates and New Findings," *International Politics* 59 (2022): 767–785.

51. Berinsky, *In Time of War*; A. Cooper Drury et al., " 'Pretty Prudent' or Rhetorically Responsive? The American Public's Support for Military Action," *Political Research Quarterly* 63, no. 1 (March 2010): 83–96; Brody, *Assessing the President*; John R. Zaller, *The Nature and Origins of Mass Opinion* (Cambridge: Cambridge University Press, 1992).

52. Jacobs and Shapiro, *Politicians Don't Pander*; Jon Western, *Selling Intervention and War* (Baltimore: Johns Hopkins University Press, 2005); Druckman and Jacobs, *Who Governs?* Saunders, "War and the Inner Circle," argues that leaders strategically manage the cues that reach the public by bargaining with the elite cue givers. This is one way in which leaders can reduce domestic constraints on foreign policy more generally. For a discussion of "malleable" constraints, see Susan D. Hyde and Elizabeth N. Saunders, "Recapturing Regime Type in International Relations: Leaders, Institutions, and Agency Space," *International Organization* 74, no. 2 (Spring 2020): 363–395.

53. Schuessler, *Deceit on the Road to War*, 3. See also John J. Mearsheimer, *Why Leaders Lie: The Truth About Lying in International Politics* (New York: Oxford University Press, 2011). For an example of the "bait and switch" tactic, see Hew Strachan, "Strategy and Democracy," *Survival* 62, no. 2 (2020): 50–54.

54. George C. Edwards, *On Deaf Ears: The Limits of the Bully Pulpit* (New Haven, CT: Yale University Press, 2006); Powlick and Katz, "Defining the American Public Opinion/Foreign Policy Nexus," 38. Druckman and Jacobs, *Who Governs?*, 127, observe that while presidents may have a "chronic *intent* to manipulate," their actual success in doing so is "selective and conditional."

55. Matthew A. Baum and Tim Groeling, *War Stories: The Causes and Consequences of Public Views of War* (Princeton, NJ: Princeton University Press, 2010); Baum and Potter, "The Relationships"; Baum and Potter, *War and Democratic Constraint*.

56. Joshua D. Kertzer and Thomas Zeitzoff, "A Bottom-Up Theory of Public Opinion About Foreign Policy," *American Journal of Political Science* 61, no. 3 (July 2017): 543–558.

57. Guisinger and Saunders, "Mapping the Boundaries of Elite Cues."

58. On partisan opponents, see Berinsky, *In Time of War*, and Baum and Potter, *War and Democratic Constraint*. On the media, see Baum and Potter, *War and Democratic Constraint*, and Baum and Groeling, *War Stories*. On the military, see James Golby, Peter Feaver, and Kyle Dropp, "Elite Military Cues and Public Opinion About the Use of Military Force," *Armed Forces & Society* 44, no. 1 (2017): 44–71. On advisors, see Saunders, "War and the Inner Circle."

59. Sarah Maxey, "Limited Spin: When the Public Punishes Leaders Who Lie About Military Action," *Journal of Conflict Resolution* 65, nos. 2–3 (February 2021): 283–312. See also Dan Reiter, "Democracy, Deception, and Entry Into War," *Security Studies* 21, no. 4 (2012): 594–623. By contrast, John Schuessler argues that leaders may be forgiven for deceptive behavior if the outcome of war is favorable, thus making deception a "calculated risk." See Schuessler, *Deceit on the Road to War*, 16–17.

60. Richard Sobel, *Impact of Public Opinion on U.S. Foreign Policy Since Vietnam* (New York: Oxford University Press, 2001); Powlick and Katz, "Defining the American Public Opinion/Foreign Policy Nexus"; Russett, *Controlling the Sword*; Aldrich et al., "Foreign Policy and the Electoral Connection"; Key, *Public Opinion and American Democracy*; Knecht, *Paying Attention to Foreign Affairs*. It should be noted that scholars seeking to challenge the liberal institutionalist perspective on democratic constraint are fully cognizant of the limits of deception and do not propose a false dichotomy—see, for instance, Schuessler, *Deceit on the Road to War*, 22.

61. Foyle, "Public Opinion and Foreign Policy"; Foyle, *Counting the Public In*.

62. Foyle, *Counting the Public In*; Knecht and Weatherford, "Public Opinion and Foreign Policy"; Powlick and Katz, "Defining the American Public Opinion/Foreign Policy Nexus"; Knecht, *Paying Attention to Foreign Affairs*.

63. Schuessler, *Deceit on the Road to War*, 3; Baum and Potter, "The Relationships."

64. Tomz, Weeks, and Yarhi-Milo, "Public Opinion."

65. Jeffrey A. Friedman, "Issue-Image Tradeoffs and the Politics of Foreign Policy: How Leaders Use Foreign Policy Positions to Shape their Personal Images," *World Politics* 75 (forthcoming).

66. Joslyn N. Barnhart et al., "The Suffragist Peace," *International Organization* 74, no. 4 (2020): 633–670; Joslyn N. Barnhart and Robert F. Trager, *The Suffragist Peace: How Women Shape the Politics of War* (New York: Oxford University Press, forthcoming).

67. Daniel L. Byman and Kenneth M. Pollack, "Let Us Now Praise Great Men: Bringing the Statesman Back In," *International Security* 25, no. 4 (2001): 107–146; Robert Jervis, "Do Leaders Matter and How Would We Know?," *Security Studies* 22, no. 2 (2013): 153–179; Michael C. Horowitz and Matthew Fuhrmann, "Studying Leaders and Military Conflict: Conceptual Framework and Research Agenda," *Journal of Conflict Resolution* 62, no. 10 (2018): 2072–2086.

68. See, for example, Alexander L. George and Eric Stern, "Presidential Management Styles and Models," in *Presidential Personality and Performance*, ed. Alexander L. George and Juliet L. George (Boulder, CO: Westview Press, 1998), 199–280.

69. For the paradigmatic account of bureaucratic drivers of decision making, see Graham T. Allison and Phillip Zelikow, *Essence of Decision: Explaining the Cuban Missile Crisis*, 2nd ed. (New York: Longman, 1999).

70. Elizabeth N. Saunders, "Elites in the Making and Breaking of Foreign Policy," *Annual Review of Political Science* 25, no. 9 (2022): 8. See also Stephen D. Krasner, "Are Bureaucracies Important? (Or Allison Wonderland?)," *Foreign Policy* 7 (Summer 1972): 166.

71. Erik Lin-Greenberg, "Soldiers, Pollsters, and International Crises: Public Opinion and the Military's Advice on the Use of Force," *Foreign Policy Analysis* 17, no. 3 (July 2021): orab009, https://doi.org/10.1093/fpa/orab009.

72. Saunders, "War and the Inner Circle."

73. Golby, Feaver, and Dropp, "Elite Military Cues."

74. See Bueno de Mesquita et al., *The Logic of Political Survival*.

75. Immanuel Kant, *Perpetual Peace and Other Essays*, trans. Ted Humphrey (Indianapolis, IN: Hackett Publishing, 1983), 113.

76. "President Thanks U.S. and Coalition Troops in Afghanistan," Office of the Press Secretary, the White House, March 1, 2006, https://georgewbush-whitehouse.archives.gov/news/releases/2006/03/20060301-3.html.

77. Among the landmark studies are Bruce Bueno de Mesquita et al., "An Institutional Explanation of the Democratic Peace," *American Political Science Review* 93, no. 4 (1999): 791–807; Michael W. Doyle, "Kant, Liberal Legacies, and Foreign Affairs," *Philosophy & Public Affairs* 12, no. 13 (1983): 205–235; Michael W. Doyle, "Kant, Liberal Legacies, and Foreign Affairs, Part 2," *Philosophy & Public Affairs* 12, no. 4 (1983): 323–353; Bruce M. Russett and John R. Oneal, *Triangulating Peace: Democracy, Interdependence, and International Organizations* (New York: Norton, 2001); James Lee Ray, *Democracy and International Conflict* (Columbia: University of South Carolina Press, 1995).

78. John E. Mueller, *War, Presidents, and Public Opinion* (New York: Wiley, 1973).

79. Gartner and Segura, *Costly Calculations*; Scott Sigmund Gartner, "The Multiple Effects of Casualties on Public Support for War: An Experimental Approach," *American Political Science Review* 102, no. 1 (2008): 95–106; Scott Sigmund Gartner and Gary M. Segura, "All Politics Are Still Local: The Iraq War and the 2006 Midterm Elections," *PS: Political Science & Politics* 41, no. 1 (2008): 95–100; Steven Casey,

When Soldiers Fall: How Americans Have Confronted Combat Losses from World War I to Afghanistan (New York: Oxford University Press, 2014). See also Eric Victor Larson, *Casualties and Consensus: The Historical Role of Casualties in Domestic Support for US Military Operations* (Santa Monica, CA: RAND Corporation, 1996).

80. Benny Geys, "Wars, Presidents, and Popularity: The Political Cost(s) of War Reexamined," *Public Opinion Quarterly* 74, no. 2 (2010): 357–374.

81. Gustavo A. Flores-Macías and Sarah E. Kreps, "Borrowing Support for War: The Effect of War Finance on Public Attitudes Toward Conflict," *Journal of Conflict Resolution* 61, no. 5 (2017): 997–1020; Sarah Kreps, *Taxing Wars: The American Way of War Finance and the Decline of Democracy* (New York: Oxford University Press, 2018).

82. Reiter and Stam, *Democracies at War*; Bueno de Mesquita et al., *The Logic of Political Survival*; Randolph M. Siverson, "Democracies and War Participation: In Defense of the Institutional Constraints Argument," *European Journal of International Relations* 1, no. 4 (1995): 481–489.

83. Benjamin A. Valentino, Paul K. Huth, and Sarah E. Croco, "Bear Any Burden? How Democracies Minimize the Costs of War," *Journal of Politics* 72, no. 2 (2010): 528–544; Casey, *When Soldiers Fall*; Thomas Waldman, *Vicarious Warfare: American Strategy and the Illusion of War on the Cheap* (Bristol, UK: Bristol University Press, 2021).

84. Flores-Macías and Kreps, "Borrowing Support for War"; Kreps, *Taxing Wars*.

85. Kurt Taylor Gaubatz, "Election Cycles and War," *Journal of Conflict Resolution* 35, no. 2 (1991): 212–244, Gaubatz, *Elections and War*. On increased presidential responsiveness before an election generally, see also Jacobs and Shapiro, *Politicians Don't Pander*; Foyle, *Counting the Public In*; Canes-Wrone, *Who Leads Whom?*

86. Gaubatz, *Elections and War*, 16–18, 55–57. See also Payne, "Trump Just De-escalated."

87. Chiozza, "Presidents on the Cycle"; Potter, "Electoral Margins." See also Auerswald, *Disarmed Democracies*. For the classic statement on "audience costs," focusing on crises and interstate bargaining disputes, see James D. Fearon, "Domestic Political Audiences and the Escalation of International Disputes," *American Political Science Review* 88, no. 3 (1994): 577–592.

88. Alexander Hamilton, James Madison, and John Jay, *The Federalist Papers*, ed. Michael A. Genovese (New York: Palgrave Macmillan, 2009), 210; Paola Conconi, Nicolas Sahuguet, and Maurizio Zanardi, "Democratic Peace and Electoral Accountability," *Journal of the European Economic Association* 12, no. 4 (2014): 997–1028; Sean Zeigler, Jan H. Pierskalla, and Sandeep Mazumder, "War and the Reelection Motive: Examining the Effect of Term Limits," *Journal of Conflict Resolution* 58, no. 4 (2014): 658–684. See also Huth and Allee, "Domestic Political Accountability," and Haynes, "Lame Ducks and Coercive Diplomacy." For an alternative perspective, see Jeff Carter and Timothy Nordstrom, "Term Limits, Leader Preferences, and Interstate Conflict," *International Studies Quarterly* 61, no. 3 (2017): 721–735.

89. Quandt, "The Electoral Cycle," 833.

90. Nincic, *Democracy and Foreign Policy*, 108.

91. Nikolay Marinov, William G. Nomikos, and Josh Robbins, in "Does Electoral Proximity Affect Security Policy?," *Journal of Politics* 77, no. 3 (2015): 762–773,

further demonstrate this point with respect to contributions to peacekeeping missions.

92. Michael C. Horowitz and Matthew S. Levendusky, "Drafting Support for War: Conscription and Mass Support for Warfare," *Journal of Politics* 73, no. 2 (April 2011): 524–534. On the civil-military "gap" more generally, see Peter D. Feaver and Richard H. Kohn, eds., *Soldiers and Civilians: The Civil-Military Gaps and American National Security* (Cambridge, MA: MIT Press, 2001); Schake and Mattis, *Warriors and Citizens*.

93. On drones in particular, see John Kaag and Sarah Kreps, *Drone Warfare* (Cambridge: Polity, 2014), 53–77. See also Waldman, *Vicarious Warfare*.

94. Tanisha M. Fazal, "Life and Limb: New Estimates of Casualty Aversion in the United States," *International Studies Quarterly* 65, no. 1 (2021): 160–172. On the underlying changes in military medicine and its impact on the wounded-to-killed ration, see also Tanisha M. Fazal, "Dead Wrong? Battle Deaths, Military Medicine, and Exaggerated Reports of War's Demise," *International Security* 39, no. 1 (Summer 2014): 95–125.

95. Jonathan D. Caverley, *Democratic Militarism: Voting, Wealth, and War* (Cambridge: Cambridge University Press, 2014).

96. Christopher Gelpi, Peter D. Feaver, and Jason Reifler, "Success Matters: Casualty Sensitivity and the War in Iraq," *International Security* 30, no. 3 (2006): 7–46; Bruce W. Jentleson, "The Pretty Prudent Public: Post Post-Vietnam American Opinion on the Use of Military Force," *International Studies Quarterly* 36, no. 1 (1992): 49–74.

97. Daniel Ellsberg, *Papers on the War* (New York: Simon and Schuster, 1972), 42–135.

98. Sarah E. Croco, "The Decider's Dilemma: Leader Culpability, War Outcomes, and Domestic Punishment," *American Political Science Review* 105, no. 3 (2011): 457–477.

99. Shawn T. Cochran, "Gambling for Resurrection Versus Bleeding the Army: Explaining Risky Behavior in Failing Wars," *Security Studies* 27, no. 2 (2018): 204–232.

100. For the classic statement of the associated "rally" hypothesis, see Mueller, *War, Presidents, and Public Opinion*. For an excellent recent overview of the literature on diversionary war theory, see Benjamin O. Fordham, "More Than Mixed Results: What We Have Learned from Quantitative Research on the Diversionary Hypothesis," in *Oxford Encyclopedia of Empirical International Relations Theory*, ed. William R. Thompson (New York: Oxford University Press, 2018), 2:549–564. For notable early examples of studies that find evidence of electorally motivated diversionary action, see Charles W. Ostrom and Brian L. Job, "The President and the Political Use of Force," *American Political Science Review* 80, no. 2 (1986): 541–566; Richard J. Stoll, "The Guns of November: Presidential Reelections and the Use of Force, 1947–1982," *Journal of Conflict Resolution* 28, no. 2 (1984): 231–246; Gregory D. Hess and Athanasios Orphanides, "War Politics: An Economic, Rational-Voter Framework," *American Economic Review* 85, no. 4 (1995): 828–846.

101. Bueno de Mesquita et al., *The Logic of Political Survival*, chap. 6. For perspectives on the "gambling for resurrection" mechanism, see George W. Downs and David M. Rocke, "Conflict, Agency, and Gambling for Resurrection: The Principal-Agent

Problem Goes to War," *American Journal of Political Science* 38, no. 2 (1994): 362–380; Giacomo Chiozza and Hein E. Goemans, "Peace Through Insecurity: Tenure and International Conflict," *Journal of Conflict Resolution* 47, no. 4 (2003): 443–467.

102. Joanne Gowa, "Politics at the Water's Edge: Parties, Voters, and the Use of Force Abroad," *International Organization* 52, no. 2 (1998): 307–324; James Meernik, "Presidential Decision Making and the Political Use of Military Force," *International Studies Quarterly* 38, no. 1 (1994): 121–138; James Meernik, *The Political Use of Military Force in US Foreign Policy* (Farnham, UK: Ashgate, 2004), 157–205; Gaubatz, "Election Cycles and War"; Potter, "Does Experience Matter?"; Zeigler, Pierskalla, and Mazumder, "War and the Reelection Motive"; Chiozza and Goemans, "Peace Through Insecurity."

103. James Meernik, "Domestic Politics and the Political Use of Military Force by the United States," *Political Research Quarterly* 54, no. 4 (2001): 889–904; James Meernik and Peter Waterman, "The Myth of the Diversionary Use of Force by American Presidents," *Political Research Quarterly* 49, no. 3 (1996): 573–590; Jack S. Levy, "Diversionary War Theory: A Critique," in *Handbook of War Studies*, ed. Manus I. Midlarsky (Boston: Unwin Hyman, 1989), 259–288.

104. Meernik, "Presidential Decision Making"; Ahmer Tarar, "Diversionary Incentives and the Bargaining Approach to War," *International Studies Quarterly* 50, no. 1 (2006): 169–188.

105. Bradley Lian and John R. Oneal, "Presidents, the Use of Military Force, and Public Opinion," *Journal of Conflict Resolution* 37, no. 2 (1993): 277–300; John R. Oneal and Anna Lillian Bryan, "The Rally 'Round the Flag Effect in US Foreign Policy Crises, 1950–1985," *Political Behavior* 17, no. 4 (1995): 379–340; Matthew A. Baum, "The Constituent Foundations of the Rally-Round-the-Flag Phenomenon," *International Studies Quarterly* 46, no. 2 (2002): 263–298; Brody, *Assessing the President*, chap. 3.

106. Johnson and Tierney, *Failing to Win*; Baum and Potter, "The Relationships."

2. Korea: Truman, Eisenhower, and America's First Limited War

Sources for chapter epigraphs: Truman, "Memoirs: Politics, Political Ethics of Presidents," Undated, PPP, Box 645, HSTL; Eisenhower, quoted in Clark, Oral History, DDEL.

1. Quoted in Harry S. Truman, *Memoirs*, vol. 2, *Years of Trial and Hope* (Garden City, NY: Doubleday, 1956), 332.

2. June 29, 1950, WHCF, Official File, Box 1454, HSTL.

3. See Larry Blomstedt, *Truman, Congress, and Korea: The Politics of America's First Undeclared War* (Lexington: University Press of Kentucky, 2016), 38–41; H. W. Brands, *The General vs. the President: MacArthur and Truman on the Brink of Nuclear War* (New York: Doubleday, 2016), 114–115; Ronald J. Caridi, *The Korean War and American Politics: The Republican Party as a Case Study* (Philadelphia: University of Pennsylvania Press, 1968), 36–37.

4. See John Lewis Gaddis, *Strategies of Containment: A Critical Appraisal of American National Security Policy During the Cold War* (New York: Oxford University Press, 2005), chaps. 2–4.

5. Prior assessments of the strategic importance of Korea would later become the subject of heavily politicized debate, however, centering around comments made by Dean Acheson in a speech before the National Press Club in January 1950, in which the secretary of state suggested that Korea lay outside of the defensive perimeter of U.S. interests in the Far East. For the speech, see United States Department of State, *Department of State Bulletin* 22, no. 551 (January 23, 1950): 111–118. For analysis, see William Stueck, *The Korean War: An International History* (Princeton, NJ: Princeton University Press, 1995), 30.

6. George F. Kennan, *Memoirs: 1950–1963* (London: Hutchinson, 1973), 24; George F. Kennan, *The Kennan Diaries*, ed. Frank Costigliola (New York: W. W. Norton, 2014), 264.

7. June 26, 1950, Acheson Papers, Box 67, HSTL.

8. June 28, 1950, Acheson Papers, Box 67, HSTL.

9. June 29, 1950, Elsey Papers, Box 71, HSTL.

10. Quoted in United States Department of State, *Department of State Bulletin* 23, no. 575 (July 10, 1950): 46.

11. Richard E. Neustadt, *Presidential Power: The Politics of Leadership from FDR to Carter* (Chichester, UK: Wiley, 1980), 93.

12. Caridi, *Korean War and American Politics*, 1–21.

13. Dean Acheson, *Present at the Creation: My Years in the State Department* (New York: W. W. Norton, 1969), 411.

14. Acheson, 416.

15. Quoted in Blomstedt, *Truman, Congress, and Korea*, 65.

16. "Background to Korea," Elsey Papers, Box 91, HSTL.

17. Quoted in Caridi, *Korean War and American Politics*, 55.

18. Quoted in Burton I. Kaufman, *The Korean War: Challenges in Crisis, Credibility, and Command* (Philadelphia: Temple University Press, 1984), 50.

19. Quoted in Caridi, *Korean War and American Politics*, 71.

20. Quoted in Steven Casey, *Selling the Korean War: Propaganda, Politics, and Public Opinion in the United States, 1950–1953* (New York: Oxford University Press, 2008), 85.

21. "Washington Wire," *New Republic*, August 21, 1950.

22. "War Now? Or When? Or Never," *Time*, September 18, 1950.

23. All quoted in Casey, *Selling the Korean War*, 76.

24. July 14, 1950, PSF, Box 188, HSTL.

25. August 14, 1950, Ayers Papers, Box 21, HSTL.

26. United States Department of State, *Foreign Relations of the United States, 1950*, vol. 7, *Korea*, ed. John P. Glennon (Washington, DC: United States Government Printing Office, 1976), doc. 344. In this and other chapters, I refer to the *Foreign Relations of the United States* series by the abbreviation *FRUS*; full publication details for each subsequent volume are listed in the bibliography.

27. *FRUS, 1950*, vol. 7, doc. 349. See also docs. 188, 278, 287, and 295.

28. Kennan, *The Kennan Diaries*, 261.

29. *FRUS, 1950*, vol. 7, doc. 365.

30. *FRUS, 1950*, vol. 7, doc. 386; emphasis added.

31. *FRUS, 1950*, vol. 7, doc. 385.

32. *FRUS, 1950*, vol. 7, doc. 422.

33. Michael H. Hunt, "Beijing and the Korean Crisis, June 1950-June 1951," *Political Science Quarterly* 107, no 3 (1992): 473.

34. Quoted in Dean Rusk, *As I Saw It* (New York: Penguin, 1990), 161. Truman would go on to accuse Dulles of instigating the "demagogic" charges made in the Republican campaign manifesto that August. See August 14 and 17, 1950, Ayers Papers, Box 21, HSTL.

35. August 10, 1950, PSF, Box 181, HSTL.

36. Rosemary Foot, *A Substitute for Victory: The Politics of Peacemaking at the Korean Armistice Talks* (Ithaca, NY: Cornell University Press, 1990), 62.

37. Quoted in Caridi, *Korean War and American Politics*, 73.

38. Quoted in Rosemary Foot, *The Wrong War: American Policy and the Dimensions of the Korean Conflict, 1950-1953* (Ithaca, NY: Cornell University Press, 1985), 69.

39. Kennan to Acheson, August 23, 1950, Acheson Papers, Box 67, HSTL.

40. J. Lawton Collins, *War in Peacetime: The History and Lessons of Korea* (Boston: Houghton Mifflin, 1969), 148.

41. Acheson, *Present at the Creation*, 446.

42. September 11, 1950, PSF, Box 181, HSTL.

43. September 27, 1950, RG-16a, Box 4, MMA.

44. Omar Bradley and Clay Blair, *A General's Life: An Autobiography by the General of the Army* (New York: Simon and Schuster, 1983), 561.

45. Bradley and Blair, 544.

46. Quoted in Collins, *War in Peacetime*, 123.

47. Quoted in Douglas MacArthur, *Reminiscences* (New York: McGraw Hill, 1964), 348.

48. Bradley and Blair, *A General's Life*, 544; MacArthur quoted in Stueck, *The Korean War*, 85. See also Courtney Whitney, *MacArthur: His Rendezvous with History* (New York: Knopf, 1956), 357–358.

49. Truman, *Memoirs*, 2:348, 358.

50. August 8, 1950, RG-6, Box 1, MMA; MacArthur quoted in Matthew B. Ridgway, *The Korean War* (New York: Da Capo Press, 1967), 37–38.

51. Harriman, Oral History Interview, RG-49, Box 5, MMA; June 8, 1951, PSF, Box 111, HSTL.

52. Harriman, Oral History Interview, RG-49, Box 5, MMA.

53. August 8, 1950, RG-37, Box 1, MMA.

54. Quoted in Casey, *Selling the Korean War*, 97.

55. October 4, 1950, SMOF/KWF, Box 5, HSTL.

56. September 27, 1950, SMOF/KWF, Box 5, HSTL.

57. On Chinese decision making, see Stueck, *The Korean War*, chap. 3; Thomas J. Christensen, *Useful Adversaries: Grand Strategy, Domestic Mobilization, and Sino-American Conflict, 1947-1958* (Princeton, NJ: Princeton University Press, 1996), chap. 5.

58. See "Daily Korea Situation" reports of October 27, 20, and 31, 1950, SMOF/KWF, Box 5, HSTL.

59. November 1, 1950, NSCF, Box 3, HSTL.

60. Bradley and Blair, *A General's Life*, 580.

61. *FRUS, 1950*, vol. 7, doc. 640.
62. October 8, 1950, RG-9, Box 45, MMA.
63. Bradley and Blair, *A General's Life*, 579; October 24, 1950, RG-16a, Box 4, MMA.
64. November 7, 1950, RG-9, Box 45, MMA.
65. See Foot, *The Wrong War*, 78–87.
66. Quoted in Kaufman, *The Korean War*, 84.
67. "The 38th Parallel," *New York Times*, September 30, 1950; "North of the 38th," *New York Times*, October 2, 1950; "A Plan for Korea," *New York Times*, September 29, 1950.
68. Casey, *Selling the Korean War*, 101.
69. September 29, 1950, Connelly Papers, Box 2, HSTL.
70. "Address by Mr. Harry S. Truman," United Nations General Assembly, Fifth Session, October 24, 1950, https://undocs.org/en/A/PV.295; August 14, 1950, Elsey Papers, Box 47, HSTL.
71. Quoted in Casey, *Selling the Korean War*, 118.
72. November 27, 1950, RG-9, Box 45, MMA.
73. December 12, 1950, PSF, Box 188, HSTL.
74. December 29, 1950, RG-16a, Box 4, MMA.
75. January 10, 1951, RG-16a, Box 4, MMA; December 30, 1950, RG-6, Box 1, MMA; Foot, *The Wrong War*, 118–130.
76. May 17, 1951, PSF, Box 188, HSTL.
77. December 2, 1950, WHCF, Official File, Box 1454, HSTL; "Daily Opinion Summary," December 4, 1950, Elsey Papers, Box 77, HSTL.
78. See Caridi, *Korean War and American Politics*, chaps. 5–6; Casey, *Selling the Korean War*, chap. 8.
79. Truman, *Memoirs*, 2:431.
80. November 28, 1950, Acheson Papers, Box 68, HSTL.
81. December 2, 1950, WHCF, Official File, Box 1454, HSTL.
82. Casey, *Selling the Korean War*, 206.
83. "Daily Opinion Summary," December 4, 1950, Elsey Papers, Box 77, HSTL; Foot, *The Wrong War*, 106–107.
84. *FRUS, 1950*, vol. 7, doc. 949.
85. December 13, 1950, Elsey Papers, Box 73, HSTL.
86. "Radio Report to the American People on Korea and on U.S. Policy in the Far East," April 11, 1951, *Public Papers of the Presidents: Truman*, 1951, bk. 1: 223–227.
87. MacArthur, *Reminiscences*, 350. See also Acheson, *Present at the Creation*, 448; Brands, *The General vs. the President*, 157.
88. October 15, 1950, Acheson Papers, Box 67, HSTL. See also Truman, *Memoirs*, 2:384
89. November 4, 1950, RG-9, Box 45, MMA.
90. November 7, 1950, RG-9, Box 45, MMA; reprinted with a November 6 date in Truman, *Memoirs*, 2:375.
91. August 23, 1950, Acheson Papers, Box 67, HSTL.
92. Draft Letter, [ca. September–October 1947], RG-16a, Box 4, MMA. See also MacArthur to Hoyt, [ca. September/October 1947]; MacArthur to Campbell, December 3, 1947; MacArthur to Hoyt, December 6, 1947; and MacArthur to MacNider, October 14, 1947, all in RG-16a, Box 4, MMA.

93. Truman, *Memoirs*, 2:443.

94. Truman, 363.

95. MacArthur, *Reminiscences*, 361; Charles A. Willoughby, *MacArthur: 1941-1951, Victory in the Pacific* (London: Heinemann, 1956), 360.

96. Quoted in Stanley Weintraub, *MacArthur's War: Korea and the Undoing of an American Hero* (New York: Free Press, 2000), 184; Whitney, *MacArthur*, 395; Acheson, *Present at the Creation*, 456.

97. Quoted in Kaufman, *The Korean War*, 91.

98. See various messages of support to MacArthur in "Telegrams, June-December 1950," RG-7, Folder 4, Box 1, MMA. MacArthur's account of the Wake Island exchange in MacArthur, *Reminiscences*, 362–363.

99. MacArthur, *Reminiscences*, 362–363.

100. November 25, 1950, PSF, Box 283, HSTL.

101. Quoted in Stueck, *The Korean War*, 66.

102. July 1, 1950, Ayers Papers, Box 20, HSTL.

103. August 20, 1950, RG-5, Box 59, MMA.

104. August 26, 1950, Elsey Papers, Box 72, HSTL.

105. Truman, *Memoirs*, 2:355–356.

106. The president must have been reassured to learn that MacArthur was in good shape. With stable blood pressure and weight, the virtual teetotaler had last taken sick leave in 1912, according to his personal physician. "His digestion and elimination," meanwhile, were "perfect." Lowe to Truman, August 8, 1950, RG-37, Box 1, MMA.

107. Robert H. Ferrell, ed., *Off the Record: The Private Papers of Harry S. Truman* (New York: Harper and Row, 1980), 46–47, 195–196.

108. August 26, 1950, Acheson Papers, Box 67, HSTL.

109. August 26, 1950, Ayers Papers, Box 21, HSTL.

110. Quoted in Merle Miller, *Plain Speaking: An Oral Biography of Harry S. Truman* (New York: G. P. Putnam, 1974), 291–292.

111. November 30, 1950, RG-7, Box 1, MMA. See also December 1, 1950, RG-5, Box 57, MMA.

112. December 6, 1950, RG-16a, Box 4, MMA.

113. August 29, 1950, and August 30, 1950, RG-10, Box 20, MMA.

114. January 18, 1952, PSF, Box 284, HSTL.

115. November 11, 1950, RG-16a, Box 4, MMA.

116. March 20, 1951, RG-5, Box 37, MMA.

117. Stueck, *The Korean War*, 178–182.

118. April 5, 1951, PSF, Box 234, HSTL.

119. April 6, 1951, PSF, Box 234, HSTL.

120. Freedman, *Command*, 25.

121. April 28, 1951, PSF, Box 111, HSTL; Bradley and Blair, *A General's Life*, 632; Truman, *Memoirs*, 2:447.

122. Truman recalls writing privately about his intention not to run as early as April 1950. However, he waited until March 1951 to discuss the prospect with his staff, just a month before dismissing MacArthur. See Truman, *Memoirs*, 2:488–497.

123. April 10, 1951, PSF, Box 234, HSTL.

124. Quoted in Blomstedt, *Truman, Congress, and Korea*, 120. See also Rusk, *As I Saw It*, 172.

125. February 8, 1952, PSF, Box 208, HSTL.

126. Truman, *Memoirs*, 2:460.

127. Marilyn B. Young, "Hard Sell: The Korean War," in *Selling War in a Media Age: The Presidency and Public Opinion in the American Century*, ed. Kenneth Osgood and Andrew K. Frank (Gainesville: University Press of Florida, 2010), 113–139.

128. Steven Casey, "Confirming the Cold War Consensus: Eisenhower and the 1952 Election," in *US Presidential Elections and Foreign Policy: Candidates, Campaigns, and Global Politics from FDR to Bill Clinton*, ed. Andrew Johnstone and Andrew Priest (Lexington: University Press of Kentucky, 2017), 82–104.

129. Foot, *A Substitute for Victory*, 136–137; Casey, *Selling the Korean War*, 335.

130. September 24, 1952, PSF, Box 189, HSTL.

131. September 24, 1952, PSF, Box 189, HSTL.

132. Quoted in Casey, *Selling the Korean War*, 395.

133. Louis Harris, *Is There a Republican Majority? Political Trends, 1952-1956* (New York: Harper, 1954), 27.

134. Adlai E. Stevenson, *Major Campaign Speeches of Adlai E. Stevenson, 1952* (New York: Random House, 1953), 185.

135. Truman to Stevenson, [n.d.], PSF, Box 284, HSTL.

136. Quoted in Ferrell, *Off the Record*, 268–269. See also Jeff Broadwater, *Adlai Stevenson and American Politics: The Odyssey of a Cold War Liberal* (New York: Twayne, 1994), 119; Truman, *Memoirs*, 2:498–499.

137. Quoted in Divine, *Foreign Policy and US Presidential Elections*, 43.

138. Quoted in John Robert Greene, *The Crusade: The Presidential Election of 1952* (Lanham, MD: University Press of America, 1985), 216.

139. Quoted in Divine, *Foreign Policy and US Presidential Elections*, 71–72.

140. October 24, 1952, AWF, Speech Series, Box 2, DDEL.

141. Truman, *Memoirs*, 2:501.

142. Bradley and Blair, *A General's Life*, 656.

143. November 6, 1952, PSF, Box 102, HSTL.

144 Acheson, *Present at the Creation*, 599.

145. See Robert Barnes, "Ending the Korean War: Reconsidering the Importance of Eisenhower's Election," *RUSI Journal* 158, no. 3 (2013): 78–87, and Robert Barnes, *The US, the UN and the Korean War: Communism in the Far East and the American Struggle for Hegemony in the Cold War* (London: I. B. Tauris, 2014), 145–174.

146. December 4, 1952, Cabinet Office Files, CAB 128/25/52, and December 30, 1952, Cabinet Office Files, CAB 128/25/58, KG.

147. Gladwyn Jebb, *The Memoirs of Lord Gladwyn* (London: Weidenfeld and Nicolson, 1972), 253.

148. *FRUS, 1952-1954*, vol. 15, pt. 1, doc. 336. See also doc. 326 in the same volume.

149. See, for instance, *FRUS, 1952-1954*, vol. 15, pt. 1, docs. 316, 319, and 324.

150. Quoted in Stueck, *The Korean War*, 299.

151. *FRUS, 1952-1954*, vol. 15, pt. 1, docs. 318, 325, and 336. See also Acheson, *Present at the Creation*, chap. 73.

152. December 15, 1952, Cabinet Office Files, CAB 129/57/41, KG.

153. November 6, 1952, AWF, Name Series, Box 33, DDEL.

154. November 15, 1952, PSF, Box 284, HSTL.

155. November 18, 1952, AWF, Name Series, Box 33, DDEL; November 20, 1952, PSF, Box 102, HSTL.

156. November 8, 1952, Brownell Papers, Box 25, DDEL.

157. November 10, 1952, Brownell Papers, Box 25, DDEL.

158. See *FRUS, 1952-1954*, vol. 15, pt. 1, docs. 346 and 347.

159. Lodge to Eisenhower, [n.d.], Reel 1, Lodge Papers, DDEL.

160. October 24, 1952, AWF, Speech Series, Box 2, DDEL.

161. Emmet John Hughes, *The Ordeal of Power: A Political Memoir of the Eisenhower Years* (London: Macmillan, 1963), 33.

162. Quoted in Clark, Oral History, DDEL.

163. Quoted in Clark, Oral History, DDEL.

164. See December 14, 1952, Dulles Papers, Subject Series, Box 8, DDEL.

165. February 12, 1953, AWF, NSC Series, Box 4, DDEL.

166. April 7, 1953, AWF, NSC Series, Box 4, DDEL.

167. May 7, 1953, AWF, NSC Series, Box 4, DDEL.

168. May 14, 1953, AWF, NSC Series, Box 4, DDEL.

169. May 23, 1953, AWF, NSC Series, Box 4, DDEL; May 19, 1953, WHO/NSCS, Disaster File, Box 60, DDEL.

170. April 2, 1953, WHO/OSANSA, NSC Series, Policy Papers Subseries, Box 4, DDEL.

171. April 7, 1953, AWF, NSC Series, Box 4, DDEL.

172. Dulles and Eisenhower, February 19, 1953, Dulles Papers, Telephone Conversations Series, Box 10, DDEL. Dulles was in fact among those inclined to go further and faster than the president. In an NSC meeting in April 1953, he proposed ripping up the terms of the emerging armistice deal then on the table and instead pursuing terms more favorable to the United States through military escalation, a suggestion the president swiftly rejected. It was "impossible to call off the armistice now and to go to war in Korea," explained Eisenhower, since "the American people would never stand for such a move." April 16, 1953, AWF, NSC Series, Box 4, DDEL.

This episode was also good illustration of the dichotomous nature of Eisenhower's leadership style more broadly, with a nonpartisan public image coupled with a "well-developed capacity for tough-minded political realism" behind closed doors. See Fred I. Greenstein, *The Hidden-Hand Presidency: Eisenhower as Leader* (New York: Basic Books, 1982), 54.

173. Dulles and Cutler, April 7, 1953, Dulles Papers, JFD Chronological Series, Box 2, DDEL.

174. See Barnes, "Ending the Korean War," 83–85; Foot, *A Substitute for Victory*, chap. 7.

175. Mark W. Clark, *From the Danube to the Yalu* (London: George C. Harrap, 1954), 249.

176. May 8, 1953, Dulles Papers, JFD Chronological Series, Box 3, DDEL.

177. May 9, 1953, Dulles Papers, JFD Chronological Series, Box 3, DDEL.

178. Clark, *From the Danube to the Yalu*, 252.

179. Dulles and Eisenhower, February 19, 1953, Dulles Papers, Telephone Conversations Series, Box 10, DDEL.

180. Dulles and Eisenhower, June 8, 1953, Dulles Papers, JFD Chronological Series, Box 3, DDEL.
181. See Stueck, *The Korean War*, chap. 3.
182. See Barnes, *The US, the UN, and the Korean War*.
183. Acheson, *Present at the Creation*, 632–633.
184. Shu Guang Zhang, *Deterrence and Strategic Culture: Chinese-American Confrontations, 1949-1958* (Ithaca, NY: Cornell University Press, 1992), 132–137; Shu Guang Zhang, *Mao's Military Romanticism: China and the Korean War, 1950-1953* (Lawrence: University of Kansas Press, 1995), 317–318.
185. Elizabeth Stanley, *Paths to Peace: Domestic Coalition Shifts, War Termination and the Korean War* (Stanford, CA: Stanford University Press, 2009), 230–233. Mao's cable in Stanley, *Paths to Peace*, 231.
186. Dwight D. Eisenhower, *Mandate for Change: The White House Years* (Garden City, NY: Doubleday, 1963), 181. For an alternative perspective, see Foot, *A Substitute for Victory*, chap. 7.

3. Vietnam: Lyndon Johnson and the "Americanization" of the War

Sources for chapter epigraphs: Bundy and Johnson, March 4, 1964, 7:26 p.m., Conversation #2347, RTTCM, LBJL; October 30, 1968, Meeting Notes, TJ, Box 4, LBJL.

1. While U.S. involvement in Vietnam predates the Johnson administration, this chapter focuses on the thirty-sixth president's handling of the war because the major escalatory decisions were made on his watch.
2. Among the many landmark historical accounts are Larry Berman, *Lyndon Johnson's War* (New York: W. W. Norton, 1989); George C. Herring, *America's Longest War: The United States and Vietnam, 1950-1975*, 4th ed. (New York: McGraw Hill, 2002); Leslie H. Gelb and Richard K. Betts, *The Irony of Vietnam: The System Worked* (Washington, DC: Brookings Institution Press, 1979); Fredrik Logevall, *Choosing War: The Lost Chance for Peace and the Escalation of the War in Vietnam* (Berkeley: University of California Press, 1999); Yuen Foong Khong, *Analogies at War: Korea, Munich, Dien Bien Phu, and the Vietnam Decisions of 1965* (Princeton, NJ: Princeton University Press, 1992); H. R. McMaster, *Dereliction of Duty: Lyndon Johnson and Robert McNamara, the Joint Chiefs of Staff and the Lies that Led to Vietnam* (New York: Harper Collins, 1997). Recent studies by Max Hastings, *Vietnam: An Epic History of a Tragic War* (London: William Collins, 2018), and Brian VanDeMark, *Road to Disaster: A New History of America's Descent Into Vietnam* (New York: Custom House, 2018), are useful additions.
3. See, most recently, Bessner and Logevall, "Recentering the United States"; Ken Hughes, *Fatal Politics: The Nixon Tapes, the Vietnam War, and the Casualties of Reelection* (Charlottesville: University of Virginia Press, 2015); Andrew L. Johns, *Vietnam's Second Front: Domestic Politics, the Republican Party, and the War* (Lexington:

University Press of Kentucky, 2010); Melvin Small, *At the Water's Edge: American Politics and the Vietnam War* (Chicago: Ivan R. Dee, 2005); Friedman, *The Commander-in-Chief Test*, 175–230.

4. December 21, 1963, *FRUS, 1961–1963*, vol. 4, doc. 374.

5. March 16, 1964, *FRUS, 1964–1968*, vol. 1, doc. 84.

6. April 22, 1964, NSF, National Security Council Meetings File, Box 1, LBJL.

7. May 24, 1964, *FRUS, 1964–1968*, vol. 1, doc. 172.

8. March 3, 1964, *FRUS, 1964–1968*, vol. 1, doc. 68.

9. May 15, 1964, *FRUS, 1964–1968*, vol. 1, doc. 159.

10. June 1, 1964, *FRUS, 1964–1968*, vol. 1, doc. 187.

11. McNamara and Johnson, June 9, 1964, 6:20 p.m., Conversation #3663, RTTCM, LBJL.

12. Quoted in VanDeMark, *Road to Disaster*, 216.

13. McNamara and Johnson, April 30, 1964, 7:50 p.m., Conversation #3220, RTTCM, LBJL. See also Fulbright and Johnson, December 2, 1963, 7:01 p.m., Conversation #248, RTTCM, LBJL.

14. Russell and Johnson, May 27, 1964, 10:55 a.m., Conversation #3520, RTTCM, LBJL.

15. For a flavor, see February 22, 1964, *FRUS, 1964–1968*, vol. 1, docs. 56 and 66. By October the Joint Chiefs were advocating an "all-out air attack on the DRV," and recommended again that Johnson "commit US and allied ground forces into Southeast Asia as required." See October 27, 1964, *FRUS, 1964–1968*, vol. 1, doc. 388.

16. May 25, 1964, *FRUS, 1964–1968*, vol. 1, doc. 388.

17. Herring, *America's Longest War*, xiii.

18. Brian VanDeMark, *Into the Quagmire: Lyndon Johnson and the Escalation of the Vietnam War* (New York: Oxford University Press, 1995), xiii.

19. Bundy and Johnson, May 27, 1964, 11:24 a.m., Conversation #3522, RTTCM, LBJL.

20. Russell and Johnson, June 11, 1964, 12:26 p.m., Conversation #3681, RTTCM, LBJL. See also Gelb and Betts, *The Irony of Vietnam*, 188–190.

21. Author interview with Francis M. Bator, telephone, March 16, 2017. See also Gelb and Betts, *The Irony of Vietnam*, 3; Dominic D. P. Johnson, *Overconfidence and War: The Havoc and Glory of Positive Illusions* (Cambridge, MA: Harvard University Press, 2004), 170–171.

22. Quoted in Gordon M. Goldstein, *Lessons in Disaster: McGeorge Bundy and the Path to War in Vietnam* (New York: Henry Holt, 2008), 98.

23. McNamara and Johnson, December 7, 1963, 5:03 p.m., Conversation #336, RTTCM, LBJL.

24. Rusk and Johnson, June 2, 1964, 4:55 p.m., Conversation #3614, RTTCM, LBJL.

25. January 13, 1964, NSF, Country File, Vietnam, Box 1, LBJL.

26. Quoted in Goldstein, *Lessons in Disaster*, 110.

27. Knight and Johnson, February 3, 1964, 5:45 p.m., Conversation #1839, RTTCM, LBJL.

28. Doris Kearns Goodwin, *Lyndon Johnson and the American Dream* (New York: Harper and Row, 1976), 252–253.

29. Lyndon B. Johnson, *The Vantage Point: Perspectives on the Presidency, 1963-1969* (New York: Holt, Rinehart and Winston, 1971), 68. See also Schuessler, *Deceit on the Road to War*, 71–78.
30. Rowe and Johnson, August 6, 1964, 1:35 p.m., Conversation #4777, RTTCM, LBJL.
31. Bundy and Johnson, July 14, 1964, 5:36 p.m., Conversation #4236, RTTCM, LBJL.
32. Rusk and Johnson, July 20, 1964, 6:50 p.m., Conversation #4281, RTTCM, LBJL.
33. Bundy and Johnson, March 24, 1964, 10:16 a.m., Conversation #2630, RTTCM, LBJL; McNamara and Johnson, April 9, 1964, 7:25 p.m., Conversation #2961, RTTCM, LBJL.
34. Bayh and Johnson, June 15, 1965, 1:20 p.m., Conversation #8135, RTTCM, LBJL.
35. Author interview with Bator.
36. March 4, 1964, *FRUS, 1964-1968*, vol. 1, doc. 70. See also Maxwell D. Taylor, *Swords and Plowshares* (New York: W. W. Norton, 1972), 309.
37. Quoted in Schuessler, *Deceit on the Road to War*, 72.
38. Bundy and Johnson, March 4, 1964, 7:26 p.m., Conversation #2347, RTTCM, LBJL.
39. Quoted in Goldstein, *Lessons in Disaster*, 97.
40. McNamara and Johnson, September 24,1964, 8:39 p.m., Conversation #5686, RTTCM, LBJL.
41. Bundy and Johnson, March 2, 1964, 12:35 p.m., Conversation #2309, RTTCM, LBJL.
42. Pierre Asselin, *Vietnam's American War: A History* (Cambridge: Cambridge University Press, 2018), 107–109.
43. John D. Negroponte, oral history interview, Association for Diplomatic Studies and Training, Foreign Affairs Oral History Project, February 11, 2000, 22, https://adst.org/OH TOCs/Negroponte-John-D.pdf.
44. VanDeMark, *Road to Disaster*, 220–221. See also Hastings, *Vietnam*, 183.
45. January 7, 1964, *FRUS, 1964-1968*, vol. 1, doc. 4.
46. November 24, 1963, MNF, Box 1, LBJL.
47. May 5, 1964, *FRUS, 1964-1968*, vol. 1, doc. 139; Russell and Johnson, May 27, 1964, 10:55 a.m., Conversation #3520, RTTCM, LBJL; Rusk and Johnson, March 2, 1964, 11:35 a.m., Conversation #2305, RTTCM, LBJL.
48. Bundy and Johnson, April 14, 1964, 1:00 p.m., Conversation #3027, RTTCM, LBJL.
49. McNamara quoted in Aurélie Basha I Novosejt, *"I Made Mistakes": Robert McNamara's Vietnam War Policy, 1960-1968* (Cambridge: Cambridge University Press, 2019), 147–148.
50. Bundy quoted in VanDeMark, *Road to Disaster*, 245.
51. "Gallup Presidential Election Trial-Heat Trends, 1936–2008," Gallup, accessed November 6, 2022, https://news.gallup.com/poll/110548/gallup-presidential-election-trial-heat-trends.aspx.
52. Friedman, *The Commander-in-Chief Test*, 179.
53. Quoted in Friedman, 180.
54. Criticism from Republicans quoted in Johns, *Vietnam's Second Front*, 61.
55. Cater to Bundy, June 12, 1964, reprinted in David, M. Barrett, *Lyndon B. Johnson's Vietnam Papers: A Documentary Collection* (College Station: Texas A&M University Press, 1997), 55–56.
56. June 10, 1964, *FRUS, 1964-1968*, vol. 1, doc. 211; June 12, 1964, *FRUS, 1964-1968*, vol. 1, doc. 210.

57. Eighty-five percent of Americans supported Johnson's actions. "Harris Poll," August 10, 1964, WHCF, Subject File, Ex ND 19/CO 312, Box 214, LBJL.

58. Quoted in Friedman, *The Commander-in-Chief Test*, 189. On the Johnson campaign's approach as summarized here, see Friedman, *The Commander-in-Chief Test*, 178–192.

59. Bundy, Unpublished Manuscript, chap. 18, 1, Bundy Papers, Box 2, LBJL.

60. November 19, 1964, *FRUS, 1964-1968*, vol. 1, doc. 417.

61. December 1, 1964, MNF, Box 1, LBJL. See also *FRUS, 1964-1968*, vol. 1, docs. 431–435, 440.

62. February 6, 1965, *FRUS, 1964-1968*, vol. 2, doc. 77.

63. On Johnson's practice of escalation by pretext in order to avoid incurring political costs, see Schuessler, *Deceit on the Road to War*, 78–88.

64. December 30, 1964, *FRUS, 1964-1968*, vol. 1, doc. 477.

65. McNamara and Johnson, February 26, 1965, 9:10 a.m., Conversation #6887, RTTCM, LBJL.

66. Taylor, *Swords and Plowshares*, 341.

67. Quoted in Johns, *Vietnam's Second Front*, 73.

68. Johnson, *The Vantage Point*, 68.

69. Quoted in Mitchell Lerner, "Vietnam and the 1964 Election: A Defense of Lyndon Johnson," *Presidential Studies Quarterly* 24, no. 4 (1995): 751–766, 754.

70. February 21, 1965, *FRUS, 1964-1968*, vol. 2, doc. 134. See also Fredrik Logevall, " 'There Ain't No Daylight': Lyndon Johnson and the Politics of Escalation," in *Making Sense of the Vietnam Wars: Local, National, and Transnational Perspectives*, ed. Mark P. Bradley and Marilyn B. Young (New York: Oxford University Press, 2008), 100–101.

71. Fulbright and Johnson, December 2, 1963, 7:01 p.m., Conversation #248, RTTCM, LBJL.

72. Russell and Johnson, March 6, 1965, 12:05 p.m., Conversation #7026, RTTCM, LBJL.

73. McNamara and Johnson, June 21, 1965, 12:15 p.m., Conversation #8168, RTTCM, LBJL.

74. Andrew Preston, *The War Council: McGeorge Bundy, the NSC, and Vietnam* (Cambridge, MA: Harvard University Press, 2006), 166–167. For an alternative perspective on the argument that Johnson received poor information, see John Garofano, "Tragedy or Choice in Vietnam? Learning to Think Outside the Archival Box: A Review Essay," *International Security* 26, no. 4 (2002): 157; Johnson, *Overconfidence and War*, 142–144, 166–169.

75. November 19, 1964, *FRUS, 1964-1968*, vol. 2, doc. 417. See also July 1, 1965, *FRUS, 1964-1968*, vol. 3, docs. 42 and 43, in which Bundy forwarded recommendations under a covering note encouraging Johnson to "listen hard to George Ball and then reject his proposal" and advocated for keeping the size of an upcoming meeting to discuss them limited even if it "cuts you off from a chance to talk freely with some other men who have expert opinions."

76. Logevall, *Choosing War*, 356. See also Andrew L. Johns, *The Price of Loyalty: Hubert Humphrey's Vietnam Conflict* (Lanham, MD: Rowman & Littlefield, 2020).

77. Logevall, *Choosing War*, 395.

78. George W. Ball, *The Past Has Another Pattern: Memoirs* (New York: W. W. Norton, 1982), 377–378.

79. Quoted in Logevall, *Choosing War*, 394. More recently, Aurélie Basha i Novosejt has argued that Robert McNamara was also bound by a rigid code of loyalty to the president, viewing his role as secretary of defense not as a mouthpiece for the views of the uniformed military nor as an independent source of advice, but instead more as a resource allocator, obliged to fulfill the president's policy preferences as efficiently as possible. See Basha I Novosejt, *"I Made Mistakes,"* especially 135–163, 180.

80. Goldstein, *Lessons in Disaster*, 153.

81. Ball, *The Past Has Another Pattern*, 389. For the memorandum, see October 5, 1964, NSF, Country File, Vietnam, Box 9, LBJL. See also Logevall, *Choosing War*, 243–250. Bundy later insisted that he had sent the memorandum to Johnson but that the president left it unread. See Goldstein, *Lessons in Disaster*, 131–132.

82. Ball, *The Past Has Another Pattern*, 382.

83. Francis M. Bator, "No Good Choices: LBJ and the Vietnam/Great Society Connection," *Diplomatic History* 32, no. 3 (2008): 313. See also Robert S. McNamara with Brian VanDeMark, *In Retrospect: The Tragedy and Lessons of Vietnam* (New York: Times Books, 1995), 173, 205–206.

84. Author interview with Bator.

85. July 27, 1965, MNF, Box 1, LBJL.

86. Quoted in Walter LaFeber, "Johnson, Vietnam and Tocqueville," in *Lyndon Johnson Confronts the World: American Foreign Policy, 1963-1968*, ed. Warren I. Cohen and Nancy Bernkopf Tucker (Cambridge: Cambridge University Press, 1994), 49.

87. Quoted in Halberstam, *The Best and the Brightest*, 530.

88. Logevall, *Choosing War*. For a powerful critique, see Garofano, "Tragedy or Choice in Vietnam?," 151–152, 165. See also Elizabeth N. Saunders, "War and the Inner Circle: Democratic Elites and the Politics of Using Force," *Security Studies* 24, no. 3 (2015): 485–490.

89. December 7, 1965, *FRUS, 1964-1968*, vol. 3, doc. 223.

90. December 9, 1965, *FRUS, 1964-1968*, vol. 3, doc. 226.

91. February 17, 1966, WHCF, Subject File, Ex ND 19/CO 312, Box 219, LBJL.

92. Quoted in Johns, *Vietnam's Second Front*, 109.

93. January 21, 1966, WHCF, Confidential File, PL/Name, Box 76, LBJL.

94. January 27, 1966, WHCF, Confidential File, PL/Name, Box 76, LBJL.

95. Quoted in VanDeMark, *Road to Disaster*, 390.

96. *FRUS, 1964-68*, vol. 4, Editorial Note, doc. 164.

97. May 10, 1966, NSF, Country File, Vietnam, Box 31, LBJL.

98. See, for instance, July 23, 1966, *FRUS, 1964-1968*, vol. 4, doc. 186; August 26, 1966, *FRUS, 1964-1968*, vol. 4, doc. 219.

99. September 15, 1966, *FRUS, 1964-1968*, vol. 4, doc. 232.

100. *FRUS, 1964-1968*, vol. 4, Editorial Note, doc. 240.

101. Carrie A. Lee, "The Politics of Military Operations" (PhD diss., Stanford University, 2015), chap. 5.

102. September 21, 1966, *FRUS, 1964-1968*, vol. 4, doc. 242.

103. "Johnson Signs L.B.J. On Casts of Wounded," *New York Times*, October 27, 1966.

104. Max Frankel, "President Terms G.I. Mission 'Vital,'" *New York Times*, October 27, 1966.

105. See, for instance, Johnson's interest in the "Sunflower" channel, January 18, 1967, *FRUS, 1964-1968*, vol. 5, doc. 19.

106. Rostow and Johnson, February 15, 1967, 9:24 a.m., Conversation #11544, RTTCM, LBJL; *FRUS, 1964-1968*, vol. 4, Editorial Note, doc. 226.

107. Quoted in Johns, *Vietnam's Second Front*, 156.

108. Fulbright in June 30, 1967, NSF, Name File, Box 3, LBJL. Javits quoted in Johns, *Vietnam's Second Front*, 140.

109. John Roche in February 6, 1967, NSF, Name File, Box 7, LBJL.

110. VanDeMark, *Road to Disaster*, 388.

111. *Public Papers of the Presidents: Johnson, 1967*, bk. 2:876–881.

112. November 1, 1967, *FRUS, 1964-1968*, vol. 5, doc. 375.

113. December 18, 1967, *FRUS, 1964-1968*, vol. 5, doc. 441.

114. November 2, 1967, *FRUS, 1964-1968*, vol. 5, doc. 378.

115. November 2, 1967, *FRUS, 1964-1968*, vol. 5, doc. 377.

116. Quoted in Gregory A. Daddis, "Choosing Progress: Evaluating the 'Salesmanship' of the Vietnam War in 1967," in *Assessing War: The Challenge of Measuring Success and Failure*, ed. Leo J. Blanken, Hy Rothstein, and Jason J. Lepore (Washington, DC: Georgetown University Press, 2015), 185.

117. On the "conversation gap" and salesmanship of the war in 1967, see Daddis, "Choosing Progress."

118. On public opinion in this period, see Gelb and Betts, *The Irony of Vietnam*, 161, 220.

119. November 21, 1967, *FRUS, 1964-1968*, vol. 4, doc. 401.

120. Johnson to Fulbright [unsent, with February 21, 1968, cover note], February 8, 1968, Office of the President File, Box 4, LBJL.

121. Johns, *Vietnam's Second Front*, 190.

122. Asselin, *Vietnam's American War*, 153–155.

123. Author email correspondence with Tom Johnson, May 4, 2016–March 29, 2017.

124. March 15, 1968, WHCF, Confidential File, PL 2, Box 77, LBJL.

125. Clifford and Johnson, March 20, 1968, 8:44 a.m., Conversation #12826, RTTCM, LBJL. Johnson's comments on the value of a total bombing halt referred to a recent proposal by UN ambassador Arthur Goldberg. See March 15, 1968, *FRUS, 1964-1968*, vol. 6, doc. 131.

126. Quoted in Lee, "The Politics of Military Operations," 143.

127. Quoted in Johns, *Vietnam's Second Front*, 185.

128. March 26, 1968, Meeting Notes, TJ, Box 2, LBJL.

129. See McNamara, *In Retrospect*, chap. 10.

130. McNamara, 311.

131. McNamara, 314.

132. September 19, 1967, Harriman Papers, Box 486, LOC.

133. March 4, 1968, Meeting Notes, TJ, Box 2, LBJL.

134. Clark Clifford with Richard Holbrooke, *Counsel to the President: A Memoir* (New York: Random House, 1991), 493.

135. March 12, 1968, Meeting Notes, TJ, Box 2, LBJL.

136. Clifford and Johnson, March 20, 1968, 8:44 a.m., Conversation #12826, RTTCM, LBJL.
137. March 26, 1968, Meeting Notes, TJ, Box 2, LBJL.
138. Clifford, *Counsel to the President*, 525–526.
139. Johnson, *The Vantage Point*, 413.
140. *Public Papers of the Presidents: Johnson, 1968–69*, bk. 1:469–76.
141. September 16, 1968, *FRUS, 1964–1968*, vol. 7, doc. 15.
142. On the ground war, see Gregory A. Daddis, *Withdrawal: Reassessing America's Final Years in Vietnam* (New York: Oxford University Press, 2017), 17–44; Casey, *When Soldiers Fall*, 175–176.
143. Dirksen and Johnson, August 27, 1968, 11:15 a.m., Conversation #13323, RTTCM, LBJL. On the prospects for peace and the 1968 election, see also Kent G. Sieg, "The 1968 Presidential Election and Peace in Vietnam," *Presidential Studies Quarterly* 26, no. 4, (1996): 1062–1080.
144. Quoted in R. W. Apple Jr., "Humphrey Vows Halt in Bombing if Hanoi Reacts," *New York Times*, October 1, 1968. See also Johns, *The Price of Loyalty*, 103–129.
145. Rusk and Johnson, October 3, 1968, 10:15 a.m., Conversation #13513, RTTCM, LBJL.
146. Murphy and Johnson, August 26, 1968, 8:04 a.m., Conversation #13314, RTTCM, LBJL.
147. Conference call (with Johnson), October 16, 1968, 11:41 a.m., Conversation #13547, RTTCM, LBJL.
148. Conference call (with Johnson), October 16, 1968, 11:41 a.m., Conversation #13547, RTTCM, LBJL.
149. Conference call (with Johnson), October 16, 1968, 11:41 a.m., Conversation #13548, RTTCM, LBJL.
150. Asselin, *Vietnam's American War*, 170.
151. On the pattern of bloody yet inconclusive struggles on the battlefield, see Ronald H. Spector, *After Tet: The Bloodiest Year in Vietnam* (New York: Vintage Books, 1993).
152. VanDeMark, *Road to Disaster*, 505.
153. October 11, 1968, *FRUS, 1964–1968*, vol. 7, doc. 58.
154. Lien-Hang T. Nguyen, *Hanoi's War: An International History of the War for Peace in Vietnam* (Chapel Hill: University of North Carolina Press, 2012), 126–128.
155. December 14, 1968, Harriman Papers, Box 521, LOC.
156. August 31, 1968, Harriman Papers, Box 458, LOC.
157. August 31, 1968, Harriman Papers, Box 458, LOC.
158. December 14, 1968, Harriman Papers, Box 521, LOC.
159. Negroponte, oral history.
160. Rusk and Johnson, October 24, 1968, 10:08 a.m., Conversation #13591, RTTCM, LBJL.
161. Author interview with John D. Negroponte, Washington, DC, March 27, 2018.
162. See, for instance, Walter LaFeber, *The Deadly Bet: LBJ, Vietnam and the 1968 Election* (Lanham, MD: Rowman & Littlefield, 2005), 162.
163. Humphrey and Johnson, October 31, 1968, 6:52 p.m., Conversation #13620, RTTCM, LBJL.

4. VIETNAM AND RICHARD NIXON

164. October 14, 1968, Meeting Notes, TJ, Box 4, LBJL.

165. October 27, 1968, Meeting Notes, TJ, Box 4, LBJL; October 23, 1968, NSF, Country File, Vietnam, Box 137, LBJL.

166. Rusk and Johnson, October 23, 1968, 9:20 a.m., Conversation #13580, RTTCM, LBJL.

167. November 17, 1968, *FRUS, 1964-1968*, vol. 7, doc. 223.

168. July 24, 1968, Meeting Notes, TJ, Box 3, LBJL.

169. Clifford, *Counsel to the President*, 571, 563.

170. Nixon and Johnson, September 30, 1968, 6:45 p.m., Conversations #13432 and #13433, RTTCM, LBJL; Dirksen and Johnson, October 1, 1968, 10:31 a.m., Conversation #1350, and 11:22 a.m., Conversation #13432, RTTCM, LBJL.

171. Clifford, *Counsel to the President*, 584.

172. Quoted in Ken Hughes, *Chasing Shadows: The Nixon Tapes, the Chennault Affair, and the Origins of Watergate* (Charlottesville: University of Virginia Press, 2014), 46.

173. John A. Farrell, *Richard Nixon: The Life* (New York: Doubleday, 2017), 342–342, 637–640.

174. Author email correspondence with Johnson.

175. December 10, 1968, Harriman Papers, Box 562, LOC. See also VanDeMark, *Road to Disaster*, 511.

176. Anna Chennault, *The Education of Anna* (New York: Times Books, 1980), 186. Interestingly, newly released Vietnamese documents reveal that officials in Saigon were incensed at rumors of Chennault's influence over their government's position, on the grounds that they did not need someone whom they considered a Washington dilettante to tell them how to deal with the communists. See Robert K. Brigham, *Reckless: Henry Kissinger and the Tragedy of Vietnam* (New York: Public Affairs, 2018), 4.

177. Quoted in VanDeMark, *Road to Disaster*, 517. Negroponte, in an interview with the author, supports this analysis, recalling that "I didn't attribute particularly sinister motives to it, really. I just thought these guys want to buy as much time as they can. That was what they wanted."

4. Vietnam: Richard Nixon and the "Vietnamization" of the War

Sources for chapter epigraphs: February 1, 1969, *FRUS, 1969-1976*, vol. 6, doc. 15; Kissinger and Nixon, March 10, 1971, 10:42 a.m., Conversation 465-008, Presidential Recordings Digital Edition, Miller Center.

1. Johns, *Vietnam's Second Front*, 196–236; Friedman, *The Commander-in-Chief Test*, 193–198.

2. Casey, *When Soldiers Fall*, 173–174; Thomas Alan Schwartz, *Henry Kissinger and American Power* (New York: Hill and Wang, 2020), 70.

3. Quoted in Casey, *When Soldiers Fall*, 182.

4. February 1, 1969, NSCF, Vietnam Subject Files, Box 64, RNL.

5. January 25, 1969, *FRUS, 1969-1976*, vol. 6, doc. 10.

6. H. R. Haldeman with Joseph DiMona, *Ends of Power* (New York: Times Books, 1978), 122.

7. Richard Nixon, *The Memoirs of Richard Nixon* (London: Sidgwick and Jackson, 1978), 382.

8. Casey, *When Soldiers Fall*, 176–180; Gregory A. Daddis, *Withdrawal*, 64–66.

9. April 15, 1969, *FRUS, 1969-1976*, vol. 6, doc. 60.

10. August 6, 1969, *FRUS, 1969-1976*, vol. 6, doc. 106.

11. Dobrynin and Kissinger, September 27, 1969, HAKTC, Box 2, RNL.

12. October 11, 1969, *FRUS, 1969-1976*, vol. 6, doc. 136.

13. 3 October 1969, HD, RNL. For an edited collection of excerpts from Haldeman's Diaries, see also H. R. Haldeman, *The Haldeman Diaries: Inside the Nixon White House* (New York: Putnam, 1994).

14. Dobrynin and Kissinger, September 27, 1969, HAKTC, Box 2, RNL; Scott D. Sagan and Jeremi Suri, "The Madman Nuclear Alert: Secrecy, Signaling and Safety in October 1969," *International Security* 27, no. 4 (Spring 2003): 150–183.

15. "Address to the Nation on the War in Vietnam," November 3, 1969, American Presidency Project, accessed November 5, 2022, https://www.presidency.ucsb.edu/documents/address-the-nation-the-war-vietnam.

16. "Informal Remarks in Guam with Newsmen," July 25, 1969, American Presidency Project, accessed November 5, 2022, https://www.presidency.ucsb.edu/documents/informal-remarks-guam-with-newsmen.

17. David L. Anderson, *Vietnamization: Politics, Strategy, Legacy* (Lanham, MD: Rowman & Littlefield, 2020), 9–20.

18. Quoted in Brigham, *Reckless*, 30.

19. March 13, 1969, *FRUS, 1969-1976*, vol. 6, doc. 38, and April 10, 1969, doc. 58.

20. March 22, 1969, *FRUS, 1969-1976*, vol. 6, doc. 44.

21. September 10, 1969, *FRUS 1969-1976*, vol. 6, doc. 117.

22. January 25, 1969, *FRUS 1969-1976*, vol. 6, doc. 10.

23. September 12, 1969, *FRUS 1969-1976*, vol. 6, doc. 120.

24. Anderson, *Vietnamization*, 43.

25. March 28, 1969, *FRUS, 1969-1976*, vol. 6, doc. 49.

26. June 8, 1969, *FRUS, 1969-1976*, vol. 6, doc. 81.

27. Nixon and Kissinger, March 20, 1970, HAKTC, Box 4, RNL.

28. April 23, 1970, HD, RNL.

29. Nixon, *The Memoirs of Richard Nixon*, 448.

30. April 23, 1970, HD, RNL.

31. October 17, 1969, *FRUS, 1969-1976*, vol. 6, doc. 137.

32. Nixon and Kissinger, May 11, 1970, HAKTC, Box 5, RNL.

33. May 4, 1970, HD, RNL.

34. Nixon, *The Memoirs of Richard Nixon*, 350.

35. July 28, 1970, *FRUS, 1969-1976*, vol. 7, doc. 1.

36. January 14, 1970, *FRUS, 1969-1976*, vol. 6, doc. 169.

37. Henry Kissinger, *The White House Years* (Boston: Little Brown & Co., 1979), 437.

38. "Address to the Nation About a New Initiative for Peace in Southeast Asia," October 7, 1970, American Presidency Project, accessed June 29, 2020, http://www

.presidency.ucsb.edu/ws/?pid=2708. On the development of this proposal, see also Brigham, *Reckless*, 121–136.

39. July 21, 1970, *FRUS, 1969–1976*, vol. 6, doc. 348.

40. See George C. Herring, "Nixon's 'Laotian Gamble:' Lam Son 719 as a Turning Point in the Vietnam War," *Army History* 119 (Spring 2021): 6–19.

41. Kissinger and Nixon, March 10, 1971, 10:42 a.m., Conversation 465-008, Presidential Recordings Digital Edition, Miller Center.

42. Kissinger and Nixon, April 21, 1971, 7:47 p.m., Conversation 484-13, Presidential Recordings Program, Miller Center.

43. December 15, 1970, HD, RNL. See also December 21, 1970, HD, RNL.

44. September 7, 1970, *FRUS, 1969–1976*, vol. 7, doc. 34.

45. Luu Van Loi and Nguyen Anh Vu, *Le Duc Tho-Kissinger Negotiations in Paris*, (Hanoi: Thê Giới Publishers, 1996), 165–66.

46. March 18, 1971, *FRUS, 1969–1976*, vol. 7, doc. 157.

47. Kissinger and Nixon, March 19, 1971, 7:03 p.m., Conversation 471-2, Presidential Recordings Program, Miller Center.

48. May 31, 1971, *FRUS, 1969–1976*, vol. 7, doc. 207.

49. Kissinger and Nixon, May 29, 1971, 8:13 a.m., Conversation 507-004, Presidential Recordings Digital Edition, Miller Center.

50. See, for instance, Kissinger and Nixon, April 21, 1971, 7:47 p.m., Conversation 484-13, Presidential Recordings Program, Miller Center; Haldeman, Ehrlichman, Kissinger and Nixon, June 23, 1971, 9:14 a.m., Conversation 527-016, WHT, RNL.

51. Nixon, *The Memoirs of Richard Nixon*, 348; Henry Kissinger, Remarks at Vietnam War Summit, Lyndon Johnson Presidential Library, Austin, Texas, April 26, 2016, available online at https://www.youtube.com/watch?v=1CsFYSC86bU. Most recently, Kissinger argues that "Nixon did not budge" in the face of Hanoi's demands concerning the political makeup of the South Vietnamese government. See Henry Kissinger, *Leadership: Six Studies in World Strategy* (London: Allen Lane, 2022), 158.

52. Haldeman, Ehrlichman, Kissinger, and Nixon, June 23, 1971, 9:14 a.m., Conversation 527-016, WHT, RNL.

53. Kissinger and Nixon, May 29, 1971, 8:13 a.m., Conversation 507-004, Presidential Recordings Digital Edition, Miller Center.

54. Henry A. Kissinger, "The Viet Nam Negotiations," *Foreign Affairs*, January 1969, 226–227; Kissinger, Haldeman, Ehrlichman, and Nixon, June 23, 1971, WHT, RNL.

55. July 9, 1971, NSCF, Presidential/HAK Memcons, Box 1033, RNL; July 10, 1971, NSCF, Presidential/HAK Memcons, Box 1033, RNL.

56. "Indochina" Section, Briefing Book, POLO I, NSCF, For the President's Files (Winston Lord)—China Trip/Vietnam, Box 850, RNL.

57. Author interview with Negroponte.

58. Hughes, *Fatal Politics*, 78–80.

59. May 27, 1972, HAKOF, Box 73, RNL. See also Friedman, *The Commander-in-Chief Test*, 213–214.

60. Weyand, Oral History, USAHEC.

61. Westmoreland, Oral History, USAHEC.

62. March 14, 1972, *FRUS, 1969-1976*, vol. 8, doc. 43.

63. Author interview with Alexander P. Butterfield, Austin, TX, April 29, 2016.

64. Asselin, *Vietnam's American War*, 191–192; Stephen P. Randolph, *Powerful and Brutal Weapons: Nixon, Kissinger, and the Easter Offensive* (Cambridge, MA: Harvard University Press, 2007), 22–31.

65. Kissinger, Haldeman and Nixon, May 1, 1972, 5:57 p.m., Conversation 716-4, WHT, RNL.

66. Randolph, *Powerful and Brutal Weapons*, 181, 338.

67. Randolph, 52–53.

68. Quoted in Hughes, *Fatal Politics*, 58.

69. May 1, 1972, *FRUS, 1969-1976*, vol. 8, doc. 106.

70. May 8, 1972, *FRUS, 1969-1976*, vol. 8, doc. 131; Laird and Kissinger, May 2, 1972, HAKTC, Box 14, RNL.

71. Randolph, *Powerful and Brutal Weapons*, 168.

72. April 3, 1972, *FRUS, 1969-1976*, vol. 8, doc. 50.

73. May 5, 1972, *FRUS, 1969-1976*, vol. 8, doc. 123.

74. Nixon and Kissinger, May 1, 1972, HAKTC, Box 14, RNL.

75. See Freedman, *Command*, 175–211; Randolph, *Powerful and Brutal Weapons*, 119–130.

76. Quoted in Douglas Brinkley and Luke A. Nichter, eds., *The Nixon Tapes: 1971-1972* (New York: Mariner Books, 2015), 472.

77. May 4, 1972, HD, RNL.

78. Kissinger, *The White House Years*, 1177.

79. May 5, 1972, *FRUS, 1969-1976*, vol. 8, doc. 123.

80. May 8, 1972, *FRUS, 1969-1976*, vol. 8, doc. 131.

81. Hughes, *Fatal Politics*, 55–56.

82. April 4, 1972, *FRUS, 1969-1976*, vol. 8, doc. 59.

83. Nixon and Kissinger, April 8, 1972, HAKTC, Box 29, RNL.

84. Nixon and Kissinger, April 9, 1972, HAKTC, Box 29, RNL.

85. May 2, 1972, HD, RNL; May 4, 1972, HD, RNL.

86. May 1, 1972, HD, RNL.

87. April 30, 1972, *FRUS, 1969-1976*, vol. 8, doc. 103.

88. Randolph, *Powerful and Brutal Weapons*, 165.

89. Bob Woodward, *The Last of the President's Men* (New York: Simon and Schuster, 2015), 116.

90. Kissinger, Haldeman, and Nixon, May 1, 1972, 5:57 p.m., Conversation 716-4, WHT, RNL.

91. April 29, 1972, HD, RNL.

92. Author interview with Butterfield.

93. "Harris Poll Finds 59% Backed Harbor Mining," *New York Times*, May 14, 1972.

94. August 11, 1972, *FRUS, 1969-76*, vol. 8, doc. 236.

95. Kissinger and Nixon, October 16, 1972, WHT, RNL.

96. Quoted in Nixon, *The Memoirs of Richard Nixon*, 700–701.

97. Kissinger and Nixon, October 16, 1972, 9:33 a.m., Conversation 799-009, WHT, RNL. On polling trends at this stage of the campaign, see, for instance, Jack

Rosenthal, "The 1972 Campaign," *New York Times*, October 18, 1972, which reported the president's lead to be as high as twenty-four percentage points according to one survey.

98. Kissinger, *The White House Years*, 1317.

99. Loi and Vu, *Le Duc Tho-Kissinger Negotiations in Paris*, 276–277.

100. Loi and Vu, 302–303.

101. Kissinger. *The White House Years*, 1345.

102. Loi and Vu, *Le Duc Tho-Kissinger Negotiations in Paris*, 276–277.

103. Author interview with Negroponte.

104. Negroponte, Oral History. See also Asselin, *Vietnam's American War*, 196–199.

105. Haig and Nixon, October 23, 1972, 11:20 p.m., Conversation 806-001, WHT, RNL.

106. Nixon, October 4, 1972, *FRUS, 1969–1976*, vol. 8, doc. 279.

107. October 12, 1972, HD, RNL.

108. Kissinger and Nixon, October 6, 1972, 9:06 a.m., Conversation 793-006, WHT, RNL.

109. Author interview with Negroponte.

110. Alexander M. Haig Jr., *Inner Circles: How America Changed the World* (New York: Warner Books, 1992), 299.

111. Kissinger and Nixon, October 6, 1972, 9:06 a.m., Conversation 793-006, WHT, RNL.

112. Nixon and Kissinger, October 27, 1972, HAKTC, Box 16, RNL.

113. October 22, 1972, *FRUS, 1969–1976*, vol. 9, doc. 43.

114. *FRUS, 1969–1976*, vol. 9, docs. 40–70.

115. November 20, 1971, *FRUS, 1969–1976*, vol. 7, doc 278.

116. Kissinger and Nixon, August 2, 1972, 10:34 a.m., Conversation 759-005, WHT, RNL.

117. Haig and Nixon, December 12, 1972, 1:30 p.m., Conversation 820-016, WHT, RNL.

118. Hughes, *Fatal Politics*, 150–58.

119. Nixon and Kissinger, December 17, 1972, HAKTC, Box 17, RNL.

120. Author interview with Negroponte.

121. Lewis Sorley, *A Better War: The Unexamined Victories and Final Tragedy of America's Last Years in Vietnam* (New York: Harcourt, 1999); Daddis, *Withdrawal*; Anderson, *Vietnamization*.

122. March 28, 1969, *FRUS, 1969–1976*, vol. 6, doc. 49.

123. Quoted in Brigham, *Reckless*, 31.

124. Kissinger, *The White House Years*, 265.

125. See Robert J. McMahon, "The Politics, and Geopolitics, of American Troop Withdrawals from Vietnam, 1968–1972," *Diplomatic History* 34, no. 3 (2010): 471–483.

126. See, for instance, Larry Berman, *No Peace, No Honor: Nixon, Kissinger, and Betrayal in Vietnam* (New York: Free Press, 2001); Jeffrey Kimball, *Nixon's Vietnam War* (Lawrence: University Press of Kansas, 1998); Jeffrey Kimball, *The Vietnam War Files: Uncovering the Secret History of the Nixon-Era Strategy* (Lawrence: University Press of Kansas, 2004). For an alternative view, attributing some strategic value to the "decent interval" Nixon ultimately secured, see Robert Jervis, "The

Politics of Troop Withdrawal: Salted Peanuts, the Commitment Trap, and Buying Time," *Diplomatic History* 34, no. 3 (2010): 512–515.

127. Johns, *Vietnam's Second Front*, 295–297.

128. October 17, 1969, *FRUS, 1969–1976*, vol. 6, doc. 137.

5. Iraq: George W. Bush and the Decision to Double Down

Source for chapter epigraph: Donald Rumsfeld, *Known and Unknown: A Memoir* (New York: Penguin, 2011), 424.

1. Quoted in Bob Woodward, *State of Denial: Bush at War, Part III* (New York: Simon and Schuster, 2006), 3.

2. "The 2000 Campaign," *New York Times*, October 4, 2000.

3. Author interview with James Jeffrey, telephone, June 28, 2018.

4. Recent book-length treatments of the invasion include Robert Draper, *To Start a War: How the Bush Administration Took America Into Iraq* (New York: Penguin, 2020); Michael J. Mazaar, *Leap of Faith: Hubris, Negligence, and America's Greatest Foreign Policy Tragedy* (New York: Public Affairs, 2019). See also Dina Badie, "Groupthink, Iraq, and the War on Terror: Explaining US Policy Shift Toward Iraq," *Foreign Policy Analysis* 6, no. 4 (2010): 277–296; Alexandre Debs and Nuno P. Monteiro, "Known Unknowns: Power Shifts, Uncertainty, and War," *International Organization* 68, no. 1 (2014): 1–31; Andrew Flibbert, "The Road to Baghdad: Ideas and Intellectuals in Explanations of the Iraq War," *Security Studies* 15, no. 2 (2006): 310–352; Chaim Kaufmann, "Threat Inflation and the Failure of the Marketplace of Ideas: The Selling of the Iraq War," *International Security* 29, no. 1 (2004): 5–48; David A. Lake, "Two Cheers for Bargaining Theory: Assessing Rationalist Explanations of the Iraq War," *International Security* 35, no. 3 (2010): 7–52; David Mitchell and Tansa George Massoud, "Anatomy of Failure: Bush's Decision-Making Process and the Iraq War," *Foreign Policy Analysis* 5, no. 3 (2009): 265–286; Aaron Rapport, "The Long and Short of It: Cognitive Constraints on Leaders' Assessments of 'Postwar' Iraq," *International Security* 37, no. 3 (2013): 133–171. For excellent discussion of the broader legacy of the war, in terms of its winners and losers as well as the wider effects on the domestic, regional, and international orders, see Louise Fawcett, "The Iraq War Ten Years On: Assessing the Fallout," *International Affairs* 89, no. 2 (March 2013): 325–343; and Louise Fawcett, "The Iraq War 20 Years On: Towards a New Regional Architecture," *International Affairs* 99, no. 2 (March 2023): iiad002, https://doi.org/10.1093/ia/iiad002.

5. On this phase of the war, see Peter D. Feaver, "The Right to Be Right: Civil-Military Relations and the Iraq Surge Decision," *International Security* 35, no. 4 (2011): 87–125; Kevin P. Marsh, "The Intersection of War and Politics: The Iraq War Troop Surge and Bureaucratic Politics," *Armed Forces & Society* 38, no. 3 (2012): 413–437; Stephen Biddle, Jeffrey A. Friedman, and Jacob N. Shapiro, "Testing the Surge: Why Did Violence Decline in Iraq in 2007?," *International Security* 37, no. 1 (2012): 7–40; Timothy Andrews Sayle et al., *The Last Card: Inside George W. Bush's Decision to Surge in Iraq* (Ithaca, NY: Cornell University Press, 2019); Andrew Payne,

"Presidents, Politics, and Military Strategy: Electoral Constraints During the Iraq War," *International Security* 44, no. 3 (2019–2020): 163–203.

6. Quoted in Ricardo S. Sanchez and Donald T. Phillips, *Wiser in Battle: A Soldier's Story* (New York: Harper Collins, 2008), 350.
7. For a frontline account of this episode, see Bing West, *No True Glory: A Frontline Account of the Battle for Fallujah* (New York: Bantam, 2005). An excellent interpretation that largely supports the argument presented here is Lee, *The Politics of Military Operations*, 121–129. See also Kenneth W. Estes, *U.S. Marine Corps Operations in Iraq, 2003-2006* (Quantico, VA: United States Marine Corps History Division, 2009).
8. L. Paul Bremer, *My Year in Iraq: The Struggle to Build a Future of Hope* (New York: Simon and Schuster, 2006), 314.
9. Sanchez and Phillips, *Wiser in Battle*, 331.
10. April 2, 2004, CENTCOM Papers, No. 446, USAHEC.
11. Jim Mattis and Bing West, *Call Sign Chaos: Learning to Lead* (New York: Random House, 2019), 129.
12. Bremer, *My Year in Iraq*, 333.
13. Quoted in Bremer, 336. See also Douglas J. Feith, *War and Decision: Inside the Pentagon at the Dawn of the War on Terrorism* (New York: Harper Collins, 2008), 483.
14. Quoted in Woodward, *State of Denial*, 250.
15. Bremer, *My Year in Iraq*, 184–185.
16. Condoleezza Rice, *Democracy: Stories from the Long Road to Freedom* (New York: Twelve, 2017), 300.
17. Quoted in Bremer, *My Year in Iraq*, 188. See also Rice, *Democracy*, 300.
18. Quoted in Sanchez and Phillips, *Wiser in Battle*, 321.
19. Jeremy Greenstock, *Iraq: The Cost of War* (London: William Heinemann, 2016), 327–330.
20. Sanchez and Phillips, *Wiser in Battle*, 288.
21. Bremer, *My Year in Iraq*, 542.
22. Bremer, 540.
23. Author interview with Negroponte.
24. Author interview with Negroponte.
25. West, *No True Glory*, 243.
26. Mattis and West, *Call Sign Chaos*, 146.
27. George W. Casey Jr., *Strategic Reflections: Operation Iraqi Freedom: July 2004-February 2007* (Washington, DC: National Defense University Press, 2012), 42.
28. Estes, *U.S. Marine Corps Operations in Iraq*, 50.
29. October 14, 2004, Box 110, Casey Papers, NDU; the substance of the presidential update and decision briefing remains classified, but the date of both (September 29) is indicated in the finding aid for this archival collection.
30. Author interview with John Sattler, telephone, July 25, 2018.
31. Thomas E. Ricks, *Fiasco: The American Military Adventure in Iraq* (New York: Penguin, 2006), 345.
32. Author interview with George Casey, Arlington, VA, March 16, 2018.
33. On this, and more generally "indirect politicization" in the Fallujah episode, see Lee, *The Politics of Military Operations*, 121–129.

34. John Negroponte, Interview with Charles Stuart Kennedy, Association for Diplomatic Studies and Training Foreign Affairs Oral History Project, August 13, 2013, 217–218.

35. Woodward, *State of Denial*, 335–336.

36. Michael Gordon and Bernard Trainor, *The Endgame: The Inside Story of the Struggle for Iraq, from George W. Bush to Barack Obama* (New York: Pantheon, 2012), 118–119.

37. Author interview with Sattler.

38. "Address to the Nation on Military Operations in Iraq," January 10, 2007, *Public Papers of the Presidents: Bush*, 2007, bk. 1:16–20.

39. Philip Zelikow, "The Surge," transcript of oral history interview by Peter Feaver and Aaron Crawford, Dallas, TX, for the Collective Memory Project, Center for Presidential History, Southern Methodist University, March 24, 2015, 12. Draft manuscript obtained by author from interviewee.

40. Author interview with Philip Zelikow, Charlottesville, VA, March 19, 2018.

41. Author interview with Jeffrey.

42. Condoleezza Rice, *No Higher Honor: A Memoir of My Years in Washington* (New York: Crown, 2011), 465, 507.

43. Author interview with Meghan L. O'Sullivan, telephone, June 11, 2018.

44. Feaver, "The Right to Be Right," 101.

45. Bob Woodward, *The War Within: A Secret White House History, 2006-2008* (New York: Simon and Schuster, 2008), 69.

46. George W. Bush, *Decision Points* (New York: Crown, 2010), 364.

47. "ODNI Camp David Scene Setter," June 12, 2006, Box 114, Casey Papers, NDU.

48. Author interview with Negroponte.

49. Woodward, *The War Within*, 73.

50. Author interview with Michael Mullen, Washington, DC, March 29, 2018.

51. "Transcript: 2006 Huddle (#1/2)," March 9, 2008, Box 104, Casey Papers, NDU.

52. Author interview with Casey.

53. Author interview with Negroponte.

54. Author interview with O'Sullivan.

55. Bush, *Decision Points*, 363. See also Bush and Hadley's comments, quoted in Sayle et al., *The Last Card*, 53–54.

56. Author interview with Zelikow.

57. Author interview with Raymond Odierno, Zoom, May 1, 2020.

58. Woodward, *The War Within*, 54–56.

59. Author interview with Jeffrey.

60. Zalmay Khalilzad, *The Envoy: From Kabul to the White House, My Journey Through a Turbulent World* (New York: St. Martin's, 2016), 234; Gordon and Trainor, *The Endgame*, 159–162.

61. Al-Rubaie to Casey and Khalilzad, November 6, 2005, Box 113, Casey Papers, NDU.

62. Author email correspondence with David H. Petraeus, March 11, 2020.

63. Author interview with Conrad C. Crane, Carlisle, PA, March 23, 2018.

64. Author interview with Crane; Headquarters, Department of the Army, and Headquarters, U.S. Marine Corps, *Counterinsurgency, FM 3-24/MWCP 3- 33.5*

(Washington, D.C., December 2006). See also Conrad C. Crane, *Cassandra in Oz: Counterinsurgency and Future War* (Annapolis, MD: Naval Institute Press, 2016).

65. Bush, *Decision Points*, 365, 367; Karl Rove, *Courage and Consequence: My Life as a Conservative in the Fight* (New York: Simon and Schuster, 2010), 476.

66. Bolten, quoted in Sayle et al., *The Last Card*, 111.

67. Rove, quoted in Sayle et al., 133.

68. Bush, *Decision Points*, 364.

69. Author interview with Casey.

70. Bush, *Decision Points*, 363.

71. Bush, 371.

72. "Fast Withdrawal of G.I.'s Is Urged by Key Democrat," *New York Times*, November 18, 2005; "Democratic Leaders Ask Bush to Redeploy Troops in Iraq," *New York Times*, August 1, 2006.

73. Warner to Pace, Abizaid, and Casey, October 25, 2006, Box 115, Casey Papers, NDU.

74. Bush, *Decision Points*, 355.

75. "CNN Poll conducted by Opinion Research Corporation, June 8–11, 2006," Polling Report.com, accessed September 20, 2019, http://pollingreport.com/iraq11.htm.

76. Bush, *Decision Points*, 375.

77. Bush, 355.

78. Author email correspondence with Meghan L. O'Sullivan, January 31, 2019.

79. Ed Donnelly, quoted in "Transcript: 2006 Iraq Huddle (#1/2)," March 9, 2008, Box 104, Casey Papers, NDU.

80. Bush, *Decision Points*, 367; Karl Rove, *Courage and Consequence*, 476; Stephen B. Dyson, "George W. Bush, the Surge, and Presidential Leadership," *Political Science Quarterly* 125, no. 4 (2011): 573.

81. Author interview with Crane.

82. Author interview with Crane.

83. Author interview with Zelikow.

84. Zelikow, "The Surge."

85. Author interview with Zelikow.

86. Quoted in Peter Baker, *Days of Fire: Bush and Cheney in the White House* (New York: Doubleday, 2013), 467.

87. Author interview with Casey; June 12, 2006, Box 114, Casey Papers, NDU; "MNF-I Staff Notes Excerpts, May–Sep 2006," CENTCOM Papers, No. 455, USAHEC.

88. Author interview with Casey.

89. Author interview with Zelikow.

90. Woodward, *The War Within*, 178–179.

91. Woodward, 201.

92. Author interview with Odierno.

93. Keane's role is particularly emphasized in Thomas E. Ricks, *The Gamble: General David Petraeus and the American Military Adventure in Iraq, 2006-2008* (New York: Penguin, 2009), especially 79–93.

94. Author interview with Zelikow. Crouch was deputy national security advisor at the time.

95. Author interview with Zelikow.
96. Bush, *Decision Points*, 372.
97. Woodward, *The War Within*, 84–85.
98. Woodward, 175.
99. Woodward, *State of Denial*, 491.
100. O'Sullivan, quoted in Sayle et al., *The Last Card*, 91.
101. Author email correspondence with Mansoor, April 30, 2020.
102. Peter R. Mansoor, *Surge: My Journey with General David Petraeus and the Remaking of the Iraq War* (New Haven, CT: Yale University Press, 2014), 46.
103. March 9, 2008, Box 104, Casey Papers, NDU.
104. Handwritten Notes, May 2006, Box 114, Casey Papers, NDU. See also "MNF-I Staff Notes Excerpts, May–Sep 2006," CENTCOM Papers, No. 455, USAHEC; and email, Donald Rumsfeld to Stephen J. Hadley, "U.S. Casualties in Iraq," May 8, 2006, Rumsfeld Papers.
105. Rumsfeld to Casey, August 2, 2006, Box 115, Casey Papers, NDU.
106. Rice, *Democracy*, 313.
107. Rice, *No Higher Honor*, 507.
108. Quoted in Sayle et al, *The Last Card*, 41.
109. Rice, *No Higher Honor*, p. 540.
110. Casey, *Strategic Reflections*, 168. See also Abizaid, quoted in Sayle et al., *The Last Card*, 128.
111. Author interview with Zelikow.
112. Author interview with Jeffrey.
113. Rumsfeld to Hadley, May 30, 2006, Box 121, Casey Papers, NDU.
114. Zelikow, "The Surge," 32.
115. Author email correspondence with James Jeffrey, June 28, 2018.
116. Rove, *Courage and Consequence*, 466. See also Sayle et al. *The Last Card*, 119–121.
117. Author interview with Jeffrey.
118. Author interview with Mullen.
119. Feaver, "The Right to Be Right," 102.
120. Author interview with Casey.
121. Author interview with Mullen.
122. Author interview with Douglas Lute, Rosslyn, Virgina, April 3, 2018.
123. Author interview with Casey.
124. Author interview with Sattler.
125. Author interview with Zelikow.
126. Woodward, *The War Within*, 234–235. See also Bush, *Decision Points*, 376.
127. "Notes from POTUS SVTC," December 8, 2006, Box 116, Casey Papers, NDU.
128. Briefing Notes, "Iraq—Security: Way Ahead," December 12, 2006, Box 117, Casey Papers, NDU.
129. "Notes from POTUS SVTC," December 8, 2006, Box 116, Casey Papers, NDU.
130. "Transcript: 2006 Iraq Huddle (#1/2)," March 9, 2008, Box 104, Casey Papers, NDU.
131. "Transcript: 2006 Iraq Huddle (#1/2)," March 9, 2008, Box 104, Casey Papers, NDU.
132. "Notes from POTUS SVTC," December 9, 2006, Box 116, Casey Papers, NDU. *The Iraq Study Group Report* contained only one sentence referring to a "surge"-like

option, buried on p. 73. See James A. Baker III and Lee H. Hamilton, *The Iraq Study Group Report* (New York: Vintage, 2006).

133. "Notes from POTUS SVTC," December 9, 2006, Box 116, Casey Papers, NDU.
134. Author interview with Zelikow.
135. Mansoor, *Surge*, 56.
136. Author interview with Crane.
137. Author email correspondence with Petraeus, March 9, 2020.
138. Joel D. Rayburn and Frank K. Sobchak, *The U.S. Army in the Iraq War,* 2 Vols. (Carlisle: United States Army War College Press, 2019), Vol. 2 112; Author interview with Odierno.
139. Author email correspondence with Petraeus, March 17, 2020.
140. Author interview with Lute.
141. Quoted in Baker, *Days of Fire*, 523.
142. See Woodward, *The War Within*, 233–251.
143. Casey, *Strategic Reflections*, 141–144.
144. "Notes from SecDef SVTC," November 16, 2006, Box 115, Casey Papers, NDU.
145. Author interview with Jeffrey.
146. "Notes from POTUS SVTC," December 8, 2006, Box 116, Casey Papers, NDU.
147. Bush, *Decision Points,* 374.
148. Woodward, *The War Within*, 264.
149. Presentation Slides, Unnamed Author [probably Nouri al-Maliki or Mowaffak al-Rubaie], August 2006, Box 115, Casey Papers, NDU.
150. "Notes from POTUS SVTC," December 8, 2006, Box 116, Casey Papers, NDU.
151. "Notes from POTUS SVTC," December 9, 2006, Box 116, Casey Papers, NDU.
152. "POTUS SVTC," December 11, 2006, Box 116, Casey Papers, NDU.
153. Newsweek Poll conducted by Princeton Survey Research Associates International, Dec. 6–7, 2006. Available online at: http://pollingreport.com/iraq9.htm (accessed September 20, 2019).
154. Los Angeles Times/Bloomberg Poll. Dec. 8–11, 2006. Available online at: http://pollingreport.com/iraq9.htm (accessed September 20, 2019).
155. Author email correspondence with Mansoor.
156. Bush, *Decision Points*, 355.
157. December 15, 2006, Box 116, Casey Papers, NDU.
158. Peter D. Feaver, "Anatomy of the Surge," *Commentary* (April 2008).
159. Author interview with Casey.
160. Author interview with Jeffrey. See also Rice, *Democracy*, 317.
161. Author interview with Zelikow.
162. Author interview with senior military officer, 2018; Bush, *Decision Points*, 385.
163. Bush, *Decision Points*, 385.
164. Odierno to Petraeus, August 2007, CENTCOM Papers, No. 9, USAHEC.
165. Author interview with Stephen Biddle, Washington, DC, March 28, 2018.
166. Author interview with Jeffrey.
167. Robert M. Gates, *Duty: Memoirs of a Secretary at War* (New York: Knopf, 2014), 49. See also Bush, *Decision Points*, 382.
168. Quoted in Mansoor, *Surge*, 225.
169. Author email correspondence with Petraeus, March 23, 2020.

170. John Allen, quoted in Colin H. Kahl and William E. Odom, "When to Leave Iraq," *Foreign Affairs*, July–August 2008, 152; Niel Smith and Sean MacFarland, "Anbar Awakens: The Tipping Point," *Military Review* (March–April 2008): 41–52. On troop withdrawals as a solution to the "commitment trap," see also Jervis, "The Politics of Troop Withdrawal," 510–511.

171. Gates, *Duty*, 57.

172. Gates, 49–79.

173. Gates, 227, 234.

174. Gates, 229.

175. Author email correspondence with Petraeus, March 5, 2020.

176. Author email correspondence with Petraeus, March 5, 2020. On the role of political considerations in the provision of military advice and development of strategy more generally, see Risa Brooks, "Paradoxes of Professionalism: Rethinking Civil-Military Relations in the United States," *International Security* 44, no. 4 (Spring 2020): 7–44; Freedman, *Command*; Lee, *Politics of Military Operations*.

177. Author email correspondence with Petraeus, March 16, 2020.

178. Author interview with Biddle.

179. Author email correspondence with Mansoor; Mansoor, *Surge*, 113.

180. Gates, *Duty*, 64.

181. Author email correspondence with Petraeus, 4 March 2020.

182. Gates, *Duty*, 93.

183. Author interview with O'Sullivan.

184. Author interview with Lute.

185. Unless otherwise stated, the following account draws from the following: author interview with Robert Loftis, Boston, MA, March 21, 2018; author interview with Lute; author interview with O'Sullivan; author interview with Negroponte.

186. Author interview with Loftis.

187. Author interview with Loftis.

188. Author interview with Lute.

189. Author interview with Lute.

190. Author email correspondence with Petraeus, March 23, 2020.

191. Gordon and Trainor, *The Endgame*, 528.

192. Gordon and Trainor, 530.

193. "Interview with Iraqi Leader Nouri al-Maliki," *Der Spiegel*, July 19, 2008.

194. Petraeus to Gates, "SecDef Weekly Update 14–20 July 2008." Copy obtained by author via email from Colonel Peter Mansoor.

195. Petraeus to Gates, "SecDef Weekly Update 4–10 August 2008." Copy obtained by author via email from Colonel Peter Mansoor.

196. Emma Sky, *The Unravelling: High Hopes and Missed Opportunities in Iraq* (London: Atlantic, 2015), 262.

197. Author interview with Lute.

198. Author interview with Mullen.

199. Author interview with Odierno.

200. Author interview with Emma Sky, Oxford, UK, February 26, 2018.

201. Author interview with Loftis.

202. Author interview with Lute.
203. Author interview with Sky.
204. Author interview with Lute.
205. Quoted in Gordon and Trainor, *The Endgame*, 555.
206. Bush, *Decision Points*, 390.
207. Author interview with Negroponte.
208. Author interview with Mullen.
209. Quoted in Gordon and Trainor, *The Endgame*, 555.
210. Author interview with Jeffrey.
211. Author interview with Negroponte.
212. Author interview with Loftis.
213. Author interview with Colin H. Kahl, Washington, DC, March 15, 2018.
214. Author interview with Lute.
215. Mattis and West, *Call Sign Chaos*, 123.
216. On leadership decapitation, see Jenna Jordan, *Leadership Decapitation of Terrorist Organizations: Strategic Decapitation of Terrorist Organizations* (Stanford, CA: Stanford University Press, 2019); Max Abrahms and Philip B. K. Potter, "Explaining Terrorism: Leadership Deficits and Militant Group Tactics," *International Organization* 69, no. 2 (2015): 311–342; Bryan C. Price, "Targeting Top Terrorists: How Leadership Decapitation Contributes to Counterterrorism," *International Security* 36, no. 4 (2012): 9–46.
217. Author interview with Casey.
218. See, for instance, Mattis and West, *Call Sign Chaos*, 139, 161–162. On the relative importance of the Sunni Awakening to the success of the "surge," see Biddle, Friedman, and Shapiro, "Testing the Surge."
219. See Biddle, Friedman, and Shapiro, "Testing the Surge"; Lebovic, *Planning to Fail*, 97–104.
220. See Casey, *Strategic Reflections*; Gian Gentile, *Wrong Turn: America's Deadly Embrace of Counterinsurgency* (New York: Free Press, 2013). See also further commentary in the conclusion of this book.
221. Author interview with Jeffrey.
222. Author interview with Negroponte.

6. Iraq: Barack Obama and the Endgame

Source for chapter epigraph: author interview with Brennan.
1. Author interview with Antony J. Blinken, telephone, June 8, 2018.
2. Author interview with Michèle Flournoy, Washington, DC, April 3, 2018.
3. "Remarks on Military Operations in Iraq at Camp Lejeune, North Carolina," February 27, 2009, *Public Papers of the Presidents: Obama*, 2009, bk. 1:158–163.
4. Obama, "My Plan for Iraq," *New York Times*, July 14, 2008.
5. Author email correspondence with Petraeus.
6. Odierno to Mullen, "RISK ASSESSMENT," December 6, 2008, Box 23, Casey Papers, NDU.

7. Author interview with Odierno.

8. Gordon and Trainor, *The Endgame*, 560–580; Author interview with Odierno.

9. Barack Obama, *A Promised Land* (New York: Crown, 2020), 314.

10. Quoted in Gordon and Trainor, *The Endgame*, 560.

11. Sky, *The Unravelling*, 272.

12. Author interview with Kahl.

13. Author interview with Sky.

14. Author interview with Odierno.

15. Quoted in Gates, *Duty*, 325. See also Obama, *A Promised Land*, 314–315.

16. Derek Chollet, *The Long Game: How Obama Defied Washington and Redefined America's Role in the World* (New York: Public Affairs, 2016), 75.

17. Quoted in Gordon and Trainor, *The Endgame*, 573.

18. Gordon and Trainor, 567–574.

19. "Remarks on Military Operations in Iraq at Camp Lejeune, North Carolina."

20. Quoted in Andrew Kenealy, "Barack Obama and the Politics of Military Force, 2009–2012," *Presidential Studies Quarterly*, 52, no. 4 (December 2022), 799.

21. Author interview with Kahl.

22. Obama, *A Promised Land*, 315.

23. Author interview with Brennan. See also John O. Brennan, *Undaunted: My Fight Against America's Enemies, at Home and Abroad* (New York: Celadon, 2020), 255.

24. Author interview with James Cartwright, Washington, DC, March 26, 2018.

25. Author interview with Brennan.

26. Gates, *Duty*, 553.

27. Leon Panetta, *Worthy Fights: A Memoir of Leadership in War and Peace* (New York: Penguin, 2014), 393.

28. Author interview with Flournoy.

29. Mattis and West, *Call Sign Chaos*, 206.

30. Author interview with Flournoy.

31. Author interview with Blinken.

32. Author interview with Lute.

33. Author interview with Mullen.

34. Author interview with Brennan.

35. Author interview with Flournoy.

36. Author interview with Kahl.

37. Author interview with Kahl.

38. Author interview with Flournoy.

39. Author interview with Odierno.

40. Obama, *A Promised Land*, 576.

41. Tim Arango, "War in Iraq Defies U.S. Timetable for End of Combat," *New York Times*, July 3, 2010; Anthony Shadid, "Iraqi Leaders Fear for Future After Their Past Missteps," *New York Times*, August 17, 2010; Peter Baker, "As Mission Shifts in Iraq, Risks Linger for Obama," *New York Times*, August 21, 2010.

42. Author interview with Kahl.

43. Author interview with Flournoy.

44. Author interview with senior military officer.

45. Author interview with Sky.

46. Author interview with Jeffrey.
47. Christopher R. Hill, *Outpost: A Diplomat at Work* (New York: Simon and Schuster, 2014), 384–386, 372–373; Sky, *The Unravelling*, 322; Gordon and Trainor, *The Endgame*, 628–635.
48. Author interview with Jeffrey.
49. Author interview with Kahl.
50. Obama, *A Promised Land*, 315.
51. Author interview with Jeffrey.
52. Author interview with Kahl.
53. Author interview with Flournoy.
54. Gordon and Trainor, *The Endgame*, 656. See also Robert M. Gates, *Exercise of Power: American Failures, Successes, and a New Path Forward in the Post–Cold War World* (New York: Alfred A. Knopf, 2020), 225–226.
55. Author interview with Mullen.
56. Author interview with Mullen. See also Rayburn and Sobchak, *The U.S. Army in the Iraq War*, 2:541–542.
57. Gordon and Trainor, *The Endgame*, 657.
58. Author email correspondence with Petraeus, March 27, 2020.
59. Author interview with Jeffrey.
60. Author interview with Mullen.
61. Author interview with Mullen.
62. Author interview with Cartwright.
63. Rayburn and Sobchak, *The U.S. Army in the Iraq War*, 2:543.
64. Quoted in "United States Forces-Iraq Quarterly Command Report, 2d Quarter (1 January–31 March 2011), FY11," May 1, 2011, No. 471, CENTCOM Papers, AMHI.
65. "United States Forces-Iraq Quarterly Command Report, 3rd Quarter, FY11 (1 April–30 June 2011)," July 1, 2011, No. 1003, CENTCOM Papers, AMHI.
66. Panetta, *Worthy Fights*, 370.
67. Author interview with Blinken.
68. Author interview with Jeffrey.
69. Author interview with Blinken. See also Kenealy, "Barack Obama," 16–18.
70. Author interview with Lute.
71. Meghan L. O'Sullivan, "The Problem with Obama's Decision to Leave Iraq," *Foreign Affairs*, October 2011.
72. Author interview with Flournoy.
73. Author interview with Flournoy. See also Mattis and West, *Call Sign Chaos*, 208.
74. Author interview with Odierno.
75. Author interview with Kahl.
76. Author interview with Jeffrey.
77. "The Third Presidential Debate," *New York Times*, October 23, 2012.
78. Author interview with Brennan. See also Brennan, *Undaunted*, 256.
79. Author interview with Casey.
80. Author interview with senior official.
81. For detailed analysis of the counterfactual, see Hal Brands and Peter Feaver, "Was the Rise of ISIS Inevitable?," *Survival* 59, no. 3 (2017): 18–30.
82. Author interview with Flournoy.

83. Author interview with Brennan. See also Brennan, *Undaunted*, 256.
84. Author interview with Odierno.
85. Author interview with Flournoy.
86. Author interview with Jeffrey.
87. Author interview with Mullen.

Conclusion

1. Kissinger and Nixon, August 3, 1972, 8:28 a.m., Conversation 760-006, WHT, RNL.
2. Quoted in Small, *Democracy and Diplomacy*, 116–117.
3. Tommy Franks, *American Soldier* (New York: Harper Collins, 2009), 373; specific quotation in Bob Woodward, *Plan of Attack* (New York: Simon and Schuster, 2004), 172.
4. Quoted in Michael Gordon and Bernard Trainor, *Cobra II: The Inside Story of the Invasion and Occupation of Iraq* (New York: Vintage, 2006), 82.
5. Quoted in Christopher Meyer (Oral Evidence), "The Transatlantic Relationship," November 26, 2009, *Report of the Iraq Inquiry*; this specific testimony is available at https://webarchive.nationalarchives.gov.uk/ukgwa/20110119123314/http://www.iraqinquiry.org.uk/transcripts/oralevidence-bydate/091126.aspx. See also Christopher Meyer, *DC Confidential: The Controversial Memoirs of Britain's Ambassador to the US at the Time of 9/11 and the Iraq War* (London: Weidenfeld & Nicholson, 2005), 255.
6. Quoted in Armacost, *Ballots, Bullets and Bargains*, 80.
7. George Stephanopoulos, quoted in Armacost, 139.
8. *FRUS, 1958-1960*, vol. 16, docs. 359, 403, and 418.
9. January 24, 1961, Clifford Papers, Box 4, LOC. On similar coordination issues between incoming and outgoing administrations, see Michaels and Payne, "One President at a Time?," 14–20.
10. Powlick and Katz, "Defining the American Public Opinion/Foreign Policy Nexus."
11. Quoted in Johnstone and Priest, *US Presidential Elections and Foreign Policy*, 172.
12. John Bolton, *The Room Where It Happened: A White House Memoir* (New York: Simon and Schuster, 2020), 301–302.
13. Fawcett and Payne, "Stuck on a Hostile Path?"
14. Multistate studies of democratic constraint include Huth and Allee, "Domestic Political Accountability"; Reiter and Tillman, "Public, Legislative, and Executive Constraints"; Clark and Nordstrom, "Democratic Variants and Democratic Variance"; Steve Chan and William Safran, "Public Opinion as a Constraint Against War: Democracies' Responses to Operation Iraqi Freedom," *Foreign Policy Analysis* 2, no. 2 (April 2006): 137–156; Baum and Potter, *War and Democratic Constraint*.
15. See Williams, "Flexible Election Timing and International Conflict."
16. Danielle Kurtzleben, "Why Are U.S. Elections So Much Longer than Other Countries?," NPR, October 21, 2015, https://www.npr.org/sections/itsallpolitics/2015/10/21/450238156/canadas-11-week-campaign-reminds-us-that-american

-elections-are-much-longer; Seth Masket, "Why Are American Elections So Long?" *Pacific Standard*, March 25, 2015, https://psmag.com/social-justice/why -are-american-elections-so-long.

17. Norman J. Ornstein and Thomas E. Mann, *The Permanent Campaign and Its Future* (Washington, DC: American Enterprise Institute, 2000). For a similar treatment applied to the Bush administration, see Scott McClellan, *What Happened: Inside the Bush White House and Washington's Culture of Deception* (New York: Public Affairs, 2008).

18. The former statement derives from "selectorate theory"—whereby the size of an incumbent's "winning margin" (i.e., the group of people a leader needs support from in order to stay in power) relative to the "selectorate" (i.e., the set of people with a say in choosing leaders) determines his or her sensitivity to democratic constraints. See Bueno de Mesquita et al., *The Logic of Political Survival*. On press freedom, see Baum and Potter, *War and Democratic Constraint*; Casey, "Confirming the Cold War Consensus"; Steven Casey, *The War Beat, Europe: The American Media at War Against Nazi Germany* (New York: Oxford University Press, 2017); Steven Casey, *The War Beat, Pacific: The American Media at War Against Japan* (New York: Oxford University Press, 2021).

19. Barnhart et al., "The Suffragist Peace"; Barnhart and Trager, *The Suffragist Peace*.

20. See Andreas Schedler, "The Logic of Electoral Authoritarianism," in *Electoral Authoritarianism: The Dynamics of Unfree Competition*, ed. Andreas Schedler (Boulder, CO: Lynne Rienner, 2006), 1–23.

21. On audience costs in authoritarian regimes, see Jessica L. P. Weeks, *Dictators at War and Peace* (Ithaca, NY: Cornell University Press, 2014).

22. Asselin, *Vietnam's American War*, 113–115, 152–154, 191–193.

23. On strategic interaction and the diversionary use of force, see Smith, "Diversionary Foreign Policy"; Benjamin O. Fordham, "Strategic Conflict Avoidance and the Diversionary Use of Force," *Journal of Politics* 67, no. 1 (February 2005): 132–153; David H. Clark, "Can Strategic Interaction Divert Diversionary Behavior? A Model of US Conflict Propensity," *Journal of Politics* 65, no. 4 (2003): 1013–1039; David H. Clark, Benjamin O. Fordham, and Timothy Nordstrom, "Preying on the Misfortune of Others: When Do States Exploit Their Opponents' Domestic Troubles?," *Journal of Politics* 73, no. 1 (2011): 248–264. On the relationship between leader turnover and the risk of military conflict, see also Robert Schub, "When Prospective Leader Turnover Promotes Peace," *International Studies Quarterly* 64, no. 3 (September 2020): 510–522.

24. Freedman, *Command*, 427–460. On the broader challenges of being a junior partner of the United States, see William D. James, "Influencing the United States: Is the Game Worth the Candle for Junior Allies?," *International Politics* 59, no. 6 (2022): 1029–1044. For the Iraq context, see Patrick Porter, *Blunder: Britain's War in Iraq* (Oxford: Oxford University Press, 2018), 132–151.

25. Reiter and Stam, *Democracies at War*; Bueno de Mesquita et al., *The Logic of Political Survival*.

26. On selection effects, see Reiter and Stam, *Democracies at War*; Bueno de Mesquita et al., *The Logic of Political Survival*. On the extraction of wealth and resources, see Bueno de Mesquita et al., *The Logic of Political Survival*; Benjamin O. Fordham

and Thomas C. Walker, "Kantian Liberalism, Regime Type, and Military Resource Allocation: Do Democracies Spend Less?," *International Studies Quarterly* 49, no. 1 (2005): 141–157. On war duration, see Scott D. Bennett and Allan C. Stam III, "The Declining Advantages of Democracy: A Combined Model of War Outcomes and Duration," *Journal of Conflict Resolution* 42, no. 3 (1998): 344–366; Branislav L. Slantchev, "How Initiators End Their Wars: The Duration of Warfare and the Terms of Peace," *American Journal of Political Science* 48, no. 4 (2004): 813–829.

27. On information and the marketplace of ideas, see Reiter and Stam, *Democracies at War*. On coalitions, see David A. Lake, "Powerful Pacifists: Democratic States and War," *American Political Science Review* 86, no. 1 (1992): 24–37. On the attributes of forces, see Reiter and Stam, *Democracies at War*.

28. Andrew Mack, "Why Big Nations Lose Small Wars: The Politics of Asymmetric Conflict," *World Politics* 27, no. 2 (1975): 175–200; Stephen Peter Rosen, "Vietnam and the American Theory of Limited War," *International Security* 7, no. 2 (1982): 83–113; Patricia L. Sullivan, "War Aims and War Outcomes: Why Powerful States Lose Limited Wars," *Journal of Conflict Resolution* 51, no. 3 (2007): 496–524; Jeffrey Record, *Beating Goliath: Why Insurgencies Win* (Dulles, VA: Potomac Books, 2007); Jonathan D. Caverley, "The Myth of Military Myopia: Democracy, Small Wars, and Vietnam," *International Security* 34, no. 3 (2009): 119–157; Alexander B. Downes, "How Smart and Tough Are Democracies? Reassessing Theories of Democratic Victory in War," *International Security* 33, no. 4 (2009): 9–51.

29. Ivan Arreguin-Toft, "How the Weak Win Wars: A Theory of Asymmetric Conflict," *International Security* 26, no. 1 (2001): 93–128; John A. Nagl, *Learning to Eat Soup with a Knife: Counterinsurgency Lessons from Malaya and Vietnam* (Chicago: University of Chicago Press, 2005).

30. Caverley, "The Myth of Military Myopia"; Downes, "How Smart and Tough Are Democracies?"

31. See Downes, "How Smart and Tough Are Democracies?"

32. On brutality in war, see Gil Merom, *How Democracies Lose Small Wars: State, Society, and the Failures of France in Algeria, Israel in Lebanon, and the United States in Vietnam* (Cambridge: Cambridge University Press, 2003). On public attitudes toward war, see Gelpi, Feaver, and Reifler, *Paying the Human Costs of War*, and chapter 1 of this book.

33. For an analogous discussion of the use of airpower as a double-edged sword, see Susan Hannah Allen and Carla Martinez Machain, "Choosing Air Strikes," *Journal of Global Security Studies* 3, no. 2 (2018): 150–162.

34. Patrick B. Johnston and Brian R. Urlacher, *Explaining the Duration of Counterinsurgency Campaigns* (Arlington, VA: RAND Corporation, 2012). This line of analysis applies most naturally to the wars in Vietnam and Iraq, given the presence of insurgencies in both, yet it might also be applied to conventional "proxy" wars like Korea, in which interest asymmetry may leave opponents with greater resolve.

35. See Record, *Beating Goliath*; Caverley, "The Myth of Military Myopia."

36. Additional studies do suggest that public opinion does materially affect decision making even in wars of "necessity." Franklin Roosevelt, for instance, while deeply concerned in private about the growing threat of war in Europe,

remained very cautious in his public comments until after the 1940 election was over, and later overruled his Joint Chiefs by explicitly ordering that the invasion of North Africa should take place prior to the 1942 midterms. See Steven Casey, *Cautious Crusade: Franklin D. Roosevelt, American Public Opinion, and the War Against Nazi Germany* (New York: Oxford University Press, 2001), chap. 1; Carrie Lee, "Operation TORCH at 75: FDR and the Domestic Politics of the North African Invasion," *War on the Rocks*, November 8, 2017, https://warontherocks.com /2017/11/16075/.

37. Berinsky, *In Time of War*; Saunders, "War and the Inner Circle."

38. Benjamin I. Page and Marshall M. Bouton, *The Foreign Policy Disconnect: What Americans Want from Our Leaders but Don't Get* (Chicago: University of Chicago Press, 2006); Stephen M. Walt, *The Hell of Good Intentions: America's Foreign Policy Elite and the Decline of U.S. Primacy* (New York: Picador, 2018); Patrick Porter, "Why America's Grand Strategy Has Not Changed: Power, Habit, and the U.S. Foreign Policy Establishment," *International Security* 42, no. 4 (2018): 9–46. For recent experimental approaches to this issue, see Joshua Busby et al., "Multilateralism and the Use of Force: Experimental Evidence on the Views of Foreign Policy Elites," *Foreign Policy Analysis* 16, no. 1 (January 2020): 118–129; and Joshua D. Kertzer, "Re-assessing Elite-Public Gaps in Political Behavior," *American Journal of Political Science* 66, no. 3 (July 2022): 539–553, who argues that the elite-public gap in political behavior may be narrower than has been suggested.

39. Quoted in Quandt, "The Electoral Cycle," 830.

40. See Peter Trubowitz, *Defining the National Interest: Conflict and Change in American Foreign Policy* (Chicago: University of Chicago Press, 1998).

41. On the erosion of constraints on presidential behavior, see James Goldgeier and Elizabeth N. Saunders, "The Unconstrained Presidency: Checks and Balances Eroded Long Before Trump," *Foreign Affairs* 97 (2018): 144. On the way in which concerns about public opinion nevertheless limit the president's willingness to exercise unilateral executive power, see Dino P. Christenson and Douglas L. Kriner, *The Myth of the Imperial Presidency* (Chicago: University of Chicago Press, 2020).

42. Jervis, "The Politics of Troop Withdrawal," 514–515.

Bibliography

PRIMARY SOURCES

Korea

Manuscript Collections

HARRY S. TRUMAN PRESIDENTIAL LIBRARY,
INDEPENDENCE, MISSOURI (HSTL)

Acheson, Dean, Papers
Anderson, Vernice E., Papers
Ayers, Eben A., Papers
Bond, Niles W., Papers
Connelly, Matthew J., Papers
Dennison, Robert L., Papers
Elsey, George M., Papers
Hechler, Kenneth, Papers
Lloyd, David D., Papers
Murphy, Charles S., Papers
National Security Council File (NSCF)
Staff Member and Office Files: Korean War File (SMOF/KWF)

Post Presidential Papers
President's Secretary's Files (PSF)
Tannenwald, Theodore J., Jr., Papers
White House Central File (WHCF)
    Official File

DWIGHT D. EISENHOWER PRESIDENTIAL LIBRARY,
ABILENE, KANSAS (DDEL)

Brownell, Herbert, Jr., Papers
Clark, Mark W. Papers
Collins, J. Lawton, Papers
Dulles, John Foster, Papers
    JFD Chronological Series
    Subject Series
    Telephone Conversations Series
    White House Memoranda Series
Eisenhower, Dwight D., Papers as President (Ann Whitman File) (AWF)
    Administration Series
    Cabinet Series
    Campaign Series
    DDE Diary Series
    Dulles-Herter Series
    Name Series
    NSC Series
    Speech Series
Eisenhower, Dwight D., Prepresidential Papers
Hagerty, James C., Papers
Harlow, Bryce, Papers
Humphreys, Robert, Papers
Jackson, C. D., Papers
Lodge, Henry Cabot, Papers
Oral History Transcripts
    Briggs, Ellis
    Brownell, Herbert, Jr.
    Clark, Mark W.
    Eisenhower, Dwight D.

Hagerty, James C.
Kendall, David
Murphy, Robert
Robertson, Walter
Sherrod, Robert L.
Stassen, Harold E.
Republican National Committee: Office of the Chairman Records
Schaefer, Earl J., Papers
White House Central File
    Confidential File Series
    President's Personal File Series
    Official File Series
White House Office: National Security Council Staff Papers (WHO/NSCS)
    Disaster File
White House Office: Office of the Special Assistant for National Security Affairs (WHO/OSANSA)
    NSC Series
White House Office: Office of the Staff Secretary

LIBRARY OF CONGRESS, WASHINGTON, DC (LOC)

Vandenburg, Hoyt S., Papers

MACARTHUR MEMORIAL ARCHIVES,
NORFOLK, VIRGINIA (MMA)

RG-5 Records of General Headquarters, SCAP, 1945–1951
RG-6: Records of Headquarters, FECOM, 1947–1951
RG-7: Records of General Headquarters, UNC, 1950–1951
RG-9: Collection of Messages (Radiograms), 1945–1951
RG-10: General Douglas MacArthur's Private Correspondence, 1848–1964
RG-16a: Papers of Major General Courtney Whitney
RG-32: Oral History Collection
RG-37: Papers of Major General Frank E. Lowe, 1950–1951
RG-45: Papers of Colonel Laurence Elliot Bunker
RG-49: James Interviews
RG-50: Papers of Philip M. Brower

NATIONAL ARCHIVES, KEW GARDENS, LONDON (KG)

Cabinet Office Files

U.S. ARMY HERITAGE AND EDUCATION CENTER,
CARLISLE, PENNSYLVANIA (USAHEC)

Ridgway, Matthew B., Papers

Published Documentary Collections

Ferrell, Robert H., ed. *Off the Record: The Private Papers of Harry S. Truman*. New York: Harper and Row, 1980.
Kennan, George F. *The Kennan Diaries*. Edited by Frank Costigliola. New York: W. W. Norton, 2014.
Public Papers of the Presidents of the United States: Harry S. Truman. 8 Vols. Washington, DC: United States Government Printing Office, 1945–1952.
Stevenson, Adlai E. *Major Campaign Speeches of Adlai E. Stevenson, 1952*. New York: Random House, 1953.
United States Department of State. *Department of State Bulletin*, vol. 23. Washington, DC: U.S. Government Printing Office, 1950.
United States Department of State. *Foreign Relations of the United States [FRUS], 1950*. Vol. 7, *Korea*. Edited by John P. Glennon. Washington, DC: United States Government Printing Office, 1976.
United States Department of State. *Foreign Relations of the United States [FRUS], 1951*. Vols. 10 and 11, *Korea and China*. 2 Parts. Edited by John P. Glennon, Harriet D. Schwar, and Paul Claussen. Washington, DC: United States Government Printing Office, 1983.
United States Department of State. *Foreign Relations of the United States [FRUS], 1952–1954*. Vol. 15, *Korea and China*. 2 Parts. Edited by Edward C. Keefer. Washington, DC: United States Government Printing Office, 1984.

Memoirs

Acheson, Dean. *Present at the Creation: My Years in the State Department*. New York: W. W. Norton, 1969.
Bradley, Omar, and Clay Blair. *A General's Life: An Autobiography by the General of the Army*. New York: Simon and Schuster, 1983.
Clark, Mark W. *From the Danube to the Yalu*. London: George C. Harrap, 1954.
Collins, J. Lawton. *War in Peacetime: The History and Lessons of Korea*. Boston: Houghton Mifflin, 1969.
Eisenhower, Dwight D. *Mandate for Change: The White House Years*. Garden City, NY: Doubleday, 1963.

Hughes, Emmet John. *The Ordeal of Power: A Political Memoir of the Eisenhower Years*. London: Macmillan, 1963.

Jebb, Gladwyn. *The Memoirs of Lord Gladwyn*. London: Weidenfeld and Nicolson, 1972.

Kennan, George F. *Memoirs: 1950-1963*. London: Hutchinson, 1973.

MacArthur, Douglas. *Reminiscences*. New York: McGraw Hill, 1964.

Ridgway, Matthew B. *The Korean War*. New York: Da Capo Press, 1967.

Rusk, Dean. *As I Saw It*. New York: Penguin, 1990.

Truman, Harry S. *Memoirs*. Vol. 2, *Years of Trial and Hope*. Garden City, NY: Doubleday, 1956.

Whitney, Courtney. *MacArthur: His Rendezvous with History*. New York: Knopf, 1956.

Willoughby, Charles A. *MacArthur: 1941-1951, Victory in the Pacific*. London: Heinemann, 1956.

Vietnam

Manuscript Collections

LYNDON B. JOHNSON PRESIDENTIAL LIBRARY,
AUSTIN, TEXAS (LBJL)

Bundy, William P., Papers
Handwriting File
Johnson, Tom, Papers (TJ)
Meeting Notes File (MNF)
National Security Files (NSF)
    Country File, Vietnam
    Files of McGeorge Bundy
    Files of Walt W. Rostow
    Memos to the President
    Name File
    National Security Council Meetings
Office Files of White House Aides
    McPherson, Harry C.
Office of the President File
Recordings and Transcripts of Telephone Conversations and Meetings (RTTCM)
White House Central Files (WHCF)
    Confidential File
    Subject File
White House Famous Names

RICHARD NIXON PRESIDENTIAL LIBRARY,
YORBA LINDA, CALIFORNIA (RNL)

H. R. Haldeman Diaries (HD)
Kissinger, Henry A., Office Files (HAKOF)
    Country Files—Far East—South Vietnam
Kissinger, Henry A., Telephone Conversation Transcripts (Telcons)
    (HAKTC)
National Security Council Files (NSCF)
    Alexander M. Haig Special File
    Cambodian Operations
    Name Files
    Presidential/HAK Memcons
    Subject Files
    Vietnam Country Files
    Vietnam Subject Files
National Security Council Institutional "H" Files
President's Personal File
White House Central Files
    Subject Files
White House Special Files
White House Special Files: Staff Member and Office Files
White House Tapes (WHT)

LIBRARY OF CONGRESS, WASHINGTON, DC (LOC)

Clifford, Clark M., Papers
Harriman, W. Averell, Papers

U.S. ARMY HERITAGE AND EDUCATION CENTER,
CARLISLE, PENNSYLVANIA (USAHEC)

Senior Officer Oral History Program
    Westmoreland, William C.
    Weyand, Frederick C.

Published Documentary Collections

Barrett, David, M. *Lyndon B. Johnson's Vietnam Papers: A Documentary Collection*. College Station, TX: Texas A&M University Press, 1997.

Beschloss, Michael R. *Reaching for Glory: Lyndon Johnson's Secret White House Tapes, 1964–1965*. New York: Simon and Schuster, 2001.

Beschloss, Michael R., ed. *Taking Charge: The Johnson White House Tapes, 1963-1964*. New York: Simon and Schuster, 1997.

Brinkley, Douglas, and Luke A. Nichter, eds. *The Nixon Tapes: 1971-1972*. New York: Mariner Books, 2015.

Gibbons, William C. *The U.S. Government and the Vietnam War: Executive and Legislative Roles and Relationships, Part 4: July 1965–January 1968*. Princeton, NJ: Princeton University Press, 1995.

Haldeman, H. R. *The Haldeman Diaries: Inside the Nixon White House*. New York: Putnam, 1994.

Presidential Recordings Digital Edition, Miller Center, University of Virginia, available online at: https://prde.upress.virginia.edu/.

Presidential Recordings Program, Miller Center, University of Virginia, available online at: https://millercenter.org/the-presidency/secret-white-house-tapes.

Public Papers of the Presidents of the United States: Lyndon B. Johnson. 10 Vols. Washington, DC: United States Government Printing Office, 1965–1970.

Public Papers of the Presidents of the United States: Richard Nixon. 5 Vols. Washington, DC: United States Government Printing Office, 1971–1975.

The Pentagon Papers: The Defense Department History of United States Decision-Making on Vietnam. Senator Gravel ed. Boston: Beacon Press, 1971.

United States Department of State. *Foreign Relations of the United States [FRUS], 1958-1960*. Vol. 16, *East Asia-Pacific Region; Cambodia; Laos*. Edited by Edward C. Keefer and David W. Mabon. Washington, DC: United States Government Printing Office, 1992.

United States Department of State. *Foreign Relations of the United States [FRUS], 1961-1963*. Vol. 4, *Vietnam, August-December 1963*. Edited by Edward C. Keefer. Washington, DC: United States Government Printing Office, 1991.

United States Department of State. *Foreign Relations of the United States [FRUS], 1964-1968*. Vol. 1, *Vietnam, 1964*. Edited by Edward C. Keefer and Charles S. Sampson. Washington, DC: United States Government Printing Office, 1992.

United States Department of State. *Foreign Relations of the United States [FRUS], 1964-1968*. Vol. 2, *Vietnam, January-June 1965*. Edited by David C. Humphrey, Ronald D. Landa, and Louis J. Smith. Washington, DC: United States Government Printing Office, 1996.

United States Department of State. *Foreign Relations of the United States [FRUS], 1964-1968*. Vol. 3, *Vietnam, June-December 1965*. Edited by David C. Humphrey, Edward C. Keefer, and Louis J. Smith. Washington, DC: United States Government Printing Office, 1996.

United States Department of State. *Foreign Relations of the United States [FRUS], 1964-1968*. Vol. 4, *Vietnam, 1966*. Edited by David C. Humphrey. Washington, DC: United States Government Printing Office, 1998.

United States Department of State. *Foreign Relations of the United States [FRUS], 1964–1968*. Vol. 5, *Vietnam, 1967*. Edited by Kent Sieg. Washington, DC: United States Government Printing Office, 2002

United States Department of State. *Foreign Relations of the United States [FRUS], 1964–1968*. Vol. 6, *Vietnam, January–August 1968*. Edited by Kent Sieg. Washington, DC: United States Government Printing Office, 2002.

United States Department of State. *Foreign Relations of the United States [FRUS], 1964–1968*. Vol. 7, *Vietnam, September 1968–January 1969*. Edited by Kent Sieg. Washington, DC: United States Government Printing Office, 2003.

United States Department of State. *Foreign Relations of the United States [FRUS], 1969–1976*. Vol. 6, *Vietnam, January 1960–July 1970*. Edited by Edward C. Keefer and Carolyn Yee. Washington, DC: United States Government Printing Office, 2006.

United States Department of State. *Foreign Relations of the United States [FRUS], 1969–1976*. Vol. 7, *Vietnam, July 1970–January 1972*. Edited by David Goldman and Erin Mahan. Washington, DC: United States Government Printing Office, 2010.

United States Department of State. *Foreign Relations of the United States [FRUS], 1969–1976*. Vol. 8, *Vietnam, January–October 1972*. Edited by John M. Carland. Washington, DC: United States Government Printing Office, 2010.

United States Department of State. *Foreign Relations of the United States [FRUS], 1969–1976*. Vol. 9, *Vietnam, October 1972–January 1973*. Edited by John M. Carland. Washington, DC: United States Government Printing Office, 2010.

Interviews/Personal Correspondence

Bator, Francis M. Deputy national security advisor to President Johnson (1965–1967). Telephone interview, March 16, 2017.

Butterfield, Alexander P. Deputy assistant to President Nixon (1969–1973). Interview, Austin, TX, April 29, 2016.

Califano, Joseph A., Jr. Special assistant to the secretary and deputy secretary of defense (1964–1965), special assistant to President Johnson (1965–1969). Telephone interview, May 1, 2013.

Johnson, Tom. Aide to President Johnson (1965–1973). Email correspondence, May 4, 2016–March 29, 2017.

Negroponte, John D. Political officer, U.S. Embassy, Vietnam (1964–1968), liaison officer, Paris peace talks (1968–1969), NSC staff (1970–1973). Interview, Washington, DC, March 27, 2018.

Shepard, Geoff. Associate director for general government (1972). Email correspondence, January 20, 2017–February 13, 2017.

Memoirs

Ball, George W. *The Past Has Another Pattern: Memoirs*. New York: W. W. Norton, 1982.

Chennault, Anna. *The Education of Anna*. New York: Times Books, 1980.

Clifford, Clark, with Richard Holbrooke. *Counsel to the President: A Memoir.* New York: Random House, 1991.

Haig, Alexander M., Jr. *Inner Circles: How America Changed the World.* New York: Warner Books, 1992.

Haldeman, H. R., with Joseph DiMona. *Ends of Power.* New York: Times Books, 1978.

Johnson, Lyndon B. *The Vantage Point: Perspectives on the Presidency, 1963–1969.* New York: Holt, Rinehart and Winston, 1971.

Kissinger, Henry. *Ending the Vietnam War: A History of America's Involvement in and Extrication from the Vietnam War.* New York: Simon and Schuster, 2003.

Kissinger, Henry. *Leadership: Six Studies in World Strategy.* London: Allen Lane, 2022.

Kissinger, Henry. *The White House Years.* Boston: Little Brown & Co., 1979.

McNamara, Robert S., with Brian VanDeMark. *In Retrospect: The Tragedy and Lessons of Vietnam.* New York: Times Books, 1995.

Nixon, Richard. *The Memoirs of Richard Nixon.* London: Sidgwick and Jackson, 1978.

Rusk, Dean. *As I Saw It.* New York: Penguin, 1990.

Taylor, Maxwell D. *Swords and Plowshares.* New York: W. W. Norton, 1972.

Iraq

Manuscript Collections

NATIONAL DEFENSE UNIVERSITY,
WASHINGTON, DC (NDU)

Casey, George W., Jr., Papers
Petraeus, David H., Papers

U.S. ARMY HERITAGE AND EDUCATION CENTER,
CARLISLE, PENNSYLVANIA (USAHEC)

CENTCOM Iraq Papers

OTHER

Papers of William J. Burns, available online at: https://carnegieendowment.org/publications/interactive/back-channel/.

Report of the Iraq Inquiry (12 vols.) and additional evidence available online at: https://webarchive.nationalarchives.gov.uk/20171123123237/http://www.iraqinquiry.org.uk/.

Rumsfeld Papers, available online at: https://papers.rumsfeld.com.

Published Documentary Collections

Baker, James A., III, and Lee H. Hamilton. *The Iraq Study Group Report*. New York: Vintage, 2006.

Headquarters, Department of the Army, and Headquarters, U.S. Marine Corps. *Counterinsurgency, FM 3-24 / MWCP 3- 33.5*. Washington, DC, December 2006.

Public Papers of the Presidents of the United States: George W. Bush. 8 Vols. Washington, DC: United States Government Printing Office, 2001–2008.

Public Papers of the Presidents of the United States: Barack Obama. 8 Vols. Washington, DC: United States Government Printing Office, 2009–2016.

Rayburn, Joel D., and Frank K. Sobchak. *The U.S. Army in the Iraq War*. 2 vols. Carlisle, PA: United States Army War College Press, 2019.

Interviews/Personal Correspondence

Biddle, Stephen. Joint Strategic Assessment Team member (2007), senior advisor to the Central Command Assessment Team (2008–2009). Interview, Washington, DC, March 28, 2018.

Blinken, Antony J. National security advisor to the vice president (2009–2013). Telephone interview, June 8, 2018.

Brennan, John O. Homeland security advisor (2009–2013), CIA director (2013–2017). Telephone interview, July 19, 2018.

Cartwright, James E. Vice chairman, Joint Chiefs of Staff (2007–2011). Interview, Washington, DC, March 26, 2018.

Casey, George W., Jr. Commander, MNF-I (2004–2007), chief of staff, U.S. Army (2007–2011). Interview, Arlington, VA, March 16, 2018.

Crane, Conrad C. Lead author, *U.S. Army Counterinsurgency Field Manual, FM3-24* (2006). Interview, Carlisle, PA, March 23, 2018.

Flournoy, Michèle. Under secretary of defense for policy (2009–2012). Interview, Washington, DC, April 3, 2018.

Jeffrey, James F. Chargé d'affaires, U.S. Embassy, Baghdad (2004–2005), special advisor for Iraq, State Department (2006–2007), deputy national security advisor (2007–2008), U.S. ambassador to Iraq (2010–12). Telephone interview, June 28, 2018. Email correspondence, June 28, 2018.

Kahl, Colin H. Deputy assistant secretary of defense for the Middle East (2009–2011). Interview, Washington, DC, March 15, 2018.

Loftis, Robert. Senior advisor for security negotiations and agreements, State Department (2004–2007). Interview, Boston, MA, March 21, 2018.

Lute, Douglas. Director of operations, CENTCOM (2004–2006), director of operations, Joint Staff (2006–2007), deputy national security advisor (2007–2010). Interview, Rossyln, VA, April 3, 2018.

Mansoor, Peter R. Executive officer to commander, MNF-I (2007–2008). Email correspondence, March 20–April 30, 2020.

Mullen, Michael G. Chief of naval operations (2005–2007), chairman of the Joint Chiefs (2007–2011). Interview, Washington, DC, March 29, 2018.

Negroponte, John D. U.S. ambassador to the United Nations (2001–2004), U.S. ambassador to Iraq (2004–2005), director of national intelligence (2005–2007), deputy secretary of state (2007–2009). Interview, Washington, DC, March 27, 2018.

Odierno, Raymond T. Commander, MNC-I (2006–2008), commander, MNF-I/USF-I (2008–2010), chief of staff, U.S. Army (2011–2015). Zoom interview, May 1, 2020.

O'Sullivan, Meghan L. Assistant to Paul Bremer, Coalition Provisional Authority (2003–2004), deputy national security advisor for Iraq and Afghanistan (2004–2007). Phone interview, June 11, 2018. Email correspondence, January 4–February 1, 2019.

Petraeus, David H. Commander, MNF-I (2007–2008), commander, CENTCOM (2008–2010). Email correspondence, March 4–July 14, 2020.

Sattler, John F. Director of operations, CENTCOM (2003–2004), commander, 1st Marine Expeditionary Force (2004–2006), director of strategic plans and policy, Joint Staff (2006–2008). Telephone interview, July 25, 2018.

Sky, Emma. Political advisor to commanding general, MNF-I (2007–2010). Interview, Oxford, UK, February 26, 2018.

Zelikow, Philip D. Counselor to the secretary of state (2005–2006). Interview, Charlottesville, VA, March 19, 2018.

Additional anonymous interviewees, 2018–2020.

Memoirs

Bremer, L. Paul. *My Year in Iraq: The Struggle to Build a Future of Hope.* New York: Simon and Schuster, 2006.

Brennan, John O. *Undaunted: My Fight Against America's Enemies, at Home and Abroad.* New York: Celadon, 2020.

Bush, George W. *Decision Points.* New York: Crown, 2010.

Casey, George W., Jr. *Strategic Reflections: Operation Iraqi Freedom: July 2004–February 2007.* Washington, DC: National Defense University Press, 2012.

Cheney, Dick. *In My Time: A Personal and Political Memoir.* New York: Threshold, 2011.

Chollet, Derek. *The Long Game: How Obama Defied Washington and Redefined America's Role in the World.* New York: Public Affairs, 2016.

Crane, Conrad C. *Cassandra in Oz: Counterinsurgency and Future War.* Annapolis, MD: Naval Institute Press, 2016.

Feith, Douglas J. *War and Decision: Inside the Pentagon at the Dawn of the War on Terrorism.* New York: Harper Collins, 2008.

Franks, Tommy. *American Soldier.* New York: Harper Collins, 2009.

Gates, Robert M. *Duty: Memoirs of a Secretary at War.* New York: Knopf, 2014.

Gates, Robert M. *Exercise of Power: American Failures, Successes, and a New Path Forward in the Post-Cold War World.* New York: Alfred A. Knopf, 2020.

Greenstock, Jeremy. *Iraq: The Cost of War.* London: William Heinemann, 2016.

Hayden, Michael V. *Playing to the Edge: American Intelligence in the Age of Terror.* New York: Penguin, 2016.

Hill, Christopher R. *Outpost: A Diplomat at Work.* New York: Simon and Schuster, 2014.

Khalilzad, Zalmay. *The Envoy: From Kabul to the White House, My Journey Through a Turbulent World.* New York: St. Martin's Press, 2016.

Kilcullen, David. *Blood Year: Islamic State and the Failures of the War on Terror.* London: Hurst, 2016.

Mansoor, Peter R. *Surge: My Journey with General David Petraeus and the Remaking of the Iraq War.* New Haven, CT: Yale University Press, 2014.

Mattis, Jim, and Bing West. *Call Sign Chaos: Learning to Lead.* New York: Random House, 2019.

McClellan, Scott. *What Happened: Inside the Bush White House and Washington's Culture of Deception.* New York: Public Affairs, 2008.

Meyer, Christopher. *DC Confidential: The Controversial Memoirs of Britain's Ambassador to the US at the Time of 9/11 and the Iraq War.* London: Weidenfeld & Nicholson, 2005.

Obama, Barack. *A Promised Land.* New York: Crown, 2020.

Panetta, Leon. *Worthy Fights: A Memoir of Leadership in War and Peace.* New York: Penguin, 2014.

Rhodes, Ben. *The World as It Is: Inside the Obama White House.* London: Bodley Head, 2018.

Rice, Condoleezza. *Democracy: Stories from the Long Road to Freedom.* New York: Twelve, 2017.

Rice, Condoleezza. *No Higher Honor: A Memoir of My Years in Washington.* New York: Crown, 2011.

Rove, Karl. *Courage and Consequence: My Life as a Conservative in the Fight.* New York: Simon and Schuster, 2010.

Rumsfeld, Donald. *Known and Unknown: A Memoir.* New York: Penguin, 2011.

Sanchez, Ricardo S., and Donald T. Phillips. *Wiser in Battle: A Soldier's Story.* New York: Harper Collins, 2008.

Sky, Emma. *The Unravelling: High Hopes and Missed Opportunities in Iraq.* London: Atlantic, 2015.

SECONDARY SOURCES

Abrahms, Max, and Philip B. K. Potter. "Explaining Terrorism: Leadership Deficits and Militant Group Tactics." *International Organization* 69, no. 2 (2015): 311–342.

Aldrich, John H. Christopher Gelpi, Peter Feaver, Jason Reifler, and Kristin Thompson Sharp. "Foreign Policy and the Electoral Connection." *Annual Review of Political Science* 9 (2006): 477–502.

Aldrich, John H., John L. Sullivan, and Eugene Borgida. "Foreign Affairs and Issue Voting: Do Presidential Candidates 'Waltz Before a Blind Audience?'" *American Political Science Review* 83, no. 1 (1989): 123–141.

Allen, Susan Hannah, and Carla Martinez Machain. "Choosing Air Strikes." *Journal of Global Security Studies* 3, no. 2 (2018): 150–162.

Allison, Graham T., and Phillip Zelikow. *Essence of Decision: Explaining the Cuban Missile Crisis.* 2nd ed. New York: Longman, 1999.

Anderson, David L. *Vietnamization: Politics, Strategy, Legacy.* Lanham, MD: Rowman & Littlefield, 2020.

Armacost, Michael H. *Ballots, Bullets, and Bargains: American Foreign Policy and Presidential Elections.* New York: Columbia University Press, 2015.

Arreguin-Toft, Ivan. "How the Weak Win Wars: A Theory of Asymmetric Conflict." *International Security* 26, no. 1 (2001): 93–128.

Asselin, Pierre. *Vietnam's American War: A History.* Cambridge: Cambridge University Press, 2018.

Auerswald, David P. *Disarmed Democracies: Domestic Institutions and the Use of Force.* Ann Arbor: University of Michigan Press, 2000.

Bacevich, Andrew J. *America's War for the Greater Middle East: A Military History.* New York: Random House, 2016.

Badie, Dina. "Groupthink, Iraq, and the War on Terror: Explaining US Policy Shift Toward Iraq." *Foreign Policy Analysis* 6, no. 4 (2010): 277–296.

Baker, Peter. *Days of Fire: Bush and Cheney in the White House.* New York: Doubleday, 2013.

Barnes, Robert. "Branding an Aggressor: The Commonwealth, the United Nations and Chinese Intervention in the Korean War, November 1950–January 1951." *Journal of Strategic Studies* 33, no. 2, (2010) 231–253.

Barnes, Robert. "Ending the Korean War: Reconsidering the Importance of Eisenhower's Election." *RUSI Journal* 158, no. 3 (2013): 78–87.

Barnes, Robert. *The US, the UN and the Korean War: Communism in the Far East and the American Struggle for Hegemony in the Cold War.* London: I. B. Tauris, 2014.

Barnhart, Joslyn N., and Robert F. Trager. *The Suffragist Peace: How Women Shape the Politics of War.* New York: Oxford University Press, forthcoming.

Barnhart, Joslyn N., Robert F. Trager, Elizabeth N. Saunders, and Allan Dafoe. "The Suffragist Peace." *International Organization* 74, no. 4 (2020): 633–670.

Barrett, David M. *Uncertain Warriors: Lyndon Johnson and his Vietnam Advisers.* Lawrence: University Press of Kansas, 1993.

Basha I Novosejt, Aurélie. *"I Made Mistakes": Robert McNamara's Vietnam War Policy, 1960–1968.* Cambridge: Cambridge University Press, 2019.

Bator, Francis M. "No Good Choices: LBJ and the Vietnam/Great Society Connection." *Diplomatic History* 32, no. 3, (2008): 309–340.

Baum, Matthew A. "The Constituent Foundations of the Rally-Round-the-Flag Phenomenon." *International Studies Quarterly* 46, no. 2 (2002): 263–298.

Baum, Matthew A., and Tim Groeling. *War Stories: The Causes and Consequences of Public Views of War.* Princeton, NJ: Princeton University Press, 2010.

Baum, Matthew A., and Philip B. K. Potter. "The Relationships Between Mass Media, Public Opinion, and Foreign Policy: Toward a Theoretical Synthesis." *Annual Review of Political Science* 11 (2008): 39–65.

Baum, Matthew A., and Philip B. K. Potter. *War and Democratic Constraint: How the Public Influences Foreign Policy.* Princeton, NJ: Princeton University Press, 2015.

Bennett, Scott D., and Allan C. Stam III. "The Declining Advantages of Democracy: A Combined Model of War Outcomes and Duration." *Journal of Conflict Resolution* 42, no. 3 (1998): 344–366.

Berinsky, Adam J. *In Time of War: Understanding American Public Opinion from World War II to Iraq*. Chicago: University of Chicago Press, 2009.

Berman, Larry. *Lyndon Johnson's War*. New York: W. W. Norton, 1989.

Berman, Larry. *No Peace, No Honor: Nixon, Kissinger, and Betrayal in Vietnam*. New York: Free Press, 2001.

Bessner, Daniel, and Fredrik Logevall. "Recentering the United States in the Historiography of American Foreign Relations." *Texas National Security Review* 3, no. 2 (Spring 2020): 38–55.

Betts, Richard K., Michael C. Desch, and Peter D. Feaver. "Correspondence: Civilians, Soldiers, and the Iraq Surge Decision." *International Security* 36, no. 3 (2011): 179–199.

Biddle, Stephen, Jeffrey A. Friedman, and Jacob N. Shapiro. "Testing the Surge: Why Did Violence Decline in Iraq in 2007?" *International Security* 37, no. 1 (2012): 7–40.

Blomstedt, Larry. *Truman, Congress, and Korea: The Politics of America's First Undeclared War*. Lexington: University Press of Kentucky, 2016.

Bolton, John. *The Room Where It Happened: A White House Memoir*. New York: Simon and Schuster, 2020.

Brands, H. W. *The General vs. the President: MacArthur and Truman on the Brink of Nuclear War*. New York: Doubleday, 2016.

Brands, Hal, and Peter Feaver. "Was the Rise of ISIS Inevitable?" *Survival* 59, no. 3 (2017): 7–54.

Brennan, Richard R., Jr., Charles P. Ries, Larry Hanauer, Ben Connable, Terrence Kelly, Michael J. McNerney, Stephanie Young, Jason H. Campbell, and K. Scott McMahon. *Ending the U.S. War in Iraq: The Final Transition, Operational Maneuver, and Disestablishment of United States Forces—Iraq*. Santa Monica, CA: RAND Corporation, 2013.

Brigham, Robert K. *Reckless: Henry Kissinger and the Tragedy of Vietnam*. New York: Public Affairs, 2018.

Broadwater, Jeff. *Adlai Stevenson and American Politics: The Odyssey of a Cold War Liberal*. New York: Twayne, 1994.

Brody, Richard. *Assessing the President: The Media, Elite Opinion, and Public Support*. Stanford, CA: Stanford University Press, 1991.

Brooks, Risa. "Paradoxes of Professionalism: Rethinking Civil-Military Relations in the United States." *International Security* 44, no. 4 (Spring 2020): 7–44.

Bueno de Mesquita, Bruce, and David Lalman. *War and Reason: Domestic and International Imperatives*. New Haven, CT: Yale University Press, 1992.

Bueno De Mesquita, Bruce, James D. Morrow, Randolph M. Siverson, and Alastair Smith. "An Institutional Explanation of the Democratic Peace." *American Political Science Review* 93, no. 4 (1999): 791–807.

Bueno de Mesquita, Bruce, and James L. Ray. "The National Interest Versus Individual Political Ambition." In *The Scourge of War: New Extensions on an Old Problem*, edited by Paul F. Diehl, 94–119. Ann Arbor: University of Michigan Press, 2004.

Bueno de Mesquita, Bruce, Alastair Smith, Randolph M. Siverson, and James D. Morrow. *The Logic of Political Survival*. Cambridge, MA: MIT Press, 2003.

Bundy, William. *A Tangled Web: The Making of Foreign Policy in the Nixon Presidency*. New York: Hill and Wang, 1998.

Busby, Joshua, Craig Kafura, Jonathan Monten, and Jordan Tama. "Multilateralism and the Use of Force: Experimental Evidence on the Views of Foreign Policy Elites." *Foreign Policy Analysis* 16, no. 1 (January 2020): 118–129.

Byman, Daniel L., and Kenneth M. Pollack. "Let Us Now Praise Great Men: Bringing the Statesman Back In." *International Security* 25, no. 4 (2001): 107–146.

Campbell, Kurt M., and James B. Steinberg. *Difficult Transitions: Foreign Policy Troubles at the Outset of Presidential Power.* Washington, DC: Brookings Institution Press, 2009.

Canes-Wrone, Brandice. *Who Leads Whom? Presidents, Policy, and the Public.* Chicago: University of Chicago Press, 2006.

Caridi, Ronald J. *The Korean War and American Politics: The Republican Party as a Case Study.* Philadelphia: University of Pennsylvania Press, 1968.

Carson, Austin. *Secret Wars: Covert Conflict in International Politics.* Princeton, NJ: Princeton University Press, 2018.

Carter, Jeff, and Timothy Nordstrom. "Term Limits, Leader Preferences, and Interstate Conflict." *International Studies Quarterly* 61, no. 3 (2017): 721–735.

Carter, Jimmy. *White House Diary.* New York: Farrar, Straus and Giroux, 2010.

Casey, Steven. *Cautious Crusade: Franklin D. Roosevelt, American Public Opinion, and the War Against Nazi Germany.* New York: Oxford University Press, 2001.

Casey, Steven. "Confirming the Cold War Consensus: Eisenhower and the 1952 Election. In *US Presidential Elections and Foreign Policy: Candidates, Campaigns, and Global Politics from FDR to Bill Clinton*, edited by Andrew Johnstone and Andrew Priest, 82–104. Lexington: University Press of Kentucky, 2017.

Casey, Steven. *Selling the Korean War: Propaganda, Politics, and Public Opinion in the United States, 1950-1953.* New York: Oxford University Press, 2008.

Casey, Steven. *The War Beat, Europe: The American Media at War Against Nazi Germany.* New York: Oxford University Press, 2017.

Casey, Steven. *The War Beat, Pacific: The American Media at War Against Japan.* New York: Oxford University Press, 2021.

Casey, Steven. *When Soldiers Fall: How Americans Have Confronted Combat Losses from World War I to Afghanistan.* New York: Oxford University Press, 2014.

Caverley, Jonathan D. "The Myth of Military Myopia: Democracy, Small Wars, and Vietnam." *International Security* 34, no. 3 (2009): 119–157.

Caverley, Jonathan D. *Democratic Militarism: Voting, Wealth, and War.* Cambridge: Cambridge University Press, 2014.

Chan, Steve, and William Safran. "Public Opinion as a Constraint Against War: Democracies' Responses to Operation Iraqi Freedom." *Foreign Policy Analysis* 2, no. 2 (April 2006): 137–156.

Chiozza, Giacomo. "Presidents on the Cycle: Elections, Audience Costs, and Coercive Diplomacy." *Conflict Management and Peace Science* 34, no. 1 (2017): 3–26.

Chiozza, Giacomo, and Hein E. Goemans. "Peace Through Insecurity: Tenure and International Conflict." *Journal of Conflict Resolution* 47, no. 4 (2003): 443–467.

Christensen, Thomas J. *Useful Adversaries: Grand Strategy, Domestic Mobilization, and Sino-American Conflict, 1947-1958.* Princeton, NJ: Princeton University Press, 1996.

Christenson, Dino P., and Douglas L. Kriner. *The Myth of the Imperial Presidency.* Chicago: University of Chicago Press, 2020.

Clark, David H. "Can Strategic Interaction Divert Diversionary Behavior? A Model of US Conflict Propensity." *Journal of Politics* 65, no. 4 (2003): 1013–1039.

Clark, David H., Benjamin O. Fordham, and Timothy Nordstrom. "Preying on the Misfortune of Others: When Do States Exploit Their Opponents' Domestic Troubles?" *Journal of Politics* 73, no. 1 (2011): 248–264.

Clark, David H., and Timothy Nordstrom. "Democratic Variants and Democratic Variance: How Domestic Constraints Shape Interstate Conflict." *Journal of Politics* 67, no. 1 (2005): 250–270.

Cochran, Shawn T. "Gambling for Resurrection Versus Bleeding the Army: Explaining Risky Behavior in Failing Wars." *Security Studies* 27, no. 2 (2018): 204–232.

Cohen, Bernard C. *The Public's Impact on Foreign Policy.* Boston: Little Brown, 1973.

Colaresi, Michael. "When Doves Cry: International Rivalry, Unreciprocated Cooperation, and Leadership Turnover." *American Journal of Political Science* 48, no. 3 (July 2004): 555–570.

Conconi, Paola, Nicolas Sahuguet, and Maurizio Zanardi. "Democratic Peace and Electoral Accountability." *Journal of the European Economic Association* 12, no. 4 (2014): 997–1028.

Craig, Campbell, and Fredrik Logevall. *America's Cold War: The Politics of Insecurity.* Cambridge, MA: Harvard University Press, 2009.

Croco, Sarah E. "The Decider's Dilemma: Leader Culpability, War Outcomes, and Domestic Punishment." *American Political Science Review* 105, no. 3 (2011): 457–477.

Daddis, Gregory A. "Choosing Progress: Evaluating the 'Salesmanship' of the Vietnam War in 1967." In *Assessing War: The Challenge of Measuring Success and Failure,* edited by Leo J. Blanken, Hy Rothstein, and Jason J. Lepore, 173–194. Washington, DC: Georgetown University Press, 2015.

Daddis, Gregory A. *Withdrawal: Reassessing America's Final Years in Vietnam.* New York: Oxford University Press, 2017.

Dallek, Robert. *Flawed Giant: Lyndon Johnson and his Times, 1961–1973.* New York: Oxford University Press, 1998.

Dallek, Robert. *Nixon and Kissinger.* New York: Harper Collins, 2007.

Debs, Alexandre, and Nuno P. Monteiro. "Known Unknowns: Power Shifts, Uncertainty, and War." *International Organization* 68, no. 1 (2014): 1–31.

Desch, Michael C. "Bush and the Generals." *Foreign Affairs,* May–June 2007.

Divine, Robert A. *Foreign Policy and US Presidential Elections.* 2 vols. New York: New Viewpoints, 1974.

Downes, Alexander B. "How Smart and Tough Are Democracies? Reassessing Theories of Democratic Victory in War." *International Security* 3, no. 4 (2009): 9–51.

Downs, George W., and David M. Rocke. "Conflict, Agency, and Gambling for Resurrection: The Principal-Agent Problem Goes to War." *American Journal of Political Science* 38, no. 2 (1994): 362–380.

Doyle, Michael W. "Kant, Liberal Legacies, and Foreign Affairs." *Philosophy & Public Affairs* 12, no. 3 (1983): 205–235.

Doyle, Michael W. "Kant, Liberal Legacies, and Foreign Affairs, Part 2." *Philosophy & Public Affairs* 12, no. 4 (1983): 323–353.

Draper, Robert. *To Start a War: How the Bush Administration Took America Into Iraq.* New York: Penguin, 2020.

Druckman, James N., and Lawrence R. Jacobs. "Lumpers and Splitters: The Public Opinion Information that Politicians Collect and Use." *International Journal of Public Opinion Quarterly* 70, no. 4 (2006): 453–476.

Druckman, James N., and Lawrence R. Jacobs. *Who Governs? Presidents, Public Opinion, and Manipulation.* Chicago: University of Chicago Press, 2015.

Drury, A. Cooper, L. Marvin Overby, Adrian Ang, and Yitan Li. "'Pretty Prudent' or Rhetorically Responsive? The American Public's Support for Military Action." *Political Research Quarterly* 63, no. 1 (March 2010): 83–96.

Dueck, Colin. *The Obama Doctrine: American Grand Strategy Today.* New York: Oxford University Press, 2015.

Dunn, David Hastings. "'Quacking Like a Duck?' Bush II and Presidential Power in the Second Term." *International Affairs* 82, no. 1 (2006): 95–120.

Dyson, Stephen B. "George W. Bush, the Surge, and Presidential Leadership." *Political Science Quarterly* 125, no. 4 (2011): 557–585.

Dyson, Stephen B. "'Stuff Happens': Donald Rumsfeld and the Iraq War." *Foreign Policy Analysis* 5, no. 4 (2009): 327–347.

Edwards, George C. *On Deaf Ears: The Limits of the Bully Pulpit.* New Haven, CT: Yale University Press, 2006.

Ellsberg, Daniel. *Papers on the War.* New York: Simon and Schuster, 1972.

Estes, Kenneth W. *U.S. Marine Corps Operations in Iraq, 2003-2006.* Quantico, VA: United States Marine Corps History Division, 2009.

Farnham, Barbara. "Impact of the Political Context on Foreign Policy Decision-Making." *Political Psychology* 25, no. 3 (2004): 441–463.

Farrell, John A. *Richard Nixon: The Life.* New York: Doubleday, 2017.

Fawcett, Louise. "The Iraq War Ten Years On: Assessing the Fallout." *International Affairs* 89, no. 2 (March 2013): 325–343.

Fawcett, Louise. "The Iraq War 20 Years On: Towards a New Regional Architecture." *International Affairs* 99, no. 2 (March 2023): iiad002. https://doi.org/10.1093/ia/iiad002.

Fawcett, Louise, and Andrew Payne. "Stuck on a Hostile Path? US Policy Towards Iran Since the Revolution." *Contemporary Politics* 29, no. 1 (February 2023): 1–21.

Fazal, Tanisha M. "Dead Wrong? Battle Deaths, Military Medicine, and Exaggerated Reports of War's Demise." *International Security* 39, no. 1 (Summer 2014): 95–125.

Fazal, Tanisha M. "Life and Limb: New Estimates of Casualty Aversion in the United States." *International Studies Quarterly* 65, no. 1 (2021): 160–172.

Fearon, James D. "Domestic Political Audiences and the Escalation of International Disputes." *American Political Science Review* 88, no. 3 (1994): 577–592.

Feaver, Peter D. "Anatomy of the Surge." *Commentary*, April 2008.

Feaver, Peter D. "The Right to Be Right: Civil-Military Relations and the Iraq Surge Decision." *International Security* 35, no. 4 (2011): 87–125.

Feaver, Peter D., and Richard H. Kohn, editors. *Soldiers and Civilians: The Civil-Military Gaps and American National Security.* Cambridge, MA: MIT Press, 2001.

Fiorina, Morris P. *Retrospective Voting in American National Elections.* New Haven, CT: Yale University Press, 1981.

Fishel, Jeff. *Presidents and Promises: From Campaign Pledge to Presidential Performance.* Washington, DC: CQ Press, 1985.

Flibbert, Andrew. "The Road to Baghdad: Ideas and Intellectuals in Explanations of the Iraq War." *Security Studies* 15, no. 2 (2006): 310–352.

Flores-Macías, Gustavo A., and Sarah E. Kreps. "Borrowing Support for War: The Effect of War Finance on Public Attitudes Toward Conflict." *Journal of Conflict Resolution* 61, no. 5 (2017): 997–1020.

Foot, Rosemary. *A Substitute for Victory: The Politics of Peacemaking at the Korean Armistice Talks*. Ithaca, NY: Cornell University Press, 1990.

Foot, Rosemary. *The Wrong War: American Policy and the Dimensions of the Korean Conflict, 1950-1953*. Ithaca, NY: Cornell University Press, 1985.

Fordham, Benjamin O. "More than Mixed Results: What We Have Learned from Quantitative Research on the Diversionary Hypothesis." In *Oxford Encyclopedia of Empirical International Relations Theory*, vol. 2, edited by William R. Thompson, 549–564. New York: Oxford University Press, 2018.

Fordham, Benjamin O. "Strategic Conflict Avoidance and the Diversionary Use of Force." *Journal of Politics* 67, no. 1 (February 2005): 132–153.

Fordham, Benjamin O., and Thomas C. Walker. "Kantian Liberalism, Regime Type, and Military Resource Allocation: Do Democracies Spend Less?" *International Studies Quarterly* 49, no. 1 (2005): 141–157.

Foyle, Douglas C. *Counting the Public In: Presidents, Public Opinion, and Foreign Policy*. New York: Columbia University Press, 1999.

Foyle, Douglas C. "Public Opinion and Foreign Policy: Elite Beliefs as a Mediating Variable." *International Studies Quarterly* 41, no. 1 (1997): 141–169.

Freedman, Lawrence. *Command: The Politics of Military Operations*. New York: Oxford University Press, 2022.

Friedman, Jeffrey A. *The Commander-in-Chief Test: How the Politics of Image-Making Shapes U.S. Foreign Policy*. Unpublished book manuscript, July 2022.

Friedman, Jeffrey A. "Issue-Image Tradeoffs and the Politics of Foreign Policy: How Leaders Use Foreign Policy Positions to Shape Their Personal Images." *World Politics* 75 (forthcoming).

Friedrichs, Gordon M. and Jordan Tama. "Polarization and US Foreign Policy: Key Debates and New Findings." *International Politics* 59 (2022): 767–785.

Gadarian, Shana K. "Foreign Policy at the Ballot Box: How Citizens Use Foreign Policy to Judge and Choose Candidates." *Journal of Politics* 72, no. 4 (2010): 1046–1062.

Gaddis, John Lewis. *Strategies of Containment: A Critical Appraisal of American National Security Policy During the Cold War*. New York: Oxford University Press, 2005.

Garofano, John. "Tragedy or Choice in Vietnam? Learning to Think Outside the Archival Box: A Review Essay." *International Security* 26, no. 4 (2002): 143–168.

Gartner, Scott Sigmund. "The Multiple Effects of Casualties on Public Support for War: An Experimental Approach." *American Political Science Review* 102, no. 1 (2008): 95–106.

Gartner, Scott Sigmund, and Gary M. Segura. "All Politics Are Still Local: The Iraq War and the 2006 Midterm Elections." *PS: Political Science & Politics* 41, no. 1 (2008): 95–100.

Gartner, Scott Sigmund, and Gary M. Segura. *Costly Calculations: A Theory of War, Casualties, and Politics*. Cambridge: Cambridge University Press, 2021.

Gartner, Scott Sigmund, and Randolph M. Siverson. "War Expansion and War Out-come." *Journal of Conflict Resolution* 40, no. 1 (1996): 4–15.

Gaubatz, Kurt Taylor. "Election Cycles and War." *Journal of Conflict Resolution* 35, no. 2 (1991): 212–244.

Gaubatz, Kurt Taylor. *Elections and War: The Electoral Incentive in the Democratic Politics of War and Peace*. Stanford, CA: Stanford University Press, 1999.

Gelb, Leslie H., and Richard K. Betts. *The Irony of Vietnam: The System Worked*. Washington, DC: Brookings Institution Press, 1979.

Gelpi, Christopher, Peter D. Feaver, and Jason Reifler. "Iraq the Vote: Retrospective and Prospective Foreign Policy Judgments on Candidate Choice and Casualty Tolerance." *Political Behavior* 29, no. 2 (June 2007): 151–174.

Gelpi, Christopher, Peter D. Feaver, and Jason Reifler. *Paying the Human Costs of War: American Public Opinion and Casualties in Military Conflicts*. Princeton, NJ: Princeton University Press, 2009.

Gelpi, Christopher, Peter D. Feaver, and Jason Reifler. "Success Matters: Casualty Sensitivity and the War in Iraq." *International Security* 30, no. 3 (2006): 7–46.

Gentile, Gian. *Wrong Turn: America's Deadly Embrace of Counterinsurgency*. New York: Free Press, 2013.

George, Alexander L., and Eric Stern. "Presidential Management Styles and Models." In *Presidential Personality and Performance*, edited by Alexander L. George and Juliet L. George, 199–280. Boulder, CO: Westview Press, 1998.

Gerges, Fawaz A. *Obama and the Middle East: The End of America's Moment?* London: Macmillan, 2012.

Geys, Benny. "Wars, Presidents, and Popularity: The Political Cost(s) of War Re-examined." *Public Opinion Quarterly* 74, no. 2 (2010): 357–374.

Gift, Thomas, and Jonathan Monten. "Who's Out of Touch? Media Misperception of Public Opinion on US Foreign Policy." *Foreign Policy Analysis* 17, no. 1 (January 2021): oraa015. https://doi.org/10.1093/fpa/oraa015.

Golby, Jim, Lindsay P. Cohn, and Peter D. Feaver. "Thanks for Your Service: Civilian and Veteran Attitudes After Fifteen Years of War." In *Warriors and Citizens: American Views of Our Military*, edited by Kori Schake and Jim Mattis, 97–141. Stanford, CA: Hoover Institution Press, 2016.

Golby, James, Peter Feaver, and Kyle Dropp. "Elite Military Cues and Public Opinion About the Use of Military Force." *Armed Forces & Society* 44, no. 1 (2017): 44–71.

Goldberg, Jeffrey. "The Obama Doctrine." *The Atlantic*, April 2016.

Goldgeier, James, and Elizabeth N. Saunders. "The Unconstrained Presidency: Checks and Balances Eroded Long before Trump." *Foreign Affairs*, September–October.

Goldstein, Gordon M. *Lessons in Disaster: McGeorge Bundy and the Path to War in Vietnam*. New York: Henry Holt, 2008.

Goodwin, Doris Kearns. *Lyndon Johnson and the American Dream*. New York: Harper and Row, 1976.

Gordon, Michael, and Bernard Trainor. *Cobra II: The Inside Story of the Invasion and Occupation of Iraq*. New York: Vintage, 2006.

Gordon, Michael, and Bernard Trainor. *The Endgame: The Inside Story of the Struggle for Iraq, From George W. Bush to Barack Obama*. New York: Pantheon, 2012.

Gowa, Joanne. "Politics at the Water's Edge: Parties, Voters, and the Use of Force Abroad." *International Organization* 52, no. 2 (1998): 307–324.

Greene, John Robert. *The Crusade: The Presidential Election of 1952.* Lanham, MD: University Press of America, 1985.

Greenstein, Fred I. *The Hidden-Hand Presidency: Eisenhower as Leader.* New York: Basic Books, 1982.

Guisinger, Alexandra, and Elizabeth N. Saunders. "Mapping the Boundaries of Elite Cues: How Elites Shape Mass Opinion Across International Issues." *International Studies Quarterly* 61, no. 2 (2017): 425–442.

Hafner-Burton, Emilie M., Stephan Haggard, David A. Lake, and David G. Victor. "The Behavioral Revolution and International Relations." *International Organization* 71, Supplement S1 (2017): S1–S31.

Halberstam, David. *The Best and the Brightest.* New York: Random House, 1972.

Hamilton, Alexander, James Madison, and John Jay. *The Federalist Papers.* Edited by Michael A. Genovese. New York: Palgrave Macmillan, 2009.

Hanhimäki, Jussi M. "Global Visions and Parochial Politics: The Persistent Dilemma of the 'American Century.'" *Diplomatic History* 27, no. 4 (2003): 423–447.

Harris, Louis. *Is There a Republican Majority? Political Trends, 1952-1956.* New York: Harper, 1954.

Hastings, Max. *Vietnam: An Epic History of a Tragic War.* London: William Collins, 2018.

Haynes, Kyle. "Lame Ducks and Coercive Diplomacy: Do Executive Term Limits Reduce the Effectiveness of Democratic Threats?" *Journal of Conflict Resolution* 56, no. 5 (2012): 771–798.

Heffington, Colton. "Do Hawks and Doves Deliver? The Words and Deeds of Foreign Policy in Democracies." *Foreign Policy Analysis* 14, no. 1 (January 2018): 64–85.

Herring, George C. *America's Longest War: The United States and Vietnam, 1950-1975.* 4th ed. New York: McGraw Hill, 2002.

Herring, George C. *LBJ and Vietnam: A Different Kind of War.* Austin: University of Texas Press, 1994.

Herring, George C. "Nixon's 'Laotian Gamble:' Lam Son 719 as a Turning Point in the Vietnam War." *Army History* 119 (Spring 2021): 6–19.

Hess, Gregory D., and Athanasios Orphanides. "War Politics: An Economic, Rational-Voter Framework." *American Economic Review* 85, no. 4 (1995): 828–846.

Higgins, Trumbull. *Korea and the Fall of MacArthur: A Precis in Limited War.* New York: Oxford University Press, 1960.

Hinckley, Ronald H. *People, Polls and Policy Makers: American Public Opinion and National Security.* New York: Free Press, 1992.

Holsti, Ole R. *Public Opinion and American Foreign Policy.* Ann Arbor: University of Michigan Press, 2004.

Horowitz, Michael C., and Matthew Fuhrmann. "Studying Leaders and Military Conflict: Conceptual Framework and Research Agenda." *Journal of Conflict Resolution* 62, no. 10 (2018): 2072–2086.

Horowitz, Michael C., and Matthew S. Levendusky. "Drafting Support for War: Conscription and Mass Support for Warfare." *Journal of Politics* 73, no. 2 (April 2011): 524–534.

Horowitz, Michael C., Allan C. Stam, and Cali M. Ellis. *Why Leaders Fight*. Cambridge: Cambridge University Press, 2015.

Howell, William G., and Jon C. Pevehouse. *While Dangers Gather: Congressional Checks on Presidential War Powers*. Princeton, NJ: Princeton University Press, 2007.

Hudson, Valerie M. "Foreign Policy Analysis: Actor-Specific Theory and the Ground of International Relations." *Foreign Policy Analysis* 1, no. 1 (2005): 1–30.

Hughes, Ken. *Chasing Shadows: The Nixon Tapes, the Chennault Affair, and the Origins of Watergate*. Charlottesville: University of Virginia Press, 2014.

Hughes, Ken. *Fatal Politics: The Nixon Tapes, the Vietnam War, and the Casualties of Reelection*. Charlottesville: University of Virginia Press, 2015.

Hunt, Michael H. "Beijing and the Korean Crisis, June 1950–June 1951." *Political Science Quarterly* 107, no. 3 (1992): 473.

Huth, Paul K., and Todd L. Allee. "Domestic Political Accountability and the Escalation and Settlement of International Disputes." *Journal of Conflict Resolution* 46, no. 6 (2002): 754–790.

Hyde, Susan D., and Elizabeth N. Saunders. "Recapturing Regime Type in International Relations: Leaders, Institutions, and Agency Space." *International Organization* 74, no. 2 (Spring 2020): 363–395.

Jacobs, Lawrence R., and Robert Y. Shapiro. *Politicians Don't Pander: Political Manipulation and the Loss of Democratic Responsiveness*. Chicago: University of Chicago Press, 2000.

Jacobson, Gary C. "George W. Bush, the Iraq War, and the Election of Barack Obama." *Presidential Studies Quarterly* 40, no. 2 (2010): 207–224.

Jacobson, Gary C. "The President's Effect on Partisan Attitudes." *Presidential Studies Quarterly* 42, no. 4 (2012): 683–718.

James, William D. "Influencing the United States: Is the Game Worth the Candle for Junior Allies?" *International Politics* 59, no. 6 (2021): 1029–1044.

Jentleson, Bruce W. "The Pretty Prudent Public: Post Post-Vietnam American Opinion on the Use of Military Force." *International Studies Quarterly* 36, no. 1 (1992): 49–74.

Jervis, Robert. "Do Leaders Matter and How Would We Know?" *Security Studies* 22, no. 2 (2013): 153–179.

Jervis, Robert. "The Politics of Troop Withdrawal: Salted Peanuts, the Commitment Trap, and Buying Time." *Diplomatic History* 34, no. 3 (2010) 507–516.

Johns, Andrew L. *The Price of Loyalty: Hubert Humphrey's Vietnam Conflict*. Lanham, MD: Rowman & Littlefield, 2020.

Johns, Andrew L. *Vietnam's Second Front: Domestic Politics, the Republican Party, and the War*. Lexington: University Press of Kentucky, 2010.

Johnson, Dominic D. P. *Overconfidence and War*. Cambridge, MA: Harvard University Press, 2004.

Johnson, Dominic D. P., and Dominic Tierney. *Failing to Win: Perceptions of Victory and Defeat in International Politics*. Cambridge, MA: Harvard University Press, 2006.

Johnston, Patrick B., and Brian R. Urlacher. *Explaining the Duration of Counterinsurgency Campaigns*. Arlington, VA: RAND Corporation, 2012.

Johnstone, Andrew, and Andrew Priest. *US Presidential Elections and Foreign Policy: Candidates, Campaigns, and Global Politics from FDR to Bill Clinton*. Lexington: University Press of Kentucky, 2017.

Jordan, Jenna. *Leadership Decapitation of Terrorist Organizations: Strategic Decapitation of Terrorist Organizations.* Stanford, CA: Stanford University Press, 2019.

Kaag, John, and Sarah Kreps. *Drone Warfare.* Cambridge: Polity, 2014.

Kaarbo, Juliet. "A Foreign Policy Analysis Perspective on the Domestic Politics Turn in IR Theory." *International Studies Review* 17, no. 2 (2015): 189–216.

Kagan Frederick, W. *Finding the Target.* New York: Encounter, 2006.

Kahl, Colin H., and William E. Odom. "When to Leave Iraq." *Foreign Affairs,* July–August 2008.

Kant, Immanuel. *Perpetual Peace and Other Essays.* Indianapolis: Hackett Publishing, 1983 [1796].

Karol, David, and Edward Miguel. "The Electoral Cost of War: Iraq Casualties and the 2004 US Presidential Election." *Journal of Politics* 69, no. 3 (2007): 633–648.

Katz, Andrew Z. "Public Opinion and Foreign Policy: The Nixon Administration and the Pursuit of Peace with Honor in Vietnam." *Presidential Studies Quarterly* 27, no. 3 (1997): 496–513.

Kaufman, Burton I. *The Korean War: Challenges in Crisis, Credibility, and Command.* Philadelphia: Temple University Press, 1984.

Kaufmann, Chaim. "Threat Inflation and the Failure of the Marketplace of Ideas: The Selling of the Iraq War." *International Security* 29, no. 1 (2004): 5–48.

Kenealy, Andrew. "Barack Obama and the Politics of Military Force, 2009–2012." *Presidential Studies Quarterly* 52, no. 4 (December 2022): 785–815.

Kertzer, Joshua D. "Re-assessing Elite-Public Gaps in Political Behavior." *American Journal of Political Science* 66, no. 3 (July 2022): 539–553.

Kertzer, Joshua D., Joshua Busby, Jonathan Monten, Jordan Tama, and Craig Kafura. "Elite Misperceptions and the Domestic Politics of Conflict." Working paper, January 21, 2022. https://jkertzer.sites.fas.harvard.edu/Research_files/NATO -Misperceptions-Web.pdf.

Kertzer, Joshua D., and Thomas Zeitzoff. "A Bottom-Up Theory of Public Opinion About Foreign Policy." *American Journal of Political Science* 61, no. 3 (July 2017): 543–558.

Key, V. O. *Public Opinion and American Democracy.* New York: Knopf, 1961.

Khong, Yuen Foong. *Analogies at War: Korea, Munich, Dien Bien Phu, and the Vietnam Decisions of 1965.* Princeton, NJ: Princeton University Press, 1992.

Kimball, Jeffrey. *Nixon's Vietnam War.* Lawrence: University Press of Kansas, 1998.

Kimball, Jeffrey. *The Vietnam War Files: Uncovering the Secret History of the Nixon-Era Strategy.* Lawrence: University Press of Kansas, 2004.

Knecht, Thomas. *Paying Attention to Foreign Affairs: How Public Opinion Affects Presidential Decision Making.* University Park: Pennsylvania State University Press, 2010.

Knecht, Thomas, and M. Stephen Weatherford. "Public Opinion and Foreign Policy: The Stages of Presidential Decision Making." *International Studies Quarterly* 50, no. 3 (2006): 705–727.

Koch, Michael T., and Stephen P. Nicholson. "Death and Turnout: The Human Costs of War and Voter Participation in Democracies." *American Journal of Political Science* 60, no. 4 (October 2016): 932–946.

Krasner, Stephen D. "Are Bureaucracies Important? (Or Allison Wonderland?)." *Foreign Policy* 7 (Summer 1972): 159–179.

Krebs, Ronald R., Robert Ralston, and Aaron Rapport. "No Right to Be Wrong: What Americans Think About Civil-Military Relations." *Perspectives on Politics*, March 11, 2021. doi:10.1017/S1537592721000013.

Kreps, Sarah. *Taxing Wars: The American Way of War Finance and the Decline of Democracy.* New York: Oxford University Press, 2018.

Kreps, Sarah E., Elizabeth N. Saunders, and Kenneth A. Schultz. "The Ratification Premium: Hawks, Doves, and Arms Control." *World Politics* 70, no. 4 (October 2018): 479–514.

Kriner, Douglas L. *After the Rubicon: Congress, Presidents, and the Politics of Waging War.* Chicago: University of Chicago Press, 2010.

Kull, Steven, I. M. Destler, and Clay Ramsay. *The Foreign Policy Gap: How Policymakers Misread the Public. Program on International Policy Attitudes.* College Park, MD: Center for International and Security Studies at Maryland, 1997.

Kull, Steven, and Clay Ramsay. "How Policymakers Misperceive US Public Opinion on Foreign Policy." In *Navigating Public Opinion: Polls, Policy and the Future of American Democracy*, edited by Jeff Manza, Fay Lomax Cook, and Benjamin I. Page, 201–218. New York: Oxford University Press, 2002.

LaFeber, Walter. *The Deadly Bet: LBJ, Vietnam and the 1968 Election.* Lanham, MD: Rowman & Littlefield, 2005.

LaFeber, Walter. "Johnson, Vietnam and Tocqueville." In *Lyndon Johnson Confronts the World: American Foreign Policy, 1963-1968*, edited by Warren I. Cohen and Nancy Bernkopf Tucker, 31–56. Cambridge: Cambridge University Press, 1994.

Lake, David A. "Powerful Pacifists: Democratic States and War." *American Political Science Review* 86, no. 1 (1992): 24–37.

Lake, David A. "Two Cheers for Bargaining Theory: Assessing Rationalist Explanations of the Iraq War." *International Security* 35, no. 3 (2010): 7–52.

Larson, Eric Victor. *Casualties and Consensus: The Historical Role of Casualties in Domestic Support for US Military Operations.* Santa Monica, CA: RAND Corporation, 1996.

Lawrence, Mark A. *The Vietnam War: A Concise International History.* New York: Oxford University Press, 2008.

Lebovic, James H. *Planning to Fail: The US Wars in Vietnam, Iraq, and Afghanistan.* New York: Oxford University Press, 2019.

Lee, Carrie. "Operation TORCH at 75: FDR and the Domestic Politics of the North African Invasion." War on the Rocks, November 8, 2017. https://warontherocks.com /2017/11/16075/.

Lee, Carrie A. "Polarization, Casualty Sensitivity, and Military Operations: Evidence from a Survey Experiment." *International Politics* 59 (2022): 981–1003.

Lee, Carrie A. *The Politics of Military Operations.* PhD Dissertation, Stanford University, 2015.

Lerner, Mitchell. "Vietnam and the 1964 Election: A Defense of Lyndon Johnson." *Presidential Studies Quarterly* 24, no. 4 (1995): 751–766.

Levy, Jack S. "Diversionary War Theory: A Critique." In *Handbook of War Studies*, edited by Manus I. Midlarsky, 259–288. Boston: Unwin Hyman, 1989.

Lian, Bradley, and John R. Oneal. "Presidents, the Use of Military Force, and Public Opinion." *Journal of Conflict Resolution* 37, no. 2 (1993): 277–300.

[311]

Lin-Greenberg, Erik. "Soldiers, Pollsters, and International Crises: Public Opinion and the Military's Advice on the Use of Force." *Foreign Policy Analysis* 17, no. 3 (July 2021): orab009. https://doi.org/10.1093/fpa/orab009.

Logevall, Fredrik. " 'There Ain't No Daylight': Lyndon Johnson and the Politics of Escalation." In *Making Sense of the Vietnam Wars: Local, National, and Transnational Perspectives*, edited by Mark P. Bradley and Marilyn B. Young, 91–108. New York: Oxford University Press, 2008.

Logevall, Fredrik. *Choosing War: The Lost Chance for Peace and the Escalation of the War in Vietnam*. Berkeley: University of California Press, 1999.

Logevall, Fredrik, and Andrew Preston, eds. *Nixon in the World: American Foreign Relations, 1969-1977*. New York: Oxford University Press, 2008.

Loi, Luu Van, and Nguyen Anh Vu. *Le Duc Tho-Kissinger Negotiations in Paris*. Hanoi: Thế Giới Publishers, 1996.

Mack, Andrew. "Why Big Nations Lose Small Wars: The Politics of Asymmetric Conflict." *World Politics* 27, no. 2 (1975): 175–200.

Mann, James. *The Obamians: The Struggle Inside the White House to Redefine American Power*. New York: Penguin, 2012.

Mann, James. *Rise of the Vulcans: The History of Bush's War Cabinet*. New York: Penguin, 2004.

Marinov, Nikolay, William G. Nomikos, and Josh Robbins. "Does Electoral Proximity Affect Security Policy?" *Journal of Politics* 77, no. 3 (2015): 762–773.

Marsh, Kevin P. "The Intersection of War and Politics: The Iraq War Troop Surge and Bureaucratic Politics." *Armed Forces & Society* 38, no. 3 (2012): 413–437.

Mattes, Michaela, and Jessica L. P. Weeks. "Hawks, Doves, and Peace: An Experimental Approach." *American Journal of Political Science* 63, no. 1 (January 2019): 53–66.

Maxey, Sarah. "Limited Spin: When the Public Punishes Leaders Who Lie About Military Action." *Journal of Conflict Resolution* 65, nos. 2–3 (February 2021): 283–312.

Mazaar, Michael J. *Leap of Faith: Hubris, Negligence, and America's Greatest Foreign Policy Tragedy*. New York: Public Affairs, 2019.

McMahon, Robert J. "The Politics, and Geopolitics, of American Troop Withdrawals from Vietnam, 1968-1972." *Diplomatic History* 34, no. 3 (2010): 471–483.

McMaster, H. R. *Dereliction of Duty: Lyndon Johnson and Robert McNamara, the Joint Chiefs of Staff and the Lies that Led to Vietnam*. New York: Harper Collins, 1997.

Mearsheimer, John J. *Why Leaders Lie: The Truth About Lying in International Politics*. New York: Oxford University Press, 2011.

Meernik, James. "Domestic Politics and the Political Use of Military Force by the United States." *Political Research Quarterly* 54, no. 4 (2001): 889–904.

Meernik, James. *The Political Use of Military Force in US Foreign Policy*. Farnham, UK: Ashgate, 2004.

Meernik, James. "Presidential Decision Making and the Political Use of Military Force." *International Studies Quarterly* 38, no. 1 (1994): 121–138.

Meernik, James, and Peter Waterman. "The Myth of the Diversionary Use of Force by American Presidents." *Political Research Quarterly* 49, no. 3 (1996): 573–590.

Merom, Gil. *How Democracies Lose Small Wars: State, Society, and the Failures of France in Algeria, Israel in Lebanon, and the United States in Vietnam*. Cambridge: Cambridge University Press, 2003.

Michaels, Jeffrey H., and Andrew Payne. "One President at a Time? How the President-Elect Shapes US Foreign Policy During the Transition." *Presidential Studies Quarterly*, July 5, 2022. https://doi.org/10.1111/psq.12795.

Miller, Merle. *Plain Speaking: An Oral Biography of Harry S. Truman.* New York: G. P. Putnam, 1974.

Milner, Helen V., and Dustin Tingley. *Sailing the Water's Edge: The Domestic Politics of American Foreign Policy.* Princeton, NJ: Princeton University Press, 2015.

Mintz, Alex. "How Do Leaders Make Decisions? A Poliheuristic Perspective." *Journal of Conflict Resolution* 48, no. 1 (2004): 3–13.

Mitchell, David, and Tansa George Massoud. "Anatomy of Failure: Bush's Decision-Making Process and the Iraq War." *Foreign Policy Analysis* 5, no. 3 (2009): 265–286.

Morrow, James D. "Electoral and Congressional Incentives and Arms Control." *Journal of Conflict Resolution* 35, no. 2 (1991): 245–265.

Mosher, Frederick C., W. David Clinton, and Daniel George Lang. *Presidential Transitions and Foreign Affairs.* Baton Rouge: Louisiana State University Press, 1987.

Most, Benjamin A., and Harvey Starr. "International Relations Theory, Foreign Policy Substitutability, and 'Nice' Laws." *World Politics* 36, no. 3 (1984): 383–406.

Mueller, John E. *War, Presidents, and Public Opinion.* New York: Wiley, 1973.

Nagl, John A. *Learning to Eat Soup with a Knife: Counterinsurgency Lessons from Malaya and Vietnam.* Chicago: University of Chicago Press, 2005.

Neustadt, Richard E. *Presidential Power: The Politics of Leadership from FDR to Carter.* Chichester, UK: Wiley, 1980.

Nguyen, Lien-Hang, T. *Hanoi's War: An International History of the War for Peace in Vietnam.* Chapel Hill: University of North Carolina Press, 2012.

Nincic, Miroslav. *Democracy and Foreign Policy: The Fallacy of Political Realism.* New York: Columbia University Press, 1992.

Nincic, Miroslav. "US Soviet Policy and the Electoral Connection." *World Politics* 42, no. 3 (1990): 370–396.

Oneal, John R., and Anna Lillian Bryan. "The Rally 'Round the Flag Effect in US Foreign Policy Crises, 1950–1985." *Political Behavior* 17, no. 4 (1995): 379–401.

Ornstein, Norman J., and Thomas E. Mann. *The Permanent Campaign and Its Future.* Washington, DC: American Enterprise Institute, 2000.

O'Sullivan, Meghan L. "The Problem with Obama's Decision to Leave Iraq." *Foreign Affairs*, October 2011.

Ostrom, Charles W., and Brian L. Job. "The President and the Political Use of Force." *American Political Science Review* 80, no. 2 (1986): 541–566.

Page, Benjamin I., and Marshall M. Bouton. *The Foreign Policy Disconnect: What Americans Want from Our Leaders but Don't Get.* Chicago: University of Chicago Press, 2006.

Payne, Andrew. "Bringing the Boys Back Home: Campaign Promises and U.S. Decision-Making in Iraq and Vietnam." *Politics* 41, no. 1 (February 2021): 95–110.

Payne, Andrew. "Presidents, Politics, and Military Strategy: Electoral Constraints During the Iraq War." *International Security* 44, no. 3 (2019–2020): 163–203.

Payne, Andrew. "Trump Just De-escalated in the Middle East. Here's Why We Shouldn't Be Surprised." *Washington Post*, January 11, 2020.

Porter, Patrick. *Blunder: Britain's War in Iraq.* Oxford: Oxford University Press, 2018.

Porter, Patrick. "Why America's Grand Strategy Has Not Changed: Power, Habit, and the U.S. Foreign Policy Establishment." *International Security* 42, no. 4 (2018): 9–46.

Potter, Philip B. K. "Does Experience Matter? American Presidential Experience, Age, and International Conflict." *Journal of Conflict Resolution* 51, no. 3 (2007): 351–378.

Potter, Philip B. K. "Electoral Margins and American Foreign Policy." *International Studies Quarterly* 57, no. 3 (2013): 505–518.

Potter, Philip B. K. "Lame-Duck Foreign Policy." *Presidential Studies Quarterly* 46, no. 4 (December 2016): 849–867.

Powlick, Philip J. "The Attitudinal Bases for Responsiveness to Public Opinion Among American Foreign Policy Officials." *Journal of Conflict Resolution* 35, no. 4 (1991): 611–641.

Powlick, Philip J. "The Sources of Public Opinion for American Foreign Policy Officials." *International Studies Quarterly* 39, no. 4 (1995): 427–451.

Powlick, Philip J., and Andrew Z. Katz. "Defining the American Public Opinion/Foreign Policy Nexus." *Mershon International Studies Review* 42, no. 1 (1998): 29–61.

Preston, Andrew, "Beyond the Water's Edge: Foreign Policy and Electoral Politics." In *America at the Ballot Box: Elections and Political History*, edited by Gareth Davies and Julian E. Zelizer, 219–237. Philadelphia: University of Pennsylvania Press, 2015.

Preston, Andrew. *The War Council: McGeorge Bundy, the NSC, and Vietnam*. Cambridge, MA: Harvard University Press, 2006.

Price, Bryan C. "Targeting Top Terrorists: How Leadership Decapitation Contributes to Counterterrorism." *International Security* 36, no. 4 (2012): 9–46.

Putnam, Robert D. "Diplomacy and Domestic Politics: The Logic of Two-Level Games." *International Organization* 42, no. 3 (1988): 427–460.

Quandt, William B. "The Electoral Cycle and the Conduct of Foreign Policy." *Political Science Quarterly* 101, no. 5 (1986): 825–837.

Randolph, Stephen P. *Powerful and Brutal Weapons: Nixon, Kissinger, and the Easter Offensive*. Cambridge, MA: Harvard University Press, 2007.

Rapport, Aaron. "The Long and Short of It: Cognitive Constraints on Leaders' Assessments of 'Postwar' Iraq." *International Security* 37, no. 3 (2013): 133–171.

Ray, James Lee. *Democracy and International Conflict*. Columbia: University of South Carolina Press, 1995.

Record, Jeffrey. *Beating Goliath: Why Insurgencies Win*. Dulles, VA: Potomac Books, 2007.

Reiter, Dan. "Democracy, Deception, and Entry Into War." *Security Studies* 21, no. 4 (2012): 594–623.

Reiter, Dan, and Allan C. Stam. *Democracies at War*. Princeton, NJ: Princeton University Press, 2002.

Reiter, Dan, and Erik R. Tillman. "Public, Legislative, and Executive Constraints on the Democratic Initiation of Conflict." *Journal of Politics* 64, no. 3 (2002): 810–826.

Ricks, Thomas E. *Fiasco: The American Military Adventure in Iraq*. New York: Penguin, 2006.

Ricks, Thomas E. *The Gamble: General David Petraeus and the American Military Adventure in Iraq, 2006-2008*. New York: Penguin, 2009.

Robinson, Linda. *Tell Me How This Ends: General David Petraeus and the Search for a Way Out of Iraq.* New York: Public Affairs, 2008.

Rosen, Stephen Peter. "Vietnam and the American Theory of Limited War." *International Security* 7, no. 2 (1982): 83–113.

Russett, Bruce M. *Controlling the Sword: The Democratic Governance of National Security.* Cambridge, MA: Harvard University Press, 1990.

Russett, Bruce M., and John R. Oneal. *Triangulating Peace: Democracy, Interdependence, and International Organizations.* New York: Norton, 2001.

Sagan, Scott D., and Jeremi Suri. "The Madman Nuclear Alert: Secrecy, Signaling and Safety in October 1969." *International Security* 27, no. 4 (Spring 2003): 150–183.

Saunders, Elizabeth N. "Elites in the Making and Breaking of Foreign Policy." *Annual Review of Political Science* 25, no. 9 (2022): 1–22.

Saunders, Elizabeth N. "Leaders, Advisers, and the Political Origins of Elite Support for War." *Journal of Conflict Resolution* 62, no. 10 (2018): 2118–2149.

Saunders, Elizabeth N. *Leaders at War: How Presidents Shape Military Interventions.* Ithaca, NY: Cornell University Press, 2011.

Saunders, Elizabeth N. "No Substitute for Experience: Presidents, Advisers, and Information in Group Decision Making." *International Organization* 71, Supplement S1 (2017): S219–S247.

Saunders, Elizabeth N. "War and the Inner Circle: Democratic Elites and the Politics of Using Force." *Security Studies* 24, no. 3 (2015): 466–501.

Sayle, Timothy Andrews, Jeffrey A. Engel, Hal Brands, and William Inboden. *The Last Card: Inside George W. Bush's Decision to Surge in Iraq.* Ithaca, NY: Cornell University Press, 2019.

Schedler, Andreas. "The Logic of Electoral Authoritarianism." In *Electoral Authoritarianism: The Dynamics of Unfree Competition,* edited by Andreas Schedler, 1–23. Boulder, CO: Lynne Rienner, 2006.

Schub, Robert. "When Prospective Leader Turnover Promotes Peace." *International Studies Quarterly* 64, no. 3 (September 2020): 510–522.

Schuessler, John M. *Deceit on the Road to War: Presidents, Politics and American Democracy.* Ithaca, NY: Cornell University Press, 2015.

Schultz, Kenneth A. "The Politics of Risking Peace: Do Hawks or Doves Deliver the Olive Branch?" *International Organization* 59, no. 1 (Winter 2005): 1–38.

Schwartz, Thomas Alan. *Henry Kissinger and American Power.* New York: Hill and Wang, 2020.

Schwartz, Thomas Alan. " 'Henry, . . . Winning an Election Is Terribly Important': Partisan Politics in the History of US Foreign Relations." *Diplomatic History* 33, no. 2 (2009): 173–190.

Shogan, Colleen J. "The Contemporary Presidency: The Sixth Year Curse." *Presidential Studies Quarterly* 36, no. 1 (2006): 89–101.

Sieg, Kent G. "The 1968 Presidential Election and Peace in Vietnam." *Presidential Studies Quarterly* 26, no. 4, (1996): 1062–1080.

Siverson, Randolph M. "Democracies and War Participation: In Defense of the Institutional Constraints Argument." *European Journal of International Relations* 1, no. 4 (1995): 481–489.

Slantchev, Branislav L. "How Initiators End Their Wars: The Duration of Warfare and the Terms of Peace." *American Journal of Political Science* 48, no. 4 (2004): 813–829.

Small, Melvin. *At the Water's Edge: American Politics and the Vietnam War.* Chicago: Ivan R. Dee, 2005.

Small, Melvin. *Democracy and Diplomacy: The Impact of Domestic Politics in US Foreign Policy, 1789-1994.* Baltimore, MD: Johns Hopkins University Press, 1996.

Smith, Alastair. "Diversionary Foreign Policy in Democratic Systems." *International Studies Quarterly* 40, no. 1 (1996): 133–153.

Smith, Niel, and Sean MacFarland. "Anbar Awakens: The Tipping Point." *Military Review* 88, no. 2 (March–April 2008): 41–52.

Sobel, Richard. *Impact of Public Opinion on U.S. Foreign Policy Since Vietnam.* New York: Oxford University Press, 2001.

Sorley, Lewis. *A Better War: The Unexamined Victories and Final Tragedy of America's Last Years in Vietnam.* New York: Harcourt, 1999.

Spector, Ronald H. *After Tet: The Bloodiest Year in Vietnam.* New York: Vintage Books, 1993.

Stanley, Elizabeth. "Ending the Korean War: The Role of Domestic Coalition Shifts in Overcoming Obstacles to Peace." *International Security* 34, no. 1 (2009): 42–82.

Stanley, Elizabeth. *Paths to Peace: Domestic Coalition Shifts, War Termination and the Korean War.* Stanford, CA: Stanford University Press, 2009.

Stoll, Richard J. "The Guns of November: Presidential Reelections and the Use of Force, 1947–1982." *Journal of Conflict Resolution* 28, no. 2 (1984): 231–246.

Strachan, Hew. "Strategy and Democracy." *Survival* 62, no. 2 (2020): 51–82.

Stueck, William. *The Korean War: An International History.* Princeton, NJ: Princeton University Press, 1995.

Sullivan, Patricia L. "War Aims and War Outcomes: Why Powerful States Lose Limited Wars." *Journal of Conflict Resolution* 51, no. 3 (2007): 496–524.

Tarar, Ahmer. "Diversionary Incentives and the Bargaining Approach to War." *International Studies Quarterly* 50, no. 1 (2006): 169–188.

Thomson, Robert, Terry Royed, Elin Naurin, Joaquín Artés, Rory Costello, Laurenz Ennser-Jedenastik, Mark Ferguson, Petia Kostadinova, Catherine Moury, François Pétry, and Katrin Praprotnik. "The Fulfillment of Parties' Election Pledges." *American Journal of Political Science* 61, no. 3 (2017): 527–542.

Tomz, Michael, and Robert P. Van Houweling. "The Electoral Implications of Candidate Ambiguity." *American Political Science Review* 103, no. 1 (February 2009): 83–98.

Tomz, Michael, Jessica L. P. Weeks, and Keren Yarhi-Milo. "Public Opinion and Decisions About Military Force in Democracies." *International Organization* 74, no. 1 (2020): 119–143.

Trager, Robert F., and Lynn Vavreck. "The Political Costs of Crisis Bargaining Rhetoric and the Role of Party." *American Journal of Political Science* 55, no. 3 (July 2011): 526–545.

Trubowitz, Peter. *Defining the National Interest: Conflict and Change in American Foreign Policy.* Chicago: University of Chicago Press, 1998.

Trubowitz, Peter. *Politics and Strategy: Partisan Ambition and American Statecraft.* Princeton, NJ: Princeton University Press, 2011.

Trubowitz, Peter, and Brian Burgoon. *Geopolitics and Democracy: The Western Liberal Order from Foundation to Fracture*. New York: Oxford University Press, 2023.

Valentino, Benjamin A., Paul K. Huth, and Sarah E. Croco. "Bear Any Burden? How Democracies Minimize the Costs of War." *Journal of Politics* 72, no. 2 (2010): 528–544.

VanDeMark, Brian. *Into the Quagmire: Lyndon Johnson and the Escalation of the Vietnam War*. New York: Oxford University Press, 1995.

VanDeMark, Brian. *Road to Disaster: A New History of America's Descent Into Vietnam*. New York: Custom House, 2018.

Waldman, Thomas. *Vicarious Warfare: American Strategy and the Illusion of War on the Cheap*. Bristol, UK: Bristol University Press, 2021.

Walt, Stephen M. *The Hell of Good Intentions: America's Foreign Policy Elite and the Decline of U.S. Primacy*. New York: Picador, 2018.

Waltz, Kenneth N. "International Politics Is Not Foreign Policy." *Security Studies* 6, no. 1 (1996): 54–57.

Weeks, Jessica L. P. *Dictators at War and Peace*. Ithaca, NY: Cornell University Press, 2014.

Weintraub, Stanley. *MacArthur's War: Korea and the Undoing of an American Hero*. New York: Free Press, 2000.

West, Bing. *No True Glory: A Frontline Account of the Battle for Fallujah*. New York: Bantam, 2005.

West, Bing. *The Strongest Tribe: War, Politics, and the Endgame in Iraq*. New York: Random House, 2008.

Western, Jon. *Selling Intervention and War*. Baltimore, MD: Johns Hopkins University Press, 2005.

Whitlark, Rachel E. *All Options on the Table: Leaders, Preventive War, and Nuclear Proliferation*. Ithaca, NY: Cornell University Press, 2021.

Wildavsky, Aaron. "The Two Presidencies." *Trans-Action* 4 (1966): 7–14.

Williams, Laron K. "Flexible Election Timing and International Conflict." *International Studies Quarterly* 57, no. 3 (2013): 449–461.

Woodward, Bob. *The Last of the President's Men*. New York: Simon and Schuster, 2015.

Woodward, Bob. *Obama's Wars*. New York: Simon and Schuster, 2010.

Woodward, Bob. *Plan of Attack*. New York: Simon and Schuster, 2004.

Woodward, Bob. *State of Denial: Bush at War, Part III*. New York: Simon and Schuster, 2006.

Woodward, Bob. *The War Within: A Secret White House History, 2006-2008*. New York: Simon and Schuster, 2008.

Young, Marilyn B. "Hard Sell: The Korean War. In *Selling War in a Media Age: The Presidency and Public Opinion in the American Century*, edited by Kenneth Osgood and Andrew K. Frank, 113–139. Gainesville: University Press of Florida, 2010.

Young, Marilyn B. *The Vietnam Wars 1945-1990*. New York: Harper Collins, 1991.

Zaller, John R. *The Nature and Origins of Mass Opinion*. Cambridge: Cambridge University Press, 1992.

Zeigler, Sean, Jan H. Pierskalla, and Sandeep Mazumder. "War and the Reelection Motive: Examining the Effect of Term Limits." *Journal of Conflict Resolution* 58, no. 4 (2014): 658–684.

Zelizer, Julian E. *Arsenal of Democracy: The Politics of National Security—from World War II to the War on Terrorism*. New York: Basic Books, 2010.

Zhang, Shu Guang. *Deterrence and Strategic Culture: Chinese-American Confrontations, 1949–1958*. Ithaca, NY: Cornell University Press, 1992.

Zhang, Shu Guang. *Mao's Military Romanticism: China and the Korean War, 1950–1953*. Lawrence: University of Kansas Press, 1995.

Index

GPSR Authorized Representative: Easy Access System Europe, Mustamäe tee 50, 10621 Tallinn, Estonia, gpsr.requests@easproject.com